W9-DGE-768

Ernest Hemingway

a reference guide
1974 – 1989

Ernest Hemingway

a reference guide
1974 – 1989

KELLI A. LARSON

G.K.HALL&CO.
70 LINCOLN STREET, BOSTON, MASS.

First published 1990
by G.K. Hall & Co.
70 Lincoln Street
Boston, Massachusetts 02111

10 9 8 7 6 5 4 3 2 1

Library of Congress Cataloging-in-Publication Data

Larson, Kelli A.
   Ernest Hemingway : a reference guide, 1974-1989 / Kelli A. Larson.
      p. cm. – (Reference guides to literature)
   Includes bibliographical references and index.
   ISBN 0-8161-8944-7
   1. Hemingway, Ernest, 1899-1961 – Bibliography.
I. Title. II. Series.
Z8396.3.L37   1990
[PS3515.E37]
016.813'52 – dc20'.285 – dc20   90-43750
                                        CIP

The paper used in this publication meets the minimum requirements of
American National Standard for Information Sciences – Permanence of Paper
for Printed Library Materials. ANSI Z39.48-1984. ♾™
MANUFACTURED IN THE UNITED STATES OF AMERICA

Contents

Introduction

More so than any other writer of the twentieth century, Hemingway continues to hold the interest and imagination of both the literary and the nonliterary public. For years we read of his exploits in the evening papers, his books and the films made from them as well as his frequent brushes with death. Paris, Pamplona, Key West – Hemingway's backyard seemed a million miles away, his adventures consistently exciting and glamorous. While we grew up to be account executives, bankers, and college teachers, Hemingway drove an ambulance on the Italian front, hunted big game in Africa, chased Nazi submarines – and then wrote about it. And what he wrote made us feel what we had missed. Now nearly thirty years after his death, the larger-than-life legend of "Papa" – a legend promoted by the man himself – continues in books, films, television programs, even his own category on "Jeopardy." In an age notably short in memory, Hemingway remains a permanent force in both American literature and culture.

Hemingway scholarship occupies a significant position in literary criticism as well, with more than a thousand essays and books published worldwide in the past decade alone – and there is no end in sight. The availability of manuscript materials at the John F. Kennedy Library in Boston since the mid-1970s, the formation of the Hemingway Society in 1980 coupled with the publication of *The Hemingway Review* the following year, and the continuous flow of posthumously published works have kept Hemingway in the forefront of critical attention since Linda W. Wagner's *Ernest Hemingway: A Reference Guide* was published in 1977. Wagner's comprehensive bibliography serves as a detailed and valuable record of Hemingway's critical reputation from the early 1920s through the mid-1970s and marks the starting point for the present study.[1] In addition, Audre Hanneman's *Ernest Hemingway: A Comprehensive Bibliography* (1967) and *Supplement* (1975) are also excellent resources for secondary and primary materials through 1973.[2]

Since the compilation of these bibliographies, the field has expanded greatly with much of the recent critical attention directed at the man himself. Memoirs and biographies abound. Sons, wives, lovers, hunting companions, and war buddies have all told their stories in an effort to reveal the man they knew and loved, the man beneath the celebrity. Of course, the inherent limitation of most memoirs, and these prove no exception, is their extensive reliance on opinions and remembrances clouded by the passage of time. Even those memoirs compiled through the use of contemporaneous journals and diaries have been reinterpreted and edited decades after the fact.

The most notable memoirs appearing in the past fifteen years paint complex and contradictory portraits of the author from vastly different perspectives: wife, son, and protégé. Mary Welsh, Hemingway's fourth and last wife, describes her seventeen years of marriage in her 1976 autobiography *How It Was*. From their first meeting in London in April, 1944 to that fateful July day in Ketchum in 1961 when Hemingway committed suicide, Mary faithfully records their often-turbulent life together: fishing in the Gulf Stream, relaxing aboard the *Pilar*, hunting in Africa, renovating the Finca Vigía, writing, loving, and quarreling. What emerges is a candid portrait of both the author's dual nature, at times happy and healthy while at others despondent and sick, and his subsequent decline into dementia.[3]

Like Welsh's autobiography, Gregory Hemingway's memoir *Papa* (1976) endeavors to describe his relationship with the author and his difficult struggle to understand and come to terms with his legendary father. Gregory makes clear from the beginning his motive in writing this account is to set the record straight. To this end Gregory presents a succession of interesting anecdotes and fond memories set in exciting locales as evidence of his contention that "in his youth, my father was not a bully, a sick bore, or a professional celebrity. ... The man I remembered was kind, gentle, elemental in his vastness, tormented beyond endurance, and although we always called him papa, it was out of love, not fear."[4]

Although we see little of Hemingway the writer, Hemingway the father is clearly illustrated here – the good and bad. And in addition, we are treated to intimate, and sometimes surprising, glimpses of the author: rescuing his son from sharks in the coral reefs, nursing him back to health after a mysterious poliolike illness, showing exuberance over Gregory's tying at the age of eleven for the Cuban shooting championship, and evincing disappointment at his plagiarizing of a short story.

Hemingway's role as mentor is explored in Arnold Samuelson's *With Hemingway: A Year in Key West and Cuba* (1984), a journal-based account written over fifty years ago but revised during the subsequent two decades. Samuelson spent a year crewing aboard the *Pilar* while the world-famous author tutored him in the fine art of writing. Although focusing on only a small portion of Hemingway's life, Samuelson offers a detailed account of day-to-day activities at the Whitehead Street home Hemingway shared with his second wife, Pauline, the time he spent with Cuban cronies, and his frequent fishing trips with family and friends aboard the *Pilar*.[5] Unfortunately, little of Hemingway's tutorial of the aspiring writer is new material, most having been published in one form or another over the past half-century.

Once heralded as the definitive Hemingway biography, Carlos Baker's 1969 *Ernest Hemingway: A Life Story* is now a stepping-stone for a number of very different biographical studies from a variety of critical and biographical perspectives.[6] While some limit their focus to particular years or subject matter, others attempt to trace and interpret the author's unfolding life history from Oak Park to Ketchum. Combined they give a detailed and valuable, although at times redundant, examination of Hemingway the man, artist, and myth. With all of this recent biographical attention, one wonders if there can be any secrets left in the Hemingway closet, or if indeed there is even a closet left at all.

Two new biographies covering the author's early years came out in the mid-1980s, Peter Griffin's *Along with Youth* (1985) and Michael Reynolds's *The Young Hemingway* (1986). Each is a first installment of a projected multivolume biography and illuminates Hemingway's boyhood and youth, ending with his first marriage to Hadley Richardson, their departure for France, and the expatriate literary scene in 1921. As a preface to a study of the Paris period during which Hemingway produced some of his finest works, knowledge of these early formative years is imperative to our understanding of Hemingway the author.

Griffin draws extensively from previously unpublished materials, including correspondence between Hemingway and the ever-tolerant and devoted Hadley in order to characterize their relationship. And he also gives the complete texts of five short stories written in 1919 and 1920. These prove valuable additions for scholars interested in assessing the author's craft prior to his Parisian apprenticeship, even though their quality testifies as to why they were not published during his lifetime.[7]

Reynolds's account, although also focused on Hemingway's youth, looks beyond 1921 by relating the early influence of family and culture to the whole of Hemingway's life. What emerges is a candid portrait of Hemingway and his family, flaws and all. Of great significance is Reynolds's examination of Hemingway's father's long medical history of chronic neurosis, depression, and paranoia. Reynolds considers the author's genetic inheritance a biological trap extending through three generations and resulting in several suicides. Of particular interest to "Grace-bashers" is the biographer's analysis of Hemingway's relationship with his mother, in which he finds Grace Hall a dominating parent but certainly not the ogre depicted in so many other accounts.[8]

Bernice Kert followed a similar vein in her earlier *The Hemingway Women* (1983) in which she describes the author's relationships with wives and "significant others" such as Grace Hall, Duff Twysden, Agnes von Kurowsky, and Adriana Ivancich. Through numerous interviews and unpublished correspondence, Kert reconstructs chronologically Hemingway's destructive patterns in choosing women and reveals what many of them thought of him as well. Here, as in Reynolds's account, Grace Hall comes off as a dominating mother simply too liberated for her time and her son. Martha Gellhorn, the author's third wife, is also vindicated in Kert's description of her as too independent for the domineering Hemingway.[9]

Norberto Fuentes's *Hemingway in Cuba* (1984) is yet another partial biography, focused this time on Hemingway's final years. In interviewing numerous Cubans and Russians, including Gregorio, captain of the *Pilar* who hunted for Nazi submarines with Hemingway, Fuentes's investigation reveals once again a complex picture of the aging author haunted by chronic depression. But perhaps Fuentes's main contribution to scholarship is his catalogue of what Mary Hemingway left behind when she removed manuscripts and other valuables from the Finca Vigía in 1961: corrected galleys of *Across the River and into the Trees*, fragments of drafts from *For Whom the Bell Tolls*, script corrections for *The Old Man and the Sea*, unpublished correspondence between family and friends (including over a dozen letters to Mary Welsh in 1944 while Hemingway was a World War II correspondent), and even portions of an untitled story.[10] Fortunately, Fuentes prints many of these in his extensive appendices.

Finally, two full-length studies appeared in the mid-1980s as well, Jeffrey Meyers's *Hemingway, A Biography* (1985) and Kenneth Lynn's *Hemingway* (1987). Meyers's biography discusses Hemingway's works at some length, relating them thematically to the author and his life. For example, Meyers argues convincingly that the author's old war buddy E.E. "Chink" Dorman-Smith served as the model for Cantwell in *Across the River and into the Trees*. Relying frequently on Freudian psychology, Meyers comments on the young Hemingway's Oedipal relationship with his mother and pays close attention to wounds (including a three-page appendix of accidents and illnesses), both physical and emotional. Meyers considers Agnes von Kurowsky's defection and Hadley's negligence in the theft of his early manuscripts from a Paris train station to be major traumatizations for the young author.[11]

Lynn's is a psychosexual approach to the author and his works, exploring the important influences in his early life and especially the supposed long-term negative effects of Grace Hall's having dressed her young son in girl's clothing. Lynn analyzes the gender twists and sexual transpositions found in Hemingway's fiction, including *The Sun Also Rises* and *A Farewell to Arms*, but reserves much of his critical energy for the posthumously published *The Garden of Eden*, rich soil indeed for such digging. Lynn also examines Hemingway's relationships with women, discussing the lesbian gossip linked to his mother and second wife Pauline's and fourth wife Mary's androgynous inclinations.[12]

Hemingway manuscript studies, like the biographies, have boomed in the last decade and a half, due to the availability of the author's manuscripts at the John F. Kennedy Library. Although smaller collections are housed at the Lilly Library, Indiana University, and the Harry Ranson Humanities Research Center in Austin, Texas, the principal collection of Hemingway materials has been housed at the Kennedy Library in Boston since the mid-1970s. Here thousands of items from complete manuscripts to personal correspondence are preserved and catalogued, awaiting critical exploration.

Recent manuscript studies tracing the transformation of jotted notes into finished art focus both on Hemingway's development as a writer and on the writing process itself. How, to what extent, and why texts were revised are the subject of numerous critical studies. They show Hemingway's innate feel for language and his consummate skill in editing his own work. They also give us a sense of the craftsman struggling with his craft, the writing and rewriting – the stumbles, together with the successful first takes, that underlie his polished prose.

An additional point of interest and important consideration to emerge through manuscript examination concerns textual problems and the need for definitive editions. Altered or deleted words, lines, and in some cases entire paragraphs and sections continue to beset critics, editors, and the general reading public alike. James Hinkle's "Dear Mr. Scribner' – About the Published Text of *The Sun Also Rises*" (1986) notes 4,000 differences between Hemingway's completed typescript and the published edition of the novel, including 125 instances of different wording – although many are certainly attributable to the author himself.[13] Peter Griffin's brief note entitled "A Substantive Error in the Text of Ernest Hemingway's 'Summer People'" (1978) wisely concludes that the transformation of "Stut" (a nickname for the heroine) into "slut" and the omission of ten lines of text seriously corrupts our reading of the story.[14] And as Leger Brosnahan demonstrates in "A Lost Passage from Hemingway's 'Macomber'" (1985), even the much-anthologized "The Short Happy Life of Francis Macomber" was well within reach of the editor's blue pencil. In comparing typescripts prepared for *Cosmopolitan* in September 1936 and the standard printing of the story in the later *The Fifth Column and the First Forty-nine Stories*, Brosnahan finds a 100-word passage near the climax of the lion hunt deleted from the Scribner edition.[15] Unfortunately, these examples represent only a fraction plaguing the author's canon. With such noted Hemingway authorities as Gerry Brenner, Robert W. Lewis, Jeffrey Meyers, Scott Donaldson, and Michael S. Reynolds all commenting on textual problems in Hemingway's published editions, it has become increasingly obvious in the last few years that a serious move to assemble and collate the various texts is long overdue.

Taking manuscript studies in a different direction, several scholars have investigated the development of the writer and his fiction through his process of composition reflected in the Kennedy materials. In his full-length critical study *Hemingway's Hidden Craft: The Writing of "A Farewell to Arms"* (1979), Bernard Oldsey relies extensively on manuscripts in discussing the forty-one different endings of the novel, including five closely related versions of the published ending. Through clustering them into variant groupings such as "The *Nada* Ending," "The Fitzgerald Ending," "The Religious Ending," and "The Live Baby Ending," this study reveals the author's struggle to achieve thematic continuity within the novel and how he finally arrived at the nihilistic void of the final published version. As Oldsey sums up, "In one sense, most of the concluding attempts . . . may be considered as artistically subsumed under what finally became *the* ending of *A Farewell to Arms*."[16]

Another full-length study, Frederic Svoboda's *Hemingway & "The Sun Also Rises": The Crafting of a Style* (1983), provides a textual examination of four scenes in *The Sun Also Rises*: the early love scene in chapter 7 between Jake and Brett, Jake and the waiter's discussion of Vincente Girones's death, Romero's performance in the bullring the day after Robert Cohn has beaten him up, and the final chapter. Svoboda concludes that in this early work, Hemingway's "narrative iceberg" theory was an important force in shaping the novel, as were his experiences in Pamplona; the latter provided the author with an initial outline, setting, and cast from which evolved, through subsequent revision, "a completely realized fictional whole."[17]

William Balassi's "The Writing of the Manuscript of *The Sun Also Rises*, with a Chart of Its Session-by-Session Development" (1986) is an interesting companion piece to Svoboda's book. Here Balassi records the sixty-seven writing sessions that resulted in the composition of *The Sun Also Rises* along with descriptions of the contents of each of the seven notebooks and the thirty-two-page text that began the original narration. In collating the manuscript with Scribner's edition, Balassi indicates additions, deletions, name changes, and errors, but he discovers surprisingly few major revisions.[18]

In another manuscript study, "'Proud and friendly and gently': Women in Hemingway's Early Fiction" (1980), Linda W. Wagner argues that prior to 1929 and the death of the author's father and the writing of *A Farewell to Arms*, Hemingway's women characters were much stronger and more sympathetically drawn, having already achieved the "semi-stoic self awareness" characteristic of the mature Hemingway hero. Wagner points to the opening chapters of *The Sun Also Rises* (later deleted at Fitzgerald's urging) depicting Brett in a much more favorable light, the revisions of "Cat in the Rain" which make George clearly unsympathetic, and the sensitive portrayal of Jig (Hadley in the manuscript) in "Hills Like White Elephants" as support for her contention that during the 1920s "Hemingway's attention was on women as themselves."[19]

Among the many well-researched essays derived from materials at the Kennedy Library is "Hemingway's Early Manuscripts: The Theory and Practice of Omission" (1983) in which Paul Smith looks first at Hemingway's conception of the theory as evidenced by his frequent references to it and then at the author's early application of it. Smith's analysis, backed by a close textual examination of the manuscripts of "The Killers," "Big Two-Hearted River," and "Up in Michigan," which serve as blueprints of what the author omitted and where, leads him to conclude that during his apprenticeship

Hemingway "was not a particularly attentive student in the informal classrooms of Ezra Pound or Gertrude Stein."[20]

Just who influenced whom is still up for critical debate judging by the amount of interest generated in this area over the past fifteen years. Not surprisingly, a number of essays are devoted to further explorations of Hemingway's professional relationships with Stein, Pound, Anderson, Eliot, and Cézanne. The issues raised by these studies and the connections found in language, theme, structure, and technique make it quite evident that we are currently balancing on the threshold of literary history and that much more needs to be done in this hazardous yet profitable area of research, especially in the way of Pound studies.

Nicholas Joost and Alan Brown in "T.S. Eliot and Ernest Hemingway: A Literary Relationship" (1978) argue that in spite of Hemingway's "generally negative personal opinion of Eliot," he modeled his writing after the imagist poet, reworking language, theme, and structure into a style artistically indebted to *The Waste Land* and other poems written by Eliot prior to 1930.[21] In another influence study entitled "The Prose Style of Selected Works by Ernest Hemingway, Sherwood Anderson, and Gertrude Stein" (1980), Ahmad Ardat gives a detailed linguistic analysis of syntactic elements in works by all three authors, concluding that although they generally "write more like one another than they write differently," their styles are marked by striking distinctions. Ardat finds Stein's style to be the most individualistic but concludes that even so, one would hardly confuse a page of prose written by Anderson with one written by Hemingway.[22] All of this, of course, may be read as support or repudiation of Hemingway's claim that Stein and Anderson had no literary influence on him – depending on whether the reader views the glass as half-full or half-empty.

One acknowledged influence on the author, artist Paul Cézanne, has also garnered a bit of attention from Hemingway critics over the past decade. Meyly Chin Hagemann's important "Hemingway's Secret: Visual to Verbal Art" (1979) identifies and describes the Cézanne paintings that Hemingway studied at the Luxembourg Museum and at the Bernheim exhibit during the 1920s. She explores the author's translation of visual techniques into literary ones in short stories he wrote under Cézanne's influence, including "Indian Camp" and "Out of Season."[23] Kenneth Johnston's later "Hemingway and Cézanne: Doing the Country" (1984) further investigates the impressionist artist's influence by comparing the depiction of landscape in the pre-Cézanne piece "Up in Michigan" with the post-Cézanne "Big Two-Hearted River," determining a definite connection in the selection, restructuring, and omission of detail. Johnston concludes that Hemingway's study of Cézanne's landscape techniques greatly increased the young author's subtlety and unity of narration.[24]

What we recognize in Hemingway's writing, the debt owed to literary influence, is partly the direction of creative impulse; Hemingway was an original thinker who looked to others for insight. And what he learned became his own through the force of creative genius. Two full-length studies appearing in 1981 have helped immensely in piecing together the puzzle of Hemingway's literary heritage. Michael S. Reynolds's *Hemingway's Reading, 1910-1940: An Inventory* (1981)[25] and James D. Brasch and Joseph Sigman's *Hemingway's Library: A Composite Record* (1981)[26] compile lists and subject indexes for the thousands of books and periodicals read, owned, and borrowed by the author during his lifetime. The Brasch and Sigman collaboration is the more extensive of the two compilations since it includes nearly 6,000 titles from the Finca Vigía library in Cuba. What emerges from the mass is a keen sense of Hemingway's diverse interest in literature, art, biography, history, military history, hunting, and fishing.

Of specific interest and use to scholars engaged in influence studies are those sections devoted to literature and literary criticism. As the inventories confirm, Hemingway was a voracious and eclectic reader; and as influence studies up till now have demonstrated, one who assimilated a great deal of what he read. French and Russian writers such as Flaubert, de Maupassant, Tolstoy, and Dostoyevsky, British authors Kipling and Conrad, and Americans Hawthorne, Melville, Twain, James, and Crane make up only a portion of Hemingway's extensive literary tastes and clearly mark the future direction of worthwhile scholarship in this area.

Influence studies moving in the opposite direction, that is tracing Hemingway's influence on other writers, are the subject of several interesting articles as well. From Ellison to Spillane, Hemingway's presence in twentieth-century fiction is a force to be reckoned with, even when it serves as a negative influence as Allan Chavkin suggests in "Fathers and Sons: 'Papa' Hemingway and Saul Bellow" (1983). Chavkin argues that Bellow's oversimplified reading of Hemingway's writing leads him to reject the "hard-boiled-dom" he finds there in order to break out of Hemingway's oppressive literary shadow and forge his own art.[27] In a positive venture, Frank McConnell's "Stalking Papa's Ghost" (1986) traces the lasting influence on some of this country's leading authors – Mailer, Pynchon, and Vonnegut – concluding that the rumblings of Hemingway's spirit "are an inescapable part of the splendid dissonance that is contemporary American fiction."[28]

In addition to his permanent place in American letters, Papa's presence looms large over the Hollywood movie industry as well. No other modern American author has been translated into film as often as Ernest Hemingway – the larger-than-life legend of the man seemingly in accord with the glamour and hype of Hollywood. Since 1932 when the first film adaptation of *A Farewell to Arms* was made, there have been nearly twenty more movies based on Hemingway's works, with some like "The Killers" and *To Have and Have Not* produced two and three times each. Even as the present bibliography is being compiled, work on an adaptation of "Indian Camp" is progressing at full speed.

Unfortunately, big stars like Gary Cooper, Ingrid Bergman, and Humphrey Bogart, lavish sets, and the talented direction of Frank Borzage, Howard Hawks, and Henry King have failed, for the most part, in capturing the awesome power of Hemingway's prose on celluloid–much to the consternation of the author, critics, and filmgoers alike. Two full-length studies and a recent collection of essays, all examining the relationship between fiction and film, provide fresh insight into the problems associated with adapting Hemingway's works to the big screen. Gene Phillips's *Hemingway and Film* (1980) offers a near-chronological, movie-by-movie analysis of sixteen film versions of Hemingway's works, complete with close comparisons of their respective texts. Phillips contends throughout that "despite Hemingway's feelings to the contrary, every one of these movies retains at least some moments that are true to his original work, and that at least some of them rank as examples of superior cinema, just as the novels and short stories on which they are based rank as superior fiction."[29]

Frank M. Laurence's *Hemingway and the Movies* (1981) is by far the broader and more extensive of the two studies, offering in addition to film/source comparisons a detailed account of casting, production, and promotion. He includes information on the reception of the various film versions by critics, audiences, and even the author himself. Laurence also explores in depth the exploitive relationship between Hemingway and Hollywood that resulted in the production of those commercialized box-office adaptations that displeased the author so much.[30]

A Moving Picture Feast: The Filmgoer's Hemingway (1989), edited by Charles M. Oliver, is a collection of fifteen diverse essays categorized into three sections: "General Criticism of Hemingway Films," "Films from Novels," and "Films from Short Stories." Essays cover a range of topics, from cinematic style and technique to the distorted Hollywood image of the writer created by studio publicists to the aesthetic relationship between cinematic art and fiction that makes faithful adaptation so difficult.[31] Focusing on fiction and film alike, these essays combined with the two previously published studies by Phillips and Laurence provide scholars, critics, and filmgoers with a firm grounding in Hemingway's often reluctant role in and legendary impact on the movie industry. And fortunately, with the advent of the VCR, cinema "classics" such as *A Farewell to Arms* are now as close and convenient as the nearest video rental store, thus opening the field of literature and film integration to those movie buffs like myself who, as the years pass, find it increasingly difficult staying awake for the late, late, late show.

Judging by the volume of articles and books produced on the author since the first reference guide was published nearly fifteen years ago, we are now in the midst of a Hemingway renaissance. New generations of scholars are breathing new life into texts once thought critically eviscerated–new insight garnered through new approaches. Code studies have declined as dramatically as deconstructionist, feminist, and contextual studies have increased. Clearly the novel most often analyzed is still *The Sun Also Rises*, with *A Farewell to Arms* and *For Whom the Bell Tolls* bringing up a distant second and third. But our focus has changed in the reenvisioning of these texts, and we have discovered in the process the richness that is Hemingway.

Studies of his short fiction have also increased considerably, with "The Short Happy Life of Francis Macomber" narrowly edging out "A Clean, Well-Lighted Place," "Big Two-Hearted River," and "Hills Like White Elephants" in the critical stakes. Although traditional biographical, thematic, and source studies are still heavily represented, new insight is being offered through linguistic and semiotic approaches as well. Two important full-length investigations focusing on the author's short-story canon appeared in 1989, Susan Beegel's *Hemingway's Neglected Short Fiction: New Perspectives* and Paul Smith's *A Reader's Guide to the Short Stories of Ernest Hemingway*. Smith devotes a chapter to each of the fifty-five short stories published during the author's lifetime – from "Up in Michigan" to "A Man of the World," including brief discussions of their respective composition, publication, sources, and important criticism.[32] Beegel's is a collection of essays on Hemingway's lesser-known short stories designed to bring them into the critical light. Sadly, as Beegel points out in her informative and well researched introduction, "to date, we lack a carefully researched and edited text that collects and arranges in chronological order of their composition all of Hemingway's efforts in the genre, both previously published and otherwise."[33] Unfortunately, a significant portion of Hemingway's short fiction remains either unpublished or uncollected and thus virtually inaccessible to critics, students, and the general reading public alike.

Attention is now being directed toward the posthumous works, and only time will reveal whether they are capable of withstanding the intense critical scrutiny their predecessors received. It is unfortunate that Hemingway's literary reputation has sagged with their publication, but perhaps even more disturbing are the changes and revisions made during the editing of these unfinished manuscripts and the unanswerable questions concerning the ways Hemingway would have revised them had he been given the opportunity. Still, they provide ready grist for the ever-revolving critical mill and serve to keep the author at the center of literary controversy. Hemingway has been dead for nearly thirty years but for me and for everyone who reads literature, he lives on and always will – until the last page of the last book is turned.

It has been said that bibliographies date faster than last year's hem lines and this volume proves no exception. By the date of its publication, hundreds of new articles and dozens of new books will have emerged. As critics and scholars we stand each day on the threshold of discovery; as educators we are an integral and vital part of it. Reference guides serve as tools for furthering that discovery process by providing insight into past research, its relevance for scholars of today, and, by omission, direction for future critical studies.

This bibliography begins where Linda W. Wagner's first *Ernest Hemingway: A Reference Guide*, compiled back in 1975, left off and includes materials as recent as 1989. Entries are arranged alphabetically by author within the year of their publication. Items that were unavailable for actual reading are marked by an asterisk (*) with the source of their listing given in place of the usual summary annotation. For some annotations, I have relied primarily on direct quotation when those quotations expressed concisely the nature of the works. Finally, I have been gradually convinced in the last year that comprehensive bibliographies are never totally complete nor completed. Although I have attempted to include all serious contributions to Hemingway scholarship published in English (with the exception of dissertations, which are listed in *Dissertation Abstracts International* available at most substantial libraries), I have probably overlooked some and for this I apologize.

My thanks to Dr. Linda Wagner-Martin for providing me with the initial impetus for this project and for her continued guidance, editorial advice, and encouragement. I am also indebted to the library staffs at Michigan State University and to Alan Larson whose enduring patience and perseverance in tracking down and photocopying materials have proven that he is truly my better half.

Notes

1. Linda W. Wagner, *Ernest Hemingway: A Reference Guide* (Boston: G.K. Hall, 1977).

2. Audre Hanneman, *Ernest Hemingway: A Comprehensive Bibliography* and *Supplement to Ernest Hemingway, A Comprehensive Bibliography* (Princeton, N.J.: Princeton University Press, 1967 and 1975).

3. Mary Welsh Hemingway, *How It Was* (New York: Knopf, 1976).

4. Gregory Hemingway, *Papa* (Boston: Houghton Mifflin, 1976).

5. Arnold Samuelson, *With Hemingway: A Year in Key West and Cuba* (New York: Random House, 1984).

6. Carlos Baker, *Ernest Hemingway: A Life Story* (New York: Charles Scribner's Sons, 1969).

7. Peter Griffin, *Along with Youth* (New York: Oxford University Press, 1985).

8. Michael Reynolds, *The Young Hemingway* (New York: Basil Blackwell, 1986).

9. Bernice Kert, *The Hemingway Women* (New York: W.W. Norton, 1983).

10. Norberto Fuentes, *Hemingway in Cuba* (Secaucus, New Jersey: Lyle Stuart, 1984).

11. Jeffrey Meyers, *Hemingway, A Biography* (New York: Harper & Row, 1985).

12. Kenneth Lynn, *Hemingway* (New York: Simon & Schuster, 1987).

13. James Hinkle, "'Dear Mr. Scribner'–About the Published Text of *The Sun Also Rises*," *The Hemingway Review* 6.1 (Fall 1986): 43-64.

14. Peter Griffin, "A Substantive Error in the Text of Ernest Hemingway's 'Summer People,'" *American Literature* 50.3 (November 1978): 471-73.

15. Leger Brosnahan, "A Lost Passage from Hemingway's 'Macomber,'" *Studies in Bibliography* 38 (1985): 328-30.

16. Bernard Oldsey, *Hemingway's Hidden Craft: The Writing of "A Farewell to Arms"* (University Park: Pennsylvania State University Press, 1979).

17. Frederic Svoboda, *Hemingway & "The Sun Also Rises": The Crafting of a Style* (Lawrence: University Press of Kansas, 1983).

18. William Balassi, "The Writing of the Manuscript of *The Sun Also Rises*, with a Chart of Its Session-by-Session Development," *The Hemingway Review* 6.1 (Fall 1986): 65-78.

19. Linda W. Wagner, "'Proud and friendly and gently': Women in Hemingway's Early Fiction," *College Literature* 7.3 (Fall 1980): 239-47.

20. Paul Smith, "Hemingway's Early Manuscripts: The Theory and Practice of Omission," *Journal of Modern Literature* 10.2 (June 1983): 268-88.

21. Nicholas Joost and Alan Brown, "T.S. Eliot and Ernest Hemingway: A Literary Relationship," *Papers on Language and Literature* 14.4 (Fall 1978): 425-49.

22. Ahmad Ardat, "The Prose Style of Selected Works by Ernest Hemingway, Sherwood Anderson, and Gertrude Stein," *Style* 14.1 (Winter 1980): 1-21.

23. Meyly Chin Hagemann, "Hemingway's Secret: Visual to Verbal Art," *Journal of Modern Literature* 7.1 (February 1979): 87-112.

24. Kenneth Johnston, "Hemingway and Cézanne: Doing the Country," *American Literature* 56.1 (March 1984): 28-37.

25. Michael S. Reynolds, *Hemingway's Reading, 1910-1940: An Inventory* (Princeton, N. J.: Princeton University Press, 1981).

26. James D. Brasch and Joseph Sigman, *Hemingway's Library: A Composite Record* (New York: Garland, 1981).

27. Allan Chavkin, "Fathers and Sons: 'Papa' Hemingway and Saul Bellow," *Papers on Language and Literature* 19.4 (Fall 1983): 449-60.

28. Frank McConnell, "Stalking Papa's Ghost," *Wilson Quarterly* 10.1 (1986): 160-72.

29. Gene Phillips, *Hemingway and Film* (New York: Ungar, 1980).

30. Frank M. Laurence, *Hemingway and the Movies* (Jackson: University Press of Mississippi, 1981).

31. Charles M. Oliver, *A Moving Picture Feast: The Filmgoer's Hemingway* (New York: Praeger, 1989).

32. Paul Smith, *A Reader's Guide to the Short Stories of Ernest Hemingway* (Boston: G.K. Hall, 1989).

33. Susan F. Beegel, *Hemingway's Neglected Short Fiction: New Perspectives* (Ann Arbor: University of Michigan Research Press, 1989).

Hemingway's Major Works

Three Stories & Ten Poems. Paris and Dijon: Contact Publishing Co., 1923.

in our time. Paris: Three Mountains Press, 1924.

In Our Time. New York: Boni & Liveright, 1925.

The Torrents of Spring. New York: Scribner's, 1926.

The Sun Also Rises. New York: Scribner's, 1926.

Men without Women. New York: Scribner's, 1927.

A Farewell to Arms. New York: Scribner's, 1929.

Death in the Afternoon. New York: Scribner's, 1932.

Winner Take Nothing. New York: Scribner's, 1933.

Green Hills of Africa. New York: Scribner's, 1935.

To Have and Have Not. New York: Scribner's, 1937.

The Fifth Column and the First Forty-Nine Stories. New York: Scribner's, 1938.

For Whom the Bell Tolls. New York: Scribner's, 1940.

Across the River and into the Trees. New York: Scribner's, 1950.

The Old Man and the Sea. New York: Scribner's, 1952.

A Moveable Feast. New York: Scribner's, 1964.

Islands in the Stream. New York: Scribner's, 1970.

The Dangerous Summer. New York: Scribner's, 1985.

The Garden of Eden. New York: Scribner's, 1986.

Hemingway's Short-Story Collections

Three Stories & Ten Poems. Paris and Dijon: Contact Publishing Company, 1923.

"Up in Michigan"
"Out of Season"
"My Old Man"

In Our Time. New York: Boni and Liveright, 1925.

"On the Quai at Smyrna" (first published as the introduction to the 1930 edition of *In Our Time*)
"Indian Camp"
"The Doctor and the Doctor's Wife"
"The End of Something"
"The Three-Day Blow"
"The Battler"
"A Very Short Story"
"Soldier's Home"
"The Revolutionist"
"Mr. and Mrs. Elliot"
"Cat in the Rain"
"Out of Season"
"Cross-Country Snow"
"My Old Man"
"Big Two-Hearted River"
"L'Envoi"

Men without Women. New York: Scribner's, 1927.

"The Undefeated"
"In Another Country"
"Hills Like White Elephants"

"The Killers"
"Che Ti Dice la Patria?"
"Fifty Grand"
"A Simple Enquiry"
"Ten Indians"
"A Canary for One"
"An Alpine Idyll"
"A Pursuit Race"
"Today Is Friday"
"Banal Story"
"Now I Lay Me"

Winner Take Nothing. New York: Scribner's, 1933.

"After the Storm"
"A Clean, Well-Lighted Place"
"The Light of the World"
"God Rest You Merry, Gentlemen"
"The Sea Change"
"A Way You'll Never Be"
"The Mother of a Queen"
"One Reader Writes"
"Homage to Switzerland"
"A Day's Wait"
"A Natural History of the Dead"
"Wine of Wyoming"
"The Gambler, the Nun, and the Radio"
"Fathers and Sons"

The Fifth Column and the First Forty-Nine Stories. New York: Scribner's, 1938. Reprints stories from above collections with the following additions:

"The Short Happy Life of Francis Macomber"
"The Capital of the World"
"The Snows of Kilimanjaro"
"Old Man at the Bridge"

The Fifth Column and Four Stories of the Spanish Civil War. New York: Scribner's, 1969.

"The Denunciation"
"The Butterfly and the Tank"
"Night before Battle"
"Under the Ridge"

The Complete Short Stories of Ernest Hemingway. New York: Scribner's, 1987. Reprints stories from above collections with the following additions:

"One Trip Across"
"The Tradesman's Return"
"Nobody Ever Dies"
"The Good Lion"
"The Faithful Bull"
"Get a Seeing-Eyed Dog"
"A Man of the World"
"Summer People"
"The Last Good Country"
"An African Story"
"A Train Trip"
"The Porter"
"Black Ass at the Cross Roads"
"Landscape with Figures"
"I Guess Everything Reminds You of Something"
"Great News from the Mainland"
"The Strange Country"

Writings about Ernest Hemingway, 1974-1989

1974

1 ASSELINEAU, ROGER. "Ernest Hemingway–A Rebel Rediscovers Tradition or the Destruction and Rehabilitation of Traditional Values in E. Hemingway's Fiction." In *Studien zur Englischen und Amerikanischen Sprache und Literatur: Festschrift für Helmut Papajewski*. Edited by Paul G. Buchloh, Inge Leimberg, and Herbert Rauter. Neumünster: Wacholtz, pp. 387-404.

　　　Examination of the author's evolving system of values, concluding that Hemingway rejected ready-made solutions in favor of a practical and nontheological philosophy of life. After eventually rejecting nihilism, Hemingway rebuilt an ethic "both pragmatic and heroic in order to help us save our souls–even if we have none–and give value and meaning to our lives–even if we are only 'brief candles.'"

2 BELL, H.H., Jr. "Hemingway's 'The Short Happy Life of Francis Macomber.'" *Explicator* 32, no. 9 (May): item 78.

　　　Comments on Wilson's application of the professional hunter's code to both animals and humans alike.

3 BRAUN, RICHARD E. "Echoes from the Sea: A Hemingway Rubric." *Fitzgerald/Hemingway Annual*, pp. 201-5.

　　　After discussing themes of ownership, use, and loss in *To Have and Have Not*, Braun suggests Philostratus's *Life of Apollonius of Tyana* as a possible source for the novel.

4 BRENAN, GERALD. *Personal Record: 1920-1972*. London: Jonathan Cape, pp. 367-68.

1

Describes his 1959 meeting with Hemingway in Churriana where he found it difficult to talk with the writer. "It was as though he wanted to emphasize that he was not a writer but a sportsman, a good mixer in bars, a man whose friends were either simple uneducated people or else very rich like himself."

5 BRUCCOLI, MATTHEW J. "Interview with Allen Tate." *Fitzgerald/Hemingway Annual*, pp. 101-13.

Tate reminisces about Hemingway and Fitzgerald in Paris, including comments on Hemingway's interest in bicycle racing, his first three wives, his animosity toward Zelda Fitzgerald and Ford Madox Ford, and his sparring match with Morley Callaghan.

6 BUTTITA, TONY. *After the Good Gay Times: Asheville–Summer of '35, a Season with F. Scott Fitzgerald*. New York: Viking Press, 173 pp.

Numerous references to Hemingway, including commentary on the author's loss of respect for Fitzgerald as a writer, the modeling of Bill Gorton and the initial help Hemingway received from Fitzgerald in advancing his career. Evidently Fitzgerald never lost his admiration for Hemingway.

7 CLARK, C.E. FRAZER, Jr. "American Red Cross Reports on the Wounding of Lieutenant Ernest M. Hemingway–1918." *Fitzgerald/Hemingway Annual*, pp. 131-36.

Contains copies of two Red Cross reports and two Oak Park newspaper articles published after his return home.

8 CROZIER, ROBERT D., S.J. "For Thine Is the Power and the Glory: Love in *For Whom the Bell Tolls*." *Papers on Language and Literature* 10:76-97.

Interprets the *La Gloria* passages of the novel in light of the mystical writings of St. John of the Cross.

9 DAIKER, DONALD A. "The Affirmative Conclusion of *The Sun Also Rises*." *McNeese Review* 21:3-19.

Considers book 3 with its images of cleansing, selection of detail, and scenes showing Jake's emotional growth as crucial to an affirmative reading of the novel in which the main character has finally learned how to live.

10 DEMOTT, BENJAMIN. "The Art of Poetry XVIII: Archibald MacLeish." *Paris Review*, no. 58, pp. 52-81.

Interview. MacLeish considered Hemingway a close friend during much of the twenties and thirties and "still the great prose stylist of the century." Is saddened that the heroic myth surrounding the public figure of Hemingway eventually eclipsed his work.

11 DOODY, TERRENCE. "Hemingway's Style and Jake's Narration." *Journal of Narrative Technique* 4, no. 3:212-25.
Is bothered by Jake's lack of narrative autonomy due to his proximity to the author. Finds that "Jake is more a function of the style than its source."

12 DUGGAN, MARGARET M. "General Checklist." *Fitzgerald/Hemingway Annual,* pp. 331-32.
Lists articles and books written in 1972 and 1973 relating to Fitzgerald, Hemingway, and modernism.

13 _____. "Hemingway Checklist." *Fitzgerald/Hemingway Annual*, pp. 323-29.
Lists items written mainly between 1971 and 1973.

14 FARRELL, JAMES T. "The 1920s in American Life and Literature." *Fitzgerald/Hemingway Annual,* pp. 115-28.
Revised version of 1957 lecture at Duke University. Places Hemingway in a subordinate position during the 1920s. "The influential voices were Dreiser, Nathan, Mencken, Sinclair Lewis, and Sherwood Anderson; to some degree Carl Sandburg, Edgar Lee Masters and James Branch Cabell." Contends that by emphasizing leisure and consumption in his works, Hemingway is mirroring the changing attitudes of the 1920s.

15 GROSSMAN, EDWARD. "The Past Refinished." *Commentary* 57, no. 2 (February): 88-90.
Book review of Lillian Hellman's *Pentimento: A Book of Portraits*. Grossman criticizes Hellman's use of the "tough code" prose style reminiscent of Hemingway and Hammett as too mannered and self-limiting.

16 HOFFMAN, FREDERICK J. "Ernest Hemingway." In *Sixteen Modern American Authors: A Survey of Research and Criticism*. Rev. ed. Edited by Jackson R. Bryer. Durham, N.C.: Duke University Press, pp. 367-92.
Bibliographic essay of selected material, including bibliography, editions, biography, and criticism. Concludes with a supplement by Melvin J. Friedman updating the original 1968 study by Hoffman.

17 INGLIS, DAVID L. "Morley Callaghan and the Hemingway Boxing Legend." *Notes on Contemporary Literature* 4, no. 4 (September): 4-7.
Examines the myth of Hemingway's legendary boxing prowess.

18 KALLAPUR, S.T. "Ernest Hemingway's Conception of Love and Womanhood." *Banasthali Patrika* 19:37-47.

Sees all Hemingway heroines as basically the same, obedient and subservient – their role being to ensure the comfort of their men. "Love, which is a union of two souls, an understanding between two minds and an adaptation between two bodies, which together finally creates a being superior to themselves, is not there." Love in Hemingway's fiction seldom transcends the physical.

19 KANN, HANS-JOACHIM. "Ernest Hemingway and the Arts: A Necessary Addendum." *Fitzgerald/Hemingway Annual,* pp. 145-54.

Feels the contents of Hemingway's private library in Cuba should have been taken into account by Emily Stipes Watts in her *Ernest Hemingway and the Arts* (Urbana: University of Illinois Press, 1971). A library checklist reveals a considerable number of his volumes devoted to art.

20 KERRIGAN, WILLIAM. "Something Funny about Hemingway's Count." *American Literature* 46, no. 1 (March): 87-93.

In viewing Count Mippipopolous as a model for Jake, Kerrigan discusses both men's impotence and relationship to Brett.

21 KOBLER, J.F. "The Short Happy Illusion of Francis Macomber." *Quartet* 45-46:62-66.

Argues that Macomber's assumed bravery at the time of his death is really "temporary illusion," a self-deception.

22 KOONTZ, LEAH RICE. "My Favorite Subject Is Hadley." *Connecticut Review* 8, no. 1:36-41.

Interview with Hadley Richardson in which she reminisces about her marriage to Hemingway and their time spent in Paris and Spain during the 1920s.

23 KVAM, WAYNE. "Hemingway's 'Banal Story.'" *Fitzgerald/Hemingway Annual,* pp. 181-91.

Manuscript study. Treats Hemingway's parody of the style, thought, and format of the *Forum* by tracing sections of "Banal Story" to specific authors, articles, and issues. Sees the main conflict to be Hemingway's "deliberate contrast" of the *Forum's* abstract responses to life with the real responses of the writer found at the beginning, middle, and end of the short story.

24 LANEY, RUTH. "A Conversation with Ernest Gaines." *Southern Review* 10, no. 1 (January): 1-14.

Gaines feels Hemingway's short stories influenced him "much more than any one particular [Hemingway] novel."

25 LAURENCE, FRANK M. "Death in the Matinée: The Film Endings of Hemingway's Fiction." *Literature/Film Quarterly* 2, no. 1 (Winter): 44-51.

Examines the distorted endings of several film versions of Hemingway's novels, remarking on Hollywood's reliance upon sentimentality and emotional gratification in the adaptations. Reprinted with minor revision: 1989.38.

26 ____. "5000 Grand: The Plagiarism Suit against Hemingway." *Fitzgerald/Hemingway Annual*, pp. 193-99.

Recounts John Igual De Montijo's 1941 suit against Hemingway for allegedly plagiarizing two of his plays in *For Whom the Bell Tolls*. His case was dismissed.

27 LIGHT, MARTIN. "Sweeping Out Chivalric Silliness: The Example of *Huck Finn* and *The Sun Also Rises*." *Mark Twain Journal* 17, no. 3:18-21.

Sees the characters in both novels as archetypes of Cervantes's *Don Quixote*. The quixotic Tom Sawyer and Robert Cohn, after reading romantic literature, are inspired to pursue fanciful adventures while Huck Finn and Jake Barnes, in their adherence to practicality and common sense, resemble the realist Sancho Panza.

28 LUCID, ROBERT F. "Three Public Performances: Fitzgerald, Hemingway, Mailer." *American Scholar* 43, no. 3 (Summer): 447-66.

Theorizes that the above three authors became cultural heroes because of the "personal presence" found in their works and their individualist roles as artists in society. Lucid traces Hemingway's transformation from public figure to legend, suggesting that "readers sought him out to learn the secret of how to win."

29 McCARTHY, HAROLD T. "Hemingway and Life as Play." In *The Expatriate Perspective: American Novelists and the Idea of America*. Rutherford, N.J.: Fairleigh Dickinson University Press, pp. 136-55.

Categorizes Hemingway as a "Neo-Transcendentalist." Relying heavily on biographical material, McCarthy contends that by living in Paris, Hemingway was able to transcend his narrow cultural attitudes and recognize both his individual freedom in unity with nature and the reality of his existence as a minute part of the whole of the universe.

30 McCLELLAN, DAVID. "Is Custer a Model for the Fascist Captain in *For Whom the Bell Tolls*?" *Fitzgerald/ Hemingway Annual*, pp. 239-41.

Points to the foolish actions and physical description of the Fascist captain in chapter 27 as proof that he might have been modeled after Custer. Includes other references to Custer Hemingway made elsewhere.

31 MANSELL, DARREL. "*The Old Man and the Sea* and the Computer." *Computers and the Humanities* 8:195-206.

Based on computer and statistical analysis, Mansell contends that *The Old Man and the Sea* more closely resembles "The Capital of the World" written in 1936 than other works written around 1951, the accepted date of *The Old Man and the Sea*.

32 MERRILL, ROBERT. "Tragic Form in *A Farewell to Arms*." *American Literature* 45, no. 4:571-79.

Reads *A Farewell to Arms* as a new form of tragedy (unlike Aristotelian tragedy) in which the protagonist acts admirably but is doomed to suffer regardless of his actions.

33 MILES, ROSALIND. *The Fiction of Sex: Themes and Functions of Sex Difference in the Modern Novel*. New York: Barnes & Noble, pp. 111-14.

Briefly looks at Hemingway's negative treatment of women, finding the writer's manipulation of the masculine romance implicitly antifeminist.

34 MOLYNEUX, THOMAS. "The Affirming Balance of Voice." *Shenandoah* 25, no. 2 (Winter): 27-43.

Refers briefly to the "artificial manner" of Hemingway's diction.

35 MONTEIRO, GEORGE. "Addenda to Hanneman's Hemingway: Books on Trial." *Papers of the Bibliographical Society of America* 71, no. 4:514-15.

Lists reviews of Hemingway's works in *Books on Trial* and the *Critic* not mentioned in Audre Hanneman's 1967 *Ernest Hemingway: A Comprehensive Bibliography* (Princeton) and her 1975 *Supplement*.

36 _____. "Hemingway on Dialogue in 'A Clean, Well-Lighted Place.'" *Fitzgerald/Hemingway Annual*, p. 243.

Comments on the incredible amount of scholarship devoted to straightening out the ambiguous dialogue. Points out that Hemingway thought the story was clear as originally published.

37 MURPHY, MICHAEL. "Ernest Miller Hemingway." In *Hemingway, a 75th Anniversary Tribute*. Edited by Vincent Starrett and Michael Murphy. St. Louis: Autolycus Press, pp. 37-54.

Biographical account of Hemingway's early years spent in Oak Park and its influence on him. Looks briefly at his father's suicide, his mother's artistic abilities, and his early contributions to the school newspaper *Trapeze*. Appeared originally in *Inland*.

38 _____. Introduction to *Heritage ... For My Children*, by Grace Hall Hemingway. St. Louis: Autolycus Press, pp. 1-4.

In introducing Grace Hall's genealogical narrative, Murphy points out Hemingway's mother's own artistic abilities and speculates on the influence of the Hall lineage on the author.

39 _____. "*McNaught's Monthly*: Addenda to the Bibliographies of Cather, Dickinson, Fitzgerald, Ford, Hemingway, Hergesheimer, and Machen." *Papers of the Bibliographical Society of America* 68, no. 1:64-65.

Lists four reviews and one letter not mentioned in Audre Hanneman's 1967 *Ernest Hemingway: A Comprehensive Bibliography* (Princeton).

40 _____. "Rod and Gun." In *Hemingway, a 75th Anniversary Tribute*. Edited by Vincent Starrett and Michael Murphy. St. Louis: Autolycus Press, pp. 10-20.

Details Hemingway's interest in fishing and hunting as evidenced in works such as "Big Two-Hearted River," "Out of Season," and *The Old Man and the Sea*. Concludes that Hemingway's ability to render sporting experience derives not from book learning but from his own time spent in the outdoors.

41 NAGARAJAN, M.S. "The Structure of 'The Killers.'" *Literary Half-Yearly* 15, no. 1:114-15.

Classifying "The Killers" as a drama, Nagarajan analyzes the dramatic function of each of the four scenes.

42 NOLAN, WILLIAM F. *Hemingway: Last Days of the Lion*. Santa Barbara: Capra Press, 38 pp.

Reprint of 1964 original with minor revisions. Brief biographical sketch of Hemingway's last years, focusing on his physical and psychological deterioration. Concerning Hemingway's suicide, Nolan writes, "When a lion is wounded it must be destroyed; that's the law of safari, the code Hemingway strictly held to." Includes poem on Hemingway by Nolan entitled "Now Never There" and a biographical checklist.

43 _____. "The Man behind the Masks: Hemingway as a Fictional Character." *Fitzgerald/Hemingway Annual*, pp. 207-13.

Authors have found the "larger-than-life" Hemingway an appropriate source for their own fiction. Nolan looks at their treatment of him in several such novels, including *Chosen Country* by Dos Passos and *The Sound of the Trumpet* by Leicester Hemingway.

44 RODGER, WILLIAM. "The Immortal Hemingway." *Hobbies* 79 (September): 154-55.
Provides information on Hemingway's manuscripts, letters, and other items of interest to the collector.

45 RODGERS, BERNARD F., Jr. "The Nick Adams Stories: Fiction or Fact?" *Fitzgerald/Hemingway Annual*, pp. 155-62.
Is bothered by Young's biographical approach in arranging *The Nick Adams Stories* (Scribner's, 1972). Internal evidence such as adolescent dialogue and references to baseball, drinking, and literature show "The End of Something" and "The Three-Day Blow" to be both prewar experiences.

46 ROSEN, KENNETH. "Ten Eulogies: Hemingway's Spanish Death." *Bulletin of the New York Public Library* 77:276-77.
Lists ten Spanish eulogies written in 1961. "The notion that Hemingway's final act [suicide] is existential and completely understandable and in full accord with the philosophy expressed in his writings is a pervasive one in these Spanish responses."

47 SINHA, KRISHNA NANDAN. "*The Old Man and the Sea*: An Approach to Meaning." In *Indian Studies in American Fiction*. Edited by M.K. Naik, S.K. Desai, and S. Mokashi-Punekar. Dharwar: Karnatak University; Delhi: Macmillan India, pp. 219-28.
Primarily concerned with the central theme of incarnation. In looking at the spiritual nature of the text, Sinha finds that for Hemingway "a deep and powerful response to experience brings him closer to the understanding of the human condition which the scriptures present with religious sanction. There is more of Christ in the sea-novel than anywhere else, and, in this sense, Hemingway is the most religious of novelists."

48 SKIPP, FRANCIS E. "Metempsychosis in the Stream, or What Happens in 'Bimini'?" *Fitzgerald/Hemingway Annual*, pp. 137-43.
Analyzes the crucifixion imagery surrounding David Hudson during his struggle with the broadbill, contending that David's crucifixion redeems the guilty Roger Davis, thus freeing his creative powers.

49 STARK de VALVERDE, DOROTHY. "An Analysis of 'The Killers' and the Work of Ernest Hemingway." *Revista de la Universidad de Costa Rica* 39:129-37.

Analyzes the primary elements of the short story including characterization, setting, and plot. Finds the basic style, conflict, and theme of "The Killers" representative of the Hemingway canon.

50 STARRETT, VINCENT. "Where's Papa?" In *Hemingway, A 75th Anniversary Tribute*. Edited by Vincent Starrett and Michael Murphy. St. Louis: Autolycus Press, pp. 21-35.

Gives a brief biographical assessment of Hemingway's early influences, focusing on both the vitality and creativity of his maternal side and his eventual alienation from family. Believes the ever-expanding Hemingway canon will long provide grist for the critical mill. Appeared originally in the *Chicago Tribune*.

51 TANNER, STEPHEN L. "Hemingway: The Function of Nostalgia." *Fitzgerald/Hemingway Annual*, pp. 163-74.

Finds Hemingway's focus on nostalgia serves as a source of realism in converting experience into art. Contends that Hemingway wrote often of his wounding in Italy not to exorcise himself of the memory but to cherish the experience, for it enabled him to write accurately about war, death, and violence.

52 TUTUNJIAN, JERRY. "A Conversation with Ross Macdonald." *Tamarack Review* 62:66-85.

Crime novelist Macdonald mentions briefly that he admires the works of Hemingway.

53 UNRUE, JOHN. "The Valley of Baca and *A Farewell to Arms*." *Fitzgerald/Hemingway Annual*, pp. 229-34.

Applies Psalm 84 to chapter 37, finding that Catherine and Frederic misinterpret the symbolic significance of the rain upon their arrival in Switzerland as they sing praises for their deliverance. "The rain that greets them is, in fact, the same foreboding, foreshadowing rain, symbolic of disaster, that Hemingway scholars have pointed to for years."

54 VAIDYANATHAN, T.G. "The Nick Adams Stories and the Myth of Initiation." In *Indian Studies in American Fiction*. Edited by M.K. Naik, S.K. Desai, & S. Mokashi-Punekar. Dharwar: Karnatak University; Delhi: Macmillan India, pp. 203-18.

Objects to reading the early stories as initiations, contending that even when Nick is the center of the experience little evidence of real change or self-discovery is revealed. Instead, the young Nick responds to unfamiliar situations by denying their reality, refusing to think about them, or fleeing.

55 WALCUTT, CHARLES C. "Hemingway's *The Sun Also Rises*." *Explicator* 32:item 57.

Objects to Twitchell's reading (*Explicator* 30:item 24) of the main characters as adolescents. Walcutt sees them as shattered people struggling to survive in a spiritually troubled world.

56 WARNER, STEPHEN D. "Hemingway's *The Old Man and the Sea*." *Explicator* 33:item 9.

Briefly comments on the narrative function of the five references to Africa and the lions on the beach.

57 WATSON, JAMES GRAY. "'A Sound Basis of Union': Structural and Thematic Balance in 'The Short Happy Life of Francis Macomber.'" *Fitzgerald/Hemingway Annual*, pp. 215-28.

In finding the faulty marriage to be thematically central to the story, Watson contends that the Macomber relationship based on mutual dependence is proof that Margot shot at the buffalo.

58 WEEKS, LEWIS E., Jr. "Two Types of Tension: Art vs Campcraft in Hemingway's 'Big Two-Hearted River.'" *Studies in Short Fiction* 11:433-34.

Argues that Hemingway deliberately depicted the pitching of the tent improperly in order to symbolize Nick's emotional strain and need for security. Weeks points out that artists sometimes have to sacrifice realism for art's sake.

59 WELLS, DAVID J. "Hemingway in French." *Fitzgerald/Hemingway Annual*, pp. 235-38.

In comparing French translations of *The Snows of Kilimanjaro and Other Stories* and *In Our Time* with the originals, Wells finds that true Hemingway style is sometimes sacrificed in French translations for the sake of audience.

60 WHITE, WILLIAM. "Hemingway on a Cuban Postage Stamp." *American Book Collector* 25, no. 1:34.

Describes in detail the set of 1963 Cuban stamps depicting either scenes from Hemingway's novels or the Finca Vigía.

61 _____. "An Inflationary Note on Hemingway." *Literary Sketches* 14, no. 3:4.

Notes that in 1946 he paid $10 for a bound cloth edition of *God Rest You Merry, Gentlemen* and $30 for a signed edition of *A Farewell to*

Arms. Twenty-seven years later the former is selling for $200 while the latter is up to $450.

62 WOODRESS, JAMES. "Ernest Hemingway (1898-1961)." In *American Fiction, 1900-1950: A Guide to Information Sources*. Vol. 1. Detroit: Gale Research, pp. 117-23.
    Bibliographical essay listing bibliographies, manuscripts, editions and reprints, biographies, and important criticism.

63 YANNELLA, PHILLIP R. "Notes on the Manuscript, Date, and Sources of Hemingway's 'Banal Story.'" *Fitzgerald/Hemingway Annual*, pp. 175-79.
    Manuscript study. References to specific boxing and bullfighting events suggest the date to be 1925. Gives evidence that "Banal Story" parodies the January 1925 issue of the *Forum*.

1975

1 ADAIR, WILLIAM. "*A Farewell to Arms*: A Dream Book." *Journal of Narrative Technique* 5, no. 1 (January): 40-56.
   Discusses the novel's resemblance to romance literature while stylistically and structurally examining its dreamlike quality. Concludes that the novel is a "dreamscape across which the protagonist flees from time and death, reenacting the primordial event of the story (the wounding) until it is exorcised in the death of Frederic's other self, in the death of Catherine." Reprinted: 1987.6.

2 ____. "Time and Structure in *A Farewell to Arms*." *South Dakota Review* 13, no. 1:165-71.
   Traces time's symbolic embodiment in linear imagery throughout the novel, concluding that the passage of time leads eventually to change and death – both beyond Frederic's control.

3 ASTRO, RICHARD. "Phlebas Sails the Caribbean: Steinbeck, Hemingway, and the American Waste Land." In *The Twenties: Fiction, Poetry, Drama*. Edited by Warren French. Deland, Fla.: Everett/Edwards, pp. 215-33.
   Compares Steinbeck's wasteland vision in *Cup of Gold* with Hemingway's in *To Have and Have Not*. Outlines similarities in characterization and theme but concludes that only Hemingway's novel holds the possibility of recovery.

4 BAKER, CARLOS. "Hemingway's Empirical Imagination." In *Individual and Community: Variations on a Theme in American Fiction*.

Edited by Kenneth H. Baldwin and David K. Kirby. Durham, N.C.: Duke University Press, pp. 94-111.

Discusses Hemingway's acute powers of observation and early practice of transforming authentic experience into literature. However, in later works "such as *Across the River, Islands in the Stream,* and even *The Old Man and the Sea,* one finds an ulterior and perhaps subconscious tendency to exploit his personal experiences not objectively, to enrich his prose from the empirical springs, but subjectively, as a means of justifying himself and his actions in the eyes of the great world."

5 BARBOUR, JAMES, and SATTELMEYER, ROBERT. "Baseball and Baseball Talk in *The Old Man and the Sea.*" *Fitzgerald/Hemingway Annual,* pp. 281-87.

Examines the historical context of the baseball references in relation to Santiago's struggle with the sea. Finds baseball and "baseball talk" serving as an initiation into adulthood for Manolin and an example of heroic action for Santiago.

6 BARGER, JAMES. *Ernest Hemingway: American Literary Giant.* Charlottesville, N.Y.: SamHar Press, 28 pp.

Surface biography focused on the larger-than-life image of the writer.

7 BECK, WARREN. "The Shorter Happy Life of Mrs. Macomber–1955." *Modern Fiction Studies* 21, no. 3 (Autumn): 363-85.

Reprint of original 1955 article (*Modern Fiction Studies* 1:28-37) with a 1975 addenda defending his original reading of the story which has come under attack by Mark Spilka. Beck questions both Wilson's credibility as a narrator and his ability to understand Margot Macomber. See 1976.84 for additional discussion.

8 BIGSBY, C.W.E. "Hemingway: The Recoil from History." In *The Twenties: Fiction, Poetry, Drama.* Edited by Warren French. Deland, Fla.: Everett/Edwards, pp. 203-13.

Sees Hemingway's protagonists responding to the wasteland by devising strategies that impose order and balance on an otherwise disordered world. Cut off from the once-supportive structures of the past, these characters must codify their experiences in order to find meaning and dignity in their continued existence.

9 BRUCCOLI, MATTHEW J. *The O'Hara Concern: A Biography of John O'Hara.* New York: Random House, 417 pp.

Numerous references to Hemingway, including commentary on O'Hara's well-known and controversial *New York Times* book review of

Across the River and into the Trees aimed at reaffirming Hemingway's literary stature.

10 _____. "Stan Ketchel and Steve Ketchel: A Further Note on 'The Light of the World.'" *Fitzgerald/ Hemingway Annual*, pp. 325-26.

Although positive that the Steve Ketchel mentioned in the short story is middleweight champion Stan Ketchel and that Alice is telling the truth, Bruccoli comments on another Steve Ketchel, a Chicago-area fighter with whom Hemingway may also have been familiar.

11 BRÜNING, EBERHARD. "Progressive American Writers' Organizations and Their Impact on Literature during the Nineteen Thirties." *Zeitschrift für Anglistik und Amerikanistik* 23, no. 3:208-16.

Discusses briefly Hemingway's involvement in the Spanish civil war, his writing of *The Fifth Column* and *For Whom the Bell Tolls*, and his speech denouncing fascism at the Second American Writers' Congress.

12 CHATMAN, SEYMOUR. "Towards a Theory of Narrative." *New Literary History* 6, no. 2 (Winter): 295-318.

Mentions briefly that "Hills Like White Elephants" requires the reader to infer a great deal.

13 CROZIER, ROBERT D., S.J. "Home James: Hemingway's Jacob." *Papers on Language and Literature* 11:293-301.

Looks closely at Hemingway's use of the Jacob motif in his works, citing major literary sources in the Bible and the writings of St. John of the Cross.

14 DAIKER, DONALD A. "The Pied Piper in *The Sun Also Rises.*" *Fitzgerald/Hemingway Annual*, pp. 235-37.

Comments on the allusion in book 2, Chapter 15 to Browning's poem, which "anticipates Jake's loss of control, his behaving in childish ways, and, consequently, his at least temporary failure to learn how to live."

15 DUGGAN, MARGARET M. "General Checklist." *Fitzgerald/Hemingway Annual*, pp. 369-70.

Lists books and articles written between 1973 and 1975 relating to Fitzgerald, Hemingway, and modernism.

16 FALBO, ERNEST S. "Carlo Linati: Hemingway's First Italian Critic and Translator." *Fitzgerald/Hemingway Annual*, pp. 293-306.

Establishes Linati as the first Italian critic-observer to report on the American expatriate writers. Also credits Linati with the first Italian translation of the author's work ("Soldier's Home"), which appeared in 1925.

17 FISHER, EDWARD. "What Papa Said." *Connecticut Review* 8, no. 2:16-20.

Recollections of the great 1935 Labor Day Hurricane in Matecumbe Key where many veterans were drowned. After viewing the bodies and wreckage, Hemingway remarked to Fisher, "No man alone now has got a bloody [obscenity] chance." In 1937 Fisher recognized this line as "a man alone ain't got no bloody f---ing chance" in *To Have and Have Not*.

18 FORD, HUGH. *Published in Paris: American and British Writers, Printers, and Publishers in Paris, 1920-1939*. New York: Macmillan Publishing Co., pp. 13-14, 49-50, 57, 104-8, 221-22, 225, 226.

Numerous references to Hemingway, including brief comments on his relationships with Sylvia Beach, Gertrude Stein, Robert McAlmon, and Caresse Crosby and the publication of some of his early works such as *Three Stories & Ten Poems* and *in our time*.

19 FRIEDMAN, NORMAN. "Plot and Symbol in the Novel: Hardy, Hemingway, Crane, Woolf, Conrad." In *Form and Meaning*. Athens: University of Georgia Press, pp. 318-39.

Argues against standard interpretations that Frederic Henry in *A Farewell to Arms* is either being punished for his immorality or victimized by war; instead, finds biology at the center of his misfortunes. Describes the war "as playing a strictly subordinate role causally and as serving otherwise mainly as an appropriate background."

20 ____. "Self and Universe in Hemingway." In *Form and Meaning*. Athens: University of Georgia Press, pp. 266-86.

Defines and interprets Hemingway's transcendent vision, placing him within the transcendental tradition that views the world as false while still recognizing it as a potential source of reality and truth. Like that of Henry James, Hemingway's vision, "while incapable of seeing human life and history in terms of some grand design, does nevertheless find a transcendent meaning in experience – a meaning that inheres in the living of a person's 'greater moments,' moments of courage, honesty, generosity, acceptance, and integrity."

21 GAJDUSEK, R.E. "Death, Incest, and the Triple Bond in Later Plays of Shakespeare." *American Imago* 31, no. 2:109-159.

Mentions briefly *King Lear* and *Macbeth* as thematic sources for Hemingway's *Across the River and into the Trees*.

22 GRIMES, CARROLL. "Hemingway's 'Defense of Dirty Words': A Reconsideration." *Fitzgerald/Hemingway Annual*, pp. 217-27.
    Looks closely at Hemingway's opinions on censorship found in his 1934 *Esquire* letter, "Defense of Dirty Words," and the critical backlash they generated.

23 GRIMES, LARRY. "Night Terror and Morning Calm: A Reading of Hemingway's 'Indian Camp' as Sequel to 'Three Shots.'" *Studies in Short Fiction* 12, no. 4 (Fall): 413-15.
    Sees the death and violence of "Indian Camp" thematically concluding "Three Shots." Explores the possibility that Uncle George is the father of the Indian woman's baby.

24 HAGOPIAN, JOHN V. "Hemingway: Ultimate Exile." *Mosaic* 8, no. 3:77-87.
    Biographical approach concerned with Hemingway's exile from America, society, and love. Hagopian concludes that Hemingway transcribed his separation from the "good life" into literature, thus revealing the horror of being alone.

25 HERNDON JERRY A. "No 'Maggie's Drawers' for Margot Macomber." *Fitzgerald/Hemingway Annual*, pp. 289-91.
    Argues against earlier criticism exonerating Margot of murder because of her inability to control such a heavy rifle. In actuality, the mild recoil of the 6.5 Mannlicher makes it quite suitable for women shooters.

26 HOLLAND, NORMAN N. "Further Evidence: Sam, Saul, Shep, Sebastian, and Sandra Read Fitzgerald's 'Winter Dreams' and Hemingway's 'The Battler.'" In *5 Readers Reading*. New Haven, Conn.: Yale University Press, pp. 300-394.
    From a psychoanalytic theoretical base Holland demonstrates the ways individual readers respond to and interpret literature in terms of their own identities.

27 ISLAM, SHAMSUL. "The Kipling and Hemingway Codes: A Study in Comparison." *Explorations* 2, no. 2 (Winter): 22-28.
    Draws biographical, stylistic, and thematic comparisons between Kipling and Hemingway. Sees both authors as sharing a dark and hostile vision of the world where "even in defeat a kind of victory is possible if one preserves one's integrity and honour."

28 JAIN, SUNITA. "Of Women and Bitches: A Defense of Two Hemingway Heroines." *Journal of the School of Languages* 3, no. 2:32-35.

Sympathetic reading of both women, contending that "Catherine Barkley is Brett Ashley in another country, in another role, reminding us portentously what a woman can be."

29 JUSTUS, JAMES H. "Hawthorne's Coverdale: Character and Art in *The Blithedale Romance*." *American Literature* 47, no. 1 (March): 21-36.

Mentions briefly that Miles Coverdale is the fictional forerunner "to the desperate expatriates of Fitzgerald's and Hemingway's fiction and to the hollow men of Eliot's earlier poems."

30 KAPOOR, S.D. "Ernest Hemingway: The Man and the Mask." *Rajasthan University Studies in English* 8:36-53.

Traces biographical efforts up to the present. Includes Hemingway's negative responses to those published during his lifetime.

31 KINGTON, M. "Exclusive–Four Unpublished Early Masterpieces." *Critic* 34, no. 1:54-57.

Short-story parody of Hemingway's characteristic style.

32 KOBLER, J.F. "Hemingway's Four Dramatic Short Stories." *Fitzgerald/Hemingway Annual,* pp. 247-57.

Discusses the dramatic structure of "The Killers," "The Sea Change," "Hills Like White Elephants," and "A Clean, Well-Lighted Place," but finds that only the last "reaches near perfection by remaining within a dramatic mode, yet at the same time taking advantage of narrative and modified stream-of-consciousness techniques."

33 KRETZOI, CHARLOTTE. "Hemingway on Bullfights and Aesthetics." In *Studies in English and American.* Vol. 2. Edited by Erzsébet Perényi and Frank Tibor. Budapest: Department of English, L. Eotvos University, pp. 277-96.

Analyzes the close connection between death and art (Hemingway's theory of aesthetics) found in *Death in the Afternoon.* Parallels the two essential aspects of a great writer, loneliness and integrity, with those of the bullfighter who too must maintain dignity while facing the bull alone.

34 LAJOIE, RONALD, and LENTZ, SALLY. "Is Jake Barnes Waiting?" *Fitzgerald/Hemingway Annual,* pp. 229-33.

Discusses Hemingway's reference in *The Sun Also Rises* to Mason's "The Crystal Trench." Parallels the stoic protagonists of both works who wait in vain for the love of their lives.

35 LAYMAN, RICHARD. "Hemingway's Library Cards at Shakespeare and Company." *Fitzgerald/Hemingway Annual,* pp. 191-206.

Copies of Hemingway's borrowing records from Sylvia Beach's Shakespeare and Company for 1925-29, 1931, 1933, 1937, and 1938.

36 LEIGH, DAVID J., S.J. *"In Our Time*: The Interchapters as Structural Guides to a Psychological Pattern." *Studies in Short Fiction* 12, no. 1 (Winter): 1-8.

Structural examination in the light of psychological patterning, with special emphasis placed upon the character of Nick Adams and existential neurosis. Reprinted: 1983.98.

37 LEWIS, JANET. "Fitzgerald's 'Philippe, Count of Darkness.'" *Fitzgerald/Hemingway Annual,* pp. 7-32.

Discussion of Fitzgerald's Philippe stories in which "the Dark Ages serve as a metaphor for the troubled Thirties, the language imitates tough guy jargon and Philippe, the Hemingway figure, appears as a precursor of the modern hero." The brash, proud, and tough personality of Hemingway comes through in Fitzgerald's protagonist.

38 LODGE, DAVID. "Metaphor and Metonymy in Modern Fiction." *Critical Quarterly* 17, no. 1 (Spring): 75-93.

Using Roman Jakobson's distinction between metaphor and metonymy, Lodge looks briefly at the metonymic style of Hemingway's "In Another Country" in which repetition supports metaphor.

39 McCARTHY, PAUL. "Opposites Meet: Melville, Hemingway, and Heroes." *Kansas Quarterly* 7, no. 4:40-54.

Comparison of *Redburn* with the Nick Adams stories. McCarthy finds similar themes of skepticism, experience, and quest along with comparable techniques and structural patterns.

40 McCORMICK, JOHN. "The Anachronous Hero: Hemingway and Montherlant." In *Fiction as Knowledge: The Modern Post-Romantic Novel.* New Brunswick, N.J.: Rutgers University Press, pp. 109-31.

Compares Hemingway with Montherlant in the light of the romantic movement, commenting on both authors' frequent joining of eroticism and death. In his comparison of *A Farewell to Arms* with *Le Songe*, McCormick finds a historical continuity in Montherlant's work that is missing in Hemingway's.

41 McHANEY, THOMAS L. "Anderson, Hemingway, and the Origins of *The Wild Palms*." In *William Faulkner's "The Wild Palms": A Study.* Jackson: University Press of Mississippi, pp. 3-24.

Recounts Faulkner's and Hemingway's break from Anderson, distinguishing Hemingway's as the more permanent. In discussing their debt to Anderson, McHaney points to similarities in theme, character, and point of view in Anderson's *Dark Laughter*, Faulkner's *The Wild Palms*, and *A Farewell to Arms*.

42 McWILLIAMS, WILSON CAREY. "Natty Bumppo and the Godfather." *Colorado Quarterly* 24, no. 2:133-44.

The old vision in literature of taming the new frontier and making the way for civilization took a long time to fade but we see intimations of it in *For Whom the Bell Tolls*: "Hemingway's Natty Bumppo, Robert Jordan, moved on a stage in which shadowy puppeteers used his virtues for their own purposes."

43 MANN, JEANETTE W. "Toward New Archetypal Forms: Jean Stafford's *The Catherine Wheel*." *Critique: Studies in Modern Fiction* 17, no. 2:77-92.

Mentions briefly that Jean Stafford's *The Catherine Wheel* is more like a Hawthorne romance than a post-Hemingway novel.

44 MANSELL, DARREL. "When Did Ernest Hemingway Write *The Old Man and the Sea*?" *Fitzgerald/Hemingway Annual*, pp. 311-24.

An analysis of subject, style, length, and form points to the novel having been written in 1935 or 1936 and not 1951 as Hemingway claimed.

45 MARDER, DANIEL. "Exiles at Home in American Literature." *Mosaic* 8, no. 3:49-75.

Briefly includes Hemingway as one of the American exiles seeking spiritual refuge and lost culture abroad.

46 MONTEIRO, GEORGE. "Santiago, DiMaggio, and Hemingway: The Ageing Professionals of *The Old Man and the Sea*." *Fitzgerald/Hemingway Annual*, pp. 273-80.

Gives historical information on the baseball references. DiMaggio's courageous endurance of and recovery from a painful heel spur provides Santiago with a powerful example of victory in the face of adversity.

47 MURDOCH, CHARLES. "Essential Glassco." *Canadian Literature*, no. 65 (Summer), pp. 28-41.

Mentions briefly that John Glassco's *Memoirs of Montparnasse* contains recollections of those making literary history in Paris during the 1920s, including Hemingway, Joyce, and Stein.

48 MURRAY, DONALD M. "*The Day of the Locust* and *The Sun Also Rises*: Congruence and Caricature." *Fitzgerald/Hemingway Annual*, pp. 239-45.

Points out similarities in style, theme, and character in the cockfight episode of *The Day of the Locust* (chapter 21) and the bullfight in *The Sun Also Rises*. ". . .There is a significant reduction in scale and dignity that parodies the earlier novel. Hemingway mounts a serious drama in a great arena; West stages a chicken-fight in a garage."

49 "New & Notable." *Princeton University Library Chronicle* 37, no. 1 (Autumn): 53.

Announces additions to the Department of Rare Books and Special Collections, including the autograph manuscript of Hemingway's "A Day's Wait" and the corrected typescript of "Bull Fighting, Sport, and Industry."

50 PRESCOTT, HERMAN. "Hemingway vs Faulkner: An Intriguing Feud." *Lost Generation Journal* 3, no. 3 (Fall): 18-19.

Traces the long-standing Hemingway-Faulkner feud, which was, for the most part, carried on indirectly through courier-friends, editors, and press articles.

51 RAEBURN, JOHN. "Hemingway in the Twenties: 'The Artist's Reward.'" *Rocky Mountain Review of Language and Literature* 29:118-46.

Traces Hemingway's meteoric rise to fame during the 1920s, emphasizing his conscious manipulation of his public image.

52 RAO, E. NAGESWARA "Syntax as Rhetoric: An Analysis of Ernest Hemingway's Early Syntax." *Indian Linguistics* 36, no. 3:296-303.

Finds that Hemingway's early use of sequential syntactic connectives rather than causal connectives reflects his vision of the world as chaotic and irrational.

53 REDINGTON, JOAN WHEELER. "Before the Corrida." *Fitzgerald/Hemingway Annual,* pp. 309-10.

Recounts her brief meeting with Hemingway in a French café in 1959.

54 REINHOLD, ROBERT. "Hemingway Papers Open for Study in a Setting That Belies Their Vitality." *New York Times*, 31 January, pp. 35, 66.

Announces the opening of a portion of the Hemingway collection at the temporary home of the Kennedy Library.

55 SARASON, BERTRAM D. "Krebs in Kodiak." *Fitzgerald/Hemingway Annual,* pp. 209-15.

Attempts to piece together Hemingway's relationship with Krebs Friend whose name appears in some Hemingway letters, in "Soldier's

Home," and in Baker's *Hemingway: The Writer as Artist*. Suspects the true nature of their dealings has yet to be uncovered.

56 SCHONHORN, MANUEL. "*The Sun Also Rises*: I: The Jacob Allusion; II: Parody as Meaning." *Ball State University Forum* 16, no. 2 (Spring): 49-55.

Refutes earlier criticism expounding the irony of Jacob Barnes's biblical name, instead focusing upon the relationship between Barnes and the heroic and affirmative Jacob myth in which the Hebrew warrior struggles to gain a true understanding of himself and his place in the world.

57 SEATOR, LYNETTE HUBBARD. "The Antisocial Humanism of Cela and Hemingway." *Revista de Estudios Hispanicos* 9, no. 3 (October): 425-39.

Compares Hemingway's novels set in Spain with those of Camilo José Cela, finding similarities in subject, theme, characterization, and humanist attitudes.

58 SHAW, PATRICK W. "How Earnest Is the Image: Hemingway's Little Animals." *CEA Critic* 37, no. 3:5-8.

Looks in detail at Hemingway's use of small and domestic animals and animal imagery in *A Farewell to Arms* and briefly in other texts, concluding that Hemingway's real heroes are like the scrounging dogs and burning ants, those who struggle to survive – and those who endure.

59 SMITH, LEVERETT T., Jr. "How to Live in It." In *The American Dream & the National Game*. Bowling Green: Bowling Green University Popular Press, pp. 51-103.

Looks at the ways in which the evolving cultural perspective regarding work and play is reflected in such novels as *The Sun Also Rises* and *The Old Man and the Sea*. By the 1950s, play, "originally a challenge to work as an ideal, becomes a new concept of work, or at least has been made to operate within a context of work." Translating this concept of professionalism into an aesthetic ideal, Hemingway found parallel changes occurring with the role of artist as well.

60 SOMERS, PAUL, Jr. "Sherwood Anderson Introduces His Friend Ernest Hemingway." *Lost Generation Journal* 3, no. 3 (Fall): 24-26.

Contains excerpts of letters written by Anderson on the young Hemingway's behalf introducing him into the American expatriate and literary circles of 1920s Paris.

61 STEWART, DONALD OGDEN. *By a Stroke of Luck! An Autobiography*. New York: Paddington Press, pp. 115-44.

Numerous references to Hemingway. Stewart discusses his 1923 meeting with Hemingway in Paris and their growing friendship, including subsequent reunions in Pamplona for the fiesta of San Firmin. Stewart writes of the author, "I admired him tremendously as an honest unsentimental man who was trying to write the truth about life."

62 STRODE, HUDSON. *The Eleventh House: Memoirs*. New York: Harcourt Brace Jovanovich, pp. 91, 93, 167-71, 175.

Several references to Hemingway, including commentary on his writing habits and his place in American literature.

63 STUCKEY, W.J. "'The Killers' as Experience." *Journal of Narrative Technique* 5, no. 2 (May): 128-35.

Rejects the established view of the story as Nick's initiation into evil and Ole as representative of the Hemingway "code" hero. Stuckey contends that the author relates the real with the irrational in "a carefully contrived fictional 'experience' in which we are required to feel rather than to think."

64 UPDIKE, JOHN. "Papa's Sad Testament." In *Picked-Up Pieces*. New York: Alfred A. Knopf, pp. 422-27.

Review of *Islands in the Stream*. Finds in this "sad broken testament" that "the tension of art has been snapped and the line between sensitive vision and psychopathy has been crossed."

65 VANDERWERKEN, DAVID L. "One More River to Cross: The Bridge Motif in *The Sun Also Rises*." *CEA Critic* 37, no. 2:21-22.

Sees each of Jake's bridge crossings as symbolic steps in his "pilgrimage from the corruption of Paris to the purity of Burguete" and as a larger metaphor for art that connects the creator's imagination with the world.

66 WHITE, WILLIAM. "Hemingway Checklist." *Fitzgerald/Hemingway Annual,* pp. 351-68.

Lists 201 reviews, articles, and books written mainly in 1973.

67 _____. "Hemingway's 'Collected Poems.'" *Literary Sketches* 15, no. 4 (April): 1-3.

Traces the reprintings of several editions of Hemingway's poetry, remarking that although the poems themselves are of "little merit," the editions are still valuable to collectors.

68 _____. "Hemingway's Stature." *New Statesman* 89 (30 May): 724-25.

Disagrees with David Leitch's opinion (in May 16 issue) that Hemingway's stature has "virtually evaporated." Numerous editions and translations currently available point to the contrary.

69 WILSON, EDMUND. *The Twenties: From Notebooks and Diaries of the Period.* Edited by Leon Edel. New York: Farrar, Straus & Giroux, pp. 94, 375, 514.

Comments briefly on Fitzgerald's early adoration of Hemingway, mentions a letter from Hemingway on Charles Lindbergh, and also includes him on the guest list of an ideal party.

70 WINSLOW, RICHARD. "A Bibliographical Correction." *Fitzgerald/Hemingway Annual,* p. 307.

Corrects earlier statement that Hemingway's *Toronto Daily Star* article entitled "Buying Commission Would Cut Out Waste" appeared on 20 April 1920. The actual date was 26 April 1920.

71 ____. "'A Good Country': Hemingway at the L Bar T Ranch, Wyoming." *Fitzgerald/Hemingway Annual,* pp. 259-72.

Describes his visit to the L Bar T Ranch where Hemingway wrote off and on during the 1930s.

72 ZAYAS-BAZÁN, EDUARDO. "Hemingway: His Cuban Friends Remember." *Fitzgerald/Hemingway Annual,* pp. 153-90.

Interviews with Elicio Arguelles, Mario Menocal, and Thórbald Sánchez in which they recall their time spent with Hemingway in Cuba drinking, fishing, and shooting. Includes commentary on the Cuban revolution, Hemingway's writing and reading habits, and the filming of *The Old Man and the Sea.*

1976

1 BADVE, V.V. "The 'Camera Eye' Technique in Hemingway's Short Stories." *Journal of the Shivaji University* 9:81-86.

Looks at the levels of objectivity achieved in "In Another Country," "Hills Like White Elephants," "The Killers," and "Today Is Friday." Sees a definite progression from conventional narrative technique toward a more objective method as Hemingway attempts to reinforce subject matter with style.

2 BARBOUR, JAMES F. "'The Light of the World': The Real Ketchel and the Real Light." *Studies in Short Fiction* 13, no. 1 (Winter): 17-23.

Contends that an analysis of the disparity between the real boxing champion Stanley Ketchel and the fictional fighter in "The Light of the

World" reveals complex themes of "romance, reality, and the question of knowledge."

3 BASKETT, SAM S. "The Great Santiago: Opium, Vocation, and Dream in *The Old Man and the Sea*." *Fitzgerald/Hemingway Annual*, pp. 230-42.

Finds the baseball motif functioning ironically "as a symbol of that which is finally unessential to Santiago." By depicting DiMaggio's "greatness," Hemingway is able to emphasize the far greater achievements of the old man who is able to transcend the limits of vocation and entertainment through his dream.

4 BATAILLE, GEORGES. "Hemingway in the Light of Hegel." Translated by Ralph Vitello. *Semiotext(e)* 2, no. 2:5-15.

Traces Hemingway's "quest for sovereignty" back to Hegel's concept of the master, paying particular attention to Hemingway's games of life and death such as hunting, bullfighting, and warring. Reprint from *Critique*, no. 70 (March 1953).

5 BECK, WARREN. "Mr. Spilka's Problem: A Reply." *Modern Fiction Studies* 22, no. 2:256-69.

Critical exchange focused on "The Short Happy Life of Francis Macomber." Beck replies to Spilka's response (see 1976.84) regarding Beck's 1975 postscript (see 1975.7). Addresses the issue ("Spilka's problem") of "right" answers in texts.

6 BERNAD, MIGUEL ANSELMO. "Some Notes on the Influence of American Authors upon Filipino Writers." *Comparative Literature Studies* 13, no. 2 (June): 160-64.

Lists Hemingway as one of many American writers who have influenced Filipino literature.

7 BERRYMAN, JOHN. "Hemingway's 'A Clean, Well-Lighted Place.'" In *The Freedom of the Poet*. New York: Farrar, Straus & Giroux, pp. 217-221.

Notes the deceptively simple style as he looks briefly at rhythm, alliteration, religious symbolism, and the theme of *nada*. Revised reprint from *The Arts of Reading*, by Ralph Ross, Allen Tate, and John Berryman. New York: T.Y. Crowell, 1960.

8 BLUEFARB, SAM. "The Middle-Aged Man in Contemporary Literature: Bloom to Herzog." *College Language Association Journal* 20, no. 1 (September): 1-13.

Sees Cantwell's sentimental recollections of his Italian army days in *Across the River and into the Trees* as a futile attempt to recapture his youth and stave off impending death. Cantwell falls into the pattern of most middle-aged men in contemporary literature – fighting to maintain sanity "in the face of those pressures on him which constantly act as erosive and corrosive agents on that ability."

9 BOCAZ, SERGIO H. "Senecan Stoicism in Hemingway's 'The Short Happy Life of Francis Macomber.'" In *Studies in Language and Literature: The Proceedings of the 23rd Mountain Interstate Foreign Language Conference*. Edited by Charles L. Nelson. Richmond: Eastern Kentucky University, pp. 81-86.

Sees the "Hemingway Hero" displaying the same stoic characteristics as the ancient heroes described by the first-century philosopher Seneca. Parallels Seneca's stoic belief in the primacy of courage in preserving one's "manly essence" with the philosophy of Hemingway's Macomber who finds redemption through overcoming his fear of death.

10 BRACKENRIDGE, LOIS. "Analysis of 'Today Is Friday' by Ernest Hemingway." *Linguistics in Literature* 1, no. 2:1-10.

Looking carefully at the different responses of the three soldiers and wine seller, Brackenridge relates them to the Passion of Christ and finds that "all of the characters in this play are changed in some way by their participation in the drama of the crucifixion."

11 BRENNER, GERRY. "An Imitation of Dante's *Divine Comedy*: Hemingway's *Across the River and into the Trees*." *Fitzgerald/Hemingway Annual*, pp. 191-209.

Finds Hemingway consciously writing "in the spirit" of *The Divine Comedy*. Gives similarities in narrative point of view, style, themes of love and search for salvation, and historical and dream dimensions as proof that Hemingway was following the classical model. Brenner concludes by raising some provocative questions: "Is his imagination original?" "Or is it bookishly derivative?" "Do his works reveal structures that are organic or ones that are mechanically dependent upon preexisting form?"

12 BROER, LAWRENCE. "Hadley: An Engaging Person." *Lost Generation Journal* 4, no. 1 (Winter): 27-30.

Hadley Richardson and Stanley Kimmel reminisce about their days spent with Hemingway in Paris.

13 _____. "The Iceberg in 'A Clean, Well-Lighted Place.'" *Lost Generation Journal* 4, no. 2:14-15, 21.

Attributes the reader's growing awareness of nothingness, or *nada*, in the story to Hemingway's use of ironic contrast, images of isolation, and absence of emotional commentary. Sees the identities of the two old men symbolically merging.

14 BRYER, JACKSON R. "Fitzgerald and Hemingway." In *American Literary Scholarship: An Annual, 1974.* Edited by James Woodress. Durham, N.C.: Duke University Press, pp. 139-64.
Survey of criticism on both authors published during 1974. Bryer sees no "meaningful increase in worthwhile scholarly activity on either Fitzgerald or Hemingway."

15 CLIFFORD, PAULA M. "The American Novel and the French *Nouveau Roman*: Some Linguistic and Stylistic Comparisons." *Comparative Literature Studies* 13, no. 14:348-58.
Refers to Hemingway only briefly as she acknowledges the debt of the French *nouveau roman* of the late 1950s to American novels of the 1930s.

16 COUSINS, NORMAN. "The Hemingway Letters." *Saturday Review*, 2 October, pp. 4-6.
Comments on unpublished letters. From 1923 to 1925 Hemingway corresponded with anthologist Edward O'Brien about publishing his short stories. And from 1949 to 1951 he corresponded with Fitzgerald biographer Arthur Mizener. Although differences in tone and style are remarkable, Hemingway's emotional and professional insecurities are clearly present in both exchanges of letters.

17 DANGULOV, SAVVA. "Hemingway As Illustrated by Orest Vereisky." Translated by Alex Miller. *Soviet Literature* 9:161-64.
Contains several illustrations by Vereisky of scenes from Hemingway's works. As artists, Vereisky and Hemingway must both rely upon imagination in order to "reproduce all the complexity which is known as the truth of life."

18 DAS GUPTA, H. "Ernest Hemingway and the Spanish Bullfight." *Indian Journal of American Studies* 6, no. 1-2:55-64.
Looking at *Death in the Afternoon* and *The Sun Also Rises*, Das Gupta stresses that Hemingway saw bullfighting as embodying a philosophy of life corresponding closely to his own code. In order to live intensely and fully, Hemingway sought out the proximity to death found in the bullring.

19 DeFALCO, JOSEPH M. "Hemingway and Revolution: *Mankinde* Not Marx." In *Renaissance and Modern: Essays in Honor of Edwin M. Moseley.* Edited by Murray J. Levith. Saratoga Springs, N.Y.: Skidmore College, pp. 143-59.

Analyzes Hemingway's political writings of the middle period (*For Whom the Bell Tolls, To Have and Have Not, The Fifth Column*), finding that "from the mid-thirties on Hemingway evolved out of his lost generation flirtation with nihilism and moved toward a strongly humanistic and affirmative view of existence." Sees Robert Jordan rejecting the egocentricity marking earlier heroes as he makes the supreme altruistic sacrifice.

20 DUGGAN, MARGARET M. "General Checklist."
Fitzgerald/Hemingway Annual, pp. 273-74.
Lists books and an article written mainly in 1975 relating to Fitzgerald, Hemingway, and modernism.

21 DURHAM, PHILIP. "Ernest Hemingway's Grace under Pressure: The Western Code." *Pacific Historical Review* 45, no. 3 (August): 425-32.
Points to the many western settings and references to the West found in Hemingway's works, concluding that the Hemingway hero, although fully realized, follows the code of the traditional western hero.

22 ELLIOTT, GARY D. "*For Whom the Bell Tolls*: Regeneration of the Hemingway Hero." *CEA* 38, no. 4:24-29.
Equates destroying the bridge with spiritual dedication, seeing Jordan's commitment to duty as a substitute for religious faith.

23 FARRELL, JAMES T. *James T. Farrell Literary Essays, 1954-1974.* Edited by Jack Alan Robbins. Port Washington, N.Y.: Kennikat Press, pp. 23-25, 88-89.
Collection of Farrell's criticism and memoirs. Includes a brief biographical sketch of Hemingway, concluding with an equally brief assessment of his literary contribution. Recounts a 1936 Key West meeting with the author in which sports dominated the conversation. Reprint from 1968 *Chicago Daily News* article entitled "A Remembrance of Ernest Hemingway."

24 FETTERLEY, JUDITH. "*A Farewell to Arms*: Hemingway's 'Resentful Cryptogram.'" *Journal of Popular Culture* 10, no. 1 (Summer): 203-14.
Is concerned with the attitude of "immense hostility" toward women underlining the novel, from the death of Catherine to the treatment of the whores. "In reading it one is continually struck by the disparity between its overt fabric of idealized romance and its underlying vision of the radical limitations of love, between its surface idyll and its subsurface critique." Reprinted with minor revision: 1977.33, 1978.28, and 1987.6.

25 FOLEY, LOUIS. "Editing á la Hemingway." *CEA Forum* 6, no. 3:4-5, 16.

Speculates on the spelling and punctuation corrections made in the posthumously published *Islands in the Stream*. Put off by common grammatical errors found in many of Hemingway's texts.

26 FRENCH, WARREN, ed. *The Thirties: Fiction, Poetry, Drama*. 2d ed. Deland, Fla.: Everett Edwards, 259 pp.

Reprint with revisions of original 1967 edition, including additional bibliography of American literature and the Spanish Civil War.

27 FRIEDRICH, OTTO. *Going Crazy: An Inquiry into Madness in Our Time*. New York: Simon & Schuster, pp. 111-15.

Briefly traces Hemingway's increasing dementia, believing the author "may have been slowly going mad all of his life – certainly the eccentricities were all there, the manic role-playing and self-delusion, the half-repressed violence, the Münchausen sense of his own heroism. . . ."

28 GARRETY, MICHAEL. "Love and War: R.H. Mottram, *The Spanish Farm Trilogy*, and Ernest Hemingway's *A Farewell to Arms*." In *The First World War in Fiction: A Collection of Critical Essays*. Edited by Holger Klein. London and Basingstoke: Macmillan Press, pp. 10-22.

Compares the conjunction of love and war found in the works, contending that although *A Farewell to Arms* is "classed as a 'war novel' it might be better described as a novel of love set against a background of war, which by its violence enhances the transience of human life and hope."

29 GOODMAN, MARK. "At Sea with Hemingway." *Motor Boating and Sailing* 137 (June): 43, 115-16, 118.

Recounts some of Hemingway's larger-than-life fishing expeditions and more briefly their translation in such works as *The Old Man and the Sea* and *Islands in the Stream*.

30 GORDON, DAVID J. "The Son and the Father: Responses to Conflict in Hemingway's Fiction." In *Literary Art and the Unconscious*. Baton Rouge: Louisiana State University Press, pp. 171-97.

Psychological approach tracing chronologically Hemingway's response to inner conflict through nearly all of his major novels and short stories. Focuses in particular on the father-son relationship, especially in connection with the Crucifixion and the martyr-hero. In a brief afterword following his essay, Gordon comments on Hemingway's martyr-hero as "a product of cultural as well as individual determinants." Revised reprint from *Literature and Psychology* 16 (1966): 122-38.

31 GORDON, GERALD T. "Survival in *The Sun Also Rises* (Hemingway's Harvey Stone)." *Lost Generation Journal* 4, no. 2:10-11, 17.

Harvey Stone's ability to survive despite his circumstances serves as a reassuring example for Jake Barnes. "Stone's plight sustains Jake's 'philosophy' of buying in the world and paying for its pleasures."

32 GOSNELL, STEPHEN. "Leave the Kid Alone." *Esquire* 85, no. 3 (March): 97, 126.

Gosnell mentions *For Whom the Bell Tolls* as his introduction at the age of twelve to "good writing."

33 GREY, M. CAMERON. "Miss Toklas Alone." *Virginia Quarterly Review* 52, no. 4 (Autumn): 687-96.

Recounts his visits with Toklas in Paris after World War II. Toklas, in recalling Hemingway's fear of impending fatherhood, jealousy of Fitzgerald, and lack of physical stamina, merely echoes Stein's comments in *The Autobiography of Alice B. Toklas*.

34 GUNN, JESSIE C. "Structural Matrix: A Stylistic Analysis of 'The End of Something.'" *Linguistics in Literature* 1, no. 2:53-60.

In examining structure, vocabulary, and lexical choice, Gunn is primarily concerned with the symbolic significance of the defunct sawmill in relation to the Nick/Marjorie breakup and the promise of Nick's regeneration through a regrowth of timber.

35 HAYES [sic], PETER L. "Conrad and Hemingway." *American Notes & Queries* 14, no. 6:87-88.

Notes parallels of word choice and subject matter in passages from Conrad's preface to *The Nigger of the "Narcissus"* and Hemingway's *Death in the Afternoon*.

36 HEMINGWAY, GREGORY H. *Papa: A Personal Memoir.* Boston: Houghton Mifflin, 119 pp.

Loving yet candid portrait of what it was like being the youngest son of a world-famous author. Includes Hemingway fishing in Bimini, rescuing Gregory from sharks in the coral reefs, chasing Nazi submarines, and hunting with Gary Cooper in Sun Valley. Also comments on his marriages, estrangement from his son, and increasing dementia. As Norman Mailer writes in his preface, "He is a father, good and bad by turns, even sensational and godawful on different days of the year, and his contradictions are now his unity, his dirty fighting and his love of craft come of the same blood."

37 HEMINGWAY, MARY WELSH. *How It Was*. New York: Alfred A. Knopf, 537 pp.

An intimate portrait by Hemingway's fourth and last wife who lived with the writer during the final years of his life. Includes quotes from unpublished Hemingway letters and twenty-four pages of photographs.

38 HILY-MANE, GENEVIÈVE. "The Manuscripts of *To Have and Have Not*: Ernest Hemingway's Social Turning Point." *Revue Française d'Études Américaines* (Paris) 2:139-47.

In looking at manuscript revisions, Hily-Mane concludes that Hemingway's original concern was with the problems facing artists and that the real hero was painter Thomas Bradley. Only last-minute changes refocused the novel on Harry Morgan and social issues.

39 HOFFER, BATES. "Hemingway's Use of Stylistics." *Linguistics in Literature* 1, no. 2:89-121.

Linguistic analysis of Hemingway's various stylistic devices (phonological, orthographic, imagistic, etc). Contends that the author's wide range of experimental techniques linked to structure and content preclude the notion of a single Hemingway style.

40 HURLEY, C. HAROLD. "The Attribution of the Waiters' Second Speech in Hemingway's 'A Clean, Well-Lighted Place.'" *Studies in Short Fiction* 13, no. 1 (Winter): 81-85.

Argues that the old waiter gives the opening line of the much-disputed second exchange, feeling that such an interpretation reflects "Hemingway's intention of delineating the waiters as distinct character types."

41 INGMAN, TRISHA. "Symbolic Motifs in 'A Canary for One.'" *Linguistics in Literature* 1, no. 2:35-41.

Relates the symbolic significance of the train and the description of the countryside with the couple on board. Also points out similarities to Hemingway's own marriage to Hadley Richardson.

42 JASON, PHILIP K. "Throw Away Your Hemingway Codebook." *Indirections* 1, no. 3-4:59-64.

Argues that by forcing each of Hemingway's works into the code, critics and teachers are exchanging opportunities of theoretical and intellectual depth for tidy oversimplifications and routine generalizations.

43 JONES, PETER G. *War and the Novelist: Appraising the American War Novel*. Columbia: University of Missouri Press, pp. 7-9.

Comments briefly on the debt owed to Hemingway by contemporary war novelists. "His use of dramatic structure, his exploitation of a biased and unreliable narrator, and his creation of an atmosphere of existential anxiety ... provided patterns for subsequent writers."

44 KANN, HANS-JOACHIM. "An Unrecorded Hemingway Letter – in German Translation." *Fitzgerald/Hemingway Annual,* pp. 187-90.
Translation of 1940 letter to "old war buddy" Hans Kahle who at the time was interned by the British in a Canadian prison camp.

45 KELLER, GARY D. "Toward a Stylistic Analysis of Bilingual Texts: From Ernest Hemingway to Contemporary Boricua and Chicano Literature." In *The Analysis of Hispanic Texts: Current Trends in Methodology.* Edited by Mary Ann Beck et al. Jamaica: Bilingual Press, York College, pp. 130-49.
Linguistic approach. Compares Hemingway's bilingual literary techniques in *For Whom the Bell Tolls* with contemporary Hispano writers, finding Hemingway able to evoke Spanish meanings and style of speech without using Spanish words.

46 KOLB, ALFRED. "Symbolic Structure in Hemingway's 'The Snows of Kilimanjaro.'" *Notes on Modern American Literature* 1 (Winter): item 4.
Looks at the symbolic effect on tone and theme of relating two separate mythtraditions (primitive Eastern and enlightened Western) in the story. "The symbols point up the noble yet frustrating struggle between man and nature (human, terrestrial, and divine), the rather romantic, rather hopeless, yet still admirable efforts to seek to know, to attempt to differentiate between what seems, what is, and what ought to be."

47 KUHN, REINHARD. *The Demon of Noontide: Ennui in Western Literature.* Princeton, N.J.: Princeton University Press, pp. 333, 335, 337.
Comments briefly on the desolate vision of the *nada* passages in "A Clean, Well-Lighted Place." Finds ennui to be a dominant theme in the twentieth century.

48 KVAM, WAYNE. "Zuckmayer, Hilpert, and Hemingway." *PLMA* 91, no. 2 (March): 194-205.
Gives the literary and historical context for the 1931 German dramatization of *A Farewell to Arms*, including the playwright's early reservations about staging the novel, the playwright's and the director's backgrounds, and the play's critical reception.

49 LANFORD, RAY. "Hemingway's 'My Old Man.'" *Linguistics in Literature* 1, no. 2:11-19.

Contends that a careful reading of the text proves Butler had already stopped fixing races at the time of his death, thus making Joe's disillusionment at the end of the story unnecessary.

50 LAYMAN, RICHARD. "C. and M. in 'The Light of the World.'" *Fitzgerald/Hemingway Annual,* pp. 243-44.

Citing Eugene Landy's *The Underground Dictionary* and Goldin, O'Leary, and Lipsius's *Dictionary of American Underground Lingo,* Layman suggests that the phrase refers to a combination of cocaine and morphine.

51 LEARY, LEWIS, and AUCHARD, JOHN. *American Literature: A Study and Research Guide.* New York: St. Martin's, pp. 104-6.

Bibliographic essay, listing biographies and important critical studies.

52 LEWIS, WYNDHAM. "Ernest Hemingway." In *Enemy Salvoes: Selected Literary Criticism by Wyndham Lewis.* Edited by C.J. Fox. New York: Barnes & Noble, pp. 132-45.

Reprints excerpts from "The Dumb Ox: A Study of Ernest Hemingway," *Life & Letters* 10 (April 1934): 33-45. Brief introduction by Fox comments on Hemingway's "violent reaction" to the piece.

53 LODGE, DAVID. "The Language of Modernist Fiction: Metaphor and Metonymy." In *Modernism, 1890-30.* Edited by Malcolm Bradbury and James McFarlane. Harmondsworth and New York: Penguin Books, pp. 481-96.

Very brief analysis of the opening of "In Another Country" in which "an essentially metonymic style is made to serve the purposes of metaphor" through the careful manipulation of repetition.

54 LOWENKRON, DAVID HENRY. "Jake Barnes: A Student of William James in *The Sun Also Rises.*" *Texas Quarterly* 19, no. 1:147-56.

In light of the lectures of William James, Lowenkron classifies Jake Barnes as a pragmatist who is "sensitive enough to be internally impelled to shop around through the various codes of behavior for items of conduct that fit in with his store of experience."

55 LOWRY, E.D. "Chaos and Cosmos in *In Our Time.*" *Literature and Psychology* 26:108-17.

Traces patterns of destruction and regeneration in the collection, finding that "behind the fragmented world mirrored by Hemingway's modernistic technique – a world consumed by time and death – lies a vision of eternity and immortality which, mitigating the terrible meaninglessness of contemporary history, may bring us 'peace in our time.'"

56 McCLELLAN, DAVID. "The Battle of the Little Big Horn in Hemingway's Later Fiction." *Fitzgerald/Hemingway Annual,* pp. 245-48.

Sees Hemingway becoming increasingly obsessed with the battle, finding references to it in *To Have and Have Not, For Whom the Bell Tolls, Islands in the Stream,* and *Across the River and into the Trees.* Detects similar battle patterns in the latter three.

57 MacNAUGHTON, W.R. "Maisie's Grace under Pressure: Some Thoughts on James and Hemingway." *Modern Fiction Studies* 22, no. 2 (Summer): 153-64.

Looks at similarities in setting, characterization, and theme in James's *What Maisie Knew* and *The Sun Also Rises,* finding the most crucial parallel in their worlds to be destructive environments which necessitate Jake and Maisie's learning "how" to live. Characterizes both authors as essentially positive. Like Hemingway, James "can look down the gun barrel of wasted lives, frustrated chances, senseless death, and still hope and wonder at the possibilities of human life. . . ."

58 MALOY, BARBARA. "The Light of Alice's World." *Linguistics in Literature* 1, no. 2:69-86.

A linguistic exploration of the religious elements (references to hell and Christ) in "The Light of the World" and literary parallels to Lewis Carroll's *Wonderland-Looking Glass* stories. Interprets the boys' eventual exit from the railroad station as a rejection of the evil found inside.

59 MANN, CHARLES. "F. Scott Fitzgerald's Critique of *A Farewell to Arms.*" *Fitzgerald/Hemingway Annual,* pp. 141-53.

Fitzgerald's notes that include, among other things, criticism of Hemingway's dialogue and characterization of Catherine Barkley. Remarks that in "Cat in the Rain" and "Hills Like White Elephants" Hemingway was "really listening to women," unlike in *A Farewell to Arms,* where he listens only to himself.

60 MECKIER, JEROME. "Hemingway Reads Huxley: An Occasion for Some Observations on the Twenties and the Apostolate of the Lost Generation." *Fitzgerald/Hemingway Annual,* pp. 154-86.

Contends Hemingway's reading during his Paris years of the English satirist Aldous Huxley had a considerable influence on the young writer in terms of tone, contrapuntal structure, and characterization of disillusioned young men and deceiving women.

Meckier suggests that Hemingway adopted in his own writings the modern myth of the twenties that originated with Huxley in which "youth, or unfounded, egotistic idealism, is invariably impaired, perhaps even destroyed, by an ultimately meretricious post-war reality generally personified by a bewitching female."

61 MESSENGER, CHRISTIAN. "Jack London and Boxing in *The Game*." *Jack London Newsletter* 9, no. 2:67-72.
      Briefly compares Genevieve's response to Joe's death with Frederic Henry's response to Catherine's. "In *A Farewell to Arms*, Hemingway shows war and love to be the same biological trap that leads to death while in *The Game*, London separated his concerns into narrower opposites ... masculinity, violence ... versus ... solace, softness, peace...."

62 MILLER, LESLIE. "'Cat in the Rain.'" *Linguistics in Literature* 1, no. 2:29-34.
      Looks at Hemingway's use of contrasting images and symbols, arguing that the cat represents the wife caught in an empty and sterile relationship.

63 MONTEIRO, GEORGE. "The Wages of Love: 'Hills Like White Elephants.'" *Fitzgerald/Hemingway Annual*, pp. 224-29.
      In his discussion of Hemingway's sympathetic treatment of the young woman in the short story, Monteiro includes possible biographical sources, suggesting that the story may be "Hemingway's attempt to 'explain' away his own apparent callousness to that unidentified 'other.'"

64 MORSBERGER, ROBERT E. "ED on Kilimanjaro." *Emily Dickinson Bulletin* 30:105-6.
      Compares the ending of "The Snows of Kilimanjaro" with Dickinson's "Because I Could Not Stop for Death," finding similarities of theme, metaphor, and approach in both authors' depiction of death and immortality.

65 ____. "'That Hemingway Kind of Love': Macomber in the Movies." *Literature/Film Quarterly* 4:54-59.
      Analyzes the 1946 film version of "The Short Happy Life of Francis Macomber," finding it the "most nearly faithful and successful" of Hollywood's attempts at adapting Hemingway to the big screen despite its drastically distorted conclusion. Reprinted with slight revision: 1989.38.

66 PALMIERI, ANTHONY F.R. "*In Dubious Battle*: A Portrait in Pessimism." *RE: Artes Liberales* 3, no. 1:61-69.

Mentions briefly that the depth of pessimism found in Steinbeck's *In Dubious Battle* makes it "almost worthy to be placed alongside the 'nada' passage in Hemingway's 'A Clean, Well-Lighted Place.'"

67 PEARSON, DONNA. "'The Gambler, the Nun, and the Radio.'" *Linguistics in Literature* 1, no. 2:21-28.

After looking closely at language devices, vocabulary, and syntax, Pearson concludes that Sister Cecilia's approach to life offers Frazer the most rewarding alternative.

68 PECKHAM, MORSE. "Hemingway: Sexual Themes in His Writing." In *Romanticism and Behavior: Collected Essays II*. Columbia: University of South Carolina Press, pp. 139-58.

Reprint from *Sexual Behavior* 1, no. 4 (July 1971): 62-70.

69 POLLIN, BURTON R. "Poe and Hemingway on Violence and Death." *English Studies* 57, no. 2 (April): 139-42.

Suggests Hemingway's focus on violence and death, and the conquering of fear, is the result not only of literary tradition but of the author's early introduction to the tales of Poe.

70 RABKIN, ERIC S. *The Fantastic in Literature*. Princeton, N.J.: Princeton University Press,

Comments briefly on the "game of love" that Frederic and Catherine agree to play in *A Farewell to Arms*. "Ultimately, the great effort expended in sustaining this mutual fantasy is seen by the protagonists as heroic and engenders real love."

71 RAO, B. RAMACHANDRA. "*The Sun Also Rises*: A Study in Structure." *Banasthali Patrika* 20:11-17.

Arranges the characters hierarchically according to the depth of their sensitivity and understanding of the world around them. Classifies the expatriates as the most aware for they "have made a self-conscious rejection of old values and have physically and spiritually alienated themselves from their native land."

72 REYNOLDS, MICHAEL S. *Hemingway's First War: The Making of "A Farewell to Arms*." Princeton: Princeton University Press, 309 pp.

Close examination of sources for and revisions of the novel. Includes numerous examples of discarded material. Reynolds shows just how little of Henry's war was based on the author's own personal experiences. Concludes with a structural analysis focused on Henry's progressive isolation – from country, family, duty, and Catherine. Reprinted in part: 1987.6.

73 RIPPIER, JOSEPH STOREY. *The Short Stories of Sean O'Faolain: A Study in Descriptive Techniques.* Gerrards Cross, England: Colin Smythe, pp. 63-64.

Comments on Hemingway's influence. Notes similarities in presentation but finds O'Faolain reluctant to excise and exclude to Hemingway's extent.

74 ROBERTS, JOHN J. "In Defense of Krebs." *Studies in Short Fiction* 13, no. 4 (Fall): 515-18.

Sees Krebs's retreat from society in "Soldier's Home" as a necessary stage toward recovery after the traumatic experiences of war. Reprinted: 1983.98.

75 ____. "Patrick W. Shaw's Hemingway: A Response." *CEA Critic* 39 (November): 20-21.

Responds to Shaw's earlier argument (see 1975.58) that Hemingway used only smaller animals as emblems of endurance. Warning against the "either-or" fallacy, Roberts concludes with "a cautionary reminder that little animals as well as killer brutes reveal Hemingway's grasp of the possibilities for endurance and heroism in our time."

76 ROVIT, EARL. "Faulkner, Hemingway, and the American Family." *Mississippi Quarterly* 29, no. 4 (Fall): 483-97.

Looks at the economic, social, and cultural conditions of the early twentieth century, arguing that Hemingway and Faulkner share a common heritage that contributes to similar "ambivalent attitudes toward the city and the female, an elitist skepticism about or disgust with the widening base of democratization and social privileges, a contempt for the bourgeois certainties which their parents held, and an internal creative rage that drove them to pursue their own idiosyncratic paths."

77 SANDERS, BARBARA. "Linguistic Analysis of 'Cross-Country Snow.'" *Linguistics in Literature* 1, no. 2:43-52.

A linguistic analysis of structure reveals the story to be a balanced series of opposites with tension as the central theme. Word repetition in a variety of grammatical forms and shifts in tense reinforce the changes experienced by the skiers and especially Nick who is left at the end in a state of unresolved tension.

78 SCAFELLA, FRANK. "Models of the Soul: Authorship as Moral Action in Four American Novels." *Journal of the American Academy of Religion* 44:459-75.

Finds a strong correspondence between Emerson's moral vision and that found in the works of Hawthorne, Twain, Faulkner, and Hemingway. Like Hester Prynne, Huck Finn, and Isaac McCaslin, Nick Adams must overcome his darkened mental state through moral action.

79 SHIRER, WILLIAM L. *Twentieth Century Journey: A Memoir of a Life and the Times/The Start, 1904-30*. New York: Simon & Schuster, pp. 229-30.

Numerous references to Hemingway and his works. Describes his first encounter with the author in Paris in the mid-twenties. Despite Shirer's desire to talk about writing, Hemingway steered clear of the subject, preferring to discuss sports instead.

80 SHOWETT, H.K. "A Note on Faulkner's Title, *These Thirteen*." *Notes on Mississippi Writers* 9, no. 2 (Fall): 120-22.

Speculates on the source of Faulkner's title for his collection of short stories, *These Thirteen*. Showett suggests that Hemingway's *Men without Women*, a collection of fourteen short stories, may have inspired a private joke of one-upmanship on Faulkner's part.

81 SOJKA, GREGORY S. "Who Is Sam Cardinella, and Why Is He Hanging between Two Sunny Days at Seney?" *Fitzgerald/Hemingway Annual*, pp. 217-23.

Notes that the Cardinella vignette (in *In Our Time*) placed between part 1 and part 2 of "Big Two-Hearted River" provides a sharp contrast to the theme of grace under pressure to which Nick Adams in "Big Two-Hearted River" is so valiantly trying to subscribe. "True to Hemingway's theory of 'iceberg' composition, Sam Cardinella's emotional panic is a reminder of what lies beneath the surface of Nick's calm."

82 SOLOVYOV, E. "The Color of Tragedy." In *20th Century American Literature: A Soviet View*. Translated by Ronald Vroon. Moscow: Progress Publishers, pp. 351-83.

Sees as a major theme in Hemingway's works "the problem of a man's personal responsibility and moral steadfastness." In looking at the tragic situations found in such novels as *A Farewell to Arms*, *The Sun Also Rises*, and *To Have and Have Not*, Solovyov finds the author depicting characters able to maintain their moral tenets in the face of a cruel and inhuman society.

83 SPIEGEL, ALAN. "The Mud on Napoleon's Boots: The Adventitious Detail in Film and Fiction." *Virginia Quarterly Review* 52, no. 2 (Spring): 248-64.

Sees Hemingway's detached, cameralike observation of seemingly insignificant and unrelated detail in the execution vignette of *In Our Time* as a dramatic device to shake the reader's presumptions about war, "to separate phenomenal appearances from preconceived mental categories."

84 SPILKA, MARK. "Warren Beck Revisited." *Modern Fiction Studies* 22, no. 2 (Summer): 245-55.

Spilka responds to Beck's 1975 postscript (see 1975.7), challenging his impressionistic approach to "The Short Happy Life of Francis Macomber." Suggests "a whole wave of critical history" has passed Beck by.

85 STUCKEY, W.J. "*The Sun Also Rises* on Its Own Ground." *Journal of Narrative Technique* 6, no. 3 (Fall): 224-32.

Argues against the orthodox reading of the novel as a prose version of *The Waste Land*. Concludes by finding here and in much of Hemingway's writings the underlying attitude "that we are all bitched from the start but that we must live with the knowledge of death and extinction, taking what pleasure we can from the senuous contemplation of that fact and some little comfort in the permanence of nature itself; generations pass away, but the earth abides."

86 TANNER, STEPHEN L. "Hemingway's Islands." *Southwest Review* 61:74-84.

Traces the symbolic functions of islands in *Islands in the Stream* in which "individual man is portrayed as an island within the stream of human life and social relationships" and his identity consists "of islands of recollection in the stream of personal experience."

87 TELESIN, JULIUS. "For Whom the Scissors Cut; How to Improve Hemingway (Moscow Style)." *Encounter* 46, no. 6 (June): 81-86.

Lists censorship cuts made in the official Soviet edition of *For Whom the Bell Tolls* and a rationale for these deletions.

88 TEUNISSEN, JOHN J. "*For Whom the Bell Tolls* as Mythic Narrative." *Dalhousie Review* 56 (Spring): 52-59.

Important reading of this novel from a mythic, Jungian perspective, relying on Mircea Eliade's terms from *Cosmos and History*. After Teunissen establishes that the novel is antihistorical, far removed from the Spanish civil war in its intention, he studies character,

totemism, and narrative leading to the sacred marriage that is the
mythic climax of the novel. Reprinted: 1987.95.

89 TUGUSHEVA, M. "The Most American Genre." In *20th Century
American Literature: A Soviet View*. Translated by Ronald Vroon.
Moscow: Progress Publishers, pp. 121-42.
    In this brief discussion of Hemingway's contribution to the
American short story, Tugusheva remarks: "Like his predecessors and
like those who followed him, Hemingway wrote of the degeneration of
the American ideal, of the loss of that former innocence, of a predatory
civilization indifferent to man's fate."

90 UNDERWOOD, JERRY. "Disquisition Concerning Style: The Evil
Influence of Ernest Hemingway." *College English* 37, no. 7 (March):
684-85.
    Sees many, including himself, "writing like Hemingway only not as
good."

91 UNFRIED, SARAH P. *Man's Place in the Natural Order: A Study of
Hemingway's Major Works*. New York: Gordon Press, 99 pp.
    Traces Hemingway's philosophical worldview that man exists as a
part of the whole of humanity despite his minuteness in the universe.
Although only a fragment in a seemingly chaotic, haphazardous, and
much larger whole, man must strive for balance in the natural order – in
a cosmos which in actuality is structured and organized. Argues that the
seeds for such an interpretation are planted in the Nick Adams stories
and reach fruition in *For Whom the Bell Tolls*.

92 VAN GELDER, LAWRENCE. "When the Sun Also Rose." In *Pages:
The World of Books, Writers, and Writing/Volume One*. Edited by
Matthew J. Bruccoli with C.E. Frazer Clark, Jr., managing editor.
Detroit: Gale Research Co., pp. 116-23.
    Using mainly newspapers of the time, Van Gelder reconstructs
the political, social, and economic climate of 1926, the year *The Sun
Also Rises* was published.

93 VERSLUYS, KRISTIAAN. "Love and Death in Hemingway's *For
Whom the Bell Tolls*." *Studia Germanica Gandensia* (Ghent, Belgium),
pp. 33-50.
    Sees Hemingway setting up a paradoxical conflict of love and
death in which Robert Jordan as "victim of his own choice" must choose
between duty and affections.

94 WAGNER, LINDA W. "The Poetry in American Fiction." *Prospects:
Annual of American Cultural Studies* 2:513-26.

In her consideration of imagism's impact on twentieth-century American prose style, Wagner uses examples from Hemingway's shorter stories to illustrate the following imagist tenets: defined image or scene, objectivity, juxtaposition, organic form, and simplicity. Reprinted: 1980.93.

95 WALKER, ROBERT G. "Irony and Allusion in Hemingway's 'After the Storm.'" *Studies in Short Fiction* 13, no. 3 (Summer): 374-76.
After examining Hemingway's subtle allusion to Plato's *The Republic*, Walker concludes that the narrator does not express the author's own views.

96 WHITE, WILLIAM. "Hemingway Checklist." *Fitzgerald/Hemingway Annual*, pp. 260-72.
Lists 134 articles, reviews, books, and dissertations. Includes several translations.

97 ____. "What Price Hemingway?" *Book Collector's Market* (November): 6-8.
Sees no decline in interest among Hemingway collectors. Quotes current auction, catalogue, and booksellers' prices for several rarer editions, manuscripts, and letters.

98 WHITLOW, ROGER. "The Destruction/Prevention of the Family Relationship in Hemingway's Fiction." *Literary Review* 20:5-16.
Examines Hemingway's undermining of the basic family unit in "Indian Camp," "The Short Happy Life of Francis Macomber," "The Doctor and the Doctor's Wife," *The Sun Also Rises*, *A Farewell to Arms*, *For Whom the Bell Tolls*, and *The Old Man and the Sea*.

99 WILLIS, MARY KAY. "Structural Analysis of 'The Battler.'" *Linguistics in Literature* 1, no. 2:61-67.
Examines the child terminology surrounding Ad and Nick, determining that Bugs represents the standard norm by which to judge Ad's bizarre behavior and Nick's growth. Shift in viewpoint reveals Ad's inability to understand his relationship with Bugs and Nick's growing awareness of "the meaning of friendship and the role of violence and even perhaps the blows a battler must face in life."

100 WILSON, DALE. "Hemingway in Kansas City." *Fitzgerald/Hemingway Annual*, pp. 211-16.
Reminiscence by a fellow *Star* reporter concerning Hemingway's early career as a newspaper reporter for *The Kansas City Star* where he began writing obituaries, working his way up to police-beat reporter.

101   ZEHR, DAVID E. "Bourgeois Politics: Hemingway's Case in *For Whom the Bell Tolls*." *Midwest Quarterly* 17:268-78.

In unraveling the complex and sometimes paradoxical political messages, Zehr interprets the novel as a warning against fascism and an affirmation of bourgeois and democratic ideals.

1977

1   ADAIR, WILLIAM. "Death the Hunter: A Note on *Across the River and into the Trees*." *Notes on Contemporary Literature* 7, no. 1:6-8.

Sees the character Baron Alvarito as a symbol for death and nothingness.

2   _____. "Landscapes of the Mind: 'Big Two-Hearted River.'" *College Literature* 4:144-51.

Using *Across the River and into the Trees*, *A Farewell to Arms*, and "A Way You'll Never Be" as sources for Nick's war past, Adair interprets "Big Two-Hearted River" as "an imitation, brief and parablelike, of Nick Adams's entire history at the front." Reprinted: 1983.98.

3   ADAMS, MICHAEL. "Hemingway Filmography."
Fitzgerald/Hemingway Annual, pp. 219-32.

Gives the fifteen screen adaptations from 1932 to 1977 of Hemingway's works, including lists of directors, producers, screenwriters, and actors. Points out that this list will soon be outdated because of forthcoming projects based on both the author and his writings.

4   ALDERMAN, TAYLOR. "Fitzgerald, Hemingway, and *The Passing of the Great Race*." *Fitzgerald/Hemingway Annual*, pp. 215-17.

Suggests that race issues found in both Fitzgerald's *The Great Gatsby* and Hemingway's *The Torrents of Spring* may be connected to Madison Grant's *The Passing of the Great Race*.

5   ALLAN, TONY. "The Lost Generation." In *Paris: The Glamour Years 1919-1940*. New York: Gallery Books, pp. 85-95.

Describes the Lost Generation and the Paris literary scene of the 1920s. Contains numerous references to Hemingway along with photographs of important and influential people and places of the time. Comments on Hemingway's fascination with boxing, bicycle and horse racing, and the infamous Callaghan-Hemingway boxing match.

6 ARMISTEAD, MYRA. "Hemingway's 'An Alpine Idyll.'" *Studies in Short Fiction* 14, no. 3 (Summer): 255-58.

Reads the sexton's account of the frozen corpse as a tall tale common to the Alpine regions. The innkeeper's response reveals his strong prejudice against peasants.

7 ARNOLD, LLOYD R. *Hemingway: High on the Wild.* New York: Grossett & Dunlap, 163 pp.

Memoir of Hemingway's days hunting, fishing, writing, and socializing in and around Ketchum and Sun Valley, Idaho. Revised version of 1968 original, including rewritten text and a reduction in the number of photographs from 150 to 80.

8 ARONOWITZ, STANLEY. "Critic as Star." *Minnesota Review*, n.s. 9 (Fall): 71-111.

Discusses Hemingway briefly as a "cinematographic" writer dependent upon pared-down language and literal description in order to present the world objectively, "as it is."

9 ASSELINEAU, ROGER. "The Impact of American Literature on French Writers." *Comparative Literature Studies* 14, no. 2 (June): 119-34.

Comments briefly on Hemingway's immense popularity in France, attributing his success to the French public's desire after World War I "for a less sophisticated literature in direct contact with life."

10 BARBOUR, JAMES. "'The Light of the World': Hemingway's Comedy of Errors." *Notes on Contemporary Literature* 7, no. 5 (December): 5-8.

Points out several textual and factual errors, maintaining that Hemingway intentionally included them as an ironic undercutting of the text.

11 BASS, EBEN. "Hemingway's Women of Another Country." *Markham Review* 6 (Winter): 35-39.

Points out Hemingway's literary allusions (by way of Eliot) to Marlowe's *The Jew of Malta* in "In Another Country" and *The Sun Also Rises*. Finds Cohn not only "the Jewish scapegoat victim of the hard malice of the Lost Generation" but also the victim of a female-dominated world.

12 BRENNER, GERRY. "Hemingway's 'Vulgar' Ethic: Revaluating *The Sun Also Rises.*" *Arizona Quarterly* 33, no. 2 (Summer): 101-15.

Looks at the opposing value systems of hedonism and traditionalism in the novel, concluding that in Jake's ethical quest for a theory of "how to live," he combines both principles into a complex moral whole.

13 BRUCCOLI, MATTHEW J. "Mary Welsh Hemingway." In *Conversations with Writers, I.* Edited by Matthew J. Bruccoli et al. Detroit: Gale Research Co., pp. 180-94.

Interview focusing on her recently published autobiography *How It Was*, a projected volume of short stories, the possibility of releasing more unpublished Hemingway works and correspondence, and the circumstances surrounding the writing of *The Old Man and the Sea*.

14 BRYER, JACKSON R. "Fitzgerald and Hemingway." In *American Literary Scholarship: An Annual.* Edited by James Woodress. Durham, N.C.: Duke University Press, pp. 167-200.

Survey of criticism on both authors published during 1975. Bryer is encouraged by the current critical shift in focus from Hemingway's life to his fiction.

15 BUNGE, NANCY L. "The Midwestern Novel: Walt Whitman Transplanted." *The Old Northwest* 3, no. 3 (September): 275-87.

Argues that Anderson, Lewis, Hemingway, and Bellow share not only midwestern backgrounds but aesthetic principles as well. "Their works reveal a fascination with the hidden depths in ordinary people, sadness at the shoddy values dominating the world their contemporaries must inhabit, and hope that a way can be found for everyone to express freely his potentialities."

16 BURNS, STUART L. "Scrambling the Unscrambleable: *The Nick Adams Stories*." *Arizona Quarterly* 33, no. 2 (Summer): 133-40.

Although certain that Hemingway intended the stories as a cycle or novel with Nick as the central character, Burns is bothered by the lack of esthetic continuity and inconsistent characterization of Nick. Suggests an arrangement of the stories by theme rather than date as a more logical critical approach.

17 BUSCH, FREDERICK. "Icebergs, Islands, Ships beneath the Sea." In *A John Hawkes Symposium: Design and Debris.* Edited by Anthony C. Santore and Michael Pocalyko. New York: New Directions, pp. 50-63.

Discussion of several Hawkes novels, including *Charivari, The Blood Oranges*, and *The Lime Twig*, in which variations of sunken-ship imagery demonstrate the impact of Hemingway's "After the Storm" on the author.

18 CALLOW, JAMES, and REILLY, ROBERT J. "Ernest Hemingway." In *Guide to American Literature from Emily Dickinson to the Present.* New York: Barnes & Noble, pp. 131-35, 244-46.

Gives a brief biography along with stylistic and thematic analyses and plot summaries of such representative works as "Big Two-Hearted

River," *The Sun Also Rises*, and *A Farewell to Arms*. Also lists editions and reprints of selected Hemingway works, bibliographies, biographies, and critical studies.

19 CANBY, VINCENT. *"Islands in the Stream* Meanders out of Control." *New York Times*, 10 March, p. 46.

Negative review of the movie version of the novel. Compares the film to riding in the back seat of a car heading nowhere. "They haven't tightened a sprawling novel to fit the screen, they've let it sprawl in other directions, with very little grace and no feeling."

20 CANTELUPE, EUGENE B. "Statues and Lovers in *A Farewell to Arms*." *Fitzgerald/Hemingway Annual*, pp. 203-5.

Looks at earlier images of "cemetery" sculpture in the novel in connection with the final statue icon at the end, arguing that they combine to support the theme of doom found in *A Farewell to Arms*.

21 CASSILL, R.V. "Hills Like White Elephants." In *Instructor's Handbook* [for] *The Norton Anthology of Short Fiction*. New York: Norton, pp. 96-97.

*Fitzgerald/Hemingway Annual 1979, p. 466.

22 CAWELTI, JOHN. "The Writer as Celebrity: Some Aspects of American Literature as Popular Culture." *Studies in American Fiction* 5, no. 1 (Spring): 161-74.

Addresses the historical development of literary celebrity and the difficulties and advantages associated with it. Sees Hemingway in the early 1930s consciously creating a celebrity persona paralleling the characters in his books, and "while brilliant as a public performance, this persona was insufficient to the demands of great fiction."

23 CHENG, YOUNG-HSIAO T. "Fact and Fiction in Hemingway's 'The Snows of Kilimanjaro.'" *American Studies* (Taiwan) 7, no. 3 (September): 41-55.

Discussion of the autobiographical elements in the short story, concluding that although Hemingway relies extensively on actual past experiences, he deliberately manipulates different symbols such as the frozen leopard to depict the immortality of art and man's own betrayal of himself and his dreams of self-fulfillment.

24 COWLEY, MALCOLM. "Can a Complete SOB Be a Good Writer?" *Esquire* 88, no. 5 (November): 120-21, 222-26.

Gives the moral code that all great writers subscribe to: recognition of the importance and immortality of art, willingness to devote one's all to achieve greatness, and the integrity to present an honest view of the world and oneself. Although Hemingway's personal and professional life may have been marred by egotism and a desire to be the first in everything he did, he subscribed to all of the above commandments and succeeded as a great writer.

25 CRIST, JUDITH. "A Precious Burst of Hemingway." *Saturday Review*, 19 March, pp. 40-41.

In her review of the film version of *Islands in the Stream*, Crist finds it "a carefully detailed adventure story that becomes, in effect, a summation of the personal and public character of both the writer and his work."

26 CROSBY, HARRY. *Shadows of the Sun: The Diaries of Harry Crosby*. Edited by Edward Germain. Santa Barbara, Calif.: Black Sparrow Press, pp. 145, 164, 280, 281.

Diary entries briefly refer to drinking and dining with Hemingway in the later twenties and Crosby's introduction to Joyce through Hemingway.

27 DeFALCO, JOSEPH M. "'Bimini' and the Subject of Hemingway's *Islands in the Stream*." *Topic* 17, no. 31 (Fall): 41-51.

Maintains that *The Old Man and the Sea* and *Islands in the Stream* are two "interlinking works" of a sea trilogy in which Hemingway intended the sea as a metaphor for "time, life, and experience." Finds the main problem of *Islands in the Stream* not with Hemingway's experimental shift of attention away from character to the metaphorical setting of the sea but with the characterization of Hudson whose "overwhelmingly negative responses so dominate his story that the metaphorical subject loses its force and is often submerged." Reprinted: 1987.95.

28 DONALDSON, SCOTT. *By Force of Will: The Life and Art of Ernest Hemingway*. New York: Viking Press, 367 pp.

Combines Hemingway's life with his writings for a deeper understanding of the true man behind the myth. With chapter headings such as "Fame", "Money", "Sport", "Art", and "Death", Donaldson constructs "a mosaic of his mind and personality"–emphasizing Hemingway's contradictory nature and divided consciousness.

29 DUGGAN, MARGARET M. "General Checklist." *Fitzgerald/ Hemingway Annual*, pp. 267-68.

Lists articles, interviews, and books written in 1975 and 1976 relating to Fitzgerald, Hemingway, and modernism.

30 ELLIOTT, GARY D. "The Hemingway Hero's Quest for Faith." *McNeese Review* 24:18-27.

Suggests that all of Hemingway's heroes are on a quest for faith in the form of a rationale for living. Sees Santiago in *The Old Man and the Sea* successfully completing the quest and finding faith composed of "paganism, code, and Christianity."

31 ____. "Hemingway's 'Hills Like White Elephants.'" *Explicator* 35, no. 4 (Summer): 22-23.

Sees the bead curtain as symbolizing a rosary, thus representing Jig's religious struggle about whether to have the abortion.

32 FERGUSON, J.M., Jr. "Hemingway's Man of the World." *Arizona Quarterly* 33, no. 2 (Summer): 116-20.

Looks at the "ironic inversion" of the initiation theme in "A Man of the World," contending that ignorance may have its own rewards but the true Hemingway hero is sensitive to life's experiences.

33 FETTERLEY, JUDITH. "*A Farewell to Arms*: Ernest Hemingway's 'Resentful Cryptogram.'" In *The Authority of Experience: Essays in Feminist Criticism*. Edited by Arlyn Diamond and Lee R. Edwards. Amherst: University of Massachusetts Press, pp. 257-73.

Reprint with minor revision of 1976.24. Reprinted with minor revision: 1978.28 and 1987.6.

34 FITCH, NOEL. "Ernest Hemingway–c/o Shakespeare and Company." *Fitzgerald/Hemingway Annual*, pp. 157-81.

Recounts Hemingway's friendship with Sylvia Beach, owner of the bookstore Shakespeare and Company where Hemingway borrowed many books during his Paris years. Comments on Hemingway's interest in Russian literature (Ivan Turgenev, in particular) and its possible influence on him as a writer. Lending records reveal that Hemingway often borrowed books that dealt with subjects similar to those he was working on at the time. For example, while writing *A Farewell to Arms* he borrowed several books on war. Includes a list of the entries on Hemingway's library records.

35 FLEMING, ROBERT E. "Hemingway's Treatment of Suicide: 'Fathers and Sons' and *For Whom the Bell Tolls*." *Arizona Quarterly* 33, no. 2 (Summer): 121-32.

Sees *For Whom the Bell Tolls* as Hemingway's "attempt to purge himself, through his art, of the debilitating psychological effects of his father's suicide." Because Jordan rejects suicide in the end and little mention of suicide appears in Hemingway's later writings, Fleming concludes that "the therapy was successful."

36 FLORA, JOSEPH M. "A Closer Look at the Young Nick Adams and His Father." *Studies in Short Fiction* 14, no. 1 (Winter): 75-78.

Refutes interpretations that see "The Doctor and the Doctor's Wife" and "Indian Camp" as concerned with the death of love. Flora suggests that reading "Three Shots" in conjunction with "Indian Camp" reveals not only Doctor Adams's weaknesses but also his love for his son.

37 FOWLER, ROGER. *Linguistics and the Novel*. London: Methuen & Co., pp. 48-54.

Linguistic analysis of the opening of "The Killers" according to textual surface structure, discourse (modality), and content (plot, character, setting, and theme).

38 GARNICA, OLGA K. "Rules of Verbal Interaction and Literary Analysis." *Poetics* 6, no. 2 (September): 155-67.

Combines psychosociological knowledge of communicative interaction with linguistics in an analysis of the terms of address and conversation sequence types (question/response and summons/ response) found in the dialogue of "Indian Camp."

39 GIGER, ROMEO. *The Creative Void: Hemingway's Iceberg Theory*. Bern, Switzerland: Francke, 109 pp.

Detailed discussion of Hemingway's technique of revelation through concealment by examining both direct statements made by the author as well as passages from his works. Closes by commenting on Hemingway's philosophical outlook on the world as it coincides with his iceberg theory. "Real communication is only possible by way of the felt experience; through it alone can the fragments of multiple reality, with their power as archetypes of existence, with all their uncertainties and irreducible ambiguities, be transposed into a valid imaginative picture of the whole."

40 GILL, BRENDAN. "Novels into Movies: *Islands in the Stream*." *Film Comment* 13 (March-April): 44-46.

Labeling it an honorable and instructive failure, Gill warns producers not to make movies from "novels as radically imperfect and therefore as risky, as *Islands*."

41 GOODMAN, PAUL. "The Sweet Style of Ernest Hemingway." *Paul Goodman*. Edited by Taylor Stoehr. New York: Free Life Editions, pp. 196-204.

Reprint from *New York Review of Books* 17, no. 11 (30 December 1971): 27-28.

42 GRANT, MARY KATHRYN, R.S.M. "The Search for Celebration in *The Sun Also Rises* and *The Great Gatsby*." *Arizona Quarterly* 33, no. 2 (Summer): 181-92.

Traces the dance motif throughout both novels, concluding that the dance scenes thematically reveal "a generation without a sense of hope, without a cause to celebrate, and without a reason to dance."

43 GUTWINSKI, WALDEMAR. *Cohesion in Literary Texts: A Study of Some Grammatical and lexical features of English Discourse*. The Hague: Mouton, 183 pp.

Linguistic study of cohesive features in passages from "Big Two-Hearted River" and *For Whom the Bell Tolls* in contrast to passages from Henry James's *The Portrait of a Lady*. Finds the authors differ markedly in their use of grammatical and lexical cohesion.

44 HAAS, RUDOLF. "Some American Contributions to World Literature." *Yearbook of Comparative and General Literature* 26:17-23.

Gives a German perspective on Hemingway's contribution to the literary scene. Sees Hemingway's greatest achievement as an Eros/Thanatos author.

45 HARDY, RICHARD E., and CULL, JOHN G. *Hemingway: A Psychological Portrait*. Sherman Oaks, Calif.: Banner Book International, 92 pp.

Combines psychological theory with biography to reveal the insecure, guilt-ridden man behind the myth. Emphasis on the early traumas and influences that formed Hemingway's character. Concludes with a psychological evaluation of his personality. Reprinted with minor revision: 1988.38.

46 HARMON, ROBERT. *Understanding Ernest Hemingway: A Study and Research Guide*. Metuchen, N.J.: Scarecrow Press, 153 pp.

Listings of major works, biographies, criticism, dissertations, theses, reviews, audiovisual materials, and reference sources. Includes chronology.

47 HARRIS, CHARLES B. "The Fisherman's Code in *The Sun Also Rises*." *Notes on Modern American Literature* 1:item 18.

Discusses Jake's violation of the trout fisherman's code at Burguete, arguing that such a failure reflects Jake's violation of the larger Hemingway code of conduct.

48 HARRISON, JIM. "Hemingway Fished Here." *Esquire*, July, pp. 38, 40.

Recounts a northern Michigan fishing trip near some of Hemingway's old haunts. Comments on the vast changes, due mainly to tourism, since Hemingway's time.

49 HARTSOCK, MILDRED. "Another Way to Heightened Consciousness." *Humanist* 37, no. 4 (July-August): 26-30.

Sees Nick Adams in "Big Two-Hearted River" as Everyman searching for renewal and expanded consciousness. Contends that reading literature can help those struggling with the chaos in their own lives.

50 "Havana Letter." *AB: Bookman's Weekly*, 19-26 September, p. 1507.

Announces the auction of Hemingway's *Havana Letter*, a possible preliminary piece for *The Old Man and the Sea*.

51 HEARN, CHARLES R. *The American Dream in the Great Depression*. Westport, Conn.: Greenwood Press, pp. 124-27.

Places *To Have and Have Not* squarely in the "tough-guy genre" of the thirties. Finds that "the bulk of the novel stands as a powerful, negative study of the viability of individualism in modern America."

52 HEMINGWAY, ERNEST. "The Author's Preface for *The Torrents of Spring*." *Fitzgerald/Hemingway Annual*, p. 113.

Facsimile of omitted author's preface in which Hemingway claims that his motivation in writing the parody was to refute "the many critics" who likened *In Our Time* to the writings of Sherwood Anderson.

53 ____. *Three Stories & Ten Poems*. Bloomfield Hills, Mich.: Bruccoli Clark Books, 58 pp.

Facsimile of 1923 edition published by Contact Publishing Co. in Paris.

54 "Hemingway Manuscript." *AB Bookman's Weekly*, 3 October, pp. 1716-17.

Announces the addition of the complete manuscript of *The Sun Also Rises* to the Alderman Library, University of Virginia.

55 HILY-MANE, GENEVIÈVE. "On Some Technical Aspects of the Manuscripts of Ernest Hemingway." *Revue Française d'Études Américaines* (Paris) 3:95-110.

Study of the Hemingway manuscripts at the Kennedy Library reveals that Hemingway made lists of possible titles both during and after composition. Tracing changes in character names shows that Hemingway often began with real people and situations, gradually altering identities and personalities. Concludes with an examination of the various endings of several short stories. Includes appendices of title and name changes.

56 HORRIGAN, WILLIAM. "Dying without Death: Borzage's *A Farewell to Arms*." In *The Classic American Novel and the Movies*. Edited by Gerald Peary and Roger Shatzkin. New York: Frederick Ungar Publishing Co., pp. 297-304.

Compares Borzage's film version with Hemingway's novel, concentrating on their differing artistic visions with "Hemingway writing the man's novel, Borzage filming the woman's picture; Hemingway emotionally distancing himself from 'l'affaire de coeur,' Borzage reviving himself in it; Hemingway's opting for action against the tendency in Borzage's melodrama to turn from action and the world."

57 HUNT, ANTHONY. "Another Turn for Hemingway's 'The Revolutionist': Sources and Meanings." *Fitzgerald/Hemingway Annual*, pp. 119-35.

Finds it improbable that Hemingway ever met an actual Hungarian Communist on which to model "The Revolutionist." Using biographical, historical, and geographical information, Hunt argues that the sketch "is the result of Hemingway's transformation of several discrete, even apparently unconnected, mental and physical experiences that occurred in a different context and time period into a single, composite, fictional cameo." Reprinted: 1983.98.

58 *In Their Time/1920-1940: Fiestas, Moveable Feasts, and "Many Fêtes" An Exhibition at the University of Virginia Library, December 1977-March 1978.* Bloomfield Hills, Mich.: Bruccoli Clark Books, 85 pp.

Record of the Hemingway, Fitzgerald, Dos Passos exhibition. Includes more than ninety photographs of people, manuscripts, and letters as well as an explanatory note on each item on display.

59 IWASA, MASAZUMI. "Beauty and Ugliness in Hemingway." *Chu-Shikoku American Literature* 13 (February): 1-12.

Sees beauty as the center of Hemingway's concept of truth. Associates the author's efforts to capture experiences in writing with his moral code. "When Hemingway refers to 'moral,' it means that he has felt the presence of something good which connotes something beautiful according to his judgment. Thus in him we can perceive the aesthetic trinity: an amalgam of truth, goodness, and beauty."

60 JOHNSTON, KENNETH G. "The Bull and the Lion: Hemingway's Fables for Critics." *Fitzgerald/Hemingway Annual*, pp. 149-56.

Regards the fables as a release for Hemingway's domestic and literary anxieties. Johnston interprets "The Faithful Bull" as both a reaffirmation of Hemingway's love for his wife and an idealization of himself as a writer. Reads "The Good Lion" as a "flattering self-portrait of a dedicated writer who faithfully adheres to his own distinctive style and subject matter, despite rejection by editors, hostile attacks by reviewers, and laughter and scorn from former friends." Reprinted with minor revision: 1987.38.

61 _____. "'Nobody Ever Dies': Hemingway's Neglected Story of Freedom Fighters." *Kansas Quarterly* 9, no. 2:53-58.

Sees "Nobody Ever Dies" as a tribute to the freedom fighters of the Spanish civil war and a rehearsal for the themes, characters, and motifs found later in *For Whom the Bell Tolls*.

62 JOY, NEILL R. "Fitzgerald's Retort to Hemingway's 'Poor Scott Fitzgerald.'" *Notes on Modern American Literature* 2:item 13.

Finds the Brimmer-Stahr fight scene in *The Last Tycoon* a thinly veiled rendering of the Eastman-Hemingway clash. Sees it as Fitzgerald's retaliation for Hemingway's reference to him as "poor Scott Fitzgerald" in "The Snows of Kilimanjaro."

63 JUNGMAN, ROBERT E. "A Note on the Ending of *The Sun Also Rises*." *Fitzgerald/Hemingway Annual*, p. 214.

Thinks the taxi scene appearing in both chapter 3 and the conclusion of the novel may be a biblical allusion to Matthew 7:13-14, suggesting that Jake and Brett are on their way to hell.

64 KAEL, PAULINE. "Stag Show." *New Yorker* 52 (14 March): 125-29.

Negative review of the movie version of *Islands in the Stream*, criticizing its stodginess and epic-scale production.

65 KANN, HANS-JOACHIM. "Perpetual Confusion in 'A Clean, Well-Lighted Place': The Manuscript Evidence." *Fitzgerald/Hemingway Annual*, pp. 115-18.

Attempts to clear up the ambiguities in the two waiters' dialogue through an analysis of the manuscript version, but finds that even in Hemingway's original the passage is obscure. Includes facsimile of section in question.

66 KAZIN, ALFRED. "Hemingway the Painter." *New Republic*, 19 March, pp. 21-28.

Biographical essay asserting that it is impossible to separate Hemingway from his writings. Pays particular attention to Hemingway's interest in Cézanne and other French painters and their influence upon his art. Reprinted: 1984.59 and 1985.12.

67 KILDAY, GREGG. "Film Clips: A Movie of Life with Papa." *Los Angeles Times*, 4 May, sec. 4, p. 16.
Announces forthcoming movie biography based in part on Mary Hemingway's *How It Was*.

68 KRIEGEL, LEONARD. "Hemingway's Rites of Manhood." *Partisan Review* 44:45-30.
Remarking that "not even Hemingway could be Hemingway," Kriegel looks at discrepancies between the man and his created persona, and in Hemingway's legacy in defining masculine behavior.

69 KROLL, JACK. "Poor Papa." *Newsweek*, 14 March, pp. 94, 96.
Negative review of the movie version of *Islands in the Stream*. Finds the one "saving grace" of the novel, the touching depiction of Hudson's relationship with his children, to be only partially captured in the film.

70 LATHAM, AARON. "A Farewell to Machismo." *New York Times Magazine*, 16 October, pp. 52-55, 80-82, 90.
Attributes Hemingway's fading popularity at the bookstores to his focus on standards of masculine behavior. "Papa seems to offend this age when men are recognizing their 'feminine' qualities and women are admitting certain 'masculine characteristics.'" Wonders if the release of *Garden of Eden*, an unpublished manuscript revealing the author's own ambiguous feelings about the subject, may rejuvenate public interest in his works. Scattered throughout this article are independent bits concerning such topics as Hemingway's alternative titles to *A Farewell to Arms*, his sense of humor, and Fitzgerald's editing of *The Sun Also Rises* and *A Farewell to Arms*.

71 LENNOX, SARA. "'We Could Have Had Such a Damned Good Time Together': Individual and Society in *The Sun Also Rises* and *Mutmassungen über Jakob*." *Modern Language Studies* 7, no. 1:82-90.
In comparing similar themes concerning the possibility of individual fulfillment within the particular society depicted in each novel, Lennox finds that Johnson's work "stands Hemingway's on its head: where Hemingway treats the individual isolated from society, seeking an individual happiness in romantic love, Johnson examines an individual seeking a social solution whom his society totally subsumes."

72 LODGE, DAVID. "Ernest Hemingway." In *The Modes of Modern Writing: Metaphor, Metonymy, and the Typology of Modern Literature*. London: Edward Arnold, pp. 155-59.

Examines Stein's influence on Hemingway as the young writer learned to balance vernacular speech and repetition in a single style combining both realism and modernism.

73 McDONALD, JAMES L. "The Incredible Richard Cantwell." *Notes on Modern American Literature* 2 (Winter): item 3.

Sees Cantwell (*Across the River and into the Trees*) as a "fantasized projection" of the author himself. Thus Cantwell's extraordinary abilities as fighter and drinker validate "Hemingway's sense of his own masculinity."

74 MAY, KEITH M. *Out of the Maelstrom: Psychology and the Novel in the Twentieth Century.* New York: St. Martin's Press, pp. 89-90.

Brief look at the existential view found in Hemingway's works. Of his characters, May writes, "What we remember is not, as in traditional portraits, a set of idiosyncrasies, but the quality of an experience. The experience almost entirely coincides with the character."

75 MEYER, WILLIAM E., Jr. "Hemingway's Novels: The Shift in Orthodoxy and Symbolism." *Arizona Quarterly* 33, no. 2 (Summer): 141-55.

Using the Spanish Civil War as a turning point, Meyer traces Hemingway's shift away from orthodox Catholicism in his war novels, noting also that the author's use of Christian symbolism paradoxically rises as the other decreases.

76 MEYERS, JEFFREY. "Ernest Hemingway's Four Wives: The Well of Loneliness." In *Married to Genius*. London: London Magazine Editions, pp. 174-89.

Biographical essay exploring the extent to which characters and themes in Hemingway's fiction are a reflection of his personal experiences with his mother, lovers, and wives.

77 MONTEIRO, GEORGE. "Addenda to Hanneman's *Hemingway: Books on Trial.*" *Papers of the Bibliographical Society of America* 71 (October-December): 514-15.

Lists seven reviews of Hemingway's works appearing in *Books on Trial* that are not included in Hanneman's 1967 *Ernest Hemingway: A Comprehensive Bibliography* (Princeton) nor her 1975 *Supplement* (Princeton).

78 _____. "Dating the Events of 'The Three-Day Blow.'" *Fitzgerald/Hemingway Annual*, pp. 207-10.

In questioning whether "The Three-Day Blow" can be dated according to its ambiguous references to baseball, Monteiro suggests (as the author himself stated in *A Moveable Feast*) that Hemingway may have written the short story in Paris during the 1920s, melding three or four years of baseball events into a composite. Reprinted: 1983.98.

79 ____. "Innocence and Experience: The Adolescent Child in the Works of Mark Twain, Henry James, and Ernest Hemingway." *Estudos Anglo-Americanos* (São José do Rio Preto) 1:39-57.

Traces the literary development of the American child from Twain's naive critic of society to Hemingway's Nick Adams in "Indian Camp" who internalizes his experiences of life and death.

80 MULLER, GILBERT. "*In Our Time*: Hemingway and the Discontents of Civilization." *Renascence* 29 (Summer): 185-92.

"Hemingway's characters become artists of the repressed scream." Using the psychoanalytic theories of Arthur Janov, Muller sees the author as well as the main characters of *In Our Time* as victims of suppressed emotion and self-destructive stoicism.

81 NIBBELINK, HERMAN. "The Meaning of Nature in *For Whom the Bell Tolls*." *Arizona Quarterly* 33, no. 2 (Summer): 165-72.

Looks at Hemingway's descriptive, metaphoric, and symbolic use of nature, concluding that Jordan's final act "is the antithesis of suicide–to become one with nature, stoically willing himself to the Whole."

82 O'BRIEN, MATTHEW. "Baseball in 'The Three-Day Blow.'" *American Notes & Queries* 16, no. 2:24-26.

Traces two baseball references to actual events that contemporary readers would remember. Through blunders, Heinie Zimmerman cost the New York Giants the 1917 World Series, and the St. Louis Cardinals were pennant contenders until their train wreck in 1911. O'Brien draws the parallel between their disasters and the Nick-Marge breakup. Although down for a time, both Zimmerman and the Cardinals returned to the field just as Nick too will survive his "disaster."

83 OGUNYEMI, CHIKWENYE OKONJO. "Order and Disorder in Toni Morrison's *The Bluest Eye*." *Critique: Studies in Modern Fiction* 19, no. 1:112-20.

Mentions briefly that Toni Morrison's simplistic style and sentence structure are reminiscent of Hemingway.

84 O'HARA, JOHN. "The Author's Name Is Hemingway." In *"An Artist Is His Own Fault"*. Carbondale and Edwardsville: Southern Illinois University Press, pp.165-73.

Reprint from the *New York Times Book Review*, 10 September 1950, pp. 1, 30-31.

85 OLDSEY, BERNARD. "The Genesis of *A Farewell to Arms*." *Studies in American Fiction* 5, no. 2 (Fall): 175-85.

Describes an undated, two-chapter version of an early opening of *A Farewell to Arms* that corresponds with later sections of the published novel. Oldsey contends that "Hemingway composed the opening and the eleven other essential chapters that constitute Book One of the novel as an afterthought."

86 ____. "The Sense of an Ending in *A Farewell to Arms*." *Modern Fiction Studies* 23, no. 4 (Winter): 491-510.

Study of the many variant conclusions now housed in the Kennedy Library. Oldsey categorizes the endings into nine separate groupings, contending in his analysis that only the final versions "demonstrate technique as discovery in the most basic sense of getting the words right, which leads to getting the right message, the right form." Reprinted: 1987.6.

87 ORR, JOHN. "Malraux and Hemingway: The Myth of Tragic Humanism." In *Tragic Realism and Modern Society: Studies in the Sociology of the Modern Novel*. Pittsburgh: University of Pittsburgh Press, pp. 143-59.

A sociological literary study comparing *For Whom the Bell Tolls* with André Malraux's *Days of Hope*, two political novels of the Spanish civil war. Examines the level of tragic realism in each work, finding the major flaw in Hemingway's to be the nature of the protagonist who remains essentially unchanged by his three-day experience.

88 "Papa's Letters." *Horizon* 19 (July): 27.

Discusses Mary Welsh Hemingway's purchase of thirty letters written by Hemingway to his parents during the 1920s. Includes commentary on publishers, vacations with Dos Passos, boxing, bullfighting, and the writing of *The Sun Also Rises*.

89 PENNER, DICK. "The First Nick Adams Story." *Fitzgerald/Hemingway Annual*, pp. 195-202.

Interprets the original opening "Three Shots" in conjunction with "Indian Camp," tracing the emergence of two interconnected themes: Nick's relationship with his father and his awareness of death. Penner argues that the key to understanding "Indian Camp" is the ambiguous ending. "On a literal, biological level, Nick's assurance that he will 'never die' is ironic. He will die. On an experiential level, however, the ending is not ironic. . . . To *experience* death, to meet it head on, as Nick does in "Indian Camp," is to know its reality."

90   PICI, J.R. "Hemingway: Openings of the Master Strategist." *Lost Generation Journal* 5, no. 1 (Spring): 9, 23.
    Applauds the mastery behind Hemingway's various short story openings that incite immediate reader interest and involvement.

91   PLIMPTON, GEORGE, ed. "Ernest Hemingway." In *Writers at Work: The Paris Review Interviews.* 2nd series. New York: Penguin, pp. 215-39.
    Reprint of *Paris Review* 5 (Spring 1958): 61-89.

92   PORTERFIELD, CHRISTOPHER. "The Big One Gets Away Again." *Time*, 21 March, p. 89.
    Negative review of the movie version of *Islands in the Stream.* Comments on the simplicity and soapiness of the script and the stilted direction.

93   RANDALL, STEPHEN. "Hemingway's *Islands in the Stream.*" *W* (New York), 7-14 January, p. 22.
    Discusses the problems associated with transcribing Hemingway's posthumous novel to the big screen, including working with child actors, shooting scenes on the water, and doing justice to the Hemingway legend.

94   RAO, E. NAGESWARA. "Hemingway and the American Tradition." In *Essays and Studies: Festschrift in Honour of Prof. K. Viswanatham.* Edited by G.V.L.N. Sarma. Machilipatnam, India: Triveni Press, pp. 61-64.
    Discusses Hemingway's borrowing of vernacular speech, naive protagonists, and themes of the American dream and male comradeship from an already well-established American literary tradition. Notes, however, that the author did contribute clean dialogue and an objective prose style.

95   ROBINSON, ROBERT. "Hemingway, by His Wife." *Listener* 97:351.
    Brief interview with Mary Welsh Hemingway about her book *How It Was.* Includes comments on Hemingway's depression, writing habits, and the publication of *The Garden of Eden.*

96   ROSENMAN, MONA G. "Five Hemingway Women." *Clafin College Review* 2, no. 1:9-15.
    In looking at Hemingway's treatment of women in five short stories ("Up in Michigan," "Cat in the Rain," "Hills Like White Elephants," "The Sea Change," and "The Short Happy Life of Francis

Macomber"), Rosenman refutes claims that Hemingway was unable to fully characterize or sympathize with women. Rather, he created "women whose *nada* existence was occasioned by their proximity to unsympathetic men, and whose courage often surpassed that of men."

97 ROTH, PHILIP. "Photography Does Not a Movie Make." In *The Classic American Novel and the Movies*. Edited by Gerald Peary and Roger Shatzkin. New York: Frederick Ungar Publishing Co., pp. 268-71.

Roth recounts conversation he had with a streetwalker over the "disappointing" 1957 film version of *The Sun Also Rises*.

98 ROVIT, EARL. "On Ernest Hemingway and 'Soldier's Home.'" In *The American Short Story*. Edited by Calvin L. Skaggs. New York: Dell Publishing Co., pp. 251-56.

Places the story squarely within both the context of disillusioned post-World War I America and the Hemingway style, concluding that "the story makes a compelling statement about the problems that divide generations and people of different experience at an historical moment of massive and incomprehensible change." Includes a screenplay adaptation by Robert Geller, pp. 232-50.

99 SHOCKLEY, MARTIN STAPLES. "Uncle Tyler Hemingway." *Fitzgerald/Hemingway Annual,* pp. 211-13.

Tells of Hemingway's wealthy Uncle Alfred Tyler Hemingway who introduced the young author to the chief editorial writer of the *Kansas City Star* in 1917. The elder Hemingway had himself published a success manual entitled *How to Make Good* in 1915.

100 SLATOFF, WALTER J. "The 'Great Sin' in *For Whom the Bell Tolls*." *Journal of Narrative Technique* 7, no. 2 (Spring): 142-48.

Attributes to Hemingway a more humane perspective on death. Although the cause that Jordan is fighting for necessitates killing, the novel "asserts absolutely and without qualification that killing is unjustifiable and sinful."

101 SMITH, WALLACE W. "On Hemingway's 'The Short Happy Life of Francis Macomber.'" *Bulletin of the Faculty of Humanities, Seikei University* (Tokyo) 13:1-14.

Gives biographical background on Hemingway's 1933 hunting trip to Africa, an experience he used in *The Green Hills of Africa*, "The Snows of Kilimanjaro," and "The Short Happy Life of Francis Macomber." Provides an overview of the latter story's structure, characterization, and plot.

102 STEINER, WENDY. "Gertrude Stein in Manuscript." *Yale University Library Gazette* 51, no. 3:156-63.

Explicates Stein's 1923 portrait of Hemingway ("He and They, Hemingway") in which their shifting teacher/student relationship is depicted. Speculates on just how influential the illustrations on her notebook cover were in writing the piece.

103 STEPHENS, ROBERT O., "Macomber and That Somali Proverb: The Matrix of Knowledge." *Fitzgerald/Hemingway Annual,* pp. 137-47.

Discusses Macomber's rite of passage as a cultural conversion from "a decadent, industrial, and commercial system of economic individualism to one of traditional and organic values in which the individual is not alone but part of a sustaining communal understanding." Macomber learns in his initiation into the formal code of the hunt that strength and courage are gained through one's sense of interdependency and community.

104 ____. ed. *Ernest Hemingway: The Critical Reception*. New York: Burt Franklin & Co., 502 pp.

Gives an extensive overview of Hemingway's critical reputation as it developed by looking at all of the reviews written during his lifetime and shortly after his death. Comprehensive survey, ranging from *Three Stories & Ten Poems* (1923) to *The Nick Adams Stories* (1972), arranged chronologically with many reviews reprinted wholly while others are excerpted and summarized. Checklists of additional reviews excluded from the text are appended. Includes an analysis of major critical trends and debates.

105 STEWART, DAVID; COWAN, ELIZABETH; and COWAN, GREGORY. "A Conversation with Mary Hemingway." *CEA Critic* 40, no. 1:29-33.

Interview with Mary Welsh Hemingway in which she comments upon critics and scholars, *The Old Man and the Sea*, and Hemingway's unpublished correspondence.

106 TOMPKINS, JANE P. "Criticism and Feeling." *College English* 39, no. 2 (October): 169-78.

Believing that criticism should be a combination of emotional response and intellectual analysis, Tompkins uses *The Sun Also Rises* as a proving ground. Put off by Hemingway's contradictory treatment of Robert Cohn, she contends that Cohn's role in the novel should be as underdog; however, this response is prevented by our awareness that he is a loser. Tompkins concludes that the novel is an example of the "repressed form" in which Hemingway disallows feeling and thought.

107 TUTTLETON, JAMES W. "'Combat in the Erogenous Zone': Women in the American Novel between the Two World Wars." In *What Manner of Woman: Essays on English and American Life and Literature.* Edited by Marlene Springer. New York: New York University Press, pp. 271-96.

Looks at Hemingway, Faulkner, and Fitzgerald's ambivalent treatment of women. Examines the recurring portrayal of women in Hemingway's fiction as either emasculating bitches or old-fashioned, self-effacing stereotypes. Sees the author as possessing a "deep fear – if not of women, at least of man's 'weakness' in 'succumbing' to his own emotional need for woman."

108 WAGNER, LINDA WELSHIMER. *Ernest Hemingway: A Reference Guide.* Boston: G.K. Hall & Co., 363 pp.

Comprehensive list with annotations of criticism from 1923 through 1974 and into 1975. In her introduction, Wagner traces the critical reputation and response to the author over the last half-century, remarking that "criticism of Hemingway's writing has never diminished."

109 _____. "Modern American Literature: The Poetics of the Individual Voice." *Centennial Review* 21, no. 4:333-54.

Using brief passages from *A Farewell to Arms* and a late unpublished fragment as examples, Wagner argues that the intense, individualistic "Hemingway voice" is present in all of his works "because it was the real self; it was – or ultimately became – the writer's identity." Reprinted: 1980.93.

110 _____. "Tension and Technique: The Years of Greatness." *Studies in American Fiction* 5, no. 1 (Spring): 65-77.

Wagner includes Hemingway's impact in her consideration of modern American fiction. Suggests that "for some contemporary readers, Hemingway's lucid and restricted style – magnificent in its purity though it is – is *so* restrictive that his characterization sometimes suffers because the reader does not know enough, does not have enough ways in." Reprinted 1980.93.

111 WALKER, ROBERT G. "Anselmo, Atonement, and Hemingway's *For Whom the Bell Tolls.*" *Notes on Contemporary Literature* 7, no. 2 (March): 7-8.

Draws parallels between Anselmo's unifying role in the novel during the climactic bridge-blowing scene and the Christian doctrine of Atonement put forward by St. Anselm of Canterbury.

112 WHITE, WILLIAM. "Hemingway Checklist." *Fitzgerald/Hemingway Annual,* pp. 255-66.

Lists articles, reviews, and books from 1971 to 1976. Includes a few earlier reviews.

113 ____. "The Short Unhappy War of Ernest Hemingway." *Lost Generation Journal* 5, no. 2 (Winter): 2-3, 22.
Biographical article recounting Hemingway's experiences on the Italian front and later convalescence at a Milan hospital during World War I.

114 WHITE, WILLIAM, and CLARK, C.E. FRAZER, Jr. "Ernest Hemingway 1899-1961." In *First Printings of American Authors: Contributions toward Descriptive Checklists*. Vol. 1. Edited by Matthew J. Bruccoli, C.E. Frazer Clark, Jr., Richard Layman, and Benjamin V. Franklin. Detroit: Gale Research Co., pp. 177-83.
*Fitzgerald/Hemingway Annual 1978, p. 462.

115 WHITTLE, AMBERYS R. "A Reading of Hemingway's 'The Gambler, the Nun, and the Radio.'" *Arizona Quarterly* 33, no. 2 (Summer): 173-80.
Argues that this story and some other Hemingway short stories cannot be fully understood unless read as modern parables.

116 "Who's Up, Who's Down." *Esquire* 88, no. 2 (August): 77-81.
Asks several well-known critics, editors, and authors which twentieth-century American writers are the most overrated and underrated. Out of thirty-two judges, Hemingway is listed as overrated three times.

117 WILLING, RICHARD. "Hemingway Manuscript Revealed." *Washington Post*, 4 April, pp. D1, D11.
Discusses a recently uncovered short-story manuscript written in 1919 entitled "The Passing of Pickles McCarty" or "The Woppian Way." Notes Hemingway's characteristic treatment of the boxer and the soldier as "macho heroes" is present even in this early manuscript.

118 WILSON, EDMUND. Introduction to *In Our Time*, by Ernest Hemingway. In *Praise from Famous Men: An Anthology of Introductions*. Edited by Guy R. Lyle. Metuchen, N.J.: Scarecrow Press, pp. 169-74.
Wilson finds the brutality of the war vignettes contrasted with the candor and sensitivity of the Nick Adams stories a key to Hemingway's later works in which "suffering and making suffer, and their relation to the sensual enjoyment of life, are the subject."

119 WILSON, ELENA, ed. *Letters on Literature and Politics 1912-1972*. New York: Farrar, Straus & Giroux, 767 pp.

Letters written by Edmund Wilson with numerous references to Hemingway and his works, including mention of the author's outrage over Wilson's publication of "Hemingway: Gauge of Morale."

120 WILSON, G.R., Jr. "Incarnation and Redemption in *The Old Man and the Sea*." *Studies in Short Fiction* 14, no. 4 (Fall): 369-73.
Examines early passages in the text in relation to the liturgical calendar, determining that the time spans mentioned refer to the sacred mysteries of the Incarnation and Redemption.

121 WINNER, VIOLA HOPKINS. "The American Pictorial Vision: Objects and Ideas in Hawthorne, James, and Hemingway." *Studies in American Fiction* 5, no. 1 (Spring): 143-59.
In defining what is truly American about American literary pictorialism, Winner finds *Islands in the Stream* subscribing to most of the conventions and themes characteristic of the tradition.

122 WINSLOW, RICHARD. "Greg and Hemmy: Writing for the *Toronto Star* in 1920." *Fitzgerald/Hemingway Annual*, pp. 183-93.
Recounts how Hemingway became a writer for the *Toronto Star*, contributing articles on boxing, fishing, and veterans, and describes his association with Gregory Clark, features editor of the newpaper.

123 WYATT, DAVID M. "Hemingway's Uncanny Beginnings." *Georgia Review* 31, no. 2 (Summer): 476-501.
"Hemingway's beginnings have the uncanny effect of raising the very specter of the end against which they are so concerned to defend." A study of his major novels (*In Our Time, The Sun Also Rises, A Farewell to Arms, Across the River and into the Trees, For Whom the Bell Tolls*) reveals that Hemingway uses the settings, characters, and dialogues described in their beginnings to anticipate their doomed endings. Reprinted: 1980.109.

124 YARDLEY, JONATHAN. *Ring: A Biography of Ring Lardner*. New York: Random House, pp. 181-83.
Comments on Lardner's influence upon the young Hemingway who imitated Lardner in his high school newspaper and later turned on him.

125 ZEHR, DAVID MORGAN. "Paris and the Expatriate Mystique: Hemingway's *The Sun Also Rises*." *Arizona Quarterly* 33, no. 2 (Summer): 156-64.
Reads *The Sun Also Rises* as Hemingway's attempt to dispel misconceptions about 1920s Paris and the expatriates living there. By depicting in detail their reasons for being there and Jake's life on the

edge of the milieu, Hemingway justifies and clarifies his own presence in Paris.

1978

1   ADAIR, WILLIAM. "Eighty-Five as a Lucky Number: A Note on *The Old Man and the Sea*." *Notes on Contemporary Literature* 8, no. 1 (January): 9.
    Points out that when eight and five are subtracted, added, and multiplied the result is three, thirteen, and forty–all significant numbers.

2   _____. "Ernest Hemingway and the Poetics of Loss." *College Literature* 5:12-23.
    Discusses the themes of loss (i.e. freedom, home, love, youthful illusions), fear of loss, and the longing following loss in several short stories and novels, tracing these recurrent patterns back to losses in the author's own life and his development of the omission theory of composition. Reprinted: 1983.1.

3   ADAMS, MICHAEL. "Gatsby, Tycoon, Islands, and the Film Critics." *Fitzgerald/Hemingway Annual,* pp. 296-306.
    Although critical reception of the Hemingway film adaptation was generally "less extreme" than for the two Fitzgerald versions, *Islands in the Stream* was derided for its sentimentality, dialogue, and direction.

4   BASKETT, SAM S. "'An Image to Dance around': Brett and Her Lovers in *The Sun Also Rises*." *Centennial Review* 22, no. 1 (Winter): 45-69.
    Looks closely at the different experiences and reactions of each of Lady Brett Ashley's lovers, arguing that their distinct differences reconcile in their fixing upon Lady Brett "as an uncertain image of great value." Reprinted: 1987.95.

5   BERG, A. SCOTT. "The Elusive Man Who Was America's Greatest Literary Editor." *Esquire* 90 (18 July): 55-58, 63-66, 68.
    Fitzgerald introduced Hemingway to Maxwell Perkins, editor for Charles Scribner's Sons. After losing an early Hemingway contract, Perkins optioned *The Sun Also Rises* without even reading it. Perkins persuaded the editorial board to publish the novel despite its profanity and questionable morality.

6   _____. *Max Perkins Editor of Genius*. New York: Dutton, pp. 87-90, 92-101, 109-113, 322-27, 418-420, etc.

Many unpublished sources, including letters, journals, and manuscripts are used in this biography of the legendary editor Maxwell Perkins. Gives an extensive overview of the American literary scene spanning the twenties, thirties, and forties, with numerous references to Hemingway, Fitzgerald, and Wolfe. Much of the book is devoted to Perkins's relationship with Hemingway, including his initial signing of the author with Charles Scribner's Sons, his defense of *The Sun Also Rises* despite its "vulgar content," and their enduring friendship.

7 BRASCH, JAMES D., and SIGMAN, JOSEPH T. "The Library at Finca Vigía: A Preliminary Report, 1977." *Fitzgerald/Hemingway Annual,* pp. 184-203.

Concerned about the deterioration of the 9,000-volume library despite the Cuban government's preservation of the Finca Vigía as a museum. Proposes that all texts be catalogued and those with marginalia be microfilmed. Includes interior and exterior photographs.

8 BROER, LAWRENCE R. "'A Clean, Well-Lighted Place.'" In *Instructor's Manual for the Art of Fiction.* Edited by R.F. Dietrich and Roger H. Sandell. 3d ed. New York: Holt, Rinehart & Winston, pp. 97-103.

*Fitzgerald/Hemingway Annual 1979, p. 465.

9 BRUCCOLI, MATTHEW J. *Scott and Ernest: The Authority of Failure and the Authority of Success.* New York: Random House, 168 pp.

Reconstructs Hemingway's friendship and literary rivalry with Fitzgerald through unearthed letters and other documents. A dark side of Hemingway emerges as it becomes evident that once the author became famous, he considered his relationship with Fitzgerald a nuisance. Includes a chronology but no index.

10 BRYER, JACKSON R. "Fitzgerald and Hemingway." In *American Literary Scholarship: An Annual.* Edited by J. Albert Robbins. Durham, N.C.: Duke University Press, pp. 141-66.

Survey of criticism on both authors published during 1976. Bryer considers it a "quiet year in Hemingway and Fitzgerald studies."

11 BUCKLEY, PETER. *Ernest.* New York: Dial Press, 162 pp.

Stunning photographs from Hemingway's personal collection together with a biographical essay by Buckley trace the author's life from early childhood until just before his 1961 suicide. Emphasis placed upon the young Hemingway growing up in Oak Park – particularly his family and other forces that influenced him.

12 BURGESS, ANTHONY. *Ernest Hemingway and His World*. New York: Scribner's, 128 pp.

> Fast-paced account of some of the most human elements of Hemingway's life, including the Spanish civil war, his many accidents, and the last days of his increasingly obvious dementia. Includes more than 100 photographs.

13 CALVERT, MARGARET CORNING. "Style and Structure in *The Sun Also Rises*." *Linguistics in Literature* 3, no. 2:1-91.

> Offers a detailed linguistic analysis of four passages in order to reveal the way Hemingway's form relates to content. Contends that style varies in connection with image patterns (war, church, sun, sports, etc.) and that these patterns represent Jake's search for self-knowledge.

14 CARBONNEAU, DENIS. "Hemingway Play Found." *Book Collector's Market* 3:40.

> Announces the discovery of *Hokum*, a 1921 three-act play written by Hemingway and Morris McNeil Musselman.

15 CASS, COLIN S. "'Nothing Happened . . .': The Tip of a Hemingway Iceberg." *Fitzgerald/Hemingway Annual*, pp. 247-59.

> Looks closely at the role of Miss Van Campen and the historical significance of the dates of Frederic Henry's convalescent leave in *A Farewell to Arms*, finding that in being forced by the superintendent to return to the war two days early Henry was in time for the retreat and escape at the Tagliamento River that labeled him a deserter. Although Cass argues that this historical connection enhances our knowledge of the symmetry and irony of book 2, he questions whether such subtleties may leave too much of the iceberg submerged.

16 CHAPMAN, MARY LEWIS. "Hometown Boy." *Literary Sketches* 18, no. 2:3-4.

> Announces the 1978 Oak Park Festival in honor of Hemingway and other famous former residents of Oak Park.

17 COWLEY, MALCOLM. "Papa and the Parricides." In *And I Worked at the Writer's Trade*. New York: Viking Press, pp. 21-34.

> Reprint with minor revision from *Esquire* 67 (June): 100-101, 103, 160, 162.

18 CRAWFORD, FRED D., and MORTON, BRUCE. "Hemingway and Brooks: The Mystery of 'Henry's Bicycle.'" *Studies in American Fiction* 6, no. 1 (Spring): 106-9.

Interprets the ironic dialogue concerning expatriate art in *The Sun Also Rises* as Hemingway's reaction against Van Wyck Brooks's assertion that an expatriate can't write.

19 CROSLAND, ANDREW. "Hemingway, Heller, and an Old Joke." *American Notes & Queries* 16, no. 5 (January): 73.

Believes that Heller's use of the Washington Irving joke in *Catch-22* was probably a coincidence since it is doubtful that he remembered its inclusion in Hemingway's "The Friend of Spain: A Spanish Letter" published in *Esquire* in 1934 when Heller was only eleven years old.

20 DAHIYA, BHIM S. *The Hero in Hemingway: A Study in Development.* New Delhi, India: Bahri, 225 pp.
    MLA Bibliography 1979, p. 217.

21 DAVIS, WILLIAM V. "'The Fell of Dark': The Loss of Time in Hemingway's 'The Killers.'" *Studies in Short Fiction* 15, no. 3:319-20.

Sees Nick's apprehension of "the dark side of the world" paralleled by the clock time in Henry's lunchroom.

22 DONALD, MILES. *The American Novel in the Twentieth Century.* Newton Abbot, England: David & Charles; New York: Barnes & Noble, pp. 27-41.

Provides a social context for many of the major works such as *The Sun Also Rises*, *A Farewell to Arms*, and *The Old Man and the Sea*. Sees the "obvious poeticism and romanticized suffering" of *A Farewell to Arms* as the first sign of Hemingway's artistic decline. Classifies Hemingway as traditional in his use of nineteenth-century themes and his depiction of the local American experience as universal.

23 DONALDSON, SCOTT. "'irony and pity': Anatole France Got It Up." *Fitzgerald/Hemingway Annual,* pp. 331-34.

Contends that the source of Bill Gorton's comments on "irony and pity" in *The Sun Also Rises* is Anatole France's *Le Jardin d'Épicure*.

24 _____. "Preparing for the End: Hemingway's Revisions of 'A Canary for One.'" *Studies in American Fiction* 6, no. 2 (Autumn): 203-11.

Examines three drafts in order to show that Hemingway made subtle revisions to lessen the shock at the end of the story of the American couple's breakup.

25 DRAKE, ROBERT. "Hemingway and Faulkner: Tracing Their Resemblances." *Christian Century* 95, no. 37:1104-6.

Categorizes Hemingway and Faulkner as similar in their fundamental concern "with behavior, deportment, human conduct in the face of formidable, even overwhelming forces."

26 ELLIS, JAMES. "Hemingway's *The Sun Also Rises*." *Explicator* 36, no. 3:24.

Sees Hemingway's humorous references to Jake's war wound as possibly connected to a "World War I joke that the British medal for gallantry, the Distinguished Service Order, stood for 'dick shot off.'"

27 FENSTERMAKER, JOHN S. "Marketing Hemingway: Scribner's Advertising in Publishers Weekly and the New York Times Book Review, 1929-1941." *Fitzgerald/Hemingway Annual*, pp. 283-95.

In this detailed account of marketing practices, Fenstermaker finds the publisher using basically the same advertising materials when targeting booksellers and the general reader alike. Interestingly enough, Scribner's seldom used biographical information when advertising.

28 FETTERLEY, JUDITH. "*A Farewell to Arms*: Hemingway's 'Resentful Cryptogram.'" In *The Resisting Reader: A Feminist Approach to American Fiction*. Bloomington: Indiana University Press, pp. 46-71.

Reprint with minor revision of 1976.24. Reprinted with minor revision: 1977.33 and 1987.6.

29 FORCZEK, DEBORAH A. "Fitzgerald and Hemingway in the Academy: A Survey of Dissertations." *Fitzgerald/Hemingway Annual*, pp. 351-85.

Along with a list of 142 dissertations, Forczek provides a breakdown by year and university as well as a commentary regarding trends in scholarship. Finds influence and stylistic studies in addition to thematic exploration of "experience, competition, and nihilism" heavily represented in the Hemingway dissertations.

30 GAITHER, LEX. "Hemingway and Wolfe." *Thomas Wolfe Newsletter* 2, no. 2:29-30.

Discusses Hemingway's seemingly unfounded dislike of Wolfe.

31 GAJDUSEK, ROBERT E. *Hemingway's Paris*. New York: Charles Scribner's Sons, 182 pp.

Photographs of Paris accompanied by excerpts from Hemingway, his contemporaries, and biographers designed to capture the essence of the city in the 1920s. Reprinted with minor revision: 1986.38.

32 GRIFFIN, PETER M. "A Substantive Error in the Text of Ernest
    Hemingway's 'Summer People.'" *American Literature* 50, no. 3
    (November): 471-73.
        Reprints ten lines of the original manuscript omitted from both
    the 1972 Scribner's edition of *The Nick Adams Stories* and the Bantam
    paperback edition, concluding that such an omission significantly mars
    the short story.

33 HAGEMANN, E.R. "A Preliminary Report on the State of Ernest
    Hemingway's Correspondence." *Literary Research Newsletter* 3:163-72.
        Finds that despite Hemingway and Mary Welsh Hemingway's
    restrictions on publication, the author's "correspondence is alive and
    doing as well as can be expected under stringent conditions." Hagemann
    reveals how 594 letters have come into public print, either in full, in
    part, or in paraphrase.

34 HAMALIAN, LEO. "Hemingway's Crucible." In *Burn after Reading*.
    New York: Ararat Press, pp. 45-50.
        Is impressed with the sincerity and energy of the newspaper
    dispatches collected in *By-Line: Ernest Hemingway*. Citing examples of
    the author's use of the 1922 Turkish conflict sketches again in his later
    fiction, Hamalian contends that Hemingway's experiences in the
    Turkish struggle "helped to forge the conscience of a great writer and a
    compassionate human being."

35 HART, JEFFREY. "*The Sun Also Rises*: A Revaluation." *Sewanee
    Review* 86 (Fall): 557-62.
        Contends that Hemingway's real novel about the thirties is *The
    Sun Also Rises*, written in 1926. Finds Hemingway "stripping the reader
    of his ordinary responses, and specifically of his bourgeois ideology, and
    by so doing bringing him to a fresh encounter with various kinds of
    actuality."

36 HEMINGWAY, JACK. "Memories of Papa." *Student*, Winter, pp. 29-
    34.
        Fitzgerald/Hemingway Annual 1979, p. 470.

37 HOFFER, BATES. "Jacob: As the Sun Rises." *Linguistics in Literature*
    3, no. 2:93-108.
        Fits the parallels between Jake Barnes and the biblical Jacob of
    Genesis into the larger picture of the Apocalypse. Finds that although
    The Sun Also Rises is not a perfect allegory of the Apocalypse,
    Hemingway "uses major biblical imagery even as the people who lived
    through the pestilence, famine, conquest, and war in World War I
    thought of it and spoke of it and wrote about it in terms of the Four

Horsemen of the Apocalypse, in terms of the final war between good and evil, which war is Armageddon."

38 HOUGH, JULIE. "Hemingway's 'The Sea Change': An Embracing of Reality." *Odyssey: A Journal of the Humanities* 2, no. 2:16-18.

Focuses on the varying degrees of vice found in the story and the different responses to it. Only the young lovers demonstrate a full realization and painful acceptance of the existence of vice in their lives.

39 JOHNSTON, CAROL. "General Checklist." *Fitzgerald/Hemingway Annual,* pp. 435-36.

Lists books written between 1975 and 1978 relating to Fitzgerald and Hemingway.

40 JOHNSTON, KENNETH G. "In the Beginning: Hemingway's 'Indian Camp.'" *Studies in Short Fiction* 15, no. 1 (Winter): 102-4.

Looks at the omitted opening of "Indian Camp" later published as "Three Shots," noting two interesting differences in the texts concerning Nick's truthfulness and a literary allusion to Plato's "parable of education and ignorance." Reprinted (expanded): 1987.38.

41 JOOST, NICHOLAS, and BROWN, ALAN. "T.S. Eliot and Ernest Hemingway: A Literary Relationship." *Papers on Language and Literature* 14 (Fall): 425-49.

Despite Hemingway's antagonism toward Eliot, the poet "filled the role of a tutor from whom Hemingway learned many valuable lessons." Explores the extent to which Hemingway's theory of writing was influenced by Eliot's imagist technique, including shared interests in sexual relationships and traditional Christianity.

42 KNOWLES, A. SIDNEY, Jr. "Hemingway's *Across the River and into the Trees*: Adversity and Art." *Essays in Literature* 5, no. 2 (Fall): 195-208.

In a biographical reading of the novel, Knowles sees Hemingway using his fiction "to pay certain tributes and settle certain scores."

43 KOBLER, J.F. "Why Does Catherine Barkley Die?" *Fitzgerald/Hemingway Annual,* pp. 313-19.

Discusses the three distinct explanations that Frederic Henry gives for Catherine Barkley's death at the end of *A Farewell to Arms*: religious, accidental, and naturalistic. Kobler finds Hemingway offering only one conclusion – "that death is the ultimate mystery."

44 KOPKA, DEBORAH. "The Private Hemingway: Recollections of a Friend." *Clifton* 6 (Spring): 34-37.

Dave Roberts reminisces about his old fishing buddy and friend, Ernest Hemingway, whom he met in Sun Valley during the mid-1940s.

45 KVAM, WAYNE. "Hemingway's 'Under the Ridge.'" *Fitzgerald/Hemingway Annual*, pp. 225-40.

In depicting the loyalist defeat during the Spanish civil war, Hemingway transforms "his own experience into the fiction writer's parabolic search for truth in wartime."

46 LEUCHTENBERGER, MARK. "The First Mrs. Hemingway: Hadley." *Student*, Winter, pp. 26-28.

Fitzgerald/Hemingway Annual 1979, p. 472.

47 MacLEISH, ARCHIBALD. *Riders on the Earth*. Boston: Houghton Mifflin Co., pp. 69-72.

Brief biographical sketch of the early Paris years commenting on Hemingway's commitment to serious writing.

48 McNEIL, MARY; LEUCHTENBERGER, MARK; and FARMER, SUE ELLEN. "Mary Hemingway: How It Was." *Student*, Winter, pp. 16-25.

Fitzgerald/Hemingway Annual 1979, p. 473.

49 MILLER, R.H. "Ernest Hemingway, Textual Critic." *Fitzgerald/Hemingway Annual*, pp. 345-47.

Comments on Hemingway's corrections to the epigraph (taken from Donne's *Devotions upon Emergent Occasions*) of *For Whom the Bell Tolls*. Miller remarks that Hemingway "wanted Donne's prose in its seventeenth-century purity, and he did a good job getting it." Includes collation of original with later versions.

50 MONK, DONALD. "Hemingway's Territorial Imperative." *Yearbook of English Studies* 8:125-40.

Looks at the Hemingway hero in the light of Conrad's and Lorenz's theories of territorial instinct. Monk writes, "Caught in his true vulnerability he holds just enough space to live, his right to that space being that he has measured what factors will make it defensible."

51 MONROE, H. KEITH. "Garbo as Guerilla: *Queen Christina* and *For Whom the Bell Tolls*." *Fitzgerald/Hemingway Annual*, pp. 335-38.

Analyzes two references to Greta Garbo, concluding that Hemingway may have modeled the Robert-Maria love story after the 1933 film *Queen Christina* in which Garbo poses as a male but meets and falls in love with a foreigner who is killed in the end.

52 MONTEIRO, GEORGE. "Additions to Hanneman: Early Unrecorded Hemingway Items." *Papers of the Bibliographical Society of America* 72, no. 2:245-46.

Lists three reviews and five items from 1925 to 1927 not mentioned in Hanneman's 1967 *Ernest Hemingway: A Comprehensive Bibliography* (Princeton) nor her 1975 *Supplement* (Princeton).

53 _____. "Hemingway's Nun's Tale." *Research Studies* 46, no. 1 (March): 50-53.

Concerns the biographical basis of "The Gambler, the Nun, and the Radio." Relates the short story to Hemingway's 1930 automobile accident in Montana and subsequent recuperation at St. Vincent's Hospital.

54 _____. "Hemingway's Unnatural History of the Dying." *Fitzgerald/Hemingway Annual*, pp. 339-42.

Looks at the reprinting of "A Natural History of the Dead" in Hemingway's third collection of short stories, *Winner Take Nothing*. Monteiro points out that the doctor, in denying the dying soldier treatment, is simply following the system of triage in which medical attention is administered according to chances of patient survival.

55 _____. "Justice Holmes on Hemingway." *Markham Review* 8 (Fall): 7-8.

Includes excerpts of letters Holmes wrote to friends regarding his opinions of Hemingway's writing. Holmes spends much time pondering why such ordinary people and events make for such interesting reading.

56 MORRIS, WRIGHT. "Ernest Hemingway." In *Earthly Delights, Unearthly Adornments*. New York: Harper & Row, pp. 141-46.

Discusses the impact of Hemingway's style on both reader and author alike. Finds Hemingway's ability to capture emotion the secret to his style and ultimate literary success.

57 MOSES, CAROLE. "Language as Theme in *For Whom the Bell Tolls*." *Fitzgerald/Hemingway Annual*, pp. 215-23.

Discusses the "limitations of language" as a subtheme. "As a political tool, as a means of communication, and as an art form, language again and again fails to describe reality adequately, even though many characters express idealistic views about the potential of language." Moses argues that the inaccurate and ephemeral nature of language undermines the articulation of experience and creates isolation.

58 NADEAU, ROBERT L. "Film and Mythic Heroism: Sturges's Old Man." In *The Modern American Novel and the Movies*. Edited by Gerald

Peary and Roger Shatzkin. New York: Frederick Ungar Publishing Co., pp. 199-203.

Thinks Sturges unable to capture an accurate image of Santiago on film because "the mythic dimensions of Santiago render him a good deal *larger* than life."

59 NAKAJIMA, KENJI. "Nick as 'The Battler.'" *Kyushu American Literature* 19:45-48.

Describes the mutually dependent relationship between Ad and Bugs as similar to that of mother and child. Nick learns from his experiences that he must reject self-pity and be constantly on guard if he is to navigate life successfully.

60 NAUMANN, MARINA T. "Tolstoyan Reflections in Hemingway: *War and Peace* and *For Whom the Bell Tolls.*" In *American Contributions to the Eighth International Congress of Slavists, Zagreb and Ljubljana, September 3-9, 1978, Volume 2.* Edited by Victor Terras. Columbus, Ohio: Slavica Publishers, Inc., pp. 550-69.

Considers *For Whom the Bell Tolls* to be "certainly Tolstoyan in its conception." In comparing the two novels, Naumann cites parallels in viewpoint (emotional/romantic/nationalistic), characterization, theme (war/death/love), setting (personification of nature), and a cyclical vision of life and death.

61 NICHOLS, KATHLEEN L. "The Morality of Asceticism in *The Sun Also Rises*: A Structural Reinterpretation." *Fitzgerald/Hemingway Annual,* pp. 321-30.

Traces Jake's progress from romantic to realist as he learns "how to live" in a world made up of emotional relationships. Jake's new perspective allows him to adopt an ascetic morality based on discipline and integrity as he faces the loss of his romantic dreams.

62 O'HARA, JOHN. *Selected Letters of John O'Hara.* Edited by Matthew J. Bruccoli. New York: Random House, pp. 329-30, 348-50.

Numerous references to Hemingway, including his meteoric rise and subsequent downfall. Considers him "the most important writer of our time and the most important writer since Shakespeare."

63 PALMIERI, ANTHONY F.R. "A Note on the Hemingway-Anderson Rupture." *Fitzgerald/Hemingway Annual,* p. 349.

Gives evidence that Hemingway apologized to Anderson over the publishing of *The Torrents of Spring.*

64 PFEIL, FRED. "Icons for Clowns: American Writers Now." *College English* 39, no. 5 (January): 525-40.

Disappointed that Hemingway misuses his clean, powerful style to "craft the same vision of manhood and courage and toughness that appears on the Marlboro billboards looming over our freeways, or comes off the pages of *Argosy* magazine."

65 PHOL, CONSTANCE. "The 'Unmaking' of a Political Film." In *The Modern American Novel and the Movies*. Edited by Gerald Peary and Roger Shatzkin. New York: Frederick Ungar Publishing Co., pp. 317-24.

Discusses Paramount Pictures' and specifically director Sam Wood's successful efforts at stripping politics from their film adaptation of *For Whom the Bell Tolls* – at the request of the State Department and the Franco government.

66 POWELL, ANTHONY. *To Keep the Ball Rolling: The Memoirs of Anthony Powell*. Vol. 2. New York: Holt, Rinehart & Winston, pp. 109-112.

Comments briefly on his initial impressions of *The Sun Also Rises* and Hemingway's influence on his own writing.

67 RAO, E. NAGESWARA. "Forms of Irony in Hemingway's Work." *Littcrit* 6:44-46.

Annual Bibliography of English Language and Literature 1978, p. 589.

68 ROBINSON, SHARON. "Hemingway, Emerson, and Nick Adams." *Studies in the Humanities* 7, no. 1:5-9.

Despite Hemingway's avowed dislike of Emerson's writings, Robinson traces similar themes of mysticism, intuition, self-knowledge, and the importance of nature found in Emerson's theories and *In Our Time*.

69 ROTHMAN, WILLIAM. "*To Have and Have Not* Adapted a Novel." In *The Modern American Novel and the Movies*. Edited by Gerald Peary and Roger Shatzkin. New York: Frederick Ungar Publishing Co., pp. 70-79.

Analyzes the extent to which Hawks's film adaptation follows the novel, noting similarities and differences in character, theme, emotional intensity, and tone.

70 ROWELL, CHARLES H. "'This Louisiana Thing That Drives Me': An Interview with Ernest J. Gaines." *Callaloo* 1, no. 3 (May): 39-51.

Gaines discusses briefly the influence of Hemingway's theme of grace under pressure in his own writing.

71   RUDNICK, LOIS P. "*Daisy Miller* Revisited: Ernest Hemingway's 'A Canary for One.'" *Massachusetts Studies in English* 7, no. 1:12-19.

Sees "A Canary for One" as an updated adaptation of the themes, culture, and moral concerns presented in James's *Daisy Miller*.

72   SAHA, P.K. "Style, Stylistic Transformations, and Incorporators." *Style* 12, no. 1 (Winter): 1-22.

Saha's stylistic analysis of brief passages from *The Sun Also Rises* and "Cross-Country Snow" explains the dynamic vigor and sense of immediacy found in Hemingway's writing.

73   SANFORD, STERLING S. "Hemingway Genealogy." *Fitzgerald/Hemingway Annual*, pp. 343-44.

Genealogical chart tracing the family back to Ralph Hemingway, born in England but "known to have been living in Roxbury, Massachusetts, as early as 1633." Shows Ernest distantly related to presidents Taft and Nixon.

74   SAROTTE, G.-M. "Ernest Hemingway: The (Almost) Total Sublimation of the Homosexual Instinct." In *Like a Brother, Like a Lover: Male Homosexuality in the American Novel and Theatre from Herman Melville to James Baldwin*. Translated by Richard Miller. New York: Doubleday, pp. 262-78.

Despite characteristics of latent homosexuality in Hemingway's works (male comradeship, contempt and fear of women, manly men), Sarotte finds no evidence of repressed homosexuality, instead classifying the writer as "the All-American boy."

75   SCHMID, HANS. "The Switzerland of Fitzgerald and Hemingway." *Fitzgerald/Hemingway Annual*, pp. 261-71.

Discusses each author's visits to Switzerland and briefly the ways each made use of his experiences in his writing. Describes the Chalet at Camby and the Posthotel Rossli at Gstaad where Hemingway skied, hiked, and fished during the 1920s. Includes photographs.

76   SELTZER, LEON F. "The Opportunity of Impotence: Count Mippipopolous in *The Sun Also Rises*." *Renascence* 31 (Autumn): 3-14.

Interprets the count as an older and more experienced Jake Barnes. Unlike Barnes, Mippipopolous is able to transcend his impotence through detachment, by subduing his sexual needs and altering his values so that he controls love without having love control him.

77 SINGER, GLEN W. "Huck, Ad, Jim, and Bugs: A Reconsideration–*Huckleberry Finn* and Hemingway's 'The Battler.'" *Notes on Modern American Literature* 3:item 9.

Reads "The Battler" as a modern version of the American myth found in Twain's novel.

78 SKERRETT, JOSEPH T., Jr. "Ralph Ellison and the Example of Richard Wright." *Studies in Short Fiction* 15, no. 2 (Spring): 145-53.

Mentions that before arriving in New York in 1937, Ellison had spent much of his spare time reading both old and new authors including Pound, Stein, Hemingway, Melville, and Twain.

79 SOJKA, GREGORY S. "The American Short Story into Film." *Studies in Short Fiction* 15, no. 2 (Spring): 203-4.

Mentions that "Soldier's Home" was cinematically adapted for the 1977 "American Short Story" film series.

80 SPOFFORD, WILLIAM K. "Beyond the Feminist Perspective: Love in *A Farewell to Arms*." *Fitzgerald/Hemingway Annual*, pp. 307-12.

Refutes feminist attacks on Catherine's subservient role and lack of identity. In analyzing the Frederic-Catherine relationship, Spofford argues that their devotion to each other results in mutual dependence and self-denial.

81 STEWART, JACK F. "Christian Allusions in 'Big Two-Hearted River.'" *Studies in Short Fiction* 15, no. 2 (Spring): 194-96.

Interprets Nick's coffee-making scene and subsequent memories of Hopkins as a ritual communion that spiritually unites past with present, directing Nick toward self-sufficiency and restored faith in himself.

82 STOLTZFUS, BEN. "Hemingway's Battle with God." In *Gide and Hemingway: Rebels against God*. Port Washington, N.Y.: Kennikat, pp. 39-79.

Two separate essays on each author's challenge of God from a traditional Christian perspective. Focusing on dialogue, narrative description, and symbolism in *The Old Man and the Sea*, Stoltzfus shows how the theme of pride underscores the "long prose poem."

83 TAVERNIER-COURBIN, JACQUELINE. "'Striving for Power': Hemingway's Classical Neurosis and Creative Force." *Midamerica* 5:76-95.

Hemingway's neurotic competitiveness and quest for power demonstrated throughout his life may have contributed to his inability to deal with the changes in his life and self-image brought about by advancing age. Also printed with minor revision in *Journal of General Education* 30, no. 3 (Fall): 137-53.

84 TRAXLER, PATRICIA. "Imitation Hemingway: 'Come Here, My Little Gerbil." *Odyssey: A Journal of the Humanities* 3, no. 1:28-29.
Winning entry in the First International Imitation Hemingway Competition. Parody at its best (or worst).

85 UNRUE, JOHN. "Duke Remembers Papa." *Fitzgerald / Hemingway Annual,* pp. 205-14.
Reminiscence by Forrest ("Duke") MacMullen, friend and hunting companion of Hemingway. Focuses mainly on their relationship between 1958 and 1960 in Idaho. MacMullen's memories of these later years shed a different light than Aaron Hotchner's "dramatically distorted" account in *Papa Hemingway*.

86 VILLARD, HENRY S. "In a World War I Hospital with Hemingway." *Horizon* (New York) 21, no. 8 (August): 85-93.
Reminiscence about his time spent at the American Red Cross Hospital in Milan where he was nursed by Agnes von Kurowsky and convalesced with the wounded Hemingway. Villard speculates on Hemingway's use of them as models in *A Farewell to Arms* and the true relationship between von Kurowsky and Hemingway. Both Villard and von Kurowsky agreed in a brief 1975 reunion that the adulation Hemingway received while convalescing may have contributed to "the self-centeredness that would transform his fresh, boyish character in the years to come." Reprinted with minor revision: 1979.95.

87 WHITE, GERTRUDE M. "We're All 'Cats in the Rain.'" *Fitzgerald/Hemingway Annual,* pp. 241-46.
Questions orthodox interpretations of the story that sympathize with the woman and despise the insensitivity of the man. White suggests that Hemingway is once again depicting the larger theme that we must all live in a world that opposes our expectations and dreams.

88 WHITE, RAY LEWIS. "*The Fifth Column and Four Stories of the Spanish Civil War*: 38 Additional Reviews." *Fitzgerald/Hemingway Annual,* pp. 273-82.
Lists and annotates reviews published in 1969 and 1970 not included in Hanneman's 1975 *Supplement* (Princeton).

89 ____. "Hemingway's *Islands in the Stream*: A Collection of Additional Reviews." *Library Chronicle* 43:81-98.
Annotates reviews written in 1970 not mentioned in Hanneman's 1975 *Supplement* (Princeton).

90 WHITE, WILLIAM.   "Addenda to Hanneman: Hemingway's
Islands in the Stream." *Papers of the Bibliographical Society of America*
72, no. 2:247-49.
    Lists a 1971 Bantam edition and a 1974 Slovak and 1971 Greek
translation of *Islands in the Stream* not mentioned in Hanneman's 1975
Supplement (Princeton).

91 ____. "Further Addenda to Hanneman's Hemingway Bibliography."
Papers of the Bibliographical Society of America 72, no. 2:249.
    Lists an anthology containing Hemingway's poem "Champ
d'Honneur" not mentioned in Hanneman's 1975 *Supplement*
(Princeton).

92 ____. "Hemingway Checklist." *Fitzgerald/Hemingway Annual*, pp. 449-
63.
    Lists 172 items written mainly between 1973 and 1977.

93 ____. "A Misprint in Hemingway's *Winner Take Nothing*." *Papers of the
Bibliographical Society of America* 72, no. 3:360-61.
    Points out a typographical error ("wo" instead of "two") in
Scribner's 1933 *Winner Take Nothing* which continued in subsequent
printings through 1968.

94 WHITLOW,   ROGER.   "*Across   the   River   and   into   the
Trees* – Hemingway and Psychotherapy." *Illinois Quarterly* 40, no. 4
(Summer): 38-47.
    Explores Renata's role in the novel as a psychotherapist for
Cantwell who is "unable to reconcile his imminent death with the
catalog of destructive mistakes of his life as a professional soldier."

95 ____. "Critical Misinterpretation of Hemingway's Helen." *Frontiers* 3,
no. 3:52-54.
    Defends Helen in "The Snows of Kilimanjaro" against the
orthodox interpretation of "bitch-woman." Whitlow characterizes her as
a "strong, considerate, and deeply loving" woman tied to a "cowardly,
dishonest, and cruel" man. Blames misinterpretations of character on
"spillover" associations with Margot Macomber.

96 WITHERINGTON, PAUL. "Word and Flesh in Hemingway's 'On the
Quai at Smyrna.'" *Notes on Modern American Literature* 2:item 18.
    Examines narrative devices, contending that "the layered effect of
dual narrators dissolves as sophisticated verbal solutions replace active
solutions to pain and confusion, and as internalized events are
controlled as art."

97 WRIGHT, MOORHEAD. "The Existential Adventurer and War: Three Case Studies from American Fiction." In *American Thinking about Peace and War: New Essays on American Thought and Attitudes.* Edited by Ken Booth and Moorhead Wright. Sussex, England: Harvester Press; New York: Barnes & Noble, pp. 101-10.

Categorizes Frederic Henry as an existential adventurer – commenting on his passive and almost detached response to both the war and his affair with Catherine Barkley. Sees Rinaldi and the priest as the only two characters in *A Farewell to Arms* "who embody that ideal fusion of individuality and community which may be the only positive by-product of war in human terms."

98 ZIFF, LARZER. "The Social Basis of Hemingway's Style." *Poetics* 7, no. 4 (December): 417-23.

Through a stylistic analysis of a passage from chapter 10 of *The Sun Also Rises*, Ziff argues that in Hemingway's early writings his style enabled him to write about experience without destroying it. "It is a style that works effectively only in conjunction with material that supports the view that public ideals are false and truth resides solely in unverbalized private experience." Reprinted: 1987.95.

1979

1 ADAMS, PHILLIP D. "Husserl's Eidetic Object: An Approach to the Styles of Hemingway and the Cubists." In *Images and Innovations: Update '70's.* Edited by Malinda R. Maxfield. Spartanburg, S.C.: Papers of the Southern Humanities Conference, Converse College, pp. 58-67.

Adams applies Husserl's theories of eidetic reduction in his examination of the way Hemingway and cubist painters present the essence of objects, finding a stylistic relationship emphasizing the vague and imprecise in their expression of the concrete.

2 AUGUST, JO. "The Ernest Hemingway Collection." *Fitzgerald/Hemingway Annual,* pp. 237-45.

Describes the extent of the collection at the Kennedy Library in Boston. Includes photographs and portions of letters indicating the variety of material available.

3 BACKMAN, MELVIN. "Death and Birth in Hemingway." In *The Stoic Strain in American Literature.* Edited by Duane J. MacMillan. Toronto: University of Toronto, pp. 115-34.

Psychological approach examining the stoic theme present in the Hemingway code. Looks at the conjunction of birth and death ranging from *In Our Time* to *The Old Man and the Sea*, with much attention paid to womb imagery.

4 BASKETT, SAM S. "Toward a 'Fifth Dimension' in *The Old Man and the Sea*." *Centennial Review* 19, no. 4:269-86.

Examines closely the biblical allusions and aura of "strangeness" surrounding Santiago, concluding that these and other devices push the protagonist's experiences beyond "the temporal limitations of the immediate moment," toward a "fifth dimension."

5 BEIDLER, PHILIP D. "Truth-Telling and Literary Values in the Vietnam Novel." *South Atlantic Quarterly* 78, no. 2 (Spring): 141-56.

Finds the tone and style of David Halberstam's *One Very Hot Day* and Josiah Bunting's *The Lionheads* (both Vietnam War novels) reminiscent of Hemingway's and Crane's war novels.

6 BENNETT, FORDYCE RICHARD. "Manolin's Father." *Fitzgerald/Hemingway Annual*, pp. 417-19.

Suggests that Manolin's father, with his contrasting system of values, serves as a foil to Santiago. "His is the kingdom of Body, Stomach, or the Mundane; Santiago's is of Spirit, Heart, or the Heroic."

7 BENNETT, WARREN. "The Manuscript and the Dialogue of 'A Clean, Well-Lighted Place.'" *American Literature* 50, no. 4 (January): 613-24.

By examining a previously undiscovered manuscript of the short story, Bennett attempts to resolve some of the confusions in dialogue identification and to explain how they came about. See 1982.38 for additional discussion.

8 BHATNAGAR, O.P. "The Sixth Dimension in *The Woman and the Sea* and *The Old Man and the Sea*." *Osmania Journal of English* 15:31-41.

Discusses similar themes, symbolism, and imagery found in the novels, stressing both authors' achievement of the "Sixth Dimension" – the merging of the conscious self with the unconscious in a state of nonbeing.

9 BIRNBAUM, MILTON. "Ernest Hemingway Read Anew." *Modern Age* 23 (Summer): 276-81.

Finds Hemingway's literary future assured not by the "readability" of his writing but by its "re-readability, its capacity to offer new meanings and reinterpretations." Relies primarily on embedded meaning in *The Sun Also Rises* to prove his point.

10 BOOHER, EDWIN R. "The Image in the Prose: Ezra Pound's Influence on Hemingway." *Illinois Quarterly* 42, no. 1 (Fall): 30-39.

Contends that general aesthetic principles shared by the two authors are the result of Pound's influence. Looks at Hemingway's adaptation of imagist methods of detail selection, symbolism, and presentation.

11 BOX, TERRY. "Hemingway's *A Farewell to Arms*." *Explicator* 37, no. 4 (Summer): 7.

Reads the novel as "a perfect reversal" of the Pygmalion-Galatea myth. While Venus cares enough to bring Galatea to life, the cruel and indifferent Hemingway God turns Catherine to stone.

12 BREIDLID, ANDERS. "Courage and Self-Affirmation in Ernest Hemingway's 'Lost Generation' Fiction." *Edda: Nordisk Tidsskrift for Litteraturforskning*, pp. 279-99.

Looks closely at the existential dilemma confronting the characters of the Nick Adams stories in *In Our Time*, *The Sun Also Rises*, and *A Farewell to Arms*. Finds Hemingway's protagonists willing to affirm the self in spite of life's contingent forces that threaten to render human existence meaningless.

13 BROWN, J.S., and CASTILLO, M. DEL. *Ernest Hemingway*. New York: Peebles Press International.

*Hemingway Notes 5, no. 2:39.

14 BRYER, JACKSON R. "Fitzgerald and Hemingway." In *American Literary Scholarship: An Annual*. Edited by James Woodress. Durham, N.C.: Duke University Press, pp. 163-86.

Survey of criticism on both authors published during 1977. Bryer finds "a good deal of worthwhile scholarship and criticism," although disheartened by the lack of any full-length critical studies on either Hemingway or Fitzgerald in the last few years.

15 CALMER, NED. "The Last Time I Saw Elliot Paul." *Virginia Quarterly Review* 55, no. 1:99-105.

Mentions Hemingway as one of the new American realists contributing to *transition* magazine during the 1920s.

16 CARABINE, KEITH. "Hemingway's *in our time*: An Appreciation." *Fitzgerald/Hemingway Annual*, pp. 301-326.

In this close examination of the experimental voices in the vignettes, Carabine argues that *in our time* is a sequence of "interrelated chapters comparable in structure and purpose, if not quality," to Pound's *Hugh Selwyn Mauberley* and Eliot's *The Waste Land*.

17 CARROLL, E. JEAN. "The Hemingway-Fitzgerald Literary Intelligence Test." *Esquire* 91, no. 1 (2 January): 81-82.
    A humorous yet challenging quiz covering the lives and works of Hemingway and Fitzgerald.

18 CASHIN, EDWARD J. "In Search of Hemingway." *Lost Generation Journal* 6, no. 1 (Summer): 10-11.
    Cashin attempts to rediscover Hemingway's Europe of the 1920s but finds that after forty years only Spain has remained unchanged.

19 COBBS, JOHN L. "Hemingway's *To Have and Have Not*: A Casualty of Didactic Revision." *South Atlantic Bulletin* 44, no. 4:1-10.
    Finds that in rewriting the novel, Hemingway added too much "social consciousness" to the central story of Harry Morgan's struggles, thus ruining "what might have been the best proletarian novel of the thirties."

20 COMLEY, NANCY. "Hemingway: The Economics of Survival." *Novel: A Forum on Fiction* 12, no. 3 (Spring): 244-53.
    Looks closely at the way "money manifests itself in an economic structure of exchange values which the Hemingway Hero learns to apply to his life, most especially to his emotional relationships." Concentrating on *The Sun Also Rises*, Comley sees Hemingway's early characters as experiencing ("paying") rites of passage in which they progress from immature emotional states to ordered maturity.

21 CONRAD, BARNABY, III. "Cézanne's Influence on Hemingway." *Horizon* 22, no. 4 (April): 32-37.
    Stein introduced the young Hemingway to the paintings of Cézanne, urging him to learn from them. Conrad traces the artist's influence on the author, suggesting that "Hemingway's brief, clear sentences and precise descriptions were literary counterparts to Cézanne's short, form-giving brushstrokes."

22 CRAWFORD, JOHN W. "Robert Jordan: A Man for Our Times." *CEA Critic* 41, no. 3:17-22.
    Categorizes Jordan as a modern American hero because he is able to find meaning, value, and order in a world turned upside down.

23 CROZIER, ROBERT D., S.J. "'The Paris Church of Passy': A Note on Hemingway's Second Marriage." *Papers on Language and Literature* 15, no. 1 (Winter): 84-86.
    Locates records of Hemingway's second marriage to Pauline Pfeiffer in Paris at St. Honore d'Eylau Catholic Church. Marriage

records indicate Hemingway altered his date of birth to appear only two years younger than Pfeiffer.

24 "Cumulative Index, 1969-1979." *Fitzgerald/Hemingway Annual,* pp. 485-530.
    Lists essays, reviews, and illustrations published in the *Fitzgerald/Hemingway Annual* from 1969 through 1979.

25 DANIEL, ALIX Du POY. "The Stimulating Life with Gertrude & Co." *Lost Generation Journal* 6, no. 1:16-18.
    Reminisces about Hemingway, Stein, and others he met while in Paris during the 1920s.

26 DAVIDSON, CATHY N. "Death in the Morning: The Role of Vicente Girones in *The Sun Also Rises*." *Hemingway Notes* 5, no. 1:11-13.
    Looks at the underlying theme of mutability in the running of the bulls passage, arguing that an authorial voice replaces Jake's in order to provide a deeper perspective.

27 DEKKER, GEORGE, and HARRIS, JOSEPH. "Supernaturalism and the Vernacular Style in *A Farewell to Arms*." *PMLA* 94, no. 2 (March): 311-18.
    Dekker and Harris admire Hemingway's use of literary allusions and supernatural elements in *A Farewell to Arms* but admit that its vernacular surface may discourage a deeper reading.

28 Di ROBILANT, OLGHINA. "Hemingway and True Grit: A Memoir." *Esquire* 91, no. 6 (27 March): 38-42, 50, 52.
    Recounts her time spent with Hemingway in Italy and Spain after World War II where he was idolized by Venetian society and welcomed into the bullfighting community at Madrid. Di Robilant recalls her conversations with Hemingway about bullfighting, skiing, and risk taking.

29 EDEL, LEON. "The Figure under the Carpet." In *Telling Lives*. Edited by Marc Pachter. Washington, D.C.: New Republic Books, pp. 16-34.
    Warns biographers against accepting the routinely obvious in their search for an author's inner identity. Speculating on the man behind the myth, Edel suggests Hemingway's excessive masculinity is merely a cover for his insecurities.

30 "Editorial Apparatus for *88 Poems*." *Fitzgerald/Hemingway Annual,* pp. 383-88.
    Lists copy texts and editor's emendations for *88 Poems*, the only authorized version of Hemingway's poetry.

31 ENGEL, BERNARD F. "Say It Clean." *Society for the Study of Midwestern Literature Newsletter* 9, no. 3 (Fall): 12-13.

Outlines briefly Twain's principles on the limited use of stage directions in dialogue and finds the later Hemingway doing away with nearly all stage directions.

32 ENGELBERG, EDWARD. "Hemingway's 'True Penelope': Flaubert's *L'Éducation Sentimentale* and *A Farewell to Arms*." *Comparative Literature Studies* 16:189-206.

Comparative study of the two novels, including an exploration of similar themes of waste, failure, and the survival of disillusionment. A close examination reveals that Hemingway may have been thinking about Frederic Moreau when he developed Frederic Henry.

33 EVANS, T. JEFF. "For Whom the Earth Moves: A Fitzgerald Parody of Hemingway." *American Notes & Queries* 17, no. 8:127-28.

Sees Fitzgerald parodying Hemingway's "earth-moving" consummation scene involving Jordan and Maria in *For Whom the Bell Tolls* with a similar consummation scene in *The Last Tycoon*. After examining both authors' use of Spanish, sentimentality, immature characters, and the image of the earth moving, Evans concludes that through this parody Fitzgerald "firmly commits himself to contemporary realistic subject matter."

34 FITZGERALD, F. SCOTT. "Letter to Ernest Hemingway on *The Sun Also Rises*." *Antaeus*, no. 33, pp. 15-18.

Reprint of letter suggesting areas of the novel in need of revision and cutting. Fitzgerald warns Hemingway that with competition so stiff, authors can no longer afford to write "casually."

35 FULKERSON, RICHARD. "The Biographical Fallacy and 'The Doctor and the Doctor's Wife.'" *Studies in Short Fiction* 16, no. 1:61-65.

Contends that a close examination of the story reveals that Nick was not present during the confrontation between Dr. Adams and Dick Boulton, concluding that excessive biographical interpretation has detracted from the real subject of the story, "the life the doctor leads and Nick's responses to it." Reprinted: 1983.98.

36 GELDERMAN, CAROL. "Hemingway's Drinking Fixation." *Lost Generation Journal* 6, no. 1:12-14.

Is put off by Hemingway's preoccupation with drinking in his major novels and, for the most part, with the novels themselves.

37 GEROGIANNIS, NICHOLAS, ed. Introduction to *88 Poems*. New York: Harcourt Brace Jovanovich, pp. xi-xxviii.

First authorized American edition of Hemingway's poems, many previously unpublished. Gerogiannis traces the development of Hemingway's verse, including Stein's and Pound's influence, publication, and critical reception.

38 GERTZMAN, JAY A. "Hemingway's Writer-Narrator in 'The Denunciation.'" *Research Studies* 47, no. 4:244-52.

Speculates on the extent to which writer-narrator Enrique Emmunds approximates Hemingway's own position as writer.

39 GIBB, ROBERT. "He Made Him Up: 'Big Two-Hearted River' as Doppelgänger." *Hemingway Notes* 5, no. 1:20-24.

Looks at the relationship between Hemingway's real 1919 fishing trip at the Fox River and the imaginary (interior) world of Nick Adams's trip in "Big Two-Hearted River." Supports the orthodox reading that Nick is recovering emotionally from his war experiences. Reprinted: 1983.98.

40 GOLDKNOPF, DAVID. "Tourism in *The Sun Also Rises*." *CEA Critic* 41, no. 3:2-8.

Concludes that Jake is not the conventional camera-in-hand tourist but is instead a culturally isolated traveler in foreign countries. See 1980.61 for additional discussion.

41 GREEN, GREGORY. "The Old Superman and the Sea: Nietzsche, the Lions, and the 'Will to Power.'" *Hemingway Notes* 5, no. 1:14-19.

Using Hemingway's 1926 library cards, Green traces the lions in *The Old Man and the Sea* back to Nietzsche's *Thus Spake Zarathustra* in which lions represent a middle level between beast and superman.

42 HAGEMANN, E.R. "A Collation, with Commentary, of the Five Texts of the Chapters in Hemingway's *In Our Time*, 1923-38." *Papers of the Bibliographical Society of America* 73, no. 4:443-58.

Collates the different versions as well as giving a publication and textual history of the interchapters of *in our time* and *In Our Time*. Reprinted: 1983.98.

43 HAGEMANN, MEYLY CHIN. "Hemingway's Secret: Visual to Verbal Art." *Journal of Modern Literature* 7:87-112.

Explores Hemingway's exposure to the "new art" and its subsequent influence upon his writing. Comparing diagrams of two Cézanne paintings with three Hemingway short stories, Hagemann examines the artist's structural and stylistic techniques that the author adapted to language.

44 HART, JEFFREY. "War as Metaphor." *American Spectator* 12, no. 11 (November): 22-26.

Connects room and window imagery with the rain motif and the sense of transitoriness that permeates *A Farewell to Arms*. "The novel is thus not finally about the First World War, or about war in general. War, rather, is a kind of metaphor for our actual circumstance. Frederic desperately seeks the shelter of those rooms and he seeks the security of Catherine's love – but there is no security and no permanence. We are all moving up, up to the front."

45 HELLENGA, ROBERT R. "Macomber Redivivus." *Notes on Modern American Literature* 3, no. 2 (Spring): item 10.

Argues that Macomber achieves manhood without turning into the traditional Hemingway code hero typified by Wilson.

46 HEMINGWAY, ERNEST. "The Unpublished Opening of *The Sun Also Rises*." *Antaeus*, no. 33, pp. 7-14.

Original opening introducing the narrator and other main characters that Fitzgerald advised the author to cut out. See 1979.34.

47 HOFFMAN, DANIEL. *Harvard Guide to Contemporary American Writing*. Cambridge, Mass.: Harvard University Press, Belknap Press, pp. 93-96.

Discusses briefly Hemingway's impact on twentieth-century literature:". . . it would seem to be impossible for any American male novelist of the postwar period to escape his influence entirely, so thoroughly had he made war and masculinity two of his most important themes."

48 HOFFMAN, STEVEN K. "*Nada* and 'A Clean, Well-Lighted Place': The Unity of Hemingway's Short Fiction." *Essays in Literature* 6, no. 1 (Spring): 91-110.

Regards "A Clean, Well-Lighted Place" as "the thematic as well as the stylistic climax of Hemingway's career in short fiction" because it summarizes the possible human responses to *nada* (nothingness), a concept found throughout the Hemingway short-story canon. Reprinted: 1985.12.

49 IACONE, SALVATORE J. "Inscribed Books and Literary Scholarship." In *A Miscellany for Bibliophiles*. Edited by George Fletcher. New York: Grastorf & Lang, pp. 47-65.

Examines inscriptions in "three books by Ernest Hemingway, inscribed to Dr. Don Carlos Guffy, the man who delivered two of the author's children." Hemingway comments on the writing and publication of *in our time*, *The Torrents of Spring*, and *The Sun Also Rises*.

50 JAIN, S.P. "'Up in Michigan': Hemingway in the Workshop." *Indian Journal of American Studies* 9, no. 1:80-83.

Emphasis on the awkwardness of this early Hemingway short story, concluding that "it points to his groping in the semi-dark, in an endeavour to find his feet as a creative artist."

51 JOHNSON, DAVID R. "'The Last Good Country': Again the End of Something." *Fitzgerald/Hemingway Annual,* pp. 363-70.

Speculates on why Hemingway never finished "The Last Good Country," the longest and last of the Nick Adams stories. Suggests that Hemingway the older brother got in the way of Hemingway the artist when he realized the direction the story was taking—an assault on Littless (modeled after Hemingway's younger sister Madelaine).

52 JOHNSTON, KENNETH G. "Hemingway's 'The Denunciation': The Aloof American." *Fitzgerald/Hemingway Annual,* pp. 371-82.

Sees that Hemingway, in condemning the American narrator "for his failure, his refusal, to assume the responsibilities which come with commitment," is actually criticizing America for its neutral stance during the Spanish civil war. Reprinted: 1987.38.

53 JONES, HORACE P. "Hemingway's 'Soldier's Home.'" *Explicator* 37, no. 4 (Summer): 17.

Points out Hemingway's errors when referring to Krebs as both a "Marine" and a "soldier" in the "army" and his description of Krebs returning home "years after the war was over" when it had only been a few months. See also 1981.10 and 1981.79 for additional discussion.

54 JOSEPHS, ALLEN. "At the Heart of Madrid." *Atlantic* 244 (July): 74-77.

Gives a history of Madrid's Botin, the restaurant made famous by Hemingway's frequent visits and his staging of the last scene of *The Sun Also Rises* there. Includes Josephs's impressions of the restaurant today and the changes that have occurred in Madrid since Hemingway's time.

55 JOYCE, THOMAS J. "An Addendum to Hanneman's *Hemingway.*" *Analytical and Enumerative Bibliography* 3, no. 2 (April): 103.

Lists a reprint edition (ca. 1933) of *The Sun Also Rises* misspelling Hemingway's name not mentioned in Hanneman's 1967 *Ernest Hemingway: A Comprehensive Bibliography* (Princeton) nor her 1975 *Supplement* (Princeton).

56 KERNER, DAVID. "The Foundation of the True Text of 'A Clean, Well-Lighted Place.'" *Fitzgerald/Hemingway Annual,* pp. 279-300.

Attempts to resolve the controversy over dialogue by tracing Hemingway's modification of the conventional dialogue pattern back to Garnett's translation of Turgenev. Includes instances of the technique found in other works as well. See also 1982.47 for additional discussion.

57 KRAFT, STEPHANIE. "Hemingway and the Island in the Sun." In *No Castles on Main Street*. Chicago: Rand McNally & Co., pp. 53-61.

Biographical essay describing Hemingway's Key West years. Recounts his breaking of Wallace Stevens's jaw, his meeting with Martha Gellhorn in Sloppy Joe's Bar leading to the author's breakup with Pauline, and the 1935 hurricane that killed nearly 1,000 people in the Islamorada and Matecumbe keys.

58 KRIM, SEYMOUR. "Hemingway after Hours." *Village Voice* 24, no. 47 (19 November): 52-53.

Review of *88 Poems* in which Krim describes at least half as "playful, shrewd, and telling" while considering the others "a catalogue of peeve."

59 KVAM, WAYNE. "*The Sun Also Rises*: The Chronologies." *Papers on Language and Literature* 15, no. 2 (Spring): 199-203.

Objects to J.F. Kobler's and Kermit Vanderbilt's contentions that confusions in days and dates seriously weaken *The Sun Also Rises*. Kvam points out that only three minor one-word adjustments are needed, scarcely marring the structure of the novel.

60 KYLE, FRANK B. "Parallel and Complementary Themes in Hemingway's Big Two-Hearted River Stories and 'The Battler.'" *Studies in Short Fiction* 16, no. 4 (Fall): 295-300.

Sees Nick Adams beginning his initiation into manhood in "The Battler" and finishing it in "Big Two-Hearted River." Kyle finds similar themes of suffering, coming to terms with the past, and accepting the existence of evil in the world and common images of camp, swamp, and fire connecting the texts.

61 LASK, THOMAS. "Book Ends: Hemingway the Poet." *New York Times Book Review*, 12 August, p. 31.

Announces a forthcoming authorized edition of Hemingway's poetry entitled *88 Poems*.

62 McKENNA, JOHN J. "Macomber: The Nice Jerk." *American Notes & Queries* 17, no. 5 (January): 73-74.

Based on a brief analysis of the background of the story and Hemingway's own description of the real-life model, McKenna argues that the unknown epithet Hemingway assigns to Macomber in "The Short Happy Life of Francis Macomber" is "jerk."

63 McLAIN, RICHARD L. "Semantics and Style–with the Example of Quintessential Hemingway." *Language and Style* 12:63-78.

Applies principles of generative semantics to passages from "Big Two-Hearted River" to show the relationship between actual form and our general impression of style. McLain contends that "linguistic models are on the verge of providing important inroads into the semantic form of language, and thus into recurrent, stylistic features that have been heretofore unapproachable." Reprinted: 1987.95.

64 MAEKAWA, TOSHIHIRO. "Catherine's Death as a Lesson–a Study of *A Farewell to Arms*." *Kyushu American Literature*, no. 20, pp. 68-70.

Compares "the two initiations of death," one by Nick Adams in "Indian Camp" and the other by Frederic Henry in *A Farewell to Arms*. Nick's understanding of death never goes beyond the surface while Frederic's life is irrevocably changed by Catherine's death.

65 MARX, PAUL. "Hemingway and Ethnics." *Essays in Arts and Sciences* 8:35-44.

Contends that Hemingway's use of racial and ethnic epithets in his 1920s stories is the result of cultural influences. Marx maintains that Hemingway's minority characters are far from stereotypical and that their depiction varies from work to work. Special emphasis is placed on "The Killers," contending that Hemingway admired the professionalism of the two Jewish gangsters who were not allowed into mainstream American society. Reprinted: 1980.63.

66 MAYER, CHARLES W. "The Triumph of Honor in James and Hemingway." *Arizona Quarterly* 35, no. 4 (Winter): 373-91.

Explores parallels in creative vision, theme, character, and tone in the works of James and Hemingway. Concludes that both authors follow the transcendental tradition of celebrating the individual who is capable of maintaining honor and integrity in the face of adversity.

67 MILLER, R.H. "*For Whom the Bell Tolls*: Book-of-the-Month Club Copies." *Fitzgerald/Hemingway Annual*, pp. 407-09.

Gives evidence that 135,000 copies of the first printing were distributed by Book-of-the-Month Club.

68 MONTEIRO, GEORGE. "Addenda to Hanneman: Hemingway in Italian and Portuguese." *Papers of the Bibliographical Society of America* 73, no. 4:477-78.

Lists Italian translations of "A Clean, Well-Lighted Place" and "The End of Something" and a Portuguese translation of "The Doctor and the Doctor's Wife" not mentioned in Hanneman's 1967 *Ernest Hemingway: A Comprehensive Bibliography* (Princeton) nor her 1975 *Supplement* (Princeton).

69 _____. "Hemingway's Samson Agonistes." *Fitzgerald/Hemingway Annual*, pp. 411-16.

Looks at Hemingway's use of the redeemed "aging, disabled, or apostate professional" in his writings. Compares Harry in "The Snows of Kilimanjaro" with Milton's Samson – each in his dying hour triumphing over apostasy.

70 MOORE, BETTY. "Ernest Hemingway and Spain: Growth of a 'Spanish' Prose Style." *English Studies* (University of Valladolid) 9:227-53.

American Literary Scholarship 1980, p. 180.

71 MURRAY, DONALD M. "Thoreau and Hemingway." *Thoreau Journal Quarterly* 11, no. 3-4:13-33.

A comparison of the lives, subjects, themes, and styles of the two writers, finding similar preoccupations with nature, the need for integrity in art and life, and the revelation of truth through art.

72 NAGEL, G.S. "Women in Hemingway's Short Stories." *USA Today* 107 (January): 57-60.

Finds that a "negative view of women consistently runs through Hemingway's short stories." Sees the few female characters defined by their sexual roles – servant, temptress, emasculator, adulterer.

73 NAKAJIMA, KENJI. "Hemingway's View of Alienation in 'Soldier's Home.'" *Kyushu American Literature*, no. 20 (June), pp. 21-28.

Deals with Krebs's internal growth and voluntary alienation from society. Only by becoming indifferent to society can Krebs experience true freedom and maintain his integrity.

74 NELSON, RAYMOND S. *Hemingway: Expressionist Artist*. Ames: Iowa State University Press, 83 pp.

Argues that Hemingway's bold and vigorous style was profoundly influenced by the expressionist movement, citing similarities in depth of emotion, distortion, and violent contrasts.

75 OLDSEY, BERNARD. *Hemingway's Hidden Craft: The Writing of "A Farewell to Arms."* University Park: Pennsylvania State University Press, 123 pp.

Studies the composition of the novel using recently uncovered material, including two handwritten beginning chapters and over forty variant endings. Also discusses Hemingway's thirty-three possible titles and the relationship between the author's personal experiences in Italy and those depicted in the novel.

76 ORGAN, DENNIS. "Hemingway's 'Hills Like White Elephants.'" *Explicator* 37, no. 4 (Summer): 11.

Sees the bead curtain as symbolic of the conflict between the two main characters. For Jig, it represents her unborn child but for the man it expresses his desire to continue their nomadic existence.

77 OUSBY, IAN. "Ernest Hemingway." In *A Reader's Guide to Fifty American Novels*. New York: Barnes & Noble, pp. 227-51.

Summarizes Hemingway's major works (*The Sun Also Rises, A Farewell to Arms, For Whom the Bell Tolls,* and *The Old Man and the Sea*), giving a brief critical commentary on each novel's style, theme, and position in the Hemingway canon.

78 OWEN, FREDERICH. "Half a Century after Hemingway." *Lost Generation Journal* 6, no. 1:18-20.

Gives his impressions of Schruns, Austria, and Aigle, Switzerland, fifty years after Hemingway visited. Remarks on the "deplorable alterations" that have occurred.

79 PARTON, LINDA C. "Time: The Novelistic Cohesive in *A Farewell to Arms*." *Fitzgerald/Hemingway Annual,* pp. 355-62.

Sees time patterns in *A Farewell to Arms* as "the driver behind language, the molder of character, the purpose behind plot." Parton looks at the ways in which time holds the love story and war story together, giving a larger meaning to the text as a whole regarding the temporal nature of life and experience.

80 PEAVLER, TERRY J. "Guillermo Cabrera Infante's Debt to Ernest Hemingway." *Hispania* 62, no. 3:289-96.

After a stylistic, thematic, and structural examination of Hemingway's *In Our Time* and Infante's *Asi en la paz como en la guerra*, Peavler concludes that Infante consciously imitated Hemingway when writing his first book.

81 RADJADHURI, A. "A Study of Hemingway's *Across the River and into the Trees*." *Journal of English Studies* 2:14-23.
   *Hemingway Review 4, no. 1 (Fall): 63.

82 RAO, E. NAGESWARA. "The Motif of Luck in Hemingway." *Journal of American Studies* 13, no. 1 (April): 29-35.

Looks at the role luck plays in several Hemingway novels and short stories, arguing that the fate of many characters is determined by a "random combination of circumstances."

83 REICH, KENNETH E. "Sport in Literature: The Passion of Action." *Jack London Newsletter* 12, no. 1-3:50-62.

Comments briefly that Hemingway's works depicting sport, such as "My Old Man," "The Killers," and "The Battler," are overshadowed by death themes.

84 REYNOLDS, MICHAEL S. "The Agnes Tapes: A Farewell to Catherine Barkley." *Fitzgerald/Hemingway Annual,* pp. 251-78.

A 1970 interview with Agnes (von Kurowsky) Stanfield. Reminisces at length about her time spent at the military hospital in Milan with the recuperating Hemingway, insisting that, despite speculation that she is the model for Catherine in *A Farewell to Arms,* she and Hemingway "never had that kind of an affair." Includes photographs.

85 ROSS, IAN CAMPBELL. "Cagancho and Villalta: An Unnoted Error in English Editions of *Death in the Afternoon.*" *Library* 1, no. 3 (September): 284-85.

Points out a punctuation error that appears in all three currently available English editions.

86 SABASHNIKOVA, ELENA. "The Word of Hemingway: On the 80th Anniversary of His Birth." *Soviet Literature* 7:136-39.

Comments on Soviet television productions of *The Sun Also Rises* and *Islands in the Stream,* attributing their successful adaptation to the inclusion of Hemingway's actual words on screen.

87 SCHEEL, MARK. "Death and Dying: Hemingway's Predominant Theme." *Emporia State Research Studies* 28, no. 1 (Summer): 5-12.

Looks at various theories regarding the source of Hemingway's fixation on death and dying as well as the features, adjustments, and responses to death found in specific texts. Maintains that the author's writings on death can best be understood through the tenets of existentialism.

88 SCHWENGER, PETER. "The Masculine Mode." *Critical Inquiry* 5, no. 4 (Summer): 621-33.

Focusing primarily on the Nick Adams stories, Schwenger explains how Hemingway's reservedly "masculine" style fits into the notion of the masculine mode of writing and experience. Finds that Hemingway's detachment and intentional distancing from the self borders on noncommunication.

89 SEELYE, JOHN. "Hyperion to a Satyr: *Farewell to Arms* and *Love Story.*" *College Literature* 6, no. 2 (Spring): 129-35.

Examines common themes and situations in both texts, suggesting that an in-class comparison of Segal's "sleazy sentimentality" with Hemingway's richness of character and detail may serve as an excellent lesson in literary values. Reprinted: 1983.102.

90 SORKIN, ADAM J. "From Papa to Yo-Yo: At War with All the Words in the World." *South Atlantic Bulletin* 44, no. 4:48-65.

Looks at the changing assumptions about language found in two American war novels written over thirty years apart, *A Farewell to Arms* and Heller's *Catch-22.* Hemingway's preoccupation with concrete and simple language as a way to express true feelings and exact thinking is contrasted with Heller's distrust of the arbitrary and controlling nature of language.

91 STEINKE, JIM. "Harlotry and Love: A Friendship in *A Farewell to Arms.*" *Spectrum* 21, no. 1-2:20-24.

Looks at the eroding friendship between Henry and Rinaldi as Henry becomes more involved with Catherine Barkley.

92 STETLER, CHARLES, and LOCKLIN, GERALD. "De-coding the Hero in Hemingway's Fiction." *Hemingway Notes* 5, no. 1:2-10.

Argues against Young's concept of the code hero because it ignores the diversity of Hemingway's writing by reducing it to a formula. Encourages reading the works "as separate pieces of fiction."

93 STINE, PETER. "Ernest Hemingway and the Great War." *Fitzgerald/Hemingway Annual,* pp. 327-54.

Although Hemingway served only a brief time in World War I, "remembering the war became for him a life work." Stine looks at Hemingway's devotion to the war that shaped much of his writing including *The Sun Also Rises* and *A Farewell to Arms.*

94 TRILLING, LIONEL. "Ernest Hemingway: 'Hills Like White Elephants.'" In *Prefaces to the Experience of Literature.* New York: Harcourt Brace Jovanovich, pp. 145-49.

Speculates on why early magazine editors failed to regard the piece as a short story, commenting on its objective point of view, remoteness of the author, and lack of explicit meaning.

95 VILLARD, HENRY S. "A Prize Specimen of Wounded Hero." *Yankee* 43 (July): 72, 76.

Reminiscence about his time spent at the American Red Cross Hospital in Milan where he was nursed by Agnes von Kurowsky and convalesced with the wounded Hemingway. Villard speculates on Hemingway's use of them as models in *A Farewell to Arms* and the true relationship between von Kurowsky and Hemingway. Reprint with minor revision of 1978.86.

96 WAGNER, LINDA W. "*Barren Ground*'s Vein of Iron: Dorinda Oakley and Some Concepts of the Heroine in 1925." *Mississippi Quarterly* 32, no. 4 (Fall): 553-64.

Sees Brett's (*The Sun Also Rises*) desire for physical satisfaction redefining female sexuality in 1926.

97 WALSER, RICHARD. "On Faulkner's Putting Wolfe First." *South Atlantic Quarterly* 78, no. 2 (Spring): 172-81.

Details the 1947 lecture series at the University of Mississippi when Faulkner was asked to rank contemporary authors in order of importance. Criticizing Hemingway's cautious style, Faulkner ranked him third behind Wolfe and Dos Passos.

98 WERTHEIM, STANLEY. "Images of Exile: *The Portrait of a Lady* and *The Sun Also Rises*." *Hemingway Notes* 5, no. 1:25-27.

Pointing out similarities in theme, character, and situation, Wertheim writes that "James made the exploration of the international theme possible for Hemingway and his influence upon Hemingway's conception of the complex fate of American expatriates is apparent in their most revealing works on the experiences of Americans abroad, *The Portrait of a Lady* and *The Sun Also Rises*."

99 WESTBROOK, PERRY D. *Free Will and Determinism in American Literature*. Rutherford, N.J.: Fairleigh Dickinson University Press, pp. 244-47.

Uses Hemingway's major works to demonstrate the decline of literary determinism beginning in the mid-1920s. Categorizing *The Sun Also Rises* and *A Farewell to Arms* as restrictively deterministic, Westbrook discerns a shift toward self-assertion in *For Whom the Bell Tolls* and *The Old Man and the Sea*.

100 WHEELOCK, JOHN HALL, ed. *Editor to Author: The Letters of Maxwell E. Perkins*. New York: Charles Scribner's Sons, pp. 77-315 passim.

Numerous letters to Hemingway concerning the publication of *Death in the Afternoon*, *Green Hills of Africa*, and Perkins's initial response to *For Whom the Bell Tolls*. Letters also include references to other writers such as Wolfe, Fitzgerald, MacLeish, and Stein.

101 WHITE, WILLIAM. "Addenda to Hanneman: Hemingway's Selected Stories." *Papers of the Bibliographical Society of America* 73, no. 1:121-23.

Lists a 1951 English edition and a 1971 Russian edition of Hemingway's short stories not mentioned in Hanneman's 1967 *Ernest Hemingway: A Comprehensive Bibliography* (Princeton) nor her 1975 *Supplement* (Princeton).

102 _____. "Bibliography." *Hemingway Notes* 5, no. 1 (Fall): 34-35.

Checklist of articles, notes, and reviews on Hemingway appearing in the *Fitzgerald/Hemingway Annual* for 1976 through 1978.

103 _____. "For the Collector." *Hemingway Notes* 5, no. 1 (Fall): 28-31.

Lists British editions and publishers, editions by Bantam International, and editions misspelling Hemingway's name.

104 "Hemingway Checklist." *Fitzgerald/Hemingway Annual,* pp. 463-83.

Lists 268 reviews, articles, and books written mainly between 1974 and 1978.

105 _____. "A Misprint in Hemingway's *A Farewell to Arms*." *Papers of the Bibliographical Society of America* 73, no. 4:476-77.

Points out a misprint in the spelling of Rinaldi's name in Scribner's 1929 edition.

106 _____. "Note to Moss Hall, Imitation Hemingway: 'Big Two-Headed Writer.'" *Odyssey* 4, no. 1:23-24.

The 1979 winning entry for the Second International Imitation Hemingway Competition – parody at its best (or worst).

107 WHITLOW, ROGER. "Adoptive Territoriality in *For Whom the Bell Tolls*." *CEA Critic* 41, no. 2:2-8.

Refutes much of the negative criticism surrounding the character of Maria and the love ethic she represents. Considers Robert Jordan's putting mission before love a "poor moral choice."

108 _____. "Mission or Love, Frederick [*sic*] Henry? You Can't Have It Both Ways." *Markham Review* 8 (Winter): 33-36.

Sees Catherine Barkley as one of many Hemingway characters who is on the edge of insanity and Frederic Henry as one of many Hemingway heros who must choose between love and duty.

109 WILLIAMS, WIRT. "Tragic Patterns and Rhythms in *Across the River and into the Trees*." *Fitzgerald/Hemingway Annual*, pp. 389-405.

Sees Cantwell as a tragic hero whose fatal flaw is also his strongest virtue – his desire to meet death on his own terms, to die with dignity. Williams examines the novel's fabulistic elements, biblical associations, references to Dante, and structural reliance on conflicting musical forms.

110 WILSON, ROBERT N. "Ernest Hemingway: Competence and Character." In *The Writer as Social Seer*. Chapel Hill: University of North Carolina Press, pp. 42-55.

Although contemporary attitudes concerning male-female relationships, commitment to one's vocation, and war may differ greatly from Hemingway's, the basic truths expressed in his writings regarding the individual in society, the joy of living, and competent performance will never go out of style.

111 WORKMAN, BROOKE. *In Search of Hemingway: A Model for Teaching a Literature Seminar*. Urbana, Ill.: NCTE, 110 pp.

Outlines discussion topics, handouts, readings, and assignments for a high-school-level seminar on Hemingway. Reprinted with slight revision: 1983.131.

112 ____. "Telephone Connection: An Interview with Ernest Hemingway's Son." *Media and Methods* 16 (December): 19-20.

Gregory Hemingway responds to questions (developed by high-school students in Workman's American literature seminar) regarding his father's religious convictions, family, chauvinism, and writing.

1980

1 ALLADI, UMA K. "Existentialism in the Novels of Hemingway and Camus." *Literary Half-Yearly* 21, no. 2 (July): 43-51.

Overview of the existential themes of alienation, disillusionment, and death found in *A Farewell to Arms*, *For Whom the Bell Tolls*, *The Old Man and the Sea*, "The Short Happy Life of Francis Macomber," and "The Snows of Kilimanjaro."

2 ARDAT, AHMAD K. "The Prose Style of Selected Works by Ernest Hemingway, Sherwood Anderson, and Gertrude Stein." *Style* 14:1-21.

Linguistic analysis of the syntactic elements in works by all three authors. Concludes that although they generally "write more like one another than they write differently," their styles are marked by striking distinctions in complexity, sentence length, and use of modifiers.

3 ASSELINEAU, ROGER. "Hemingway, or 'Sartor Resartus' Once More." In *The Transcendentalist Constant in American Literature*. New York: New York University Press, pp. 137-52.

Contends that Hemingway's life and works "were carried away by a dialectical movement which, to some extent, parallels the movement of *Sartor Resartus*." Asselineau traces connections between Hemingway's and Carlyle's work, paying close attention to the progression of stages found in each: innocence to experience, disillusionment, nihilism, and eventual recovery.

4 AUGUST, JO. "A Note on the Hemingway Collection." *College Literature* 7, no. 3 (Fall): introductory note.

Discusses how the collection at the Kennedy Library came into being.

5 BAKER, CARLOS. "The Champion and the Challenger: Hemingway and O'Hara." *John O'Hara Journal* 3, no. 1-2 (Fall-Winter): 22-30.

Looks at Hemingway's relationship with O'Hara, remarking that despite their similar backgrounds and education, the two authors differ greatly in method, vision, and quality.

6 BENOIT, RAYMOND. "Again with Fair Creation: Holy Places in American Literature." *Prospects* 5:315-30.

Briefly discusses Nick's camp in "Big Two-Hearted River" as a holy area within the context of the American literary tradition.

7 BIER, JESSE. "Liquor and Caffeine in *The Sun Also Rises*." *American Notes and Queries* 18, no. 9:143-44.

Contends that Cohn is modeled, in part, after Fitzgerald.

8 _____. "A Note on Twain and Hemingway." *Midwest Quarterly* 21, no. 2 (Winter): 261-65.

Stylistically compares passages from *The Sun Also Rises*, "The Snows of Kilimanjaro," and *Huckleberry Finn* in order to show Twain's influence. Briefly notes Twain's innovative rendering of "heard voice."

9 BOELHOWER, WILLIAM. "Antonio Gramsci and the Myth of America in Italy during the 1930s." *Minnesota Review*, n.s. 15 (Fall): 34-52.

Comments briefly on Hemingway's popularity in Italy during the 1930s and 1940s.

10 BRASCH, JAMES D., and SIGMAN, JOSEPH. "Hemingway's Library: Some Volumes of Poetry." *College Literature* 7:282-88.

Explains that the author's library included 229 volumes of poetry, of which those by Ezra Pound, T.S. Eliot, Charles Baudelaire, and Lord Byron may be the most significant. He also owned a number of books by Marianne Moore, William Carlos Williams (prose as well as poetry), William Butler Yeats, Archibald MacLeish, W.H. Auden, and Edna St. Vincent Millay. He also continued to read Shakespeare's sonnets. Reprinted: 1981.86.

11 "Brief Mention." *American Literature* 52 (March): 151.
Mixed review of Hemingway's *88 Poems*. Mentions the helpfulness of the editing and photographs but fails to comment on the quality of the poetry.

12 BRKIC, SVETOZAR. "Ernest Hemingway." In *Yugoslav Perspectives on American Literature*. Edited by James L. Thorson. Ann Arbor, Mich.: Ardis, pp. 89-101.
Broad overview of Hemingway's life and works, offering no new insight.

13 BRYER, JACKSON R. "Fitzgerald and Hemingway." In *American Literary Scholarship: An Annual, 1978*. Edited by J. Albert Robbins. Durham, N.C.: Duke University Press, pp. 153-78.
Survey of criticism on both authors published during 1978. Pleased by the number of valuable full-length examinations and shorter essays appearing this year.

14 CAHALAN, JAMES M. "Hemingway's Last Word about the Ending of 'Macomber.'" *Hemingway Notes* 5, no. 2 (Spring): 33-34.
Believes the "core" of "The Short Happy Life of Francis Macomber" to be the parallel between the courageous lion and the rejuvenated Macomber. "Both are victims; both face death courageously." Reprints Hemingway's 1959 comment expressing concern for both victims in the story.

15 CENTING, RICHARD R. "Ohio Magazines." *Ohioana Quarterly* 23, no. 1:23-24.
Announces the revival of *Hemingway Notes* to be published each October and April by Ohio Northern University.

16 COOLEY, JOHN R. "Nick Adams and 'The Good Place.'" *Southern Humanities Review* 14:57-68.
Concentrates on the image of "the calm and sacred place"–a cathedrallike grove of pines nestled between a despoiled region of land and an ominous swamp in both "The Last Good Country" and "Big Two-Hearted River." Concludes that in "the good place," all the "dangers and

distractions are minimized and values are clarified. Here Nick does not have to risk *all* to gain strength, inspiration, and renewed purpose for living."

17 CRANE, JOAN. "Hemingway and the Painter's Wife: A Romance." *American Book Collector*, n.s. 1, no. 5 (September-October): 4-6.

Speaks of Hemingway's attachment to Andrea del Sarto's painting, "Portrait of a Woman."

18 CROCKER, JIM. "Nine Instructional Exercises to Teach Silence." *Communication Education* 29, no. 1 (January): 72-77.

Uses "The Killers" in teaching students how to identify the various communication functions of silence found in fiction.

19 "Current Bibliography." *Hemingway Notes* 6, no. 1 (Fall): 39-40.

Items include books, articles, reviews, and foreign translations.

20 CURRY, PAMELA MALCOLM, and JIOBU, ROBERT M. "Big Mac and *Caneton À L'Orange*: Eating, Icons and Rituals." In *Rituals and Ceremonies in Popular Culture*. Edited by Ray B. Browne. Bowling Green: Bowling Green University Popular Press, pp. 248-57.

Brief attention to the eating rituals in "The Short Happy Life of Francis Macomber" that exemplify Curry and Jiobu's thesis that habitual behaviors become institutionalized regardless of the conditions under which they are played out.

21 DONALDSON, NORMAN, and DONALDSON, BETTY. "Ernest Hemingway." In *How Did They Die?* New York: St. Martin's Press, pp. 165-66.

Briefly summarizes Hemingway's mental and physical condition at the time of his death as well as the events leading up to it.

22 DONALDSON, SCOTT. "Hemingway of the *Star*." *College Literature* 7:263-81.

Traces the writer's contributions to journalism and studies the influence of Hemingway's brand of journalism on his fiction. Reprinted: 1981.86.

23 EDMONDS, DALE. "When Does Frederic Henry Narrate *A Farewell to Arms*?" *Notes on Modern American Literature* 4:item 14.

Argues that a reference to Babe Ruth by Henry sets the novel's date of narration at 1928, ten years after Catherine's death.

24 "Etcetera: Bad Hemingway." *Horizon* 23:10-11.

Reprints winning entries for the 1980 Third International Imitation Hemingway Competition. Parody at its best (or worst).

25 FINKELSTEIN, DAVID, and LONDON, JOHN. "Hemingway's Cuba Revisited." *Horizon* 23, no. 1 (January): 44-49.

Combines a modern visitor's view of Cuba with a recounting of Hemingway's time spent there – fishing, drinking, and writing. Although much has changed since Hemingway's day, one can still visit his villa or drink in one of his favorite bars.

26 FLETCHER, MARY DELL. "Hemingway's 'Hills Like White Elephants.'" *Explicator* 38, no. 4 (Summer): 16-18.

Looks at the way the differing landscape imagery illuminates the conflict between the couple, but warns against interpreting the American's shifting of the bags to the fruitful side of the station as a positive sign.

27 FLORES, OLGA EUGENIA. "Eros, Thanatos, and the Hemingway Soldier." *American Studies International* 18, no. 3-4:27-35.

Treats the polarity of the life-death imagery in *A Farewell to Arms* and *For Whom the Bell Tolls*, tracing each protagonist's initiation and movement from the isolated world of Thanatos toward an increased sense of individuality and, paradoxically, community found in Eros.

28 GARGAN, WILLIAM. "'Death Once Dead': An Examination of an Alternative Title to Hemingway's *A Farewell to Arms*." *Notes on Modern American Literature* 4:item 26.

Argues that Hemingway's source for the alternative title is Shakespeare's Sonnet 146, which shares with the novel "a number of important themes including the transitory nature of human life, the constant struggle between the flesh and the spirit, and the search for durable values that transcend man's limitations."

29 GEROGIANNIS, NICHOLAS. "Ernest Hemingway." In *Dictionary of Literary Biography. American Writers in Paris, 1920-1939*. Vol. 4. Edited by Karen Lane Rood. Detroit: Bruccoli Clark Books/Gale Research, pp. 187-211.

Discusses Hemingway's expatriate years in Paris. Gives a biographical overview focusing on his literary and journalistic efforts and his relationship with contemporaries such as James Joyce, Ezra Pound, and Gertrude Stein.

30 _____. "Hemingway's Poetry: Angry Notes of an Ambivalent Overman." *College Literature* 7:248-62.

Traces much of Hemingway's aesthetic to his belief in a Nietzschean overman. Proving that Hemingway had read both *Thus Spake Zarathustra* and books about Nietzsche, this author also emphasizes the influence of Gabriele D'Annunzio, the Italian Lord Byron, and Eleonora Duse's lover, whose affair was the basis for his novel *The Flame*, 1920. Hemingway's *Across the River and into the Trees* shows this influence. Reprinted: 1981.86 and 1987.95.

31 GERVAIS, RONALD J. "The Trains of Their Youth: The Aesthetics of Homecoming in *The Great Gatsby, The Sun Also Rises*, and *The Sound and the Fury*." *American-Austriaca: Beiträge zur Amerikakunde* 6:51-63.
     MLA Bibliography 1980, p. 237.

32 GODINE, AMY. "Notes toward a Reappraisal of Depression Literature." *Prospects* 5:197-239.
     Comments briefly on the influence of *The Sun Also Rises* on Horace McCoy's *They Shoot Horses, Don't They?*, pointing out similarities in situation, character, and style. However, Godine considers the separate peace that Gloria and Robert embrace (Robert's shooting of Gloria) to be a rejection of Hemingway's romanticism.

33 GUETTI, JAMES. *Word-Music: The Aesthetic Aspect of Narrative Fiction*. New Brunswick, N.J.: Rutgers University Press, pp. 139-49.
     Looks at the symbiotic relationship of the visual (sequential) and aural (repetitive) aspects of Hemingway's narrative. Concludes that Hemingway's fiction favors the musical though it often begins with the visual.

34 HAGEMANN, E.R. "'Dear Folks . . . Dear Ezra': Hemingway's Early Years and Correspondence, 1917-1924." *College Literature* 7:202-212.
     Draws on the Lilly Library's holdings of family correspondence to chart Hemingway's years both before going to Paris and in Paris. Reprinted: 1981.86.

35 _____. "'Only Let the Story End As Soon As Possible': Time-and-History in Ernest Hemingway's *In Our Time*." *Modern Fiction Studies* 26, no. 2 (Summer): 255-62.
     Arranges the interchapters chronologically to demonstrate Hemingway's preoccupation with death and to show further how the author reconstructed the deadly decade of 1914-23 in his text.

36 _____. "Word-Count and Statistical Survey of the Chapters in Ernest Hemingway's *In Our Time*." *Literary Research News* 5, no. 1 (Winter): 21-30.

Using computer analysis, Hagemann examines statistically the 760 different words used in the sixteen chapters of *In Our Time*. Finds interconnected images of death and violence as well as a heavy reliance upon the third-person plural "they" and the second-person singular and plural "you" pronouns within the repetitive and simplistic vocabulary.

37 HARKEY, JOSEPH H. "The Africans and Francis Macomber." *Studies in Short Fiction* 17, no. 3 (Summer): 345-48.
Points out the irony of Macomber's name, which sounds like the Swahili word for "leader" or "master". "During most of the story the latent pun identifies Macomber as the opposite of 'master,' and only in the end does he become worthy of his own name."

38 HAYASHI, TETSUMARO. *Steinbeck and Hemingway: Dissertation Abstracts and Research Opportunities*. Metuchen, N.J.: Scarecrow Press, 228 pp.
Chronological list with abstracts of dissertations from 1950 to 1977. Designed to assist scholars in finding out what areas have already been explored. See also 1980.71.

39 HEMINGWAY, LORIAN. "The Young Woman and the Sea." *New York Times Magazine*, 21 September, pp. 48-50, 55-63.
Talks about her Key West fishing trip, frequently referring to her grandfather (Ernest Hemingway).

40 HOVEY, RICHARD B. "*Islands in the Stream*: Death and the Artist." *Hartford Studies in Literature* 12 no. 3:173-94.
Biographical and psychological study of Thomas Hudson, arguing that Davis, as Hudson's alter ego, embodies all that Hudson-Hemingway wished for in life. The protagonist finds his ultimate release in combat but implicit in the novel is the theme that the heroic code doesn't work. The machismo-death idea neglects the inner self, thus destroying the masculine self it professes to support. Reprinted: 1983.86.

41 HOWELL, JOHN M. "Hemingway, Faulkner, and 'The Bear.'" *American Literature* 52, no. 1 (March): 115-26.
Finds "The Bear" closely paralleling *For Whom the Bell Tolls* in theme and imagery. Explores in both the nature of brotherhood, precognition, and how each work "underlines the tragedy of idealism and the ultimate isolation of its hero by introducing a metaphysical debate."

42 HURLEY, C. HAROLD. "Hemingway's 'The Short Happy Life of Francis Macomber.'" *Explicator* 38, no. 3 (Spring): 9.

Contends that Wilson deliberately puns on the word "topping" in order to show his dominance and contempt for the Macombers. See also 1983.36.

43 JACKSON, PAUL R. *"For Whom the Bell Tolls*: Patterns of Joking and Seriousness." *Hemingway Notes* 6, no. 1 (Fall): 15-24.

Examines the way Hemingway balances humor with gravity, thus revealing character and theme. "Knowing when to joke and when to be serious, essentially a case of dignity, and what to joke about or treat with seriousness, a case of values, define important differences among most of the characters, Spanish and foreign."

44 _____. "Point of View, Distancing, and Hemingway's 'Short Happy Life.'" *Hemingway Notes* 5, no. 2 (Spring): 2-16.

Analyzes the shifting point of view in "The Short Happy Life of Francis Macomber" that results in "the distancing of reader from character and character from event." Finds that Margot's shooting parallels her husband's earlier shooting of the lion.

45 JOHNSTON, KENNETH G. "Hemingway's 'Night before Battle': Don Quixote, 1937." *Hemingway Notes* 6, no. 1 (Fall): 26-28.

Explicates Hemingway's allusions to Cervantes and *Don Quixote* in his story of Al Wagner, a quixotic American idealist fighting for the Republic during the Spanish civil war.

46 KANJO, EUGENE R. "A Fable for Hunters." *Hemingway Notes* 5, no. 2 (Spring): 26-28.

Arguing that life is presented as immoral in "The Short Happy Life of Francis Macomber," Kanjo contends that hunting stands as "a metaphor for the 20th century human condition."

47 KAWIN, BRUCE F. "Introduction: No Man Alone." In *To Have and Have Not*. Wisconsin/Warner Bros. Screenplay Series. Madison: University of Wisconsin Press, pp. 9-53.

Reprints the screenplay of *To Have and Have Not* written by Jules Furthman and William Faulkner. Lengthy introduction chronicles the transformation of the novel onto the big screen. Details Hemingway's limited contribution, the different versions of the script, Faulkner's revisions, governmental interference, Bogart and Bacall's relationship, production aspects, and the film's critical reception.

48 KOBLER, J.F. "Hemingway's 'Hills Like White Elephants.'" *Explicator* 38, no. 4 (Summer): 6-7.

Discusses the symbolic significance of the beaded curtain as a "touchstone" for the couple's conflicting emotions.

49 KORT, WESLEY A. "Human Time in Hemingway's Fiction." *Modern Fiction Studies* 26, no. 4 (Winter): 579-96.

Applies the construct of human time to much of the author's canon, concluding that Hemingway's fiction "grants access to a human time which is primary, which is rhythmic, and which is productive of healing, wisdom and peace." Reprinted: 1986.13.

50 LAL, MALASHRI. "The Spanish Civil War and Ernest Hemingway: Form Reportage to Novel." *Indian Journal of American Studies* 10 (January): 65-77.

Analysis of the marked contrast in tone and content of Hemingway's early war dispatches and his later fictional representation of the war in *For Whom the Bell Tolls*. "The war reports look acutely and swiftly into pockets of action in Spain; the novel comes of the writer's camera eye dwelling long and leisurely on a selected scene."

51 LAURENCE, FRANK M. "The Hemingway Radio Broadcasts: 'The Short Happy Life of Francis Macomber.'" *Hemingway Notes* 5, no. 2 (Spring): 22-25.

Treats the 1948 hour-long radio adaptation, finding both script and production "quite worthy of the story."

52 _____. "The Pack and the Lunch Box: Hemingway's Stylistic Influence on Russell Hoban." *Hemingway Notes* 6, no. 1 (Fall): 29-31.

Suggests that Hoban's Frances stories were significantly influenced by Hemingway's writings. Compares Nick's ritual of preparing and eating his meal in "Big Two-Hearted River" with a similar scene in Hoban's *Bread and Jam for Frances*.

53 _____. "'That Hemingway Kind of Love': The Publicity Campaign for the Movie Version of 'The Short Happy Life of Francis Macomber.'" *Hemingway Notes* 5, no. 2 (Spring): 18-21.

Overview of the sensational promotional campaign for the film *The Macomber Affair*, including photographs of the actual 1947 movie posters distributed to theaters.

54 LEBLANC, ROBERT. "An English Teacher's Fantasy." *English Journal* 69, no. 7 (October): 35-36.

Suggests, because of their similar historic themes, pairing the adolescent novel *Across Five Aprils* by Irene Hunt with *For Whom the Bell Tolls* in order to facilitate for younger readers the transition from adolescent to classic literature.

55 LEE, DORIS. "Tracking Hemingway in Paris." *Horizon* 23, no. 11 (November): 42-45.

Uses a Michelin guide and *A Moveable Feast* to retrace Hemingway's footsteps, visiting his old haunts. Concludes that even after all these years, Hemingway's "Paris is still there, and, with a few exceptions, just as he left it."

56 LEVIN, HARRY. "Observations on the Style of Ernest Hemingway." In *Memories of the Moderns*. New York: New Directions, pp. 81-104.
    Abridged reprint from *Contexts of Criticism* (Cambridge: Harvard University Press, 1957), pp. 140-67.

57 LOCKLIN, GERALD, and STETLER, CHARLES. "Ernest Hemingway: Best of All He Loved the Fall." *Snowy Egret* 43, no. 1:18-24.
    Treats Hemingway's love of nature and conservationist attitudes expressed through such works as *In Our Time, The Sun Also Rises*, and *Across the River and into the Trees*. Also relies on Mary Welsh's recollections in *How It Was* and in later interviews. Reprinted: 1981.66.

58 ____. "Response from Stetler-Locklin." *Hemingway Notes* 6, no. 1 (Fall): 13-14.
    Defend their position against Young's categorizing of Hemingway's works according to the code-hero or wound theory. Such oversimplification limits our interpretations and blinds us to the richness of Hemingway's writing. See also 1980.66.

59 LODGE, DAVID. "Analysis and Interpretation of the Realist Text: A Pluralistic Approach to Ernest Hemingway's 'Cat in the Rain.'" *Poetics Today* 1, no. 4 (Summer): 5-22.
    Describes briefly a variety of critical approaches to fiction, including "narratology," poetics of fiction, and rhetorical analysis. Structuralist reading of the short story, looking at the quest for the cat in relation to the husband-wife relationship. Categorizes the work as both realistic and modern. Reprinted with minor revision: 1981.67.

60 LOUNSBERRY, BARBARA. "The Education of Robert Wilson." *Hemingway Notes* 5, no. 2 (Spring): 29-32.
    Traces Wilson's education into character (both the Macombers and his own), through a series of lessons involving misunderstandings and mistaken assessments. Finds that "Wilson assesses, questions, and reassesses according to the unfolding circumstances, just as the reader does."

61 LYNCH, DENNIS. "Tourism Per Se Is Not a Technique." *CEA Critic* 42, no. 4 (May): 39.
    Takes exception with David Goldknopf's reading (see 1979.40) of Jake's "touristic awareness." Lynch argues that the many references to

Jake's expenditures serve to reinforce "the picture of Jake as a man of honor concerned with even the smallest details. . . ."

62 McGILLIGAN, PATRICK. "Movies Are Better Than Ever on Television." *American Film* 5 (March): 50-54.

Briefly mentions the withdrawal from television of the movie version of "The Killers" in the wake of John F. Kennedy's assassination.

63 MARX, PAUL. "Hemingway and Ethnics." In *Seasoned Authors for a New Season: The Search for Standards in Popular Writing.* Edited by Louis Filler. Bowling Green, Ohio: Bowling Green University Popular Press, pp. 43-50.

Reprint of 1979.65.

64 MONTEIRO, GEORGE. "Addenda to the Bibliographies of Boyle, Conrad, De Forest, Eliot, Ford, Hemingway, Huxley, Wharton, and Woolf." *Papers of the Bibliographical Society of America* 74, no. 2:153-55.

Adds two reviews of Hemingway works (*Winner Take Nothing* and *The Old Man and the Sea*) to Hanneman's *Ernest Hemingway: A Comprehensive Bibliography* (Princeton, 1967) and *Supplement* (Princeton, 1975).

65 MORROW, PATRICK D. "The Bought Generation: Another Look at Money in *The Sun Also Rises*." In *Money Talks: Language and Lucre in American Fiction.* Edited by Roy R. Male. Norman: University of Oklahoma Press, pp. 51-69.

Comments on Hemingway's obsession with money in the novel, noting 142 direct and 71 indirect references to it. Maintains that money and the waste associated with it not only serve to reveal character morality but also the continued circular and senseless motion of the characters who live their lives without purpose. Also printed in *Genre* 13 (Spring): 51-69.

66 MORTON, BRUCE. "An Interview with Philip Young." *Hemingway Notes* 6, no. 1:2-13.

Young comments on his influential 1952 *Ernest Hemingway*, criticism by other critics, and the future of Hemingway scholarship. See also 1980.58.

67 _____. "The Irony and Significance of the Early Faulkner and Hemingway Poems Appearing in the Double Dealer." *Zeitschrift für Anglistik und Amerikanistik* 28:254-58.

Reprints Faulkner's "Portrait" and Hemingway's "Ultimately," both appearing on the same page of the June 1922 issue. "Thematically and stylistically both poems indicate an aesthetic philosophy, and a means by which that philosophy is to be communicated. The poems are self-fulfilling prophecies."

68 NAKAJIMA, KENJI. "Shot, Alive, and Was Glad: On Hemingway's Chapter VI, *In Our Time*." *Kyushu American Literature* 21:13-17.
   Sees Nick's sole concern to be the establishment of his individual self, which he achieves through injury (i.e., the wound is evidence of his initiation into manhood).

69 OLDSEY, BERNARD. "Hemingway's Beginnings and Endings." *College Literature* 7:213-38.
   A thorough and provocative discussion of the author's strategies in shaping his short fiction, drawing upon the manuscripts of "Indian Camp," "Big Two-Hearted River," and "The Short Happy Life of Francis Macomber." Reprinted: 1981.86 and 1987.95.

70 OLIVER, CHARLES M. "Have You Read This One?" *Hemingway Notes* 5, no. 2 (Spring): 28.
   Recommends Cyril Falls's *The Battle of Caporetto* (1966) for its historical insight on the battle fictionalized in *A Farewell to Arms*.

71 PETERSON, RICHARD F. "Research Opportunities." In *Steinbeck and Hemingway: Dissertation Abstracts and Research Opportunities*, by Tetsumaro Hayashi. Metuchen, N.J.: Scarecrow, pp. 191-201.
   Presents an overview of the scholarship and argues that Hemingway has been "overdone" in repeated craft and code-hero studies. He warns scholars to steer clear of these areas unless they have a new approach and directs attention toward potentially profitable areas such as women, film, and comparative studies. See also 1980.38.

72 PHILLIPS, GENE D. *Hemingway and Film*. New York: Ungar, 192 pp.
   Near-chronological analysis of sixteen film versions of Hemingway's fiction, including close comparisons with their respective texts. Discusses the problems associated with translating Hemingway's fiction to the big screen and the variant adaptations of these texts, such as *To Have and Have Not* and "The Killers," that have been filmed more than once. Also interviews directors and others who worked on Hemingway film productions.

73 PLIMPTON, GEORGE. "JFK and Hemingway." *College Literature* 7:181-88.
   Addresses the relationship between President Kennedy and the writer, and describes his own dealings with Hemingway at the time of *The Paris Review* interview.

74 PRICE, S. DAVID. "Hemingway's *The Old Man and the Sea*." *Explicator* 38, no. 3 (Spring): 5.

    Points to Hemingway's comparison of Santiago's fishing line with a pencil as further evidence of the allegorical interpretation that Santiago represents the writer while the sharks represent the critics.

75 RADELJKOVIĆ, ZVONIMIR. "Initial Europe: 1918 as a Shaping Element in Hemingway's *Weltanschauung*." *College Literature* 7:304-9.

    Discusses the influence of Hemingway's European experiences on his writing. Four of his best novels are set in Europe: "Italy, France and Spain, perhaps not in that order, were all at some time his second countries, lands whose culture, civilization and characteristic world-view helped him at least to appreciate his own". Reprinted 1981.86.

76 _____. "A Long Journey to Hope: Hemingway's *The Old Man and the Sea*." In *Yugoslav Perspectives on American Literature: An Anthology*. Ann Arbor, Mich.: Ardis, pp. 103-6.

    Briefly summarizes the plot, arguing that Hemingway's depiction of the hopelessness of man's condition found in his earlier works is absent in this later novella, for Santiago's courage, humility, and endurance ensure his victory.

77 RAO, P.G. RAMA. *Ernest Hemingway: A Study in Narrative Technique*. New Delhi, India: Chand, 235 pp.

    Looks at the evolution of Hemingway's narrative technique in the light of his subject matter and aesthetic principles, paying particular attention to shifts in technique and style that came about through changes in theme following the publication of *Green Hills of Africa* – Rao sees paradox replacing irony as the dominant motif after 1935. Discusses Hemingway's literary inheritance from both the British realist and American romance traditions, his simplicity of style and adherence to the iceberg principle, his use of symbolism, and his evolving narrative perspective. Believes the "contrapuntal theme" running through Hemingway's works to be the juxtaposition of passing generations and the abiding earth.

78 "Review of Ernest Hemingway, *88 Poems*." *Booklist* 76, no. 11 (1 February): 752.

    Disappointed in the quality of the poetry that ranges "from the trivial to the bland to the preposterous."

79 REYNOLDS, MICHAEL S. "False Dawn: *The Sun Also Rises* Manuscript." In *A Fair Day in the Affections: Literary Essays in Honor of Robert B. White, Jr*. Edited by Jack D. Durant and M. Thomas Hester. Raleigh, N.C.: Winston Press, pp. 171-86.

Compares the holograph manuscript with the final draft, noting additions, deletions, and revisions. Argues that Hemingway originally intended to focus on the corruption and possible death of Nino de la Palma, the promising bullfighter whose name served as the working title through much of the first draft of the novel. Reprinted: 1983.86 and 1987.7.

80 _____. "Unexplored Territory: The Next Ten Years of Hemingway Studies." *College Literature* 7:189-201.

Predicts new directions in research on Hemingway's works, as a result of the acquisition of the valuable manuscript collection at the Kennedy. Reynolds calls for a moratorium on nostalgia, and advocates the challenge of becoming explorers, relearning our trade. Reprinted: 1981.86.

81 RYAN, FRANK L. *The Immediate Critical Reception of Ernest Hemingway.* Washington D.C.: University Press of America, 71 pp.

Brief synopsis and summary of major reviews, with notes. Starts with *Three Stories & Ten Poems* and goes through *Islands in the Stream.* Includes *Winner Take Nothing, The Fifth Column, Men at War,* besides the obvious. Ryan contends that "a study of the immediate response to each work indicates that there was a sustained tension between Hemingway and his critics or, more accurately, between what Hemingway achieved and what the critics wished him to achieve." Not exhaustive. More for public library use.

82 SANDERSON, STEWART F. "Hemingway, Ernest." In *20th Century American Literature.* New York: St. Martin's Press, pp. 271-74.

Includes a brief biography and list of published books along with a selected list of bibliographies and important critical studies. Concludes with a brief overview of the Hemingway canon.

83 SCHULZ, GRETCHEN, and ROCKWOOD, R.J.R. "In Fairyland, without a Map: Connie's Exploration Inward in Joyce Carol Oates' *Where Are You Going, Where Have You Been?*" *Literature and Psychology* 30:155-67.

Notes the similarity of a line in Oates's story uttered by Connie who is unable to comprehend a world that has "so much land that Connie had never seen before and did not recognize except to know that she was going to it" with the dying Harry's remark in "The Snows of Kilimanjaro" that "there was where he was going."

84 SHABER, SARAH R. "Hemingway's Literary Journalism: The Spanish Civil War Dispatches." *Journalism Quarterly* 57, no. 3 (Autumn): 420-25, 535.

Concludes that Hemingway was a literary journalist who "wrote non-fiction with the broad goals of a writer of fiction and an arsenal of tested literary devices." Rather than adopting a traditional journalistic perspective, Hemingway concentrated on communicating to his audience a feeling or sense of the Spanish civil war.

85 SLATTERY, WILLIAM C. "The Mountain, the Plain, and San Siro." *Papers on Language and Literature* 16 (Fall): 439-42.

Supports Baker's earlier reading of the mountain/plain symbolism through a close examination of chapter 20 of *A Farewell to Arms*, with its crooked horse racing on the Lombardy plain set against the backdrop of the beautiful and purifying mountains in the distance.

86 SPENDER, STEPHEN. "Stephen Spender: The Art of Poetry XXV." *Paris Review* 22, no. 77:119-54.

Spender reminisces about his time spent with Hemingway during the Spanish civil war (p. 124). See also 1981.37 for Gellhorn's response.

87 SRIVASTAVA, RAMESH KUMAR. *Hemingway and His "For Whom the Bell Tolls."* Amritsar, India: Guru Nanak Dev University Press, 174 pp.

Annual Bibliography of English Language and Literature for 1983, 58:650-51.

88 TAVERNIER-COURBIN, JACQUELINE. "The Mystery of the Ritz Hotel Papers." *College Literature* 7:289-303.

Discusses the evolution of *A Moveable Feast* and its relation to the supposed discovery of manuscripts in old trunks Hemingway found in the Ritz Hotel in Paris in 1957. Reprinted: 1981.86.

89 TAYLOR, CHARLES. "*The Old Man and the Sea*: A Nietzschean Tragic Vision." *Dalhousie Review* 61, no. 4 (Winter): 631-43.

Argues against the traditional reading of the novel as a parable of sin and punishment. Taylor uses Nietzsche's theory of tragedy to demonstrate that Santiago's voyage is a positive participation in and reaffirmation of life.

90 THORNE, CREATH S. "The Shape of Equivocation in Ernest Hemingway's *For Whom the Bell Tolls*." *American Literature* 51, no. 4 (January): 520-35.

Argues that Hemingway fails in the novel to achieve the level of narrative tragedy found in his earlier works. Points to Jordan's indecisive and equivocal interior monologues and the novel's abstraction of values as major flaws in a work that "finally has talked itself to death."

91 TRILLING, LIONEL. "An American in Spain." In *Speaking of Literature and Society*. New York: Harcourt Brace Jovanovich, pp. 170-76.
    Reprint of *Partisan Review* 8 (January-February 1941): 63-67.

92 _____. "Hemingway and His Critics." In *Speaking of Literature and Society*. New York: Harcourt Brace Jovanovich, pp. 123-34.
    Reprint of *Partisan Review* 6 (Winter 1939): 52-60.

93 WAGNER, LINDA W. *American Modern: Essays in Fiction and Poetry*. Port Washington, N.Y.: Kennikat, 263 pp.
    Reprints 1976.94, 1977.109, and 1977.110.

94 _____. "'Proud and friendly and gently': Women in Hemingway's Early Fiction." *College Literature* 7:239-47.
    Emphasizes that the women characters in "Up in Michigan," "Indian Camp," "The End of Something," "The Three-Day Blow," and "Cross-Country Snow" have already reached "that plateau of semi-stoic self awareness which Hemingway's men have, usually, yet to attain." Wagner uses the manuscripts of *The Sun Also Rises*, "The Last Good Country," and "Cat in the Rain" to show how positively Hemingway viewed many of his women characters. Reprinted 1981.86.

95 WALDRON, EDWARD E. "*The Pearl* and *The Old Man and the Sea*: A Comparative Analysis." *Steinbeck Quarterly* 13, no. 3-4 (Summer-Fall): 98-106.
    Points out similarities in characterization, style, natural imagery, and themes. Both novels depict triumph in the face of adversity and the endurance of the human spirit.

96 WEEKS, LEWIS E., Jr. "Hemingway Hills: Symbolism in 'Hills Like White Elephants.'" *Studies in Short Fiction* 17, no. 1 (Winter): 75-77.
    Discusses the symbolic significance of the story's title image, pointing out the paradoxical nature of something that is both valuable and rare while also worthless and burdensome.

97 WHITE, GERTRUDE M. Review of *88 Poems*. *Hemingway Notes* 6, no. 1 (Fall): 37-38.
    Comments on the rawness of emotion found in the unadorned poetry. Feels Hemingway had no skill as a poet.

98 WHITE, RAY LEWIS. "Anderson's Private Reaction to *The Torrents of Spring*." *Modern Fiction Studies* 26, no. 4 (Winter): 635-37.
    Drawing on correspondence between the two, White shows Anderson's reaction to be very mild.

99 WHITE, WILLIAM. "For the Collector." *Hemingway Notes* 5, no. 2 (Spring): 17.

Provides information on the latest Hemingway "discovery," a romantic comedy entitled *Hokum: A Play in Three Acts.* Apparently written in 1920 or 1921 by Hemingway and high-school friend Morris McNeil Musselman.

100 _____. "For the Collector." *Hemingway Notes* 6, no. 1 (Fall): 34-35.

Gives information on German editions of interest to the collector.

101 _____. "General Bibliography." *Hemingway Notes* 5, no. 2 (Spring): 38-40.

List of mostly recent articles, books, and dissertations on Hemingway.

102 _____. "Imitation Hemingway Contest: 3." *Hemingway Notes* 6, no. 1 (Fall): 32-33.

Reprints the winning entry for the Third International Imitation Hemingway Competition, Richard Wiltshire's "The Short Hapless Life of Robert Wilson." Parody at its best (or worst).

103 _____. "Macomber Bibliography." *Hemingway Notes* 5, no. 2 (Spring): 35-38.

Lists more than 100 items on "The Short Happy Life of Francis Macomber."

104 WIDMER, KINGSLEY. "Protestant American Fate: Hemingway and Faulkner." In *Edges of Extremity: Some Problems of Literary Modernism.* Monograph Series no. 17, Tulsa, Oklahoma: University of Tulsa, pp. 42-57.

Briefly discusses the insect fable near the end of *A Farewell to Arms* as an example of "antinomian pessimism."

105 WILSON, EDMUND. *The Thirties.* Edited by Leon Edel. New York: Farrar, Straus & Giroux, 753 pp.

Reminiscences of Hemingway and Fitzgerald (301-3), on Hemingway's "taking back" an insult (474), and other incidents.

106 WILSON, MARK. "Ernest Hemingway as Funnyman." *Thalia* 3, no. 1 (Spring-Summer): 29-34.

Interested in the "consistent strain of humor" in Hemingway's writing, focusing on the author's reliance on two techniques familiar to southwestern humor and particularly found in Mark Twain – the deadpan narrator and the juxtaposition of two contrasting voices or levels of speech. Looks at Hemingway's application of humor in *Death in the Afternoon, To Have and Have Not, For Whom the Bell Tolls*, and others.

107 WORKMAN, BROOKE. "A Semester of Hemingway for Gifted High School Students." *Journal of Reading* 23, no. 7 (April): 598-600.
  Outlines a high-school-level seminar course on Hemingway which emphasizes oral readings, discussion, seminar reports, and group evaluation.

108 WYATT, DAVID M. "The Hand of the Master." *Virginia Quarterly Review* 56, no. 2 (Spring): 312-19.
  Contends that from 1940 on, Hemingway "self-consciously" used metaphoric language – specifically the metaphor of the hand to express his fear of failing creative powers.

109 ____. "Hemingway's Uncanny Beginnings." In *Prodigal Sons: A Study in Authorship and Authority*. Baltimore: Johns Hopkins University Press, pp. 52-71.
  Reprint of 1977.123.

110 WYLDER, DELBERT E. "The Two Faces of Brett: The Role of the New Woman in *The Sun Also Rises*." *Kentucky Philological Association Bulletin*, pp. 27-33.
  Argues against the interpretation of Brett as bitch-goddess, contending that such a limited view prohibits critics from seeing her both as a mother/protector figure and as an example of the new, emancipated woman of the twentieth century.

111 YAGODA, BEN. "American Writers in Paris." *Horizon* 23, no. 11 (November): 25-31.
  Discusses Paris's unique attraction for the expatriate American writers. Considers *The Sun Also Rises* to be "probably the best single work to come out of the Parisian twenties; ironically, by publicizing and glamorizing the expatriate movement, it hastened its end. Before long, crowds of Americans with no interest in literature were invading; Paris had become a fad."

112 YOUNG, PHILIP. "Hemingway Papers, Occasional Thoughts." *College Literature* 7:310-18.
  Serves as a summary of work done, and work yet to do, from the man who has spent a career assessing and interpreting Hemingway's work. Reprinted: 1981.86.

1981

1 ABLEMAN, PAUL. "A Kind of Superman." *Times Educational Supplement*, no. 3384 (1 May), p. 25.

Review of *Ernest Hemingway: Selected Letters, 1917-1961*. Recommends the book for the close-up view it gives of the "whirlwind life and mind of a mighty fisherman and hunter who happened also to be one of the most influential writers of the twentieth century." Finds the index lacking.

2 ADAMS, PHOEBE-LOU. Review of *Ernest Hemingway: Selected Letters, 1917-1961. Atlantic* 247 (May): 84.

Favorable. "One has the impression, reading this collection, that half-a-dozen different voices are speaking, each saying something of interest."

3 AMORY, MARK. "Downhill All the Way." *Spectator* 246, no. 7973 (2 May): 21-22.

Negative review of *Ernest Hemingway: Selected Letters, 1917-1961*. Although the early years make for some interesting reading, the last half of the collection is little more than a vehicle for the author's posturing.

4 ATLAS, JAMES. "The Private Hemingway." *New York Times Magazine*, 15 February, pp. 23-32, 64-71, 83-87, 91.

Prints excerpts from *Ernest Hemingway: Selected Letters*, with an introduction by Atlas praising the volume for the insight it gives into the private side of Hemingway's life. "This side of Hemingway, the self-doubting, even dependent nature seldom reflected in his public image, dominates the correspondence."

5 BAKER, CARLOS. Introduction to *Ernest Hemingway: Selected Letters, 1917-1961*. New York: Scribner's, pp. ix-xxi.

Outlines Hemingway's letter-writing habits and remarks on his difficulties with spelling and punctuation, his tendency toward gossip, and his capacity for friendship.

6 BAKER, RUSSEL. "I Remember Papa." *New York Times Magazine*, 25 October, p. 25.

Humorous anecdotes of "alleged" Hemingway incidents involving Fitzgerald, Stein, and others.

7 BALITAS, VINCENT D. Review of *Ernest Hemingway: Selected Letters, 1917-1961. America* 144 (23 May): 430.

Suggests that the greater contribution of the collection is not to Hemingway scholarship but that it may draw old and new readers back to the works themselves.

8 BENDER, BERT. "Margot Macomber's Gimlet." *College Literature* 8, no. 1 (Winter): 12-20.

Warns critics against reading their own changing cultural attitudes into the story. "'The Short Happy Life of Francis Macomber' runs rife with sexist values but this does not justify our exoneration of Margot."

9 BOUTELLE, ANN EDWARDS. "Hemingway and 'Papa': Killing of the Father in Nick Adams Fiction." *Journal of Modern Literature* 9, no. 1:133-46.

Locates at the heart of the Nick Adams stories the disguised secret of killing the father figure, an unapproachable fantasy linking the image of the dead Indian with the wished-for dead father.

10 BOYD, JOHN D. "Hemingway's 'Soldier's Home.'" *Explicator* 40, no. 1 (Fall): 51-53.

Suggests that Jones (see 1979.53), in pointing out Hemingway's alleged errors concerning the date of Krebs's return from the war, missed Hemingway's deliberate irony.

11 BRASCH, JAMES DANIEL, and SIGMAN, JOSEPH. *Hemingway's Library: A Composite Record.* New York: Garland, 558 pp.

Catalogues all the books in the Cuban library, Finca Vigía, as well as information about his reading habits and other holdings.

12 BRESNAHAN, ROGER J. "Ernest Hemingway: A Reader's Perspective." *Midamerica* 8:22-35.

Relates Hemingway's theory of the iceberg to Wolfgang Iser's theories of the reading process that emphasize the interactive role of the reader in reacting to and creating text. Demonstrates how readers continually readjust their projections based on authorial cues through a reading of "The Short Happy Life of Francis Macomber."

13 BURGESS, ANTHONY. "Opening Hemingway's Mail." *Saturday Review* 8 (April): 64-65.

Review of *Ernest Hemingway: Selected Letters, 1917-1961.* Feels that because the letters hold "no literary effects, [they are] all the more a kind of literature – direct, pungent, highly idiosyncratic, and breathing speech more than lamp oil."

14 ____. "Straight from the Heart." *Observer*, 26 April, n.p.

Review of *Ernest Hemingway: Selected Letters, 1917-1961*. Admires Hemingway's openness and bluntness in his correspondence, remarking that "it is sound refreshing stuff."

15 CARPENTER, CAROL. "Exercises to Combat Sexist Reading and Writing." *College English* 43, no. 3 (March): 293-300.
Outlines a number of reading and writing activities at the college-freshman level designed to examine sexist thought and language. Uses examples from *A Farewell to Arms*.

16 CASEWIT, CURTIS. *The Literary Guide to the United States*. Edited by S. Benedict. New York: Facts on File, p. 182.
Mentions Hemingway's attachment to Idaho.

17 CASS, COLIN S. "The Look of Hemingway's 'In Another Country.'" *Studies in Short Fiction* 18, no. 3 (Summer): 309-13.
Discusses the central motif of looking and windows along with the significance of the title image in relation to its source in Marlowe's *The Jew of Malta*. Finds the imagery serving to tie together the story of the American soldier and Italian major.

18 "Clarified Image." *Economist* 279 (13 June): 92-93.
Review of *Ernest Hemingway: Selected Letters, 1917-1961*. Values the collection for the portrait it presents of the man behind the legend.

19 COLEMAN, ARTHUR. "Francis Macomber and Sir Gawain." *American Notes & Queries* 19 (January-February): 70.
Considers "The Short Happy Life of Francis Macomber" to be a modern rendition of the theme and situation dramatized in the medieval romance *Sir Gawain and the Green Knight*. Briefly compares the knightly code with the Hemingway code.

20 CORE, GEORGE. Review of *88 Poems*. *Sewanee Review* 89, no. 2 (Spring): 89.
Negative review, characterizing Hemingway's poetry as chatty, flabby, petty, and obscene.

21 CURLEY, ARTHUR. Review of *Ernest Hemingway: Selected Letters, 1917-1961*. *Library Journal* 106, no. 6 (15 March): 662.
Favorable. Contends that Hemingway's "background to the novels and stories and his most private views on life and literature lend a richness to this volume which even Baker's own excellent biography cannot match."

22 DAVIS, ALEXANDER. "Historic Houses: Ernest Hemingway,
    Memories of Literary Creativity in Key West." *Architectural Digest* 38,
    no. 1 (January): 94-98.
    Tour of the Hemingway house in Key West. Includes interior and
    exterior photographs.

23 De PUY, HARRY. "Imitation Hemingway: 'Bull in the Night.'" *Odyssey*
    4, no. 2:23-24.
    Prints 1981 winning entry for the Fourth International Imitation
    Hemingway Competition. Parody at its best (or worst).

24 Di DOMENICO, FRANK, Jr. "For the Collector." *Hemingway Notes* 6
    (Spring): 38.
    Describes rare edition of *The Old Man and the Sea*.

25 DONALDSON, SCOTT. "Fitzgerald and Hemingway." In *American
    Literary Scholarship: An Annual, 1979*. Edited by James Woodress.
    Durham, N.C.: Duke University Press, pp. 155-76.
    Survey of criticism on both authors published during 1979. Finds
    "that the most significant publications resulted from gathering
    previously uncollected and somewhat peripheral writings of Fitzgerald
    and Hemingway themselves."

26 _____. "The Case of the Vanishing American and Other Puzzlements in
    Hemingway's Fiction." *Hemingway Notes* 6, no. 2 (Spring): 16-19.
    Sums up some of the more puzzling textual problems in
    Hemingway's fiction (i.e., disappearing characters, changed names, and
    contradictions), concluding from his inspection of the Kennedy Library
    manuscripts that at times it was Hemingway's fault and at others it was
    his editors'.

27 _____. "Gertrude Stein Reviews Hemingway's *Three Stories & Ten
    Poems*. *American Literature* 53, no. 1 (March): 114-15.
    Reprints Stein's review – "apparently the first review of
    Hemingway's first book."

28 EGRI, PETER. "European Origins and American Originality: The Case
    of Drama." *Zeitschrift für Anglistik und Amerikanistik* 29, no. 3:197-206.
    Commenting briefly, Egri sees the growing tension between
    Jordan and Pablo as a prime example of a retrogressive motif that
    diverts the dramatic action from the course of its intended goal in *For
    Whom the Bell Tolls*.

29 EHRESMANN, JULIA M. Review of *Ernest Hemingway: Selected
    Letters, 1917-1961. Booklist* 77 (1 February): 731.

Considers the collection of "gigantic importance" but feels the general reading public may be lost without a biography to refer to.

30 ELLIOTT, GARY D. "Hemingway's 'The Light of the World.'" *Explicator* 40, no. 1 (Fall): 48-50.

Sees the title reinforcing Nick's role in the story but admits that "Nick finds great difficulty in shining as a light into the darkness."

31 EWART, GAVIN. "There Is Good News about Hemingway, As Well As Bad." *Listener* 105 (23 April): 545-46.

Review of *Ernest Hemingway: Selected Letters, 1917-1961*. Believes the letters served as a form of relaxation and therapy for the author.

32 FEAR, JACQUELINE, and McNEIL, HELEN. "The Twenties." In *Introduction to American Studies*. Edited by Malcolm Bradbury and Howard Temperley. New York: Longman, pp. 199-219 passim.

Briefly comments on both *The Sun Also Rises* as Hemingway's true war novel and its influence on the sexual revolution of the twenties. Reads Jake's impotence as a defense against Brett's aggressive sex drive.

33 FIELD, ROSS. Review of *Ernest Hemingway: Selected Letters, 1917-1961. Nation* 233, no. 22 (26 December): 712.

Considers the collection "an unmatched romance-of-ego."

34 FLEMING, ROBERT E. "When Hemingway Nodded: A Note on Firearms in 'The Short Happy Life.'" *Notes on Modern American Literature* 5, no. 3 (Summer): item 17.

Notes Hemingway's error concerning Wilson's rifle having "a muzzle velocity of two tons." Velocity is measured in feet per second.

35 GAJDUSEK, ROBERT E. "On the Definition of a Definitive Text." *Hemingway Review* 1, no. 1 (Fall): 18-22.

Argues against standard editions because "the errors are of a sort that really could not have been missed by Hemingway, not by the Hemingway we know, and that is a far greater argument for leaving them intact than is our own confusion."

36 GEBHARDT, RICHARD C. "Hemingway's Complex Values." *Hemingway Review* 1, no. 1 (Fall): 2-10.

Bothered by oversimplified readings of the values implied in Hemingway's fiction as either nihilistic or optimistic. Feels the author's complex value system "can best be understood not from any single focus ... but from the essentially dual drive to deny and affirm values simultaneously." Gebhardt points to this phenomenon appearing consistently throughout the Hemingway canon and especially in "Up in Michigan," "The Short Happy Life of Francis Macomber," *The Sun Also Rises*, and *The Old Man and the Sea*.

37 GELLHORN, MARTHA. "*On Apocryphism.*" *Paris Review* 23, no. 79 (Spring): 280-301.

Takes Stephen Spender (see 1980.86) and Lillian Hellman (see *An Unfinished Woman*, Boston: Little, Brown, 1969) to task for printing untrue anecdotes about Hemingway. Gellhorn sets the record straight concerning alleged morgue visits, ghoulish pictures, and other falsities. See also 1981.104 for Spender's response.

38 GLADSTEIN, MIMI R. "Ma Joad and Pilar: Significantly Similar." *Steinbeck Quarterly* 14, no. 3-4 (Summer-Fall): 93-104.

Sees the women as representing optimistic possibilities in a pessimistic milieu. Both, having endured, continue to suffer and overcome hardship and provide hope for the future.

39 GREEN, GREGORY. "'A Matter of Color': Hemingway's Criticism of Race Prejudice." *Hemingway Review* 1, no. 1 (Fall): 27-32.

Provides background information on the racial issues surrounding boxing in the early 1900s, relating the characters of Morgan and Gans to the real-life boxers Stanley Ketchel and champion Jack Johnson. "Even though Ketchel gave away some fifty pounds to the black champion, he carried into the fight with him the club of public prejudice and racial hatred." In "A Matter of Color" Hemingway reverses history and restores blind justice.

40 HAAS, RUDOLF. "'God Bless Tauchnitz': Some Observations on Hemingway's Paris Sketches." In *Forms and Functions of History in American Literature: Essays in Honor of Ursula Brumm*. Edited by Winfried Fluck, Jürgen Peper, and Willi Paul Adams. Berlin: Verlag, pp. 149-59.

Reassesses Hemingway's fame as a writer in light of his limited attitudes toward and knowledge of European culture, history, and politics as evidenced in the posthumous *A Moveable Feast*. Concludes "that the echo of his work is greater than its literary qualities."

41 HAGEMANN, E.R. "The Feather Dancer in 'A Way You'll Never Be.'" *Hemingway Notes* 6, no. 2 (Spring): 25-27.

Gives background information on Hemingway's reference to dancers Gaby Deslys and Harry Pilcer who performed in Paris during World War I. A comparison of their show schedule with Hemingway's sojourn in Paris in 1918 reveals that Hemingway never actually saw them perform.

42 HART, JEFFREY. "Swell Letters: The (Mostly) Sunlit Hemingway."
    National Review 33 (29 May): 618-19.
       Review of *Ernest Hemingway: Selected Letters, 1917-1961*. Grants
    the collection occasionally gives a glimpse of the dark side of
    Hemingway, but sees it as generally presenting a positive and warm
    portrait of the author.

43 HAUPTMAN, ROBERT. Review of *Ernest Hemingway: Selected
    Letters, 1917-1961*. *World Literature* 55 (Autumn): 679-80.
       Laments the quality of the letters. "Hemingway is writing for his
    correspondents, not the future."

44 HAYS, PETER. "Hemingway, Faulkner, and a Bicycle Built for Death."
    Notes on Modern American Literature 5, no. 4 (Fall): item 28.
       Concludes that although policeman Percy Grimm pursues Joe
    Christmas on a bicycle in *Light in August* (1932), Hemingway did not
    borrow from Faulkner the image of bicycle policemen as a symbol of
    death in "The Snows of Kilimanjaro" (1936). Notes the frequency of
    Hemingway's references to bicycles as early as 1926 in *The Sun Also
    Rises*.

45 HECK, FRANCIS S. "*The Old Man and the Sea* and Rimbaud's *Le
    Bateau Ivre*: 'Solidaire'/ 'Solitaire.'" *North Dakota Quarterly* 49, no. 1:61-
    67.
       Traces the theme of the rite of manhood through *The Old Man
    and the Sea* and *Le Bateau Ivre*. Sees Santiago's and Rimbaud's boats as
    symbols of the authors themselves.

46 HEMINGWAY, ERNEST. "The Art of the Short Story." *Paris Review*
    23 (Spring): 85-102.
       Prints the unedited version of Hemingway's address on the
    methods of short-story writing in which the author comments on his
    own short stories and his theory of omission.

47 _____. *Ernest Hemingway: Selected Letters, 1917-1961*. Edited by Carlos
    Baker. New York: Scribner's, 948 pp.
       Reprints nearly 600 uncut letters written over the course of forty-
    five years. Each letter includes the name of the recipient, place of
    origin, and date, along with frequent informative notes. Contains index.

48 HERNDON, JERRY A. "'Macomber' and the 'Fifth Dimension.'"
    Notes on Modern American Literature 5, no. 4 (Fall): item 24.
       Argues that the flatly objective statement that "Mrs. Macomber, in
    the car, had shot at the buffalo" echoes what Wilson will testify to at the

inquest but not what really happened in "The Short Happy Life of Francis Macomber."

49 HIGGS, ROBERT J. "Apollo." In *Laurel & Thorn: The Athlete in American Literature*. Lexington: University Press of Kentucky, pp. 22-90 passim.

Sees Cohn as the failed Renaissance man who tries to live a life of sport and leisure but is undermined by circumstance; the war, anti-Semitism, and psychological aberrations combine to bring out the brute in Cohn.

50 HILL, DOUGLAS. "Epistle-Packing Papa." *Books in Canada* 10, no. 6 (June-July): 24-25.

Review of *Ernest Hemingway: Selected Letters, 1917-1961*. Concludes that, overall, "there's just too much unpleasantness, stupidity, xenophobia, pomposity, paranoia. One tires soon of Hemingway's life. As he eventually did."

51 HOTCHNER, A.E. "Ernest Hemingway: An American Original." *TV Guide* 29, no. 33 (15 August): 26-27.

Comments on Hemingway's thirst for adventure, dedication to writing, and abundant generosity.

52 HOWE, IRVING. "Messages from a Divided Man." *New York Times Book Review*, 29 March, pp. 28-29.

Review of *Ernest Hemingway: Selected Letters, 1917-1961*. Finds only a "handful of letters are strong and memorable in their own right." Saddened by the contents of many that serve only to deflate the author's image even more.

53 HURD, MYLES. "The Cat in the Rain in Bullins' 'Clara's Ole Man.'" *Notes on Contemporary Literature* 11 (May): 2.

Points out that like Hemingway's "Cat in the Rain," Bullins's play uses a cat to symbolize a deteriorating relationship that is lacking in some way.

54 JACKSON, PAUL R. "Hemingway's 'Out of Season.'" *Hemingway Review* 1, no. 1:11-17.

Feels Hemingway's shifting point of view creates confusion regarding the narrative's central focus, the story of Peduzzi.

55 JOHNSTON, KENNETH. "Nick/Mike Adams? The Hero's Name in 'Cross-Country Snow.'" *American Notes & Queries* 20, no. 1-2:16-18.

Manuscript evidence shows that originally Hemingway intended Nick to be named Mike. Johnston suggests that Hemingway used both in the final version to connote boyhood comradeship. Reprinted with minor revision: 1987.38.

56 KAZIN, ALFRED. "The Battler." *New York Review of Books* 28, no. 6 (April): 3-4.

Review of *Ernest Hemingway: Selected Letters, 1917-1961.* As Kazin says, these "'selected' letters make a sometimes unbearably continuous and too emphatic record of the man's life, vehemence by vehemence."

57 KENNER, HUGH. "Writing by Numbers: Hemingway's Letters." *Harper's* 262 (April): 93-95.

Discusses Hemingway's obsession with daily word counts of his writing and the honest portrait of the man and author that emerges from *Ernest Hemingway: Selected Letters, 1917-1961.*

58 KRILE, IVO. "Nice and Fine in the Translation of Ernest Hemingway's *A Farewell to Arms.*" *Studia Romanica et Anglica Zagrabiensia* 26:297-308.

Focuses on the ambiguities surrounding the use of the words *nice* and *fine* in the novel and the problems associated with finding translation equivalents in Serbo-Croatian.

59 KVAM, WAYNE. "The Melville Legacy in Hochhuth's *Tod eines Jägers.*" *Melville Society Extracts* 45 (February): 9-10.

Describes in detail German dramatist Rolf Hochhuth's two-act play which loosely recreates Hemingway's final hours. Depicts Hemingway's turning to the troubled legacy of Melville in a last-ditch effort for solace.

60 LANSER, SUSAN SNIADER. "Point of View as Ideology and Technique." In *The Narrative Act: Point of View in Prose Fiction.* Princeton, N.J.: Princeton University Press, pp. 246-76.

Paying attention to the relation between textual structure and ideology, Lanser looks closely at the self-effacing narrative voice in "The Killers." Concludes that while dodging visibility, the narrator "also refuses to give up his own identity or to hand over the focalizing role to a character. In a sense, then, the narrator is like Nick Adams, setting up a small but significant resistance to the pressures that would silence or eliminate him."

61 LAURENCE, FRANK M. *Hemingway and the Movies.* Jackson: University Press of Mississippi, 329 pp.

In addition to film-text comparisons of big screen adaptations of Hemingway, Laurence provides a detailed account of casting, production, and promotions. Includes information on the critical reception of the various film versions by critics, audiences, and Hemingway alike. Also explores the exploitative Hemingway-Hollywood relationship that resulted in the production of those commercialized box-office adaptations that displeased the author so much. Includes a thorough and valuable filmography.

62 LAWSON, CAROLINA DONADIO. "Hemingway, Stendhal, and War" *Hemingway Notes* 6, no. 2:28-33.
    Suggests that Hemingway modeled the retreat from Caporetto in *A Farewell to Arms* after Stendhal's account of the battle of Waterloo in *The Charterhouse of Parma*.

63 LEHMANN-HAUPT, CHRISTOPHER. Review of *Ernest Hemingway: Selected Letters, 1917-1961*. *New York Times*, 31 March, p. C20.
    Praises the collection for the light it sheds on the man and author. Comments on Hemingway's adoption of masks, even in his personal correspondence.

64 LEVIN, GAIL. "Edward Hopper's 'Nighthawks.'" *Arts Magazine* 55, no. 9 (May): 154-61.
    Finds echoes of the setting and mood of "The Killers" in Hopper's later painting *Nighthawks*.

65 LEWIS, ROBERT W. Review of *Ernest Hemingway: Selected Letters, 1917-1961*. *Hemingway Review* 1, no. 1 (Fall): 59-60.
    Judges Baker's selection overall to be "very good," feeling the volume to be an "autobiography and Hemingway's longest 'book.'"

66 LOCKLIN, GERALD, and STETLER, CHARLES. "Ernest Hemingway: 'Best of All He Loved the Fall.'" *Hemingway Notes* 6, no. 2 (Spring): 20-24.
    Reprint of 1980.57.

67 LODGE, DAVID. "Analysis and Interpretation of the Realist Text: Ernest Hemingway's 'Cat in the Rain.'" In *Working with Structuralism*. Boston: Routledge & Kegan Paul, pp. 17-36.
    Reprint with minor revision of 1980.59.

68 LUDINGTON, TOWNSEND. "Papa Agonistes." *New Republic* 184, no. 18 (2 May): 32-36.
    Review of *Ernest Hemingway: Selected Letters, 1917-1961*. Praises Baker's selection and footnoting, feeling that the editor has done an "excellent job of presenting Hemingway's career and personality."

69 LYNN, KENNETH S. "Hemingway's Private War." *Commentary* 72, no. 1 (July): 24-33.

Argues against the orthodox interpretation of "Big Two-Hearted River," contending that Edmund Wilson's original reading, which permeated later critical studies, describing "Hemingway's hero as the psychological victim of a brutal war was a measure of the extent to which his literary sensibility was ruled by political nausea." Reprinted: 1983.72. See also 1984.12.

70 McCANN, RICHARD. "To Embrace or Kill: 'Fathers and Sons.'" *Iowa Journal of Literary Studies* 3, no. 1-2:11-18.

Treats the past and Nick's ambivalent feelings toward his father. "As Nick Adams travels back into his father's country he is claimed by the past, a past which, like the father, will neither wholly die nor nourish him."

71 McILVAINE, ROBERT. "Robert Cohn and *The Purple Land*." *Notes on Modern American Literature* 5, no. 2 (Spring): item 8.

Draws connections between *The Sun Also Rises* and W.H. Hudson's *The Purple Land*, commenting on how the romantic adventures of the hero in Hudson's novel influence the naive Cohn.

72 McKENNA, JOHN J., and PETERSON, MARVIN V. "More Muddy Water: Wilson's Shakespeare in 'The Short Happy Life of Francis Macomber.'" *Studies in Short Fiction* 18, no. 1 (Winter): 82-85.

Points to Hemingway's blunder of having Wilson utter the "God of death" quote from one of Shakespeare's fools in Henry IV, for it undermines and discredits Wilson's character.

73 MAGILL, FRANK N., ed. "Ernest Hemingway." In *American Novel: Crane to Faulkner*. Pasadena, Calif.: Salem Press, pp. 305-340.

Reference guide providing an overview of forty authors' lives and major works. Includes character analyses, plot summaries, critical evaluations, and bibliographies for *The Sun Also Rises*, *A Farewell to Arms*, *For Whom the Bell Tolls*, and *The Old Man and the Sea*.

74 MALOFF, SAUL. "Hemingway Alive." *Commonweal* 108, no. 10 (22 May): 302-3.

Favorable review of *Ernest Hemingway: Selected Letters, 1917-1961*, calling it an "autobiography-in-letters."

75 MÁRQUEZ, GABRIEL GARCÍA. "Gabriel García Márquez Meets Ernest Hemingway." *New York Times Book Review*, 27 July, pp. 1, 16-17.

Recounts his one sighting of Hemingway on a Paris street in 1957 and then goes on briefly to compare his writing with Faulkner's, finding that Faulkner touched his soul but Hemingway taught him about writing.

76   MARTIN, LAWRENCE H., Jr. "Stories That Can't Be Hung: Miss Stein's Use of 'Inaccrochable.'" *Hemingway Notes* 6, no. 2 (Spring): 34-35.
    Treats Stein's criticism of "Up in Michigan" as recounted in Hemingway's *A Moveable Feast*. Stein considered the story "inaccrochable" (unpublishable) because of its sexual explicitness.

77   MESSENGER, CHRISTIAN K. "The School Sports Hero as Satiric Emblem: Hemingway and Faulkner." In *Sport and the Spirit of Play in American Fiction: Hawthorne to Faulkner*. New York: Columbia University Press, pp. 208-28.
    Examines the evolution of the ritual, school, and popular sports hero over time, arguing that Cohn in *The Sun Also Rises* and Labove in *The Hamlet* are satiric figures representing the overturned schoolboy ideal and the decline of the school sports hero. Analyzes Cohn's failure to make it in an uncertain environment foreign to the college hero in light of Hemingway's own experiences with and suspicion of school sport.
    Pp. 231-61: "Hemingway: Exemplary Heroism and Heroic Witnessing." Considers *The Sun Also Rises* to be Hemingway's major treatise on ritualistic sport, both for the participant and spectator. Sees the sports ritual as a means by which a solitary human being can achieve self-knowledge about personal identity and the limits of capability. "Ritual sport for Hemingway was a defense against life that could not be confronted other ways."
    Pp. 291-309: "Sport Approaches the Sacred: Hemingway and Faulkner." Looks at each author's depiction of play and sport and the desire of the protagonists/hunters (Santiago in *The Old Man and the Sea* and Ike McCaslin in *Go Down, Moses*) to be part of a natural ritual. Sees sport as the entrance "into the sacred environment but in this environment sport falls away before larger questions and realities."

78   MITCHELL, J. LAWRENCE. "The Language of the Thirties: Some Literary Evidence." *Centrum*, n.s. 1, no. 2 (Fall): 120-32.
    Credits Hemingway with popularizing the Spanish term "the moment of truth."

79   MONTEIRO, GEORGE. "Hemingway's 'Soldier's Home.'" *Explicator* 40, no. 1 (Fall): 50-51.
    Suggests that Jones (see 1979.53), in pointing out Hemingway's alleged errors concerning the date of Krebs's return from the war, missed Hemingway's deliberate irony.

80 MOORE, GEOFFREY. "Hemingway, Ernest." In *Makers of Modern Culture*. Edited by Justin Wintle. New York: Facts on File, pp. 223-24.

Brief overview of Hemingway's literary career and contribution to modern American literature.

81 MUDRICK, MARVIN. "A No-Good Self-Righteous Bragging Boasting Chickenshit Character." *Hudson Review* 34 (Autumn): 441-55.

Essay review of *Ernest Hemingway: Selected Letters, 1917-1961*. Comments on Hemingway's correspondence with Charles Scribner and his feelings toward psychoanalytic critics and first wife Hadley years after their marriage. Mudrick suggests that "Hemingway's letters are his Boswell."

82 NAKAJIMA, KENJI. "*Lacrimae Rerum* in 'My Old Man.'" *Kyushu American Literature* 22 (May): 18-23.

Analyzes the dual nature of Joe's narration (what he feels and how he perceives) and his indirectness in interpreting reality. Finds that the humor in the garrulous style possesses a "quiet sadness, akin to *lacrimae rerum*, it being expressed without sentimentality."

83 NEWLOVE, DONALD. *Those Drinking Days*. New York: Horizon Press, pp. 34-35, 62, 137-38.

Autobiography coupled with commentary on other alcoholic authors like himself. Several references to Hemingway and his drinking habits. Briefly chronicles his decline into dementia and subsequent suicide.

84 "Newsreel." *American Film* 6, no. 7 (May): 12.

Points to a 1956 letter to Gary Cooper included in the recently published *Ernest Hemingway: Selected Letters, 1917-1961* as evidence of Hemingway's strong aversion to working in Hollywood.

85 NICHOLS, OLIVIA MURRAY. "An Example of Folklore in Hemingway's 'Indian Camp.'" *Kentucky Folklore Record* 27, no. 1-2:33-35.

Explains the folk tradition of *couvade* (sympathetic connection between expectant fathers and their wives), commonly practiced among North American Indians, in relation to Hemingway's extreme example in "Indian Camp," when the father cuts his own throat as the doctor cuts the wife's abdomen.

86 OLDSEY, BERNARD, ed. *Ernest Hemingway, The Papers of a Writer*. New York: Garland, 147 pp.

Papers presented at the July 1980 Hemingway conference commemorating the opening of the Hemingway Room at the John F. Kennedy Library in Boston. Contents:

Pp. xi-xv: Introduction by Bernard Oldsey. Explains the occasion, the kinds of research possible in the Hemingway papers and archival collection, and the role of Mary Hemingway.

Pp. xxi-xxii: "A Note on the Hemingway Collection" by Jo August, curator of the collection.

Pp. 11-23: "Unexplored Territory: The Next Ten Years of Hemingway Studies" by Michael S. Reynolds. Reprint of 1980.80.

Pp. 25-35: "'Dear Folks . . . Dear Ezra': Hemingway's Early Years and Correspondence, 1917-1924" by E.R. Hagemann. Reprint of 1980.34.

Pp. 37-62: "Hemingway's Beginnings and Endings" by Bernard Oldsey. Reprint of 1980.69. Reprinted: 1987.95.

Pp. 63-71: "'Proud and friendly and gently': Women in Hemingway's Early Fiction" by Linda W. Wagner. Reprint of 1980.94.

Pp. 73-87: "Hemingway's Poetry: Angry Notes of an Ambivalent Overman" by Nicholas Gerogiannis. Reprint of 1980.30. Reprinted 1987.95.

Pp. 89-107: "Hemingway of the *Star*" by Scott Donaldson. Reprint of 1980.22.

Pp. 109-115: "Hemingway's Library: Some Volumes of Poetry" by James D. Brasch and Joseph Sigman. Reprint of 1980.10.

Pp. 117-31: "The Mystery of the Ritz Hotel Papers" by Jacqueline Tavernier-Courbin. Reprint of 1980.88.

Pp. 133-38: "Initial Europe: 1918 as a Shaping Element in Hemingway's *Weltanschauung*" by Zvonimir Radeljković. Reprint of 1980.75.

Pp. 139-47: "Hemingway Papers, Occasional Remarks" by Philip Young. Reprint of 1980.112.

87 _____. "Papa's Private World." *Nation* 232, no. 18 (9 May): 575-77.
Review of *Ernest Hemingway: Selected Letters, 1917-1961.* Considers the collection to serve as a "rough biography," at times providing valuable insight into the writer's craft.

88 PALMIERI, ANTHONY F. "The Hemingway-Anderson Feud: A Letter from Boni." *Hemingway Review* 1, no. 1 (Fall): 56-58.
Records the circumstances of the Hemingway-Anderson split and reprints portions of a 1965 letter from Albert Boni expressing his own resentment over Hemingway's treatment of Anderson.

89 PIAZZA, PAUL. Review of *Ernest Hemingway: Selected Letters, 1917-1961.* *Smithsonian* 12 (April): 151-53.

Favorable review, calling it an "extraordinary collection" for the light it sheds on both the man and writer.

90 PRENDERGAST, ALAN. "The Hemingway Heartland." *Rocky Mountain Magazine* 3:33-37.

Focuses on the lives and careers of Hemingway's three granddaughters – Muffet, Margaux, and Mariel – with only marginal references to the author.

91 PRESCOTT, PETER S. Review of *Ernest Hemingway: Selected Letters, 1917-1961. Newsweek*, 23 March, pp. 76-78.

Regards the collection as fascinating because of the author's unguardedness and openness in writing the letters. "Hemingway emerges from these pages as close to life as we shall ever see him: blustering, aggrieved, courteous, malicious, determined, funny, profane and increasingly obscene."

92 "Review of *Ernest Hemingway: Selected Letters, 1917-1961.*" *Business Week*, 20 April, p. 14.

Praises the collection for revealing the true man behind the legend.

93 "Review of *Ernest Hemingway: Selected Letters, 1917-1961. Choice* 18, no. 11-12 (July-August): 1545.

Commends the collection for its candid and insightful portrait of the man and author.

94 "Review of Ernest Hemingway's *The Nick Adams Stories.*" *New York Times Book Review*, 8 March, p. 35.

Considers the collection "indispensable for an understanding of Hemingway's development as man and artist."

95 REYNOLDS, MICHAEL S. *Hemingway's Reading, 1910-1940: An Inventory*. Princeton: Princeton University Press, 236 pp.

Compilation of books and periodicals owned and borrowed by the author up to 1940 (prior to his move to Cuba). Includes a valuable index categorizing entries under such subjects as biography, history, and literature. Future direction for worthwhile source and influence studies springs from this seemingly objective listing.

96 ____. "Words Killed, Wounded, Missing in Action." *Hemingway Notes* 6, no. 2 (Spring): 2-9.

Citing textual problems in several of Hemingway's works, Reynolds calls for standard editions, especially of *The Sun Also Rises* and *A Farewell to Arms*.

97 REYNOLDS, STANLEY. "Yours, Papa." *Punch* 280 (22 April): 646.
Review of *Ernest Hemingway: Selected Letters, 1917-1961*. Sees the
collection as chronicling Hemingway's growth into a self-obsessed
monster.

98 SAGE, LORNA. "Advertisive Life." *Times Literary Supplement*, 22 May,
p. 571.
Along with a review of recent critical studies, Sage looks at
Baker's *Ernest Hemingway: Selected Letters, 1917-1961*. Discusses the
difficulties associated with separating the man from the legend.

99 SCHAUBER, ELLEN, and SPOLSKY, ELLEN. "Stalking a Generative
Poetics." *New Literary History* 12, no. 3 (Spring): 397-413.
Argues that when sophisticated readers connect the palm-reading
scene with the first scene in which Jordan lies on the ground listening to
his heart beat, there can be little doubt, despite varied interpretive
response, that Jordan is about to die.

100 SCHOONOVER, DAVID E. Review of *Ernest Hemingway: Selected
Letters, 1917-1961*. *Yale Review* 71, no. 1 (October): x-xiii.
Commends the collection for the light it sheds on both the man
and writer.

101 SEYDOW, JOHN J. "Francis Macomber's Spurious Masculinity."
Hemingway Review 1, no. 1 (Fall): 33-41.
Argues against traditional readings of "The Short Happy Life of
Francis Macomber" that insist Francis redeems himself at the end and
proves his manhood, contending instead that Francis, unable to
transcend Wilson's narrow definition of masculinity, dies "full of
illusions."

102 SHEPPARD, R.Z. "Papa's Moveable Treats." *Time*, 6 April, pp. 79-80.
Overall favorable review of *Ernest Hemingway: Selected Letters,
1917-1961*, commenting on the honest portrait the collection presents of
the author.

103 SIGGINS, CLARA M. Review of *Ernest Hemingway: Selected Letters,
1917-1961*. *Best Sellers* 41, no. 2 (May): 68.
Discusses the broad range of subject and time period
encompassed by the collection.

104 SPENDER, STEPHEN. "Stephen Spender Replies." *Paris Review* 23,
no. 79 (Spring): 304-6.

Responds to Gellhorn's labeling him a liar (see 1981.37), defending his original statements concerning Hemingway in Spain. See also 1980.86.

105 STAFFORD, WILLIAM. "Benjy Compson, Jake Barnes, and Nick Carraway: Replication in Three 'Innocent' American Narrators of the 1920s." In *Books Speaking to Books: A Contextual Approach to American Fiction*. Chapel Hill: University of North Carolina Press, pp. 27-50.

Sees Jake Barnes of *The Sun Also Rises* as representing the unconscious innocent who records the world around him with only limited personal reflection on what events mean, thus forcing the reader to formulate meaning from Jake's observations.

106 STANTON, EDWARD F. "The Correspondent and the Doctor: A Spanish Friendship." *Hemingway Review* 1, no. 1 (Fall): 53-55.

Reconstructs Hemingway's thirty-year relationship with Dr. Juan Madinaveitia, quoting liberally from correspondence.

107 STEPHENSON, EDWARD R. "The 'Subtle Brotherhood' of Crane and Hemingway." *Hemingway Review* 1, no. 1 (Fall): 42-52.

Draws parallels between Crane's "The Open Boat" and *The Old Man and the Sea*, contending that "what these works share, specifically, is a vital tension between withdrawal from a brutal, brutalizing environment and the human commitment to others necessary for spiritual and psychological wholeness."

108 STETLER, CHARLES, and LOCKLIN, GERALD. "Does Time Heal All Wounds? A Search for the Code Hero in *The Sun Also Rises*." *McNeese Review* 28:92-100.

Argues against Young's interpretation of Jake Barnes as a typical Hemingway hero, citing the protagonist's continued rejection of the code at every turn.

109 STRAUCH, EDWARD. "*The Old Man and the Sea*: A Numerological View." *Aligarh Journal of English Studies* 6, no. 1:89-100.

Gives mythical or religious associations for each of the numbers mentioned in the text.

110 STUCKEY, WILLIAM JOSEPH. "Celebrities and Best Sellers." In *Pulitzer Prize Novels: A Critical Backward Look*. Norman: University of Oklahoma Press, pp. 165-80.

Considers Hemingway's 1953 Pulitzer prize for *The Old Man and the Sea*, although long overdue, was given for a book "much inferior" to his earlier fiction.

111 STUTTAFORD, GENEVIEVE. Review of *Ernest Hemingway: Selected Letters, 1917-1961*. *Publishers Weekly* 219, no. 8 (20 February): 83.
 Considers the collection the closest we'll come to an autobiography.

112 TAVERNIER-COURBIN, JACQUELINE. "The Manuscripts of *A Moveable Feast*." *Hemingway Notes* 6, no. 2 (Spring): 9-15.
 Questions Hemingway's claim that *A Moveable Feast* resulted from the discovery of thirty-year-old material in the basement of the Ritz Hotel, and also looks at his borrowing from other manuscripts in his writing of the memoir, Mary's editing of it, and those sections deleted from the final published text.

113 ____. "The Paris Notebooks." *Hemingway Review* 1, no. 1 (Fall): 23-26.
 Physical description of each of the Paris notebooks along with a list of their contents.

114 THOMPSON, IRENE. "The Left Bank Apéritifs of Jean Rhys and Ernest Hemingway." *Georgia Review* 35 (Spring): 94-106.
 Discusses the parallel literary careers of Rhys and Hemingway that both began in Paris during the 1920s. Points out similarities in innovative style and autobiographical subject matter and speculates on why Hemingway's work eventually eclipsed Rhys's. Thompson calls for an expanded canon that includes *all* writers of merit.

115 UPDIKE, JOHN. "Hem Battles the Pack; Wins, Loses." *New Yorker* 57 (13 July): 96-106.
 Extended review of *Ernest Hemingway: Selected Letters, 1917-1961*, quoting liberally from the collection and commenting on the content – especially the author's repetitive posturing. "It cannot be said that these letters add anything substantial to the picture of Hemingway's life already provided by his own fiction and journalism, by the heavy publicity he received while alive, by the personal accounts of A.E. Hotchner and Mary Hemingway and others, and by Mr. Baker's own biography." Reprinted: 1983.118.

116 WALLACE, IRVING; WALLACE, AMY; WALLECHINSKY, DAVID; and WALLACE, SYLVIA. "Macho Writer." In *The Intimate Sex Lives of Famous People*. New York: Delacorte Press, pp. 140-43.
 Brief biographical essay outlining Hemingway's relationships with his four wives and various other women including prostitutes, mistresses, and girlfriends.

117 WEDIN, WARREN. "Trout Fishing and Self-Betrayal in *The Sun Also Rises*." *Arizona Quarterly* 37, no. 1:63-74.

Contrasts the passionate and energetic descriptions of trout fishing in "Big Two-Hearted River," "The Last Good Country," and "Now I Lay Me" with the heavy and flat description found in *The Sun Also Rises*. Blames Jake's amateurish efforts and lack of intensity at Burguete upon his failure with Brett and jealousy of Cohn. Jake "betrays the Hemingway Code of the passionate fisherman and loses his chance for emotional renewal."

118 WEXLER, JOYCE. "E.R.A. for Hemingway: A Feminist Defense of *A Farewell to Arms*." *Georgia Review* 35, no. 1:111-23.

Identifies Catherine as a fully developed Hemingway hero. "She is a shellshocked victim of the war who chooses love as a method of rechanneling self-destructive feelings of guilt and remorse." Sees Catherine's progression from self-denial to self-transcendence as instrumental to Frederic's own growth and development.

119 WHITE, RICHARD L. "F. Scott Fitzgerald: The Cumulative Portrait." *Biography* 4, no. 2 (Spring): 154-68.

Contrasts trends in Hemingway and Fitzgerald biography along with the images of the authors presented in these biographies. Regards the Hemingway biographies to be "less scholarly and more sensational; they tend to be closer to memoirs."

120 WHITE, WILLIAM. "Addendum to Hanneman: Hemingway in *Game Fish of the World*." *Papers of the Bibliographical Society of America* 75, no. 4:449.

Adds two versions of *Game Fish of the World* published by Nicholson & Watson, in which Hemingway's article "Cuban Fishing" appears, to Hanneman's *Ernest Hemingway: A Comprehensive Bibliography* (Princeton, 1967).

121 _____. "Current Bibliography." *Hemingway Notes* 6 (Spring): 39-40.

Lists current items, including articles, reviews, dissertations, and books.

122 _____. "Current Bibliography." *Hemingway Review* 1, no. 1 (Fall): 64-68.

Lists current items, including articles, reviews, dissertations, books, and translations.

123 _____. "For the Collector: Addenda to Hanneman, German Editions." *Hemingway Review* 1, no. 1 (Fall): 63.

Adds several German items to Hanneman's *Ernest Hemingway: A Comprehensive Bibliography* (Princeton, 1967) and *Supplement* (Princeton, 1975).

124 ____. "Imitation Hemingway Contest: 4." *Hemingway Review* 1 (Fall):
61-62.
Reprints the winning entry in the Fourth International Imitation
Hemingway Competition, Harry De Puy's "Bull in the Night." Parody at
its best (or worst).

125 ____. "A Play on Hemingway's Suicide." *Hemingway Notes* 6 (Spring):
38.
Describes the trials and tribulations of tracking down a copy of
Hochhuth's out-of-print *Tod eines Jägers*, a monodrama based on
Hemingway's suicide.

126 WIDMAYER, JAYNE A. "Hemingway's Hemingway Parodies: The
Hypocritical Griffon and the Dumb Ox." *Studies in Short Fiction* 18, no.
4 (Fall): 433-38.
Reads the 1951 fables "The Good Lion" and "The Faithful Bull"
not only as "satiric attacks on pretensions and affectations" but also as
self-parodies of the author. However, in comparing them with *Across
the River and into the Trees* (written at the same time), Widmayer finds
that Hemingway is also showing that his heroes are considerably more
complex than the parodies would suggest.

127 WILL, GEORGE F. "Literary Voyeurism: Publishing Hemingway
Letters Hurtful." *Detroit News*, 19 April, p. 15A.
Is bothered that Hemingway's private correspondence was
published despite his desire that it remain private.

128 WILLIAMS, WIRT. *The Tragic Art of Ernest Hemingway*. Baton Rouge:
Louisiana State University Press, 240 pp.
Contends that Hemingway "was one of the century's greatest
makers of tragedy." Systematically analyzes each novel and short-story
collection within a broad definition of tragedy and tragic design,
demonstrating how the author progressively moved toward transcendent
tragedy, culminating in *The Old Man and the Sea*. Williams argues that
Hemingway used structures in musical composition in order to unify his
novels.

129 WINN, HARBOUR. "Hemingway's African Stories and Tolstoy's
'Illich.'" *Studies in Short Fiction* 18, no. 4 (Fall): 451-53.
Finds that in "The Short Happy Life of Francis Macomber" and
"The Snows of Kilimanjaro" Hemingway manages to measure his work
against a classic by building upon Tolstoy's "The Death of Ivan Illich"
and yet still individualize the deaths of Macomber and Harry.

130 WOLCOTT, JAMES. "On the Ropes: Can Ernest Hemingway's *Selected Letters* Revive His Flagging Reputation?" *Esquire* 95 (May): 17-18.

> Finds the new collection gossipy and brash, and sure to further deflate Hemingway's already sagging reputation.

1982

1 ADAIR, WILLIAM. "*For Whom the Bell Tolls*: Oedipus in Spain." *Notes on Contemporary Literature* 12, no. 2 (March): 2.

> Brings out Oedipal elements in the novel, centering on Jordan's inability to kill Pablo the father figure.

2 ALLEN, WILLIAM RODNEY. "All the Names of Death: Walker Percy and Hemingway." *Mississippi Quarterly* 36 (Winter): 3-19.

> Considers Hemingway to be the "one American writer who seems to haunt Percy more than all the others, one who appears, rather thinly disguised, in each of his five novels." Looks at both authors' treatment of suicide and Percy's rejection of the stoic Hemingway code.

3 BARNES, DANIEL R. "Traditional Narrative Sources for Hemingway's *The Torrents of Spring*." *Studies in Short Fiction* 19, no. 2 (Spring): 141-50.

> Discusses Hemingway's use of two folktales in his satire of Anderson's *Dark Laughter*, suggesting that the author was also parodying the folk and their traditions.

4 BARRON, CYNTHIA M. "The Catcher and the Soldier: Hemingway's 'Soldier's Home' and Salinger's *The Catcher in the Rye*." *Hemingway Review* 2, no. 1 (Fall): 70-73.

> Looks at the considerable literary influence "Soldier's Home" had on Salinger's novel, pointing out similarities in theme and character: ". . . faced with their inability to adapt to an adult world that is hypocritical and corrupt, both boys seek a return to the realm of childhood."

5 BOGDAN, DEANNE. "Is It Relevant and Does It Work? Reconsidering Literature Taught as Rhetoric." *Journal of Aesthetic Education* 16, no. 4 (Winter): 27-39.

> Begins with a discussion of those aspects of Plato's literary theory that have relevance today and then applies Platonic fallacies to specific works, including "The Killers." Argues that students may fail to see the value of the story because of our current predilection for a content-oriented approach to literature.

6 BONHEIM, HELMUT. "How Stories Begin–Devices of Exposition in 600 English, American, and Canadian Short Stories." *REAL: Yearbook of Research in English and American Literature* 1:209.

   Considers the anterior events (references to earlier happenings) depicted in the opening scene of "The Battler" certainly "exchangeable, if not expendable."

7 BRADBURY, MALCOLM. "Style of Life, Style of Art." *Hemingway Review* 1, no. 2 (Spring): 58-61.

   Reprint from *The American Novel and the Nineteen Twenties*, Stratford-upon-Avon Studies 19 (London: Edward Arnold, 1971).

8 BRASCH, JAMES D., and SIGMAN, JOSEPH. "Art at Finca Vigía: A Cuban Caricature of Hemingway." *Hemingway Review* 2, no. 1 (Fall): 62-63.

   Discusses the circumstances behind the hanging of Cuban artist Juan David's caricature of Hemingway as the "Old Man of the Sea" in the Finca Vigía dining room as a replacement for Miro's *The Farm* which had been removed by Mary Hemingway after her husband's death.

9 BRENNER, GERRY. "Are We Going to Hemingway's Feast?" *American Literature* 54, no. 4:528-44.

   Drawing on manuscript materials, Brenner pays attention to the "substantial changes" Mary Hemingway made in the text while editing. Evidence suggests that she, not Hemingway, finished the book. Reprinted: 1987.95.

10 BRYER, JACKSON R. Review of *Ernest Hemingway: Selected Letters, 1917-1961. Studies in Short Fiction* 19, no. 3 (Summer): 283-85.

   Considers the collection to be both remarkable and important for the insight it provides on the author, his time, and contemporaries.

11 CAGLE, CHARLES HAEMON. "'Cézanne Nearly Did': Stein, Cézanne, and Hemingway." *Midwest Quarterly* 23, no. 3 (Spring): 268-78.

   Provides an overview of what others have written regarding Stein's and Cézanne's influence on Hemingway as well as the author's own thoughts and writings on the subject.

12 CAMATI, ANNA STEGH. "Ritual As Indicative of a Code of Values in Hemingway's *In Our Time*." *Revista Letras* 31:11-25.

   Categorizes Nick Adams of *In Our Time* as an apprentice or code learner who is initiated into a code of values that enable him to live properly in a chaotic world lacking in love and belief.

13 CANDELARIA, CORDELIA. "Literary Fungoes: Allusions to Baseball in Significant American Fiction." *Midwest Quarterly* 23 (Summer): 411-25.

Comments briefly on the pastoral view of baseball presented in *The Old Man and the Sea* that functions as "a touchstone of human perfection and possibility."

14 CARABINE, KEITH. "'Big Two-Hearted River': A Re-Interpretation." *Hemingway Review* 1, no. 2 (Spring): 39-44.

Takes exception with the story's traditional interpretation as "a nightmare at noontide." Carabine argues for a positive reading based on Nick's euphoric pleasure gained from participating in familiar activities.

15 CARTER, RONALD. "Style and Interpretation in Hemingway's 'Cat in the Rain.'" In *Language and Literature: An Introductory Reader in Stylistics*. London: Allen & Unwin, pp. 65-80.

Stylistic analysis of the shifts in linguistic patterning found in the story. Carter focuses on three main areas (nominal group structure; verbal structure; and free indirect speech, and cohesion, repetition, and ambiguity), leading him to conclude that the story deals basically with the frustration of expectation.

16 CLARKE, GRAHAM. "Hemingway in England: Bibliography." *Hemingway Review* 1, no. 2 (Spring): 76-84.

Lists Hemingway's publications, along with selected British reviews, articles, books, and essays, from 1926 through 1981.

17 COCKBURN, ALEXANDER. "Hemingway in Spain." *Village Voice* 27 (7 December): 7.

Prints an excerpt from his father's memoirs detailing a humorous incident involving Hemingway at the Florida Hotel during the Spanish civil war.

18 COLEMAN, ARTHUR. "Hemingway's *The Spanish Earth*." *Hemingway Review* 2, no. 1 (Fall): 64-67.

Concerns Hemingway's narration for the film documentary *The Spanish Earth*. Finds that Hemingway subordinates political issues in favor of a nostalgic view of the war's threat to the Spanish culture and traditional way of life.

19 CULVER, MICHAEL. "'The Short-Stop Run': Hemingway in Kansas City." *Hemingway Review* 2, no. 1 (Fall): 77-80.

Biographical essay drawing on Hemingway letters recently made available by his sister Sunny. The correspondence identifies two unsigned articles, written by Hemingway while a cub reporter for the

Kansas City Star during 1917-18 revealing where he stayed during that time and and also his enlistment in the Missouri National Guard while in Kansas City.

20 DONALDSON, SCOTT. "Ernest Hemingway." In *Dictionary of Literary Biography Yearbook: 1981.* Detroit: Gale Research Co., pp. 89-93.

Review of *Ernest Hemingway: Selected Letters, 1917-1961.* "The letters constitute a kind of biography between the lines and are particularly useful in illuminating Hemingway's young manhood and his last years."

21 _____. "Fitzgerald and Hemingway." In *American Literary Scholarship: An Annual, 1980.* Edited by J. Albert Robbins. Durham, N.C.: Duke University Press, pp. 173-91.

Survey of criticism on both authors published during 1980. Donaldson comments cautiously on the recent trend in scholarship that seems to be pointing away from Fitzgerald and toward Hemingway.

22 _____. "The Wooing of Ernest Hemingway." *American Literature* 53, no. 4 (January): 691-710.

Discusses how Hemingway was won over to Scribner's, detailing his break from Liveright, his relationship with Fitzgerald and Scribner's editor Max Perkins, and the editing and publishing of *The Torrents of Spring, The Sun Also Rises,* and "Fifty Grand."

23 DONNELL, DAVID. *Hemingway in Toronto: A Post-Modern Tribute.* Windsor, Ontario: Black Moss Press, 61 pp.

Chronicles the four months Hemingway worked at the *Toronto Star* late in 1923, just prior to returning to Paris and serious writing. Considers this experience at such a formative time crucial to Hemingway's subsequent success as a writer. "Hemingway disliked the Toronto experience but he learned more about how to write while he was here. The syntax changed and the structure of the sentence changed, the economy increased and the generalized point of view became more exact and specific. . . ."

24 DONNELLY, HONORIA MURPHY. *Sara and Gerald.* New York: Times Books, pp. 20-26, 112-15, 134-36, 163-81, etc.

Frequent references to Hemingway and his long relationship with the Murphys.

25 FITTS, BILL D. "'The Battler': Lexical Foregrounding in Hemingway." *Language and Literature* 7, no. 1-3:81-92.

Focuses on Hemingway's systematic use of lexical patterns in order to create cohesion not only in "The Battler" but throughout the text of *In Our Time*. Concludes that life is presented as a series of battles ending in death:"... the swamp, the bullring, the courtyard, the trench, the top of the boxcar, or the hobo campfire – will eventually triumph over man."

26 FLORA, JOSEPH M. *Hemingway's Nick Adams*. Baton Rouge: Louisiana State University Press, 285 pp.

Looks at the stories as a whole, arranging them according to the stages of Nick's life rather than date of publication. Flora puts them in the context of Hemingway's life and writing, emphasizing a unity based on the bildungsroman – Nick's initiation from innocence to experience to eventual acceptance and recovery. Includes Michigan maps detailing significant settings and a Nick Adams chronology.

27 FRIBERG, INGEGERD. "The Reflection in the Mirror: An Interpretation of Hemingway's Short Story 'Cat in the Rain.'" *Moderna Sprak* 76, no. 4:329-38.

Combines linguistic and literary analysis in order to show how the central image of the reflection in the mirror brings out the theme of the repetitiveness of life.

28 GAJDUSEK, ROBERT E. "Dubliners in Michigan: Joyce's Presence in Hemingway's *In Our Time*." *Hemingway Review* 2, no. 1 (Fall): 48-61.

Treats Joyce's "considerable" literary influence on Hemingway, pointing out parallel themes, metaphors, and patterns. Contends that both authors share a common view of the condition of the world which they record in their writings.

29 GELFANT, BLANCHE. "The Hidden Mines in Ethel Wilson's Landscape." *Canadian Literature*, no. 93 (Summer), pp. 4-23.

Brief comparison of Wilson's *Hetty Dorval* with *In Our Time*, noting both authors' preoccupation with style, irony, omission, and the themes of humanity's vulnerability in the natural world and desire to lead an uncomplicated existence.

30 GIBSON, ANDREW. "Hemingway on the British." *Hemingway Review* 1, no. 2 (Spring): 62-75.

Looks at Hemingway's ambivalent attitudes toward the British in his writings and his creation of British characters. Hemingway valued the British for their coolness and reserve yet suspected that beneath the reserve lay a "lack of warmth" and a "craven reluctance to face up to coarseness, brutality, and horror."

31 GIVNER, JOAN. *Katherine Anne Porter, A Life*. New York: Simon & Schuster, pp. 203, 398, etc.

Scattered references to Hemingway (mention of Hemingway's comment that a writer writes better when in love; references to his importance as a writer; others).

32 GULLASON, THOMAS A. "The Short Story: Revision and Renewal." *Studies in Short Fiction* 19, no. 3 (Summer): 221-30.

Argues against Norman Friedman's 1958 essay describing "Hills Like White Elephants" as a "static" short story. Instead, Gullason contends that Hemingway's skillful rendering of a "brief conversation and a few gestures can reflect the entire life of a relationship."

33 HEYEN, WILLIAM, and PICCIONE, ANTHONY. "The Shine of the World: A Conversation with Archibald MacLeish." *Massachusetts Review* 23, no. 4 (Winter): 703-4.

MacLeish recites a poem written after Hemingway's suicide that begins with a quotation from Mary Hemingway regarding the circumstances of the author's death.

34 HINKLE, JIM. "Note on Importance of Reading Aloud." *Hemingway Newsletter*, no. 4, p. 4.

Contends that by reading aloud the passage in which Brett enters with a group of homosexuals, one will discover from the built-in tone of voice that Robert Prentiss is also homosexual.

35 ____. "Note on Two-Timin' at Zelli's." *Hemingway Newsletter*, no. 4, p. 3.

Identifies the song being sung by the drummer at Zelli's in *The Sun Also Rises* as a version of the 1923 "Aggravatin' Papa (Don't You Try to Two-Time Me)." Considers, among other interpretations, the relevance of the lyrics in light of Jake's relationship with Brett.

36 ____. "Seeing through It in *A Farewell to Arms*." *Hemingway Review* 2, no. 1 (Fall): 94-95.

Identifies the book that Count Greffi recommends to Henry as H.G. Wells's 1916 *Mr. Britling Sees It Through*. Discusses the significance of Wells's novel in trying to make sense of their subsequent conversation.

37 ____. Some Unexpected Sources for *The Sun Also Rises*." *Hemingway Review* 2, no. 1 (Fall): 26-42.

Contends that Hemingway consciously and unconsciously echoed other contemporary writers in his novel, pointing out nearly sixty examples from George Ade to Edgar Lee Masters. See also 1984.26.

38 HURLEY, C. HAROLD. "The Manuscript and the Dialogue of

'A Clean, Well-Lighted Place': A Response to Warren Bennett."
Hemingway Review 2, no. 1 (Fall): 17-20.

Takes exception with Bennett's interpretation (see 1979.7) of the
much-disputed dialogue, arguing that Hemingway intended the waiters
to be distinct characters. Attributes the lines expressing concern for the
soldier being picked up by the guard to the old waiter.

39 HYDE, ELIZABETH WALDEN. "Aficionado Fishes Worms: A Study
of Hemingway and Jake." *American Fly Fisher* 9, no. 2 (Spring): 2-7.

After an examination of Hemingway's previous references to
fishing in articles and stories, Hyde contends that the author's limited
knowledge of fly-fishing should not detract from the symbolic
significance of the Burguete fishing scene. "We must see in Jake's worm
the thing that it is, a graphic symbol of impotence, and in his actions as
in his life, the incomplete angler, the incomplete man."

40 ISERNHAGEN, HARTWIG. "'A Constitutional Inability to Say Yes':
Thorstein Veblen, the Reconstruction Program of the *Dial*, and the
Development of American Modernism after World War I." *REAL:
Yearbook of Research in English and American Literature* 1:153-90.

Looks at the development of the *Dial*, its changing directions
during and after World War I, and its influence on American
modernism. Suggests that "the modernist image of man is
anthropological by intention and by method: it tries to define man in the
abstract and identifies him with Original or Natural Man, and it
proceeds from there to an analysis of Historical Man." Isernhagen sees
the process reversed in the fiction of the twenties, listing Hemingway's
hunters, fishermen, and bullfighters as prime examples.

41 JACOBSON, NOLAN PLINY. "A Buddhistic-Christian Probe of the
Endangered Future." *Eastern Buddhist* 15, no. 1 (Spring): 38-55.

Concludes briefly that "Hemingway *lived* the self-destructive self,"
arguing that the author, in his "pathological individualism," was unable
to reach beyond his own self-centeredness to the vividness and intensity
of true life experience.

42 *John F. Kennedy Library Catalog of the Ernest Hemingway Collection*. 2
vols. Boston: G.K. Hall, 1:673; 2:751.

A descriptive listing and catalogue of all materials available to
researchers as of September 1981, including manuscripts, typescripts,
photographs, correspondence, and newspaper clippings.

43 JOHNSTON, KENNETH G. "'Hills Like White Elephants': Lean,
Vintage Hemingway." *Studies in American Fiction* 10, no. 2 (Autumn):
233-38.

Analyzes how the setting, theme, and characterization blend to create "a taut, tense story of conflict in a moral wasteland." Johnston points out that in the Kennedy Library manuscripts, the girl was originally named Hadley. Reprinted with slight revision: 1987.38.

44 _____. "'The Killers': The Background and the Manuscripts." *Studies in Short Fiction* 19, no. 3 (Summer): 247-51.
Discusses the evolving manuscript drafts of the story (at one point entitled "The Matadors"). Reprinted: 1987.38.

45 _____. "'The Three-Day Blow': Tragicomic Aftermath of a Summer Romance." *Hemingway Review* 2, no. 1:21-25.
Draws on biographical data in addition to tracking down the significance of the references to Meredith's *The Ordeal of Richard Feverel*, Hewlett's *The Forest Lovers*, Walpole's *Fortitude*, and the Black Sox scandal in his explication of Nick's tragicomic disillusionment with young love. Reprinted: 1987.38.

46 JOSEPHS, ALLEN. "*Death in the Afternoon*: A Reconsideration." *Hemingway Review* 2, no. 1 (Fall): 2-16.
Begins with an overview of the mixed critical reception of the novel. Claims that an understanding of Hemingway's vision of the *toreo* (bullfight) both as a paradigm for the code of grace under pressure and as an archetypal ritual is essential to our understanding the rest of the Hemingway canon.

47 KERNER, DAVID. "Fitzgerald vs. Hemingway: The Origins of Anti-Metronomic Dialogue." *Modern Fiction Studies* 28, no. 2 (Summer): 247-50.
Replies to Raymond Nelson's response (see *MFS* 1981 28, no. 2) to Kerner's essay (see 1979.56) regarding Hemingway's innovative use of antimetronomic dialogue. Nelson's pointing to Fitzgerald's use of the device simply reinforces Kerner's argument that Hemingway deliberately adapted the technique to his own writing.

48 _____. "The Manuscripts Establishing Hemingway's Anti-Metronomic Dialogue." *American Literature* 54, no. 3 (October): 385-96.
From a close manuscript study of the forty other passages using antimetronomic dialogue, Kerner argues that Hemingway intentionally attributed two consecutive lines to the same character in "A Clean, Well-Lighted Place."

49 KRILE, IVO. "On a Sentence in Ernest Hemingway's Novel *A Farewell to Arms*." *Studia Romanica et Anglica Zagrabiensia* 27:93-100.

Detailed stylistic analysis of one sentence from chapter 7 in which Frederic envisions an intimate encounter with Catherine in a Milan hotel. Focuses on the author's manipulation of the "and" connector in order to achieve a balanced unity of form and sense within the structure of the text.

50 LEWIS, ROBERT W. "Hemingway, Ernest." In *Encyclopedia of World Literature in the 20th Century*. Edited by Leonard S. Klein. New York: Ungar, pp. 353-59.

Provides an overview of Hemingway's life and works, including selected excerpts from such well-known Hemingway critics and scholars as Edmund Wilson, Earl Rovit, and Carlos Baker.

51 _____. "Hemingway in Italy: Making It Up." *Journal of Modern Literature* 9, no. 2 (May): 209-36.

Biographical approach examining Hemingway's war experiences in Italy and their fictional transcription in *A Farewell to Arms*. Unearths a number of official Italian documents in order to set the record straight regarding Hemingway's wounding and subsequent decoration. Cites G.M. Trevelyan's *Scenes from Italy's War* as a probable additional source for the novel.

52 LUKACS, PAUL. "The Hemingway Letters." *Salmagundi*, no. 57, pp. 172-80.

Negative review of *Ernest Hemingway: Selected Letters, 1917-1961*. Disappointed with both the length and selection of letters, Lukacs writes "so many hold little interest for either general reader or the Hemingway scholar."

53 MAILER, NORMAN. In *Pieces and Pontifications*. Boston: Little, Brown & Co.

Pp. 86-93: "Miller and Hemingway." Adapted from *Genius and Lust*, New York: Grove Press, 1976.

Pp. 94-96: "Papa & Son." See 1976.36.

54 MANN, ANN FERGUSON. "Taking Care of Walter Mitty." *Studies in Short Fiction* 19, no. 4 (Fall): 351-57.

Briefly points out similarities between the traditional Hemingway hero and Thurber's Walter Mitty. Both authors, with their pessimistic worldviews, depict a hostile environment intent on destroying but ultimately not defeating their protagonists.

55 MARIANI, JOHN. "Papa's Pleasures: Drinks at Sea." *Motor Boat & Sailing* 150 (September): 26, 29-30.

Discusses Hemingway's taste in and capacity for alcohol, even including the author's Bloody Mary recipe.

56 MASSA, ANN. "Ernest Hemingway." In *American Literature in Context, IV 1900-1930*. New York: Methuen, pp. 155-70.

Reprints the final scene of *The Sun Also Rises*, offering a critical interpretation aimed at giving students a sense of how this extract fits in with the rest of the novel and the author's oeuvre. Includes a discussion of the Lost Generation, the Hemingway code, and his iceberg theory of writing.

57 MAST, GERALD. "Hemingway and Chandler into Bogart-Bacall and Hawks: *To Have and Have Not* and *The Big Sleep*." In *Howard Hawks, Storyteller*. New York: Oxford, pp. 243-95.

Discusses the translation of Hemingway's novel into cinema, looking at script drafts, structure, camera strategies, political issues, and the Bogart-Bacall relationship. Sees the film's two basic narrative strands to be Harry's love for Marie and his friendship with Eddie. Suggests that "although Hawks's narrative bears little resemblance to Hemingway's there is an unmistakable Hemingway aroma and flavor about the film."

58 MEYERS, JEFFREY. *Hemingway: The Critical Heritage*. Boston: Routledge & Kegan Paul, 661 pp.

Collection of more than 100 "significant" reviews and essays by both critics and novelists, including Lionel Trilling, Edmund Wilson, F. Scott Fitzgerald, and John Dos Passos. Entries are arranged chronologically and subdivided according to individual works. Meyers's introduction traces the evolving patterns and trends that make up Hemingway's critical reputation both prior to and after his death. At times, Meyers either argues against or defends the critical reception of particular works.

59 ____. "Wallace Stevens and 'The Short Happy Life of Francis Macomber.'" *American Notes & Queries* 21, no. 3-4 (November-December): 47-49.

Suggests that the 1936 fight between Hemingway and Stevens influenced his short story about a man's cowardly flight and his later shameful attempts at covering it up.

60 MEYERSON, ROBERT E. "Why Robert Cohn? An Analysis of Hemingway's *The Sun Also Rises*." *Liberal and Fine Arts Review* 2, no. 1:57-68.

Considers Hemingway's negative treatment of the Jewish Robert Cohn to be a deliberate move to strengthen the sentimental aspects of the novel and focus on a subject the author felt infinitely more worthy of historical sentimentality–the Lost Generation. "... the most coveted niche in the pantheon of suffering is already occupied by the all-time scapegoat: the Jewish people. Hemingway had to remove the Jewish bust from this niche in order to make room for his replacement: the Lost Generation."

61 MONTEIRO, GEORGE. "Grover Cleveland Alexander in 1918: A New Kansas City Piece by Ernest Hemingway." *American Literature* 54, no. 1 (March): 116-18.
    Reprints unsigned 1918 *Star* article, attributing it to Hemingway on the basis of a letter he wrote to his father.

62 ____. "A Missing Review." *Hemingway Review* 2 (Fall): 76.
    Possible addendum to Hanneman. Cites an unverified review of *To Have and Have Not* by Evelyn Waugh that may have appeared in *Night and Day* (1937).

63 MONTEITH, MOIRA. "A Change in Emphasis: Hemingway Criticism in Britain over the Last Twenty-Five Years." *Hemingway Review* 1, no. 2:2-19.
    Survey of critical attitudes over the past twenty-five years. Concerned with ascertaining Hemingway's position within the tradition of American literature and his influence on and relationships with other writers and literary movements. Quotes liberally from a variety of critics and reviewers.

64 MORTON, BRUCE. "Hemingway's 'The Short Happy Life of Francis Macomber.'" *Explicator* 41, no. 1 (Fall): 48-49.
    Suggests that Hemingway modeled Macomber after Fitzgerald in retaliation for his 1936 "crack-up" articles that Hemingway wanted no part of but felt overtly linked to.

65 ____. "Macomber and Fitzgerald: Hemingway Gets Even in 'The Short Happy Life of Francis Macomber.'" *Zeitschrift für Anglistik und Amerikanistik* 30, no. 2:157-60.
    Adds to the argument that Hemingway "was drawing a bead on Fitzgerald in his rendition of the character of Francis Macomber." Citing similarities in name, circumstance, and marital relations, Morton concludes that Hemingway is retaliating against Fitzgerald's publishing of three "confessional" articles in *Esquire*, the second of which alluded directly to Hemingway.

66 ORIARD, MICHAEL V. *Dreaming of Heroes: American Sports Fiction,
    1868-1980*. Chicago: Nelson-Hall, pp. 10-11, 16, 21, 46, 55, 85, 99-101,
    158-59, etc.
       Many references to Hemingway. Comments briefly on how the
    Hemingway code of "grace under pressure" functions in "Fifty Grand."
    Considers the story to be not an indictment of boxing but an "indictment
    of those who take boxing to be in any way romantic."

67 PETRY, ALICE HALL. "Hemingway's 'The Light of the World.'"
    Explicator 40, no. 3 (Spring): 46.
       Referring to the *Dictionary of American Slang*, Petry claims that
    "C" and "M" stand for cocaine and morphine.

68 PORTCH, STEPHEN R. "The Hemingway Touch." *Hemingway Review*
    2, no. 1 (Fall): 43-47.
       Treats both Hemingway's use of nonverbal cues and extended
    silence to convey meaning in "Hills Like White Elephants" and "The
    Killers."

69 REYNOLDS, MICHAEL S. Review of *Ernest Hemingway: Selected
    Letters, 1917-1961*. *American Literature* 54:119-20.
       Positive review praising Baker's editing of the collection.
    Discovers in the more than 900 pages the real Hemingway beneath the
    mask.

70 ROBERTS, JOHN S. "*The Old Man and the Sea* in the Classroom."
    Indiana English 5:4-8.
       Offers several approaches to teaching the novel such as locating
    its place in the American literary tradition, exploring its religious design,
    and comparing it with earlier Hemingway works.

71 RUBIN, LOUIS D., Jr. "Hemingway and His Correspondence."
    Sewanee Review 90, no. 1 (Winter): 167-69.
       Finds the collection worthwhile for what it reveals about the man,
    myth, and writer.

72 SCHOLES, ROBERT. "Decoding Papa: 'A Very Short Story' as Word
    and Text." In *Semiotics and Interpretation*. New Haven: Yale University
    Press, pp. 110-26.
       A semiotic study in which Scholes explores the implications of the
    text-diegesis relationship of "A Very Short Story." Concludes in his
    biographical assessment that Hemingway's text "responds to a double
    motivation. It wants to be art, to be a work that is complete in itself. But
    it also wants to rewrite life, to make its surrogate protagonist more

triumphant as a lover, more active as a soldier, and more deeply victimized as a man than was the author himself."

73 SCHÖNFELDER, KARL-HEINZ. "Ernest Hemingway and Cuba." *Zeitschrift für Anglistik und Amerikanistik* 30, no. 1:5-14.
   Follows Hemingway's love for and time spent in Cuba. Emphasis on Cuba's political upheavals and the author's responses to them.

74 SHECHNER, MARK. "Papa." *Partisan Review* 49, no. 2:213-23.
   Considers the publication of *Ernest Hemingway: Selected Letters, 1917-1961* (against the author's wishes) to be both dishonorable and damaging. "They portray him as a tiresome braggart, a malicious adversary who heaped scorn on nearly everyone he knew, a racist and anti-Semite, and a shallow and boring correspondent who wrote many of his letters – maybe most of them – when too drunk to write fiction."

75 SMITH, PAUL. "Almost All Is Vanity: A Note on Nine Rejected Titles for *A Farewell to Arms*." *Hemingway Review* 2, no. 1 (Fall): 74-76.
   Lists nine more of Hemingway's tentative titles for *A Farewell to Arms*, all taken from Ecclesiastes.

76 SPANIER, SANDRA WHIPPLE. "Hemingway's 'The Last Good Country' and *The Catcher in the Rye*: More Than a Family Resemblance." *Studies in Short Fiction* 19, no. 1 (Winter): 35-43.
   A comparison of the two works yields similarities in character, plot, setting, and theme – the American romantic tradition of man's escape from corrupt civilization. Spanier suggests that "The Last Good Country" was influenced greatly by Salinger's earlier novel and that perhaps Hemingway left his manuscript unfinished because "he realized he was coming awfully close to a story that had already been written."

77 SPILKA, MARK. "Hemingway and Fauntleroy: An Androgynous Pursuit." In *American Novelists Revisited: Essays in Feminist Criticism*. Edited by Fritz Fleischman. Boston: G.K. Hall, pp. 339-70.
   Looks at the influence that growing up in an androgynous household had on both the author's later personal life and his writing. Points to androgynous strains throughout the Hemingway canon, from *The Sun Also Rises* to "The Last Good Country." Spilka contends that despite the chauvinist conception of women in Hemingway's works, "the familiar 'bitches' and 'dream girls' of his fiction become androgynous alternatives (destructive and redemptive) rather than chauvinist fantasies, and his strenuous defense of maleness becomes part of a larger struggle with his own androgynous impulses rather than a sustained form of homosexual panic."

78 STETLER, CHARLES, and LOCKLIN, GERALD. "Beneath the Tip of the Iceberg in Hemingway's 'The Mother of a Queen.'" *Hemingway Review* 2, no. 1 (Fall): 68-69.

Sees the shrewish Roger as taking on the role of surrogate mother to the homosexual bullfighter. Perceives the story to be "an attack upon the worse aspects of motherhood as represented by *both* mothers of the Queen."

79 STUBBS, MICHAEL. "Stir until the Plot Thickens." In *Literary Text and Language Study*. Edited by Ronald Carter and Deirdre Burton. London: Arnold, pp. 56-85.

Seeks to develop a methodology for analyzing narrative structures by testing the competence of schoolteachers and university students and lecturers to summarize the plot of "Cat in the Rain." Finds that the summaries emphasize Hemingway's use of ambiguity and implication.

80 TANNER, TONY. "Ernest Hemingway's Unhurried Sensations." *Hemingway Review* 1, no. 2 (Spring): 20-38.

Reprint from *The Reign of Wonder: Nativity and Reality in American Literature* (Cambridge: Cambridge University Press, 1965).

81 TOWNSEND, BEN. "Pearls from Papa." *Writer's Digest* 62 (October): 21.

Excerpts from *Ernest Hemingway: Selected Letters, 1917-1961*, dealing mainly with the craft of writing.

82 VAN ANTWERP, MARGARET A., ed. *Dictionary of Literary Biography Documentary Series: An Illustrated Chronicle*. Vol 1. Detroit: Gale Research Co., pp. 291-360.

Lists major works and biographies, and includes photographs spanning Hemingway's life. Reprints the author's "American Bohemians in Paris a Weird Lot" written while Hemingway was a foreign correspondent for the Toronto *Star Weekly* in 1922. Also includes contemporary book reviews of Hemingway's major works by such well-known authors and critics as Gertrude Stein, Edmund Wilson, F. Scott Fitzgerald, Conrad Aiken, and Alfred Kazin as well as interviews with Harvey Breit and George Plimpton. Tributes following his death by Archibald MacLeish, William Faulkner, Robert Frost, Lillian Hellman, and others are reprinted.

83 VIJGEN, THEO. "A Change of Point of View in Hemingway's 'Big Two-Hearted River.'" *Notes on Modern American Literature* 6, no. 1 (Spring-Summer): item 5.

Notes the narrative shift from limited omniscience to interior monologue in the passage where Nick has lost the big trout, arguing that as emotions ebb, the author reverts to limited omniscience in order to demonstrate Nick's movement once again toward emotional stability.

84 WALDHORN, ARTHUR. "Harold Loeb's Ants." *Hemingway Review* 2, no. 1 (Fall): 86-87.

Traces Hemingway's ant passage in *A Farewell to Arms* back to a similar ant metaphor in Harold Loeb's *The Professors Like Vodka* written two years prior.

85 WALSH, JEFFREY. "Emblematical of War: Representation of Combat in Hemingway's Fiction." *Hemingway Review* 1, no. 2 (Spring): 45-56.

Looks at how Hemingway reconstituted the traditional literary representation of warfare in much of his fiction, including *A Farewell to Arms* and *For Whom the Bell Tolls*. Hemingway sought to bring war into an authentic light, defamiliarized and unglorified.

86 ____. "Two Modernist War Novels." In *American War Literature, 1914 to Vietnam*. New York: St. Martin's Press, pp. 41-58.

Concludes that despite differences in style and language usage, both E.E. Cummings in *The Enormous Room* and Hemingway in *A Farewell to Arms* engage the modernist tenet of "breaking down in order to rebuild" and use regenerative and innovative language to counter their subject – war. "In war, their works seems to imply, historical energies bear down upon individual men and women curtailing potentialities for communal relationship and productive social interchange."

Pp. 95-111: "Hemingway and Bessie: Education in Spain." Argues that "Jordan's political reflections are essentially anti-fascist and Republican rather than Communist." Traces Jordan's "political apprenticeship," seeing the major educative force to be love, both in his solidarity with the loyalist band and with Maria.

Pp. 112-51: "Second World War Fiction: Alienation and Group Identity." Examination of Cantwell's psychological condition along with a look at the military ambiance that pervades *Across the River and Into the Trees*. Argues that the ex-general "subsumes two diametrically opposed facets of the American military ethos, a hostility towards professional soldiery and its antithesis, an involvement in the mystique and dignity supposedly conferred by war."

87 WATSON, WILLIAM B. "Discovering Hemingway's *Pravda* Article." *Washington Post*, 28 November, pp. F1, 13.

Watson writes of the drawn-out process of identifying and verifying Hemingway's propaganda piece on the Spanish civil war. See 1982.88.

88 ____. "Humanity Will Not Forgive This!" *Washington Post*, 28 November, pp. F1, 15.

Reprints in English Hemingway's article on the Spanish civil war published originally on 1 August 1938 in *Pravda*.

89 WEEKS, ROBERT P. "Wise-Guy Narrator and Trickster Out-Tricked in Hemingway's 'Fifty Grand.'" *Studies in American Fiction* 10, no. 1 (Spring): 83-91.

Looks at the story's innovative point of view and the author's adaptation of the humorous tradition of the trickster out-tricked. Points to the early "A Matter of Colour" as a preliminary version of the story.

90 WHITE, WILLIAM. "For the Collector: Hebrew Translator of *The Old Man and the Sea*." *Hemingway Review* 2 (Fall): 16.

Clarifies that the Hebrew edition of *The Old Man and the Sea* was translated by Yitschak Shenhar who also goes by the literary name Ehud Rabin.

91 ____. "Have You Read This One?" *Hemingway Review* 1, no. 2 (Spring): 57.

Points out that the narrator of Donald Hamilton's *Line of Fire* (1955) is modeled in part after Barnes in *The Sun Also Rises*.

92 ____. "Hemingway: A Current Bibliography." *Hemingway Review* 2, no. 1:90-94.

Recent items, including articles, books, reviews, new editions, and translations.

93 ____. "Imitation Hemingway Contest: 5." *Hemingway Review* 2 (Fall): 88-89.

Reprints the winning entry in the Fifth International Imitation Hemingway Competition, "Arriba Y Abajo" by Walter N. Trenerry. Parody at its best (or worst).

94 ____. "'Manner' and 'Fact'; Attributed to 'E. Hemingway.'" *Papers of the Bibliographical Society* 76, no. 3:350.

Identifies two incomplete items listed in Michael Reynolds's *Hemingway's Reading 1910-1940: An Inventory* as a German translation of *Men without Women* (Manner) and the London periodical *Fact*.

95 WICKES, GEORGE. Review of *Ernest Hemingway: Selected Letters, 1917-1961. Modern Fiction Studies* 28, no. 2 (Summer): 292-94.

Mixed review. Wishes Baker had been more selective in his choice of letters but admits the portrait they present of their author "is far more revealing than Baker's biography, for which they provided much of the documentation."

96 WINNICK, ROY H. "Archibald MacLeish: Selected Letters." *Paris Review* 24, no. 84 (Summer): 104-44.
    Reprint of selected correspondence from *Letters of Archibald MacLeish, 1907 to 1982*, including several to Hemingway.

1983

1 ADAIR, WILLIAM. "Ernest Hemingway and the Poetics of Loss." *College Literature* 10 (Fall): 294-306.
    Reprint of 1978.2.

2 ALDRIDGE, JOHN. W. *The American Novel and the Way We Live Now*. New York: Oxford University Press, 166 pp.
    Aldridge assesses a somewhat later period but comments in retrospect on Hemingway as, with Fitzgerald, a writer who needed assurance that finding "moral and emotional authenticity" was possible. To compensate for the loss of surety, both writers "were so continuously preoccupied with procedural questions, with the effort to formulate dependable rules of feeling and conduct" (149-50). Numerous references to Hemingway.

3 ALLEN, MARY. "The Integrity of Animals: Ernest Hemingway." In *Animals in American Literature*. Urbana: University of Illinois Press, pp. 177-96.
    Overview of Hemingway's wide and varied use of animals and animal imagery, from the blackened grasshoppers of "Big-Two-Hearted River" to the bulls, horses, and fish of *The Sun Also Rises*, *For Whom the Bell Tolls*, and *The Old Man and the Sea*. Allen comments on the aesthetic and ethical values attached to hunting as well as the heroic ideal and the notion of bravery in the face of death as applied both to hunter and prey.

4 ATLAS, JAMES. "Papa Lives." *Atlantic Monthly* 252, no. 40 (October): 114-20.
    Writes of Hemingway's enduring popularity on the occasion of Scribner's reissuing of four of the author's classics – *The Sun Also Rises*, *A Farewell to Arms*, *For Whom the Bell Tolls*, and *The Old Man and the Sea*. Comments on the unevenness of Hemingway's prose – sometimes soaring eloquently and collapsing into maudlin self-indulgence on the same page. Discusses the author's legendary status and eventual decline.

5 BAKKER, J. *Fiction as Survival Strategy: A Comparative Study of the Major Works of Ernest Hemingway and Saul Bellow*. Rodopi, Amsterdam: Costerus, 220 pp.

Chapters on early heroes, the search for self, the search for a philosophy, the hero as dupe, the heroes in middle age and old age, and the artist as hero. Treatment of Hemingway's work does not change greatly from his 1972 *Ernest Hemingway: The Artist as Man of Action* (Assen, the Netherlands: Van Gorcum & Co.). Does include *Islands in the Stream*, which the earlier study did not. Concludes that both writers were fascinated by the problem of identity and the fictionist's role in creating characters who puzzle after it. Sees Hemingway as a proponent of the American West, the hero who finds himself in nature, not civilization – an existential character, like Cooper's Leatherstocking.

6 BALBERT, PETER. "From Hemingway to Lawrence to Mailer: Survival and Sexual Identity in *A Farewell to Arms*." *Hemingway Review* 3, no. 1 (Fall): 30-43.

Primarily centered on "how Frederic Henry's practical, soldierly, but delimiting brand of merely 'survivalist' ideology is broadened and enriched, under the influence of Catherine Barkley, to become a courageous commitment to love, life, and family responsibility."

7 BEEGEL, SUSAN. "Note in Answer to Query on 'Natural History.'" *Hemingway Notes* 6 (July): 3.

Responds to an earlier inquiry regarding the blinding of the lieutenant in "A Natural History of the Dead." After analyzing the medical treatment described, Beegel's physician feels that Hemingway intended the situation to be ambiguous.

8 BEEVOR, ANTONY. *The Spanish Civil War*. London: Orbis, 320 pp.

Scattered references to Hemingway (74, 140, 149, 178) and to *For Whom the Bell Tolls*.

9 BIER, JESSE. "Don't Nobody Move – This Is a Sticho-Mythia (or an Unfinal Word on Typography in Hemingway)." *Hemingway Review* 3, no. 1 (Fall): 61-63.

Renews the controversy over dialogue in "A Clean, Well-Lighted Place" by pointing out a similar mislineation of dialogue in *Islands in the Stream*.

10 ____. "Jake Barnes, Cockroaches, and Trout in *The Sun Also Rises*." *Arizona Quarterly* 39, no. 2 (Summer): 164-71.

Argues that Jake's impotence is psychological and moral as well as physical. Although Jake's is the central consciousness, he is not the hero of the novel.

11 BRADBURY, MALCOLM. "Art-Style and Life-Style: The 1920s." In *The Modern American Novel*. New York: Oxford University Press, pp. 57-95.

Discusses the social and cultural milieu of the postwar 1920s and the expatriate movement in Paris. Looks at several authors' contributions to American modernism, including Hemingway's. Gives a brief introduction to Hemingway's innovative style along with a thematic overview of his canon, paying attention to psychic trauma, stoic consciousness, and the code hero.

12 BREDAHL, A. CARL. "Divided Narrative and Ernest Hemingway." *Literary Half-Yearly* 24, no. 1 (January): 15-21.

Describes the function of the divided narrative in relation to Hemingway's *In Our Time*, *A Farewell to Arms*, and *Green Hills of Africa*, looking at the themes of life and death and rejection of the illusory division between life and death.

13 BRENNER, GERRY. *Concealments in Hemingway's Works*. Columbus: Ohio State University Press, 279 pp.

Revisionist reading of Hemingway and his writing. Combining psychoanalytic, generic, and New Critical approaches, Brenner explores the five phases of Hemingway's writing career (thesis, aesthetic, Aristotelian, imitative, and antithetical) in the light of three theses: Hemingway was an experimental author until the fifties; his goal was to conceal both the artist and the art behind a facade of simplicity; and he was "father-fixated" and latently homoerotic.

14 BUTTERFIELD, HERBIE. "Ernest Hemingway." In *American Fiction: New Readings*. Edited by Richard Gray. Totowa, N.J.: Barnes & Noble, pp. 184-99.

Valuative and thematic overview of the Hemingway canon, beginning with *In Our Time* and ending with *The Old Man and the Sea*. Briefly looks at Hemingway's treatment of death, courage and the code hero, male comradeship, separation and isolation, and nature.

15 CAMPBELL, HILBERT H. "Three Unpublished Letters of Alice B. Toklas." *English Language Notes* 20, no. 3-4 (March-June): 47-51.

Toklas comments briefly on Hemingway's suicide in a letter to Eleanor Anderson, the widow of Sherwood Anderson.

16 CHAVKIN, ALLAN. "Fathers and Sons: 'Papa' Hemingway and Saul Bellow." *Papers on Language and Literature* 19:449-60.

Influence study arguing that Bellow's distorted and oversimplified reading of Hemingway's work leads him to reject the "hard-boiled-dom" he finds there in his attempt to break out of Hemingway's oppressive literary shadow.

17   COSGROVE, VINCENT. *The Hemingway Papers: A Novel*. New York: Bantam Books, 192 pp.
      Highly fictionalized account of what happened to the manuscripts that Hadley lost in 1922, as told by Sara Morgan, an old friend of Hemingway's during the 1920s.

18   COWAN, S.A. "Robert Cohn, the Fool of Ecclesiastes in *The Sun Also Rises*." *Dalhousie Review* 63 (Spring): 98-106.
      Argues that Cohn, modeled after the fool of Ecclesiastes, "symbolizes the concept of folly."

19   COX, CHRISTOPHER. *A Key West Companion*. New York: St. Martin's Press, 214 pp.
      Brief biographical sketch of Hemingway's time spent in Key West, mentioning his drinking, his friends, and old haunts such as Sloppy Joe's Bar.

20   DAVIS, RANDALL SCOTT. "A Little More Light." *Hemingway Review* 2, no. 2 (Spring): 65-66.
      Verifies from an article Hemingway wrote in 1938 that the author knew the true circumstances of Ketchel's death and purposely had the whore lie. Davis contends that Hemingway intentionally set the record straight in 1938 in order to protect himself and push critics "toward the real meaning of the story" – Alice's faith and redemption.

21   DEROUNIAN, KATHRYN ZABELLE. "An Examination of the Drafts of Hemingway's Chapter 'Nick Sat against the Wall of the Church. . . .'" *Papers of the Bibliographical Society of America* 77, no. 1:54-65.
      Analyzes three revisions of chapter 6 in *In Our Time*. Finds a gradual concentration upon Nick's experience and deletion of irrelevant details. Reprinted: 1983.98.

22   DEUTELBAUM, MARSHALL. "Showing the Strings That Don't Show: *Mise-en-scène* and Meaning in *To Have and Have Not*." *North Dakota Quarterly* 51, no. 3 (Summer): 61-77.
      Examines Howard Hawks's use of visual elements such as lighting, gesture, costume, and decor to achieve the effect of Hemingway's terse writing style in the film adaptation of *To Have and Have Not*.

23   DEVINE, KATHLEEN. "Alun Lewis's 'A Fragment.'" *Poetry Wales* 19, no. 1:37-43.

Finds thematic echoes of *For Whom the Bell Tolls* in both the short story "They Came" and the poem "A Fragment."

24 DONALDSON, SCOTT. "Fitzgerald and Hemingway." In *American Literary Scholarship: An Annual, 1981*. Edited by James Woodress. Durham, N.C.: Duke University Press, pp. 171-80.

Survey of criticism on both authors published during 1981. Donaldson declares Baker's publication of selected Hemingway letters the "major news" for the year.

25 _____. "Woolf vs. Hemingway." *Journal of Modern Literature* 10 (June): 338-42.

Concerned with Woolf's unfavorable 1927 review of *The Sun Also Rises* and *Men without Women* in which she criticizes Hemingway's subject, style, and approach. Also includes Hemingway's counterattack in correspondence to Maxwell Perkins.

26 "Dr. Bowdler Is Back." *National Review* 35, no. 16 (19 August): 984.

Blames Hemingway's sagging reputation on militant women who view his sexual politics as offensive.

27 DUFFEY, BERNARD I. Review of *Ernest Hemingway: Selected Letters, 1917-1961*. *South Atlantic Quarterly* 82, no. 4 (Autumn): 455.

Favorable review. "What emerges from them [the letters] is abundant in the background it affords to the career of an important author, but beyond that their more than 900 pages gather up the whole fabric of a life lived in unceasingly intricate participation."

28 DUKE, DAVID C. "Swords and Ploughshares: Hemingway and Dos Passos in Spain." In *Distant Obligations: Modern American Writers and Foreign Causes*. New York: Oxford University Press, pp. 165-97.

Explores Hemingway's growing friendship with Dos Passos and the eventual breakdown of that friendship. Looks at their active commitment to the Loyalist cause during the Spanish Civil War, their disagreements over that war, and their further disagreements over the filming of the documentary *The Spanish Earth* and the execution of Jose Robles.

29 EDGERTON, LARRY. "'Nobody Ever Dies!': Hemingway's *Fifth* Story of the Spanish Civil War." *Arizona Quarterly* 39, no. 2 (Summer): 135-47.

Close analysis of the story's circular structure, characterization, symbolism (laurel trees and mockingbird), and themes (love and death). Argues that at times the author crosses the thin line into parody.

30 EDMONDS, DALE. "How Now, Bocanegra? Jake's Bull in the Afternoon." *Notes on Modern American Literature* 7, no. 2 (Fall): item 10.

Establishes Bocanegra, Romero's second bull in the ring, as the sixth and final bull of the afternoon and not the third, as Jake states.

31 EVANS, GARRETT. "Laughing Wildly in the Ocean's Spray." *Communiqué* 8, no. 1:44-48.

Uneven overview of the author's contribution to American literature.

32 FICKERT, KURT J. "The Theme of a Separate Peace in Uwe Johnson's *Zwei Ansichten*." *International Fiction Review* 10, no. 2 (Summer): 104-7.

Compares *Zwei Ansichten* (1965) with *A Farewell to Arms*, pointing out similarities in style, characterization, and the theme of a separate peace. Argues that Johnson is not consciously imitating Hemingway but that the earlier novel serves as a paradigm in contemporary literature.

33 FIELD, JOHN. "Tell No Secrets." *Times Higher Education Supplement* (London), no. 544 (8 April), p. 12.

Mentions the relative ease of obtaining access to Hemingway's FBI file in comparison to obtaining similar documents on George Orwell from British authorities.

34 "Fifty Years On: *The Torrents of Spring*." *Times Literary Supplement*, no. 4174 (1 April), p. 326.

Reprints a favorable review of *The Torrents of Spring* appearing in *TLS* in 1933 in which the reviewer points out not only Hemingway's parody of Anderson but of himself as well.

35 FITCH, NOEL RILEY. *Sylvia Beach and the Lost Generation*. New York: W.W. Norton, 446 pp.

Many references to Hemingway, particularly in relation to Beach (117, 147-48, 389-90, others), to Fitzgerald (190-91), and to Stein (119-20) and in regard to his life both as a writer and as a person.

36 FLEISSNER, ROBERT F. "Hemingway's 'The Short Happy Life of Francis Macomber.'" *Explicator* 41, no. 4 (Summer): 45-47.

Building on Hurley's earlier gloss on Hemingway's "topping" pun (see 1980.42), Fleissner points to further connections with Shakespeare's *Othello*.

37 FLEMING, ROBERT E. "An Early Manuscript of Hemingway's 'Hills Like White Elephants.'" *Notes on Modern American Literature* 7, no. 1 (Spring-Summer): item 3.

Manuscript study reveals the original opening to be a biographical account of Hemingway's train trip through the Ebro valley with wife Hadley who points out the white mountains that later became the short story's title image.

38 ____. "Hemingway and Peele: Chapter I of *A Farewell to Arms.*" *Studies in American Fiction* 11, no. 1 (Spring): 95-100.

Drawing on manuscript materials, Fleming argues that Hemingway revised the opening chapter to contrast ironically with Peele's "A Farewell to Arms."

39 ____. "Hemingway's Dr. Adams: Saint or Sinner?" *Arizona Quarterly* 39, no. 2 (Summer): 101-10.

Original manuscripts of "Ten Indians" reveal that Hemingway "did not intend to depict Nick's father unfavorably but rather as a man who has suffered a good deal and knows that the boy Nickie, who has been living in a child's world where romanticized betrayed lovers suffer from 'broken hearts,' is about to enter adolescence."

40 FORD, RICHARD. "The Three Kings; Hemingway, Faulkner, and Fitzgerald." *Esquire* 100 (December): 577-88.

Ford gives his impressions of the three authors, recounting his own reading of them for the first time and coming to terms with what each was writing about. Reprinted: 1984.28.

41 GILES, JAMES R. "Nick Adams 1983: In the Manner of 'Big Two-Hearted River.'" *Arizona Quarterly* 39:148-55.

Short story written in the Hemingway tradition with a forty-year-old Nick Adams as the protagonist. Giles attempts "to merge the functions of fiction and literary criticism (in essence, to apply Hemingway's values to the realities confronted by a different generation)."

42 GILMOUR, DAVID R. "Hemingway's 'Hills Like White Elephants.'" *Explicator* 41, no. 4 (Summer): 47-49.

Discusses the function of the bamboo bead curtain as a fertility symbol.

43 GINGRICH, ARNOLD. "Coming to Terms with Scott and Ernest: Who Was the Better Writer? Who Was the Better Friend?" *Esquire* 99 (June): 54-64.

Reprint of *Esquire* 66 (December 1966): 322-25.

44 GODDEN, RICHARD. "'You've Got to See It, Feel It, Smell It, Hear It', Buy It: Hemingway's Commercial Forms." *Essays in Poetics* 8, no. 1:1-29.

Attempts to define *The Sun Also Rises*, "Big Two-Hearted River," and "Hills Like White Elephants" in terms of the commercial age of the twenties with its emphasis on the marketplace and consumption.

45 GUDMUNSSON, TURA. "Visiting Prof Exposes Hemingway's FBI File." *Collegian* (Amherst), 9 May, p. 5.

On Jeffrey Meyers's exposing of the FBI file on the author.

46 GUSSOW, ADAM. "Cheever's Failed Paradise: The Short-Story Stylist as Novelist." *Literary Review* 27, no. 1 (Fall): 103-16.

Speaks briefly of Hemingway's influence on the writings of John Cheever – the use of ironic understatement, reliance on "and" to tie long sentences together, and the notion of male friendship.

47 HEMINGWAY, ERNEST. "Judgment of Manitou." In *Michigan: A State Anthology*. Edited by David D. Anderson. Detroit: Bruccoli-Clark Books/Gale Research Co., p. 219.

Reprints the story that appeared in Oak Park High School's literary magazine (*Tabula*) when Hemingway was a senior.

48 HIGA, MIYOKO. "An Approach to Hemingway's First Wife, Elizabeth Hadley Richardson." *Kyushu American Literature* 24 (July): 15-30.

Biographical approach looking at both Hadley's influence on Hemingway the author and his depiction of her in his writings. Finds allusions to or models of Hadley in "The Snows of Kilimanjaro," *The Sun Also Rises*, *A Farewell to Arms*, and *Islands in the Stream*.

49 HINKLE, JAMES. "Hemingway's Iceberg." *Hemingway Review* 2 (Spring): 10.

Points out that both Frued and the sculptor Auguste Rodin were interested in the iceberg principle long before Hemingway adopted his theory of omission in writing.

50 ____. "Where the Indian's Razor Came from in 'Indian Camp.'" *Hemingway Review* 2, no. 2:17.

Suggests the razor in the Indian husband's upper bunk was placed there by superstitious midwives to "help cut the pain."

51 HOETKER, JAMES. "Hemingway's 'Mr. & Mrs. Elliot' and Its Readers." *Kyushu American Literature* 24 (July): 11-14.

Comments on why the short story has bombed with critics, suggesting that readers are misinterpreting the narrative method in which "the third person narrative is actually reporting, with only the grammatical person changed, an autobiographical monologue delivered by Elliot himself."

52 HOLCOMBE, WAYNE C. "The Motive of the Motif: Some Thoughts on Hemingway's Existentialism." *Hemingway Review* 3, no. 1 (Fall): 18-27.

Takes issue with Kilinger's 1960 claim that Hemingway is an existentialist, pointing out fundamental differences in worldview between Hemingway and such well-known existentialists as Camus and Sartre. For Hemingway heroes, metaphysical topics such as mortality and death are impervious to thought and thus left unexamined.

53 HOLMES, JOE. "Hemingway's Wives: You Have to Praise Them." *Lost Generation Journal* 7, no. 2 (Fall): 2-7.

Shows that despite Hemingway's dominant pose, he depended a great deal on both the emotional and financial support of his wives.

54 HOTCHNER, A.E. *Papa Hemingway: The Ecstasy and Sorrow*. New York: Quill, 322 pp.

Reprint of revised *Papa Hemingway: A Personal Memoir* (New York: Random House, 1966). Includes an additional chronology of Hemingway's life and "gossipy" postscript in which Hotchner attempts to set the record straight concerning the controversy over his earlier publishing of *Papa Hemingway* but succeeds only in raking Mary Hemingway and Philip Young over the coals.

55 IDOL, JOHN L., Jr. "Ernest Hemingway and Thomas Wolfe." *South Carolina Review* 15, no. 1:24-31.

Relates what each writer thought of the other and their respective relationships with Scribner's editor Max Perkins. Hemingway resented Wolfe for the heavy demands Wolfe made on Perkins's time. Concludes that both authors "hungered mightily for fame, and each came to defend his own style as something essentially right for himself."

56 JACKSON, PAUL [R.]. "Note on Another Earth-Moving Scene." *Hemingway Newsletter*, no. 6 (July): 3.

Suggests that Gabriel García Marquez's description of an intimate encounter in *One Hundred Years of Solitude* as an "earthquake" may be a "lingering gesture of homage" to Hemingway who describes a similar experience between Jordan and Maria in *For Whom the Bell Tolls*.

57 JOHNSTON, KENNETH G. "In Defense of the Unhappy Margot Macomber." *Hemingway Review* 2, no. 2 (Spring): 44-47.

Concludes that an examination of the circumstantial evidence, Wilson's motives, and the narrator's testimony proves that Margot really shot at the buffalo. Reprinted with slight revision: 1987.38.

58 JOSEPHS, ALLEN. "Hemingway's out of Body Experience." *Hemingway Review* 2, no. 2 (Spring): 11-17.

Connects Hemingway's statements about his soul temporarily leaving his body after his wounding in Italy to his depiction of out-of-body experiences in "Now I Lay Me" and "A Way You'll Never Be." Suggests that Hemingway's enduring trauma resulted not from the actual wound but from his subsequent out-of-body experience.

59 KARAGUEUZIAN, MAUREEN. "Irony in Robert Stone's *Dog Soldiers*." *Critique* 24, no. 2 (Winter): 65-73.

Looks at Stone's allusions to the expatriate world of *The Sun Also Rises* in his Vietnam War novel about a new generation becoming "lost" as a result of the war.

60 KENNEDY, J. GERALD. "What Hemingway Omitted from 'Cat in the Rain.'" *Les Cahiers de la Nouvelle: Journal of the Short Story in English* 1:75-81.

Biographical interpretation of the story in light of Hemingway's own marital difficulties at the time. Argues that like Hadley, the wife in the short story is also pregnant.

61 KERNER, DAVID. "Hemingway's Letters." *Biography* 6 (Winter): 76-83.

Review of *Ernest Hemingway: Selected Letters, 1917-1961*. Is bothered by omitted passages and the numerous gaps in chronological time in which no letters appear. Also bemoans the lack of a table of contents and a comprehensive index to the author's thoughts and ideas.

62 KERT, BERNICE. *The Hemingway Women*. New York: W.W. Norton, 555 pp.

Discusses Hemingway's relationships with wives and "significant others" such as Grace Hall, Duff Twysden, Agnes von Kurowsky, and Adriana Ivancich. Through interviews and unpublished correspondence, Kert reconstructs chronologically Hemingway's destructive patterns in choosing women and reveals what many of them thought of him as well. Grace Hall and Martha Gellhorn are vindicated to a certain degree, depicted as simply too independent for the domineering Hemingway. Kert identifies and treats those who served as prototypes for Hemingway's female characters and also shows that the author often used composites of various people in his creation of characters.

63 KNIGHT, CHRISTOPHER. "Ernest Hemingway's 'Under the Ridge':
A Textual Note." *Notes on Modern American Literature* 7, no. 3
(Winter): item 15.
Argues that a passage deleted during printing disrupts the
narrative continuity of the short story. Knight reprints the missing lines.

64 KRILE, IVO. "The Verb Say in the Reporting Clauses of Ernest
Hemingway's Dialogues." *Studia Romanica et Anglica Zagrabiensia*
28:197-204.
Finds Hemingway's reliance on the generic verb *say* in identifying
interlocutors adds to the vividness and drama of his dialogues and
places them directly within the narrative process.

65 KVAM, WAYNE. "Ernest Hemingway and Hans Kahle." *Hemingway
Review* 2, no. 2 (Spring): 18-22.
In reconstructing their relationship, Kvam draws on biographical
data and a Hemingway letter to the former Prussian officer who fought
for the loyalist cause during the Spanish civil war and later appeared in
For Whom The Bell Tolls.

66 LAFONTAINE, CÉCILE AURORE. "Waiting in Hemingway's 'The
Killers" and Borges' 'La Espera.'" *Revue de Littérature Comparée* 57
(January-March): 67-80.
Looks at how both authors interweave into their texts the
subpattern of waiting framed within the larger plot structure of a duel.
Contends that Ole Andreson's situation as "a trapped waiting victim"
supercedes Nick's initiation experience as the primary focus of "The
Killers."

67 LEE, A. ROBERT, ed. *Ernest Hemingway: New Critical Essays*. Totowa,
N.J.: Barnes & Noble, 216 pp.
Pp. 7-12: Introduction by the editor seeks to reevaluate
Hemingway's position in the American literary scene. Provides an
overview of the collection.
Pp. 13-35: "'The Picture of the Whole': *In Our Time*" by David
Seed. Examines how Hemingway's early journalistic experiences
influenced his writing and explores how Hemingway shaped the early *in
our time* (1924) into the unified collection of *In Our Time* (1925)
through the use of "a central composite character, common themes,
common locations, and quasi-poetical links through recurring figures or
verbal details."
Pp. 36-48: "The Short Stories after *In Our Time*: A Profile" by
Colin E. Nicholson. Surveys the recurrent features in those short stories
written after *In Our Time* in order "to examine the overall larger
patterns and configurations which carry both the struggle and the

inevitable sense of failure. . . ." Argues that Hemingway's fiction reveals despair and failed possibility as the essence of the human condition.

Pp. 49-63: "Art and Life in *The Sun Also Rises*" by Andrew Hook. After calling for a halt to biographical readings of the novel, Hook explores the importance and symbolic significance of place: Paris, Burguete, Pamplona, and San Sebastian. Suggests that each not only serves as a structuring device but also informs the central meaning of the story.

Pp. 64-78: "*A Farewell to Arms*: Radiance at the Vanishing Point" by William Wasserstrom. After a brief autobiographical note in which he recounts his 1963 meeting with Eduardo C. Mondlane, Wasserstrom contends that the greatness of *A Farewell to Arms* resides in the author's powerful style and the novel's enduring resonance. "Unlike books less long-lived, it possesses the faculty of self-renewal, generated not by its idea – principal ground of its early fame – but by its force as a work of experiment . . . it unites avant-garde experiments of language with a presiding mode of American demotic speech."

Pp. 79-102: "'Everything Completely Knit Up': Seeing *For Whom the Bell Tolls* Whole" by A. Robert Lee. Shows how the novel's form and subject blend into one another. Sees the bridge as both the structural and thematic center, with the flashbacks, insets, interior monologues, and account of camp life forming the circumference.

Pp. 103-21: "The Later Fiction: Hemingway and the Aesthetics of Failure" by James H. Justus. Places *Islands in the Stream* within the context of *The Old Man and the Sea*, *A Moveable Feast*, and the author's longtime preoccupation with the study of failure. Argues that despite the novel's "considerable" editing, *Islands* "retains enough narrative patterning to make it structurally and thematically coherent."

Pp. 122-50: "Essential History: Suicide and Nostalgia in Hemingway's Fictions" by Eric Mottran. Argues that Hemingway "explores how to make a life and a work out of the decaying body of the history of male prerogatives." The lone male wanderer, searching for happiness and true self-definition, must contend with the deterioration or erosion of male dominance in the twentieth century.

Pp. 151-71: "Hemingway – the Intellectual: A Version of Modernism" by Brian Way. Argues against the popular perception that Hemingway was a "natural" writer, incapable of serious thought. Points to the level of intellectualism found in his recently published letters, his complex narrative structures (in works prior to 1930), and his conception of the artist and art in relation to literary modernism as evidence to the contrary.

Pp. 172-92: "Hemingway and the Secret Language of Hate" by Faith Pullin. Contends that Hemingway is unable to treat human relationships fully because he views such relationships, especially those between men and women, as destructive. "The Hemingway protagonist is the archetypal loner fighting against a hostile world and an indifferent nature...."

Pp. 193-211: "Stalking Papa's Ghost: Hemingway's Presence in Contemporary American Writing" by Frank McConnell. Looks at Hemingway's influence on later American writers, including Bellow (despite his "refutation of the entire Hemingway mystique"), Vonnegut, and Pynchon. Concludes that the rumblings of Hemingway's ghost "are an inescapable part of the splendid dissonance that is contemporary American fiction."

68 LELAND, JOHN. "The Happiness of the Garden: Hemingway's Edenic Quest." *Hemingway Review* 3, no. 1 (Fall): 44-53.

Looks at Hemingway's preoccupation with the Eden symbol (a last refuge in a once-expansive wilderness turned to wasteland) and his treatment of the inevitable loss of that paradise in his writings. Pays particular attention to "Big Two-Hearted River," *The Sun Also Rises*, and *Green Hills of Africa*.

69 LINDHOLDT, PAUL J. "Ernest Hemingway's 'Summer People': More Textual Errors and a Reply." *Studies in Short Fiction* 20, no. 4 (Fall): 319-20.

Points out several more substantive errors in the story, including the editor's changing of the word *Jews* to *slobs*.

70 LINGEMAN, RICHARD. "Papa and the Feds." *Nation* 236, no. 12 (26 March): 355.

Humorous approach to Hemingway's "delusions" of FBI surveillance.

71 LOUNSBERRY, BARBARA. "*Green Hills of Africa*: Hemingway's Celebration of Memory." *Hemingway Review* 2, no. 2 (Spring): 23-31.

Considers memory and its transfiguration into art as the novel's primary focus. *Green Hills of Africa* "is not an experiment to see if 'actuality' can compete with the imagination, but an effort to demonstrate how the *memory* of actuality can extend that actuality and ultimately serve as the basis for transforming that actuality into art."

72 LYNN, KENNETH S. "Hemingway's Private War." In *The Air-Line to Seattle: Studies in Literary and Historical Writing about America*. Chicago: University of Chicago Press, pp. 108-131.

Reprint of 1981.69.

73 McCARTIN, JAMES T. "Ernest Hemingway: The Life and the Works." *Arizona Quarterly* 39, no. 2 (Summer): 122-34.

Stresses the difficulties associated with uncovering the real man beneath the legendary myth, noting Hemingway's own manipulation of his public image. Also comments on the author's obsession with violence and death, his negative relationships with women, and his stereotypical characterization of them in his works.

74 MacLEISH, ARCHIBALD. *Letters of Archibald MacLeish, 1907-1982.* Edited by R.H. Winnick. Boston: Houghton Mifflin, 471 pp.
Many references to Hemingway, both as subject in letters and as correspondent. Mention also of Pauline and Mary, and children.

75 _____. "There Is Nothing to Say." *Wolf Magazine of Letters* 49 (June-July): 11-12.
Reprints letter to Hemingway from Archibald MacLeish after Hemingway's father's suicide imploring the author not to dwell on the circumstances of the death.

76 MERIWETHER, JAMES B. "Addendum to Hanneman: Hemingway in *The Albatross Book of American Short Stories.*" *Papers of the Bibliographical Society of America* 77, no. 1:65-66.
Identifies one of the previously unknown entries in Hemingway's 1940 Key West book inventory as *The Albatross Book of American Short Stories.* Adds the anthology (which includes "The Undefeated") to Hanneman's *Ernest Hemingway: A Comprehensive Bibliography* (Princeton, 1967) and *Supplement* (Princeton, 1975).

77 MEYER, WILLIAM E., Jr. "The Artist's America: Hemingway's 'A Clean, Well-Lighted Place.'" *Arizona Quarterly* 39:156-63.
Relates America's cultural "visual bias" to Hemingway's stylistic devotion to prose imagism, claiming for his thesis that "A Clean, Well-Lighted Place" depicts "striking parallels to the mythic America of the visually biased and to the artist's dilemma in such a realm."

78 MEYERS, JEFFREY. "Ernest Hemingway." *Times Literary Supplement*, no. 4211 (16 December), p. 1403.
In response to Crace's earlier contention in his review (see *TLS*, 9 December) that Hemingway sold out to Hollywood, Meyers points out that Hemingway, unlike Fitzgerald, Faulkner, and others, never wrote screenplays for Hollywood and had little to do with the movie industry as a whole.

79 _____.   "Hemingway, Ford Madox Ford, and *A Moveable Feast.*" *Critical Quarterly* 25, no. 4 (Winter): 35-42.
Explores Hemingway's personal and professional relationship with Ford in order to explain his animosity toward Ford in *A Moveable Feast,*

The Torrents of Spring, and deleted passages from *The Sun Also Rises.* Characteristically, Hemingway repays the older writer's assistance with ingratitude. "Hemingway's inability to learn from Ford as well as profit from him, helps to account for the egotism and arrogance of *A Moveable Feast.*"

80 ____. "A Queer, Ugly Business: The Origins of 'The Short Happy Life of Francis Macomber.'" *London Magazine* 23 (November): 26-37.

Points to a real-life case of adultery and suicide in Africa in 1908 as the source and inspiration for Hemingway's short story.

81 ____. "Wanted by the FBI." *New York Review of Books* 30, no. 5 (31 March): 17-20.

Chronicles Hemingway's involvement in a private spy network in Cuba during World War II and the FBI's investigation of him. Reprinted: 1989.33.

82 MILLS, EVA B. "Ernest Hemingway and Nathan Asch: An Ambivalent Relationship." *Hemingway Review* 2, no. 2 (Spring): 48-51.

Draws on biographical data and unpublished Asch letters in order to reconstruct their rather uncertain personal and professional relationship. According to Mills, Asch "loved, hated, envied, admired, and respected Ernest Hemingway."

83 MORTON, BRUCE. "Music and Distorted View in Hemingway's 'The Gambler, the Nun, and the Radio.'" *Studies in Short Fiction* 20, no. 2-3 (Spring-Summer): 79-85.

Suggests that Frazer's reaction to Sister Cecilia and the religious faith she represents is keyed to the music. Hemingway uses "music as a device to reveal the failure of stoical realism, religion, and the assorted worldly fare of the radio to provide a salvation for Frazer's spiritual and emotional dilemma."

84 ____. "Santiago's Apprenticeship: A Source for *The Old Man and the Sea.*" *Hemingway Review* 2, no. 2 (Spring): 52-55.

Compares paragraphs on fishing taken from Hemingway's 1935 "Marlin off Cuba" with those from *The Old Man and the Sea* in order to show the extent to which the author borrowed from his article in composing his novel.

85 MOTYLEVA, TAMARA. "The Novelists' Novelist." *Soviet Literature,* no. 12 (429), pp. 150-60.

Speaks briefly of Hemingway's appreciation of Turgenev.

86 NOBLE, DONALD R., ed. *Hemingway: A Revaluation*. Troy, N.Y.:
    Whitston Publishing Co., 282 pp.
        Pp. 1-15: Introduction by the editor, calling for a revaluation of
    our past critical efforts while directing future energies toward those
    areas as yet unexplored in Hemingway criticism. Provides an overview
    of the collection.
        Pp. 17-47: "Hemingway Criticism: Getting at the Hard Questions"
    by Jackson J. Benson. Breaks both the books and periodical studies on
    Hemingway into categories and comments on the best in each.
    Condemns the redundancy and superficiality of many of the other
    studies, especially the triviality of a large portion of the influence
    studies, but looks to the recent availability of manuscript materials at
    the Kennedy Library to raise the overall level of scholarship. Offers
    direction for future worthwhile studies as well.
        Pp. 49-65: "Hemingway, Painting, and the Search for Serenity" by
    Alfred Kazin. Reprint with revision of *Saturday Review* article.
        Pp. 67-82: "Hemingway and the Magical Journey" by Leo Gurko.
    Looks at Hemingway's treatment of travel, finding that in his early
    novels, the protagonists remain unchanged by their respective journeys
    but in the later novels, the heroes "advance toward new ground."
    Compares Hemingway's treatment of the voyage motif with Conrad's,
    contending that both men "share a vision of the universe as empty, and
    define life as essentially a manichean struggle between the forces of
    light ... and the forces of darkness (the cosmic *nada*)." For both
    authors, the physical crossing of space aids the emotional crossing, thus
    supplying them with the energy to endure.
        Pp. 83-97: "Hemingway's British and American Reception: A
    Study in Values" by Robert O. Stephens. Surveys a number of British
    and American reviews, contending that during Hemingway's lifetime,
    American reviewers concentrated on the man rather than his work
    while British reviewers emphasized his writing over his legendary status.
        Pp. 99-113: "'The Truest Sentence': Words as Equivalents of Time
    and Place in *In Our Time*" by Charles G. Hoffman and A.C. Hoffman.
    Look at the ways common motifs or images (roads, fire, water, and
    walls) interact with theme, word repetition, and rhythm in order to
    achieve a novelistic whole.
        Pp. 115-34: "False Dawn: A Preliminary Analysis of *The Sun Also
    Rises* Manuscript" by Michael S. Reynolds. Reprint of 1980.79.
        Pp. 135-63: "Hemingway and Faulkner on the Road to Roncevaux"
    by H.R. Stoneback. Compares the ways each author uses Roncevaux in
    his novel (*The Sun Also Rises* and *Flags in the Dust*). Focusing on the
    symbolic landscape and religious associations of Roncevaux, Stoneback
    sees Jake as a pilgrim on a quest for spiritual value in a world singularly
    lacking in such values.

Pp. 165-85: "Frederic Henry's Escape and the Pose of Passivity" by
Scott Donaldson. Close reading of the text and manuscript, arguing that
Henry assumes a more passive and innocent pose in order to avoid
responsibility for deserting the war and impregnating Catherine
Barkley. Manuscript revisions reveal how Hemingway made Henry less
sympathetic, emphasizing his guilt for his actions and implicating him in
Barkley's death. Reprinted: 1987.6.

Pp. 187-203: "Hemingway as Artist in *Across the River and into the
Trees*" by W. Craig Turner. Considers the novel to be an experimental
work in which Hemingway pushed his craft to the limits. Looks at the
circular structure of the text together with its varied narrative technique
and symbolic image patterns of wind, scars, bridges, and journeys that
make up an integral part of Hemingway's thematic exploration of death
by disease.

Pp. 205-23: "Hemingway's Poor Spanish: Chauvinism and Loss of
Credibility in *For Whom the Bell Tolls*" by F. Allen Josephs. Looks at
Hemingway's numerous errors in Spanish, from simple misspellings to
serious usage errors, that undermine the text. Points out that the
Spanish equivalent of Jordan's nickname for Maria, "rabbit," is a vulgar
euphemism "for the female sexual organ."

Pp. 225-39: "Hemingway: The Writer in Decline" by Philip Young.
Speculating on the reasons behind Hemingway's decline in later years,
Young argues that "the author became increasingly his own, undisguised
subject." Young finds collaborating evidence for his thesis in letters
addressed to him that were never mailed now at the Kennedy Library.

Pp. 241-62: "*Islands in the Stream*: Death and the Artist" by
Richard B. Hovey. Reprint of 1980.40.

Pp. 263-80: "Art and Order in *Islands in the Stream*" by Gregory S.
Sojka. Argues that the core issue in the novel is really Hudson's struggle
to bring order to his life and maintain his self-respect through the
therapeutic and aesthetically satisfying activities of fishing and painting.
Sees Hudson's devotion to duty at the end as his redemption in which
he "regains a lost sense of pride and earns his place with the bravest of
Hemingway's matadors, soliders, hunters, and fishermen." Views the
novel as "a fictional transition between the Nick Adams short stories
and *The Old Man and the Sea*."

87 OGUNYEMI, CHIKWENYE OKONJO. "The Poetics of the War
Novel." *Comparative Literature Studies* 20, no. 2 (Summer): 203-16.

Looks at the influence of American war novels written by
Hemingway, Crane, Cummings, Mailer, and Heller on the theme,
technique, and form of Nigerian war novels such as S.O. Mezu's *Behind
the Rising Sun* and Elechi Amadi's *Sunset in Biafra*.

88 OLIVER, CHARLES M. "Language Correlative in Hemingway's Fiction." *Language and Literature* 8, no. 1-3:83-94.
Concerns the way Hemingway elicits certain emotional responses through the repetition of words, sounds, and rhythms. Points out that the repetition of "and" appears most often in emotionally charged passages such as the wound scenes in both *A Farewell to Arms* and *For Whom the Bell Tolls*. The reader feels the increase in "and" usage and simultaneously experiences intensified excitement.

89 PANDEYA, SHIVA M. "Hemingway: *The Torrents of Spring.*" In *Studies in Modern Fiction*. New Delhi, India: Vikas Publishing House, pp. 120-40.
After examining Hemingway's parody of Sherwood Anderson in *The Torrents of Spring*, Pandeya concludes that Hemingway turned on his former mentor and friend in order to assert his individuality as an author–to make himself and his writing distinct from the other modernist authors of the time whom he was alleged to be imitating.

90 PRICE, REYNOLDS. "For Ernest Hemingway." In *In Praise of What Persists*. Edited by Stephen Berg. New York: Harper & Row, pp. 194-221.
Reprint from *Things Themselves: Essays and Scenes* (New York: Atheneum, 1972).

91 PROKOSCH, FREDERIC. *Voices: A Memoir*. New York: Farrar, Straus, Giroux, pp. 27, 41, 44, 101, 155-57, 164-65, 167-69, etc.
Many references to Hemingway, including Pound's comments on the author's "swollen ego," Prokosch's first rather peculiar meeting with him in London when Hemingway matched wits with Emerald Cunard and emerged victorious, and Alice B. Toklas's recounting of Gertrude Stein's dislike of the young author.

92 RAGHUNATH, S. "The Concept of Tragedy." *Triveni* 52, no. 2:26-34.
Sees Hemingway's stoic strain and pessimism regarding the human situation as characteristic of the fatalistic Greek vision.

93 RAO, E. NAGESWARA. *Ernest Hemingway: A Study of His Rhetoric*. New Delhi, India: Arnold Heinemann, 134 pp.
Examines Hemingway's changing rhetorical devices over time, categorizing his writing into periods marked by distinct rhetorical strategies. Considers his later rhetoric "less effective than his earlier rhetoric" because of his abandonment of successful modes of persuasion and his adoption of "complex overstatements and direct emotional appeals."

94 _____. "The Quest for Happiness in Hemingway." *Indian Journal of American Studies* 13, no. 1:119-25.

Explores how a number of Hemingway heroes, including Frederic Henry, Robert Jordan, Harry Morgan, and Francis Macomber, achieve happiness or catharsis "through fishing, hunting, killing, sexual intercourse, and creative writing," even in the midst of adverse situations.

95 REYNOLDS, MICHAEL S., "Hemingway's Stein: Another Misplaced Review." *American Literature* 55, no. 3 (October): 431-34.

Believes Stein's review of *Three Stories & Ten Poems* was written in response to Hemingway's earlier review of her *Geography and Plays* in which the young author delivered a stinging attack on Lewis, Mencken, and others. Reprints both reviews.

96 _____. "Holman Hunt and 'The Light of the World.'" *Studies in Short Fiction* 20, no. 4 (Fall): 317-19.

Reveals that Hemingway's mother donated a copy of Hunt's religious painting to her church in 1905 in memory of her father. Suggests that Hemingway titled his brutal story after the painting out of resentment toward his mother.

97 _____. "Macomber: An Old Oak Park Name." *Hemingway Review* 3, no. 1 (Fall): 28-29.

Traces Macomber's name in "The Short Happy Life of Francis Macomber" back to a prominent Oak Park family and speculates on the possibility of Hemingway's having modeled the character after the Bumsteads, another Oak Park family who hunted big game.

98 _____., ed. *Critical Essays on Ernest Hemingway's "In Our Time."* Boston: G.K. Hall, 273 pp.

Collection of mostly reprinted essays on Hemingway's 1925 collection, prefaced by a helpful introduction and indexed. Contents:

Pp. 1-12: Introduction by the editor, combining biography and cultural history with aesthetic judgments about *In Our Time*.

Pp. 15-16. "Review: *In Our Time*" by Herbert J. Seligman. Praises the collection for Hemingway's "passionately bare telling of what happened," and comments on idiomatic language, precision, and delicacy. Reprint from *New York City Sun*, 17 October 1925.

Pp. 17: "A New Chicago Writer" by Mary Plum. Describes Hemingway's "harsh and unadorned" style, in keeping with his "brutal, trenchant and terse" stories. Reprint from *Chicago Post*, 27 November 1925.

Pp. 18-20: "Tough Earth" by Paul Rosenfeld. Describes *In Our Time* as the fruit of the cubism, Stein, *Le Sacre du Printemps* era:

"Emphatic, short, declarative sentences follow staunchly upon the other ... never relenting." Asserts that this is permanently valuable art, though it may take years before we recognize its strengths. Reprint from *New Republic* (November 1925): 22-23.

Pp. 20: "*In Our Time*" by an anonymous reviewer. Praises the book as "powerfully good writing" even though "unliterary, unconventional." Reprint from *Plaindealer*, 6 December 1925.

Pp. 20-21: "*In Our Time*" by J.H.R. Regrets Hemingway's poor taste, use of filth, and heavy-handed irony. Reprint from *News* (Parkersburg, W. Va.), 6 December 1925.

Pp. 22-23: "Another American Discovers the Acid in the Language" by Schuyler Ashley. Praises the book for its new language, its vigor. Reprint from *Kansas City Star*, 12 December 1925.

Pp. 23-24: "Chiselled Prose Found in Fiction of Hemingway: Realistic Stories Are Found in *In Our Time*" by Warren Taylor. Sees Hemingway taking "language as the material of art." He also praises his characters and his economy of style. Reprint from *Tennessean* (Nashville), 10 January 1926.

Pp. 24-25: "*In Our Time*" by anonymous reviewer. Questions the structure (why the short paragraphs appear when there is no ostensible connection to the stories). Reprint from *World-Herald* (Omaha, Nebraska), 10 January 1926.

P. 25: "Review: *In Our Time*" by anonymous reviewer. Says there is something wrong with the reviewer because so many people have praised the book. He or she, however, cannot. Reprint from *Portland Oregonian*, 2 May 1926.

P. 26: "Short Stories of Distinction" by Ruth Suckow. Praises the Nick Adams stories as being the best; she connects "Soldier's Home" with Hamlin Garland's "The Return of the Private." Reprint from *Register* (Des Moines, Iowa), 12 September 1926.

Pp. 29-30: "Hemingway's *In Our Time*" by E.M. Halliday. Reprint from *Explicator*, March 1949.

Pp. 31-37: "Two Hemingway Sources for *in our time*" by Michael S. Reynolds. Reprint from *Studies in Short Fiction* (Winter 1972): 81-86.

Pp. 38-60: "A Collation, with Commentary, of the Five Texts of the Chapters in Hemingway's *In Our Time*, 1923-38" by E.R. Hagemann. Reprint of 1979.42.

Pp. 61-75: "An Examination of the Drafts of Hemingway's Chapter 'Nick Sat against the Wall of the Church...'" by Kathryn Zabelle Derounian. Reprint of 1983.21.

Pp. 76-87: "The Structure of *In Our Time*" by Robert M. Slabey. Reprint from *South Dakota Review* (August 1965): 38-52.

Pp. 88-102: "The Complex Unity of *In Our Time*" by Clinton S. Burhans, Jr. Reprint from *Modern Fiction Studies* (Autumn 1968): 313-28.

Pp. 103-119: "Patterns of Connection and Their Development in Hemingway's *In Our Time*" by Jackson J. Benson. Reprint from *Rendezvous* (Winter 1970): 37-52.

Pp. 120-29: "Juxtaposition in Hemingway's *In Our Time*" by Linda W. Wagner. Reprint from *Studies in Short Fiction* (Summer 1975): 243-52.

Pp. 130-37: "*In Our Time*: The Interchapters as Structural Guides to a Psychological Pattern" by David J. Leigh, S.J. Reprint of 1975.36.

Pp. 138-40: "Neural Projections in Hemingway's 'On the Quai at Smyrna'" by Louis H. Leiter. Reprint from *Studies in Short Fiction* (Summer 1968): 384-86.

Pp. 141-43: "Hemingway's *In Our Time*" by J.M. Harrison. Reprint from *Explicator* (May 1960): item 51.

Pp. 144-45: "Hemingway's 'Indian Camp'" by G. Thomas Tanselle. Reprint from *Explicator* (February 1962): item 53.

Pp. 146-47: "Hemingway's 'The Doctor and the Doctor's Wife'" by Aerol Arnold. Reprint from *Explicator* (March 1960): item 36.

Pp. 148-49: "Hemingway's 'The Doctor and the Doctor's Wife'" by R.M. Davis. Reprint from *Explicator* (September 1966): item 1.

Pp. 150-54: "The Biographical Fallacy and 'The Doctor and the Doctor's Wife'" by Richard Fulkerson. Reprint of 1979.35.

Pp. 155-56: "Hemingway's 'The End of Something'" by Joseph Whitt. Reprint from *Explicator* (June 1951): item 58

Pp. 157-58: "Hemingway's 'The End of Something'" by Alice Parker. Reprint from *Explicator* (March 1952): item 36.

Pp. 159-71: "Ernest Hemingway's 'The End of Something': Its Independence as a Short Story and Its Place in the 'Education of Nick Adams'" by Horst H. Kruse. Reprint from *Studies in Short Fiction* (Winter 1967): 152-66.

Pp. 172-75: "Dating the Events of 'The Three-Day Blow'" by George Monteiro. Reprint of 1977.78.

Pp. 176-88: "Nick Adams on the Road: 'The Battler' as Hemingway's Man on the Hill" by Nicholas Gerogiannis. (New essay.) Called earlier "The Great Man" and "The Great Little Fighting Machine," this story was written about complex emotions, chiefly the importance of the encounter with Bugs and Ad to Nick. Gerogiannis sees "The Battler" as a gateway story for Nick's odyssey of discovery of manhood and life.

Pp. 189-98: "Hemingway's Concept of Sport and 'Soldier's Home'" by Robert W. Lewis. Reprint from *Rendezvous* (Winter 1970): 19-27.

Pp. 199-202: "In Defense of Krebs" by John J. Roberts. Reprint of 1976.74.

Pp. 203-217: "Another Turn for Hemingway's 'The Revolutionist': Sources and Meanings" by Anthony Hunt. Reprint of 1977.57.

Pp. 218-26: "The Two Shortest Stories of Hemingway's *In Our Time*" by Jim Steinke. (New essay.) "A Very Short Story" and "The Revolutionist" were originally considered vignettes by Hemingway and were titled, respectively, "Love" and "Youth" in earlier versions. Manuscripts and the history of the writing provide good insight into Hemingway's intentions with each story.

Pp. 227-34: "Hemingway's 'Out of Season' and the Psychology of Errors" by Kenneth G. Johnston. Reprint from *Literature and Psychology* (November 1971): 41-46.

Pp. 235-51: "Some Misconceptions of 'Out of Season'" by Paul Smith. (New essay.) Close reading of all manuscript versions of the story, attempting to place it both aesthetically and biographically.

Pp. 252-53: "Hemingway's 'My Old Man'" by Sidney J. Krause. Reprint from *Explicator* (January 1962): item 39.

Pp. 254-59: "He Made Him Up: 'Big Two-Hearted River' as Doppelgänger" by Robert Gibb. Reprint of 1979.39.

Pp. 260-67: "Landscapes of the Mind: 'Big Two-Hearted River'" by William Adair. Reprint of 1977.2.

99 RUBIN, LOUIS D. [, Jr.] "The Mockingbird in the Gum Tree: Notes on the Language of American Literature." *Southern Review* 19, no. 4:785-801.

Comments on Hemingway's innovative prose and the limitations of the vernacular style as well as his contributions to twentieth-century literature.

100 SANDERS, DAVE. "Dos Passos's Portrait of Hemingway." *Lost Generation Journal* 7, no. 2 (Fall): 18-22.

Looks at Dos Passos's modeling of George Elbert Warner in *Chosen Country*, *The Great Days*, and *Century's Ebb* after Hemingway. Chronicles their break over the Spanish civil war.

101 SCAFELLA, FRANK. "Imagistic Landscape of a Psyche: Hemingway's Nick Adams." *Hemingway Review* 2, no. 2 (Spring): 2-10.

Finds "remarkable imagistic parallels" between A.R. Ammons's "Terrain" and the Nick Adams stories, proposing that both "are the soul's description of itself as landscape in poetry." Pays particular attention to the psychic landscape of interchapter 6 of *In Our Time*, "In Another Country," "A Way You'll Never Be," and "Big Two-Hearted River."

102 SEELYE, JOHN. "Hyperion to a Satyr: *Farewell to Arms* and *Love Story*." *College Literature* 10:307-313.
Reprint of 1979.89.

103 SMITH, B.J. "'Big Two-Hearted River': The Artist and the Art." *Studies in Short Fiction* 20, no. 2-3 (Spring-Summer): 129-32.

Looks at Hemingway's deleted ending, suggesting that it reveals another metaphoric fishing trip representing "an attempt by Hemingway to write, perhaps for the first time, about the artist and the process of his art."

104 SMITH, PAUL. "Hemingway's Early Manuscripts: The Theory and Practice of Omission." *Journal of Modern Literature* 10, no. 2:268-88.

Looks at Hemingway's conception of the theory as evidenced by his frequent references to it and then at the author's early application of it through an examination of the manuscripts of "The Killers," "Big Two-Hearted River," and "Up in Michigan."

105 _____. "Hemingway's Iceberg." *Hemingway Review* 2, no. 2:10.

Smith shows that Hemingway may have become familiar with the iceberg principle through a 1917 issue of the *Kansas City Star* which featured a drawing of Rodin's "The Thinker" coupled with a quote from R.L. Stevenson that encapsulated the theory of omission in writing.

106 SMITH, PAUL, and TAVERNIER-COURBIN, JACQUELINE. "'Terza Riruce': Hemingway, Dunning, Italian Poetry." *Thalia* 5, no. 2:41-42.

Good-humored approach to Hemingway's knowledge of "the convoluted philological history of *terza riruce*." Reprinted: 1984.112.

107 SPENKO, JAMES LEO. "A Long Look at Hemingway's 'Up in Michigan.'" *Arizona Quarterly* 39, no. 2:111-21.

After a brief publishing history, Spenko discusses Hemingway's "finely etched" characterization of Liz Coates and how nearly all of the details in the story focus on her and her situation. Considers the story to be a "minor" but "flawed masterpiece."

108 SPILKA, MARK. "Victorian Keys to the Early Hemingway: Part I -*John Halifax, Gentleman*." *Journal of Modern Literature* 10, no. 1 (March): 125-50.

Argues that Dinah Mulock Craik's popular novel *John Halifax, Gentleman* with its emphasis on "adventurous gentility" had a lasting and profound influence on the entire Hemingway family.

109 _____. "Victorian Keys to the Early Hemingway: Part II -*Fauntleroy* and *Finn*." *Journal of Modern Literature* 10, no. 2 (June): 289-310.

Drawing on biographical data, Spilka contends that Grace Hall Hemingway sought to model her son's upbringing after Frances Hodgson Burnett's genteel *Little Lord Fauntleroy*. "They were not interested in feminizing young boys, but in sharing with them a fuller range of human possibilities than their limited spheres allowed."

110　STEINKE, JIM. "Hemingway's 'Cat in the Rain.'" *Spectrum* (University of California, Santa Barbara) 25, no. 1-2:36-44.

Argues against traditional biographical readings that interpret the story as an illustration of marital dissatisfaction and unfulfilled desires. Believes the incident in the hotel room to be the result of the couple's temporary confinement due to the weather. "This is a momentary incident, domestic, familiar in the accommodations they are making to the place and to each other."

111　STETLER, CHARLES, and LOCKLIN, GERALD. "Hemingway and the Adult Sports Story." *McNeese Review* 30:29-37.

Sees "The Undefeated," "My Old Man," and "Fifty Grand" falling into the adult sports-story genre that emphasizes character and generally a more poignant behind-the-scenes conflict.

112　STONEBACK, H.R. "'For Bryan's Sake': The Tribute to the Great Commoner in Hemingway's *The Sun Also Rises*." *Christianity and Literature* 32, no. 2:29-36.

Sees the fishing scene in Burguete in which Jake and Bill discuss William Jennings Bryan as the center of the novel. Jake's siding with Bryan over Mencken regarding the Scopes trial reveals that Jake takes his faith very seriously.

113　SVOBODA, FREDERIC JOSEPH. *Hemingway & "The Sun Also Rises"*. Lawrence: University Press of Kansas, 148 pp.

Textual examination of various drafts of *The Sun Also Rises* focusing on four scenes in the novel: the early love scene in chapter 7 between Jake and Brett; Jake and the waiter's discussion of Girones's death; Romero's performance in the bullring after Cohn has beaten him up; and the final chapter. Concludes that Hemingway's narrative iceberg theory was an important force in shaping the fiction as were his experiences in Pamplona that provided the author with an initial outline, setting, and cast.

114　TALESE, GAY. "Looking for Hemingway." *Esquire* 99 (June): 151-55.

Reprint from *Esquire* (July 1963).

115　THOMSON, GEORGE H. "'A Clean, Well-Lighted Place': Interpreting the Original Text." *Hemingway Review* 2, no. 2 (Spring): 32-43.

Provides an overview of the numerous critical studies devoted to the story's textual problems. Concludes that regardless of the confusion in lines, the reader must still "confront the desolation of Hemingway's

narrative with its fragment of light, in a night of enclosing nothingness."
See also 1984.62.

116 TILLINGHAST, B.S., Jr. "Five Perspectives for Introducing
Hemingway." *English Journal* 72, no. 8:38-39.
Outlines different approaches for introducing young people to the
richness of Hemingway's writing.

117 TURNBULL, JEANETTE. "Hemingway's Fascination with Pamplona."
Lost Generation Journal 7, no. 2 (Fall): 24-25.
Looks briefly at Hemingway's passion for the corrida, serving as
both entertainment and inspiration for the writer.

118 UPDIKE, JOHN. "Hem Battles the Pack; Wins, Loses." In *Hugging the
Shore: Essays and Criticism*. New York: Alfred A. Knopf, pp. 158-76.
Reprint of 1981.115.

119 VITACOLONNA, LUCIANO. "*The Old Man and the Sea*: Some
Aspects of a Structural Analysis." In *Micro and Macro Connexity of
Texts*. Edited by János Petöfi and Emel Sözer. Hamburg, West
Germany: Buske, pp. 287-300.
In examining textual structures, Vitacolonna divides the novel into
three macro (main) parts: the time prior to Santiago's departure, the
fishing episode, and the return journey. Looks at several aspects of
structure including: the novel's lack of chapter or section division; the
recurrence of the number three and its multiples; the levels of
description, dialogue, monologue, and represented thought; and the
ways in which structural coherence is achieved.
Pp. 301-13: "Narrative and Action Analysis: Some Structural
Aspects of *The Old Man and the Sea*." Looks at Hemingway's use of
action in the fishing passages of the novel in light of Bremond's and Van
Dijk's theories of action description. Finds the same characters
(Santiago, fish, and sharks) playing different roles in the action and
concludes "that in *OMS* nothing is gratuitous or irrelevant."

120 WATTS, CEDRIC. "Hemingway's 'Cat in the Rain': A Preter-
Structuralist View." *Studi dell'Istuto Linguistico* 6:310-23.
MLA Bibliography 1984, p. 244.

121 WHITE, WILLIAM. "For the Collector." *Hemingway Review* 2, no.
2:56-61.
Deals mainly with Hemingway translations and editions.

122 ____. "For the Collector." *Hemingway Review* 3, no. 1 (Fall): 71-72.

Includes information on foreign editions of interest to the collector.

123 _____. "Hemingway: A Current Bibliography." *Hemingway Review* 3, no. 1:73-76.
List of recent items, including articles, reviews, books, new editions, and translations.

124 _____. "Imitation Hemingway Contest: 6." *Hemingway Review* 3 (Fall): 64-65.
Reprints the winning entry for the Sixth International Imitation Hemingway Competition, Lynda Leidiger's "A Farewell to Val." Parody at its best (or worst).

125 WILSON, EDMUND. *The Forties*. Edited by Leon Edel. New York: Farrar, Straus, Giroux, 369 pp.
Scattered references to Hemingway and to Wilson's writing about him.

126 WISER, WILLIAM. *The Crazy Years: Paris in the Twenties*. New York: Atheneum, 256 pp.
Numerous references to Hemingway, his wives Hadley Richardson and Pauline Pfeiffer, his relationships with Stein, Fitzgerald, and McAlmon, and the publication of *Three Stories & Ten Poems* and *The Sun Also Rises*.

127 WITTKOWSKI, WOLFGANG. "Crucified in the Ring: Hemingway's *The Old Man and the Sea*." Translated by Bonita Veysey and Larry Wells. *Hemingway Review* 3, no. 1 (Fall): 2-17.
Looks at the way Santiago's struggle and suffering are modeled after both the fighter in the ring and Christ on the Cross, determining that the Christ model is subsumed by the fighter figure.

128 WOOD, TOM. "Ernest Hemingway 1899-1961." *Lost Generation Journal* 7, no. 2 (Fall): i, 25.
Overview of Hemingway's legendary status and contribution to twentieth-century literature and culture.

129 _____. "Hemingway House: Sightseers Flock to Historic Shrine." *Lost Generation Journal* 7, no. 2 (Fall): 8-11.
Tour of Hemingway's Whitehead Street home in Key West. Includes photographs.

130 _____. "Hemingway's Favorite Watering Hole." *Lost Generation Journal* 7, no. 2 (Fall): 12-15.

Wood describes in detail his visit to Sloppy Joe's Bar, one of Hemingway's old Key West haunts. Includes photographs.

131 WORKMAN, BROOKE.   "In Search of Ernest Hemingway." In *Writing Seminars in the Content Area: In Search of Hemingway, Salinger, and Steinbeck*. Urbana, Ill.: National Council of Teachers of English, pp. 1-116.
    Reprint with slight revision of 1979.111.

132 _____. "Twenty-Nine Things I Know about Bumby Hemingway." *English Journal* 72, no. 2 (February): 24-26.
    Lists facts related to Hemingway's eldest son, John.

133 WYDEN, PETER. *The Passionate War, The Narrative History of the Spanish Civil War*. New York: Simon & Schuster, 575 pp.
    Many references to Hemingway, in his relationships with John Dos Passos and Martha Gellhorn, and in his propagandizing and military roles.

134 WYLDER, DELBERT E. "The Critical Reception of Ernest Hemingway's *Selected Letters, 1917-1961*." *Hemingway Review* 3, no. 1 (Fall): 54-60.
    Overview of the critical response to Baker's collection along with Wylder's own assessment of the volume. "All in all, the reviews are less enthusiastic than the criticism of his most famous novels and less vicious than reviews of his other novels." Quotes liberally from the letters and reviews.

1984

1 BAKKER, J. "In Search of Reality: Two American Heroes Compared." *Costerus*, n.s. 43:37-53.
    An extended comparison of several Hemingway heroes including Harry Morgan, Richard Cantwell, and Santiago with Bellow's Henderson, Herzog, and Sammler. Concludes that the Hemingway hero, in his struggle to reconcile the duality of "man as killer and as having a moral nature, places himself outside the community of men" while the Bellow protagonist places himself squarely within the community as he attempts to solve his problem of identity. "Man as a killer is recognized as blocking the road to change, to his availability to all of life's possibilities."

2 BEEGEL, SUSAN F. "Cowley Gives Lecture, Interview." *Hemingway Newsletter* 8 (June): 2.

Reports on a recent lecture by Malcolm Cowley at Yale University entitled "Hemingway's Wound."

3 ____. "Hemingway Gastronomique: A Guide to Food and Drinking in *A Moveable Feast* (with Glossary)." *Hemingway Review* 4, no. 1 (Fall): 14-26.

Treatment of food and beverages, showing how Hemingway uses the imagery of food and drink to develop the central concerns of his memoirs – the Lost Generation, the fate of the artist, and his relations with wife Hadley and other writers.

4 BERG, A. SCOTT. "Hemingway and Fitzgerald – Where Would They Have Been Without Him?" *New York Times Book Review*, 16 September, p. 38.

Discusses Scribner's editor Max Perkins's wide-ranging influence on and support of numerous authors, including Hemingway.

5 BRAHAM, JEANNE. "A Separate Peace." In *A Sort of Columbus: The American Voyages of Saul Bellow's Fiction*. Athens: University of Georgia Press, pp. 76-98.

Examines the Bellow hero within the paradigm of Hemingway's fiction. Argues that Bellow's resistance to the Hemingway code hero, stoic consciousness, and protagonist/author as "reality" instructor results in his heroes being less concerned with rebirth than with recovery. "The insight Bellow's heroes come to endorse repeatedly is that life is open, is possibilities, is freedom."

6 BRUCCOLI, MATTHEW J., "Yet More Re Hinkle's Polo Shirt Query." *Hemingway Newsletter* 7 (January): 3.

Clarifies the type of shirt worn by Cohn in *The Sun Also Rises*. "By 'polo shirt' EH meant a Brooks Brothers button-down shirt."

7 ____. ed. *James Gould Cozzens, Selected Notebooks, 1960-1967*. Columbia, S.C., and Bloomfield Hills, Mich.: Bruccoli Clark Publishers, 104 pp.

Numerous references to Hemingway and other fellow writers including Faulkner, Porter, Dreiser, and Mailer. Cozzens remarks on the amount of publicity surrounding Hemingway's death, his "hard-boiled" reputation, and the "horrible experience" of reading *A Moveable Feast*.

8 BURROUGHS, WILLIAM S. "Creative Reading." *Review of Contemporary Fiction* 4, no. 1 (Spring): 4-8.

Review of Hemingway's creative process and contribution to twentieth-century literature. Feels that the author's distinct style limited his potential as a writer.

9 CAROTHERS, JAMES B. "Faulkner's Short Stories: 'And Now What's to Do.'" In *New Directions in Faulkner Studies*. Edited by Doreen Fowler and Ann J. Abadie. Jackson: University Press of Mississippi, pp. 202-226.

Compares Faulkner's "Lugger" stories with "The Killers," suggesting that Faulkner deliberately adapted key elements of Hemingway's story in ironic response to Scribner's criticism that his own work lacked "the real core" of a story.

10 CARR, VIRGINIA SPENCER. *Dos Passos: A Life*. Garden City, N.Y.: Doubleday, pp. 201-2, 274, 340, 348, 368-70, 374-76, etc.

Numerous references to Hemingway, including his growing friendship with Dos Passos and eventual estrangement from him due in part to their disagreements over the Spanish civil war. Comments on Hemingway's various wives and the publication of several of his works.

11 CASAS, PENELOPE. "Pamplona in July: Viva San Fermín!" *New York Times*, 29 April, sec. 10, pp. 19, 45.

Finds during her recent visit that "Hemingway remains a powerful presence in Pamplona."

12 COWLEY, MALCOLM. "Hemingway's Wound – and Its Consequences for American Literature." *Georgia Review* 38, no. 2:223-39.

Seemingly written in response to Kenneth Lynn's review of *Ernest Hemingway: Selected Letters, 1917-1961* (see 1981.69). Cowley defends his introduction to the 1944 Viking *Portable Hemingway* by presenting his view of literary history and denying that his introduction was politically motivated. Cowley also supports his original "spooky" reading of "Big Two-Hearted River" through personal correspondence with Hemingway that reveals the author was indeed writing about the war without mentioning it. See also 1984.66 and 1984.135 for additional discussion.

13 ____. "Reader's Forum." *Georgia Review* 38, no. 3:670-72.

In response to Young (see 1984.135), Cowley contends that "the wound in Italy was in the background of my thinking when I wrote an introduction to the *Portable Hemingway* in 1944."

14 CROZIER, ROBERT D., S.J. "The Mask of Death, the Face of Life: Hemingway's Feminique." *Hemingway Review* 4, no. 1 (Fall): 2-13.

In examining the participatory role of women in *For Whom the Bell Tolls* and *Across the River and into the Trees*, Crozier isolates distinct feminine characteristics that are both understood and needed by men. Concludes that Hemingway envisioned a "strong, new and enduring unity of the sexes." Reprinted: 1987.95.

15 CURTIS, JAMES M. "Hemingway." In *Solzhenitsyn's Traditional Imagination*. Athens: University of Georgia Press, pp. 169-81.

Begins by describing the Soviet "rediscovery" of Hemingway during the late 1950s and early 1960s, relating it to Solzhenitsyn's own introduction to the author in 1961 through a translation of *For Whom the Bell Tolls*. Points to similarities in theme (war and revolution) and style (restraint, irony, and understatement) in his analysis of Hemingway's impact on the Russian author.

16 DIETZE, RUDOLPH F. "Crainway and Son: Ralph Ellison's *Invisible Man* As Seen through the Perspective of Twain, Crane, and Hemingway." *DeltaES* 18:25-46.

Sees the common link between all four writers to be their "shared view of life as a sort of ongoing civil war and a common concern for the morality, the moral continuity of American life."

17 DOHERTY, JIM. "Hemingway's River." *Audubon* 86, no. 5:10-15.

Account of his real-life duplication of Nick Adams's fishing trip in "Big Two-Hearted River." Frequent references to Hemingway and the story.

18 DONALDSON, SCOTT. "Fitzgerald and Hemingway." In *American Literary Scholarship: An Annual, 1982*. Edited by J. Albert Robbins. Durham, N.C.: Duke University Press, pp. 167-82.

Survey of criticism on both authors published during 1982. Donaldson finds the quality of scholarship for the year "unusually high" overall.

19 EBY, CECIL D. "The *Soul* in Ernest Hemingway." *Studies in American Fiction* 12, no. 2:223-26.

Examines Hemingway's evolving conception of "soul" in relation to his World War I wounding. In "Now I Lay Me" soul is a synonym for life but in *A Farewell to Arms* the soul is depicted as separate and distinct from the body.

20 EDEL, LEON. "Myth." In *Writing Lives: Principia Biographica*. New York: Norton, pp. 162-64.

Writes of the difficulties associated with reaching beyond the mythic Hemingway legend to the man beneath.

21 ELLMANN, RICHARD. "Freud and Literary Biography." *American Scholar* 53:465-78.

Suggests briefly that Hemingway biographers may wish to comment on the author's anal erotic tendencies of gathering, hoarding, and withholding. "He prided himself on his secrets, and his method of writing was to offer information as sparingly as possible."

22 FAULKNER, WILLIAM. "A Review." *Shenandoah* 35, no. 2-3:123.

Reprints Faulkner's 1952 review of *The Old Man and the Sea* in which he writes: "His Best. Time may show it to be the best single piece of any of us, I mean his and my contemporaries."

23 "The FBI File on Hemingway." *International Herald Tribune* (Paris), 16 March, p. 14.

Hemingway Review 4, no. 1 (Fall 1984): 64.

24 FERRELL, KEITH. *Ernest Hemingway: The Search for Courage*. New York: M. Evans & Co., 236 pp.

Simplistic biography geared toward younger readers. Although offering no new information or interpretation, Ferrell provides a well-organized and straightforward account of those people, places, and events of importance in Hemingway's life and also summarizes novels and stories. Includes index.

25 FLEMING, ROBERT E. "Hemingway's 'The Killers': The Map and the Territory." *Hemingway Review* 4, no. 1 (Fall): 40-43.

Looks at the way Hemingway deliberately built faulty signs and misunderstandings into the text in order to illustrate his theme that the new generation can no longer rely on the codes of the previous generation in interpreting life. "Life sets traps for honest, straightforward people who believe what they hear and what they read."

26 ____. "Re Sources for *The Sun Also Rises*." *Hemingway Newsletter* 8 (June): 3.

In response to James Hinkle's earlier article (see 1982.37), Fleming argues that the line in question ("He sat in the outer room and read the papers, and the Editor and Publishers and I worked hard for two hours") actually means that Cohn was reading both papers and the trade journal *Editor & Publisher* while Jake worked in the inner office.

27 FONTANA, ERNEST. "Hemingway's 'A Pursuit Race.'" *Explicator* 42, no. 4 (Summer): 43-45.

Identifies Willie Campbell's "wolf" as his homosexual lover, thus, asserting that his greatest horror is his homosexuality.

28   FORD, RICHARD. "The Three Kings: Hemingway, Faulkner, and Fitzgerald." In *Fifty Who Made the Difference*. An *Esquire* Press Book. New York: Villard Books, pp. 499-514.
      Reprint of 1983.40.

29   FRENCH, WILLIAM. "Fragment of a Letter." *Yale Literary Magazine* 150:154-60.
      Concentrates on Hemingway's lengthy friendship with Ezra Pound and prints a portion of a letter written by Hemingway to Pound while the poet was incarcerated at St. Elizabeth's Hospital.

30   FUENTES, NORBERTO. *Hemingway in Cuba*. Translated by Consuelo E. Corwin. Secaucus, N.J.: Lyle Stuart, 453 pp.
      Biography focused on Hemingway's final years. Interviews numerous Russians and Cubans, revealing a complex picture of the aging author haunted by chronic depression. Includes a valuable catalogue of what Mary Welsh Hemingway left behind when she removed manuscripts and other materials from the Finca Vigía in 1961: corrected galleys of *Across the River and into the Trees*, fragments of drafts from *For Whom the Bell Tolls*, script corrections for *The Old Man and the Sea*, unpublished correspondence, and portions of an untitled story. Many reprinted in the extensive appendices.

31   GAJDUSEK, ROBERT E. *Hemingway and Joyce: A Study in Debt and Repayment*. Corte Madera, Calif.: Square Circle Press, 50 pp.
      Monograph aimed at determining Joyce's influence on Hemingway in terms of theme, structure, and technique. Gives an overview of past scholarship on the subject along with a brief look at Hemingway's associations with Joyce. Taking nearly all of Hemingway's major works into account, Gajdusek pays particular attention to how Hemingway adapts Joyce's fascination with cyclical patterns, crossover and transcendence, and ritual.

32   GARCIA, WILMA. *Mothers and Others: Myths of the Female in the Works of Melville, Twain, and Hemingway*. New York: Peter Lang, 180 pp.
      Sees the rigid and limited role of women in Hemingway's works, especially as sexual partner, prescribed by cultural tradition. Garcia categorizes Hemingway's protagonists as true heroes who, having undergone a traumatic experience, are unable to return to the life they once knew. The female characters in *The Sun Also Rises*, *For Whom the Bell Tolls*, and *A Farewell to Arms* share the trials of the heroic journey but still embody mythic conventions assigned to them such as the archetypal image of renewed life and innocence amid destruction.

33 GARRETT, GEORGE. *James Jones*. New York: Harcourt Brace Jovanovich, 218 pp.

Many references to Hemingway, as a model for Jones (Jones went first to Scribner's because of their long association with the important modernist writers, 18-20) and as an influence.

34 GELFANT, BLANCHE H. "'Lives' of Women Writers: Cather, Austin, Porter/and Willa, Mary, Katherine Anne." *Novel* 18, no. 1 (Fall): 64-80.

Using Hemingway's life (literary art and career) as emblematic of the male author, Gelfant looks at literary biography's differing treatment of writers of both sexes. Reprinted in *Women Writing in America: Voices in Collage* (Hanover, NH: University Press of New England, 1984).

35 GILLIGAN, THOMAS MAHER. "Topography in Hemingway's 'Hills Like White Elephants.'" *Notes on Modern American Literature* 8, no. 1:item 2.

Uncovering parallels between the surrounding landscape and the couple depicted in the short story, Gilligan reveals the shallowness of their relationship.

36 GLENDAY, MICHAEL K. "*Deliverance* and the Aesthetics of Survival." *American Literature* 56, no. 2 (May): 149-61.

Briefly draws a parallel between Robert Jordan in *For Whom the Bell Tolls* and Ed Gentry in James Dickey's *Deliverance*, finding that both protagonists "savor the prospect of killing as an aesthetic exercise."

37 GRADOLI, MARINA. "Italy in Ernest Hemingway's Fiction." *Rivista di Studi Anglo-Americani* 3, no. 4-5:145-52.

Breaks Hemingway's Italian visits into three categories and, accordingly, the works produced at those times. In analyzing Hemingway's changing attitudes concerning Italy, Gradoli traces the author's "movement from indifference to involvement" as evidenced in the early *A Farewell to Arms* and the later *Across the River and into the Trees*.

38 GREEN, MARTIN. "Hemingway's *Green Hills of Africa*." In *The Great American Adventure: Action Stories*. Boston: Beacon Press, pp. 167-83.

Includes *Green Hills of Africa* in his examination of the adventure tradition in American literature. Discusses the nineteenth-century context that Hemingway was working out of and the influence of British author Rudyard Kipling on American modernists. Argues from a Marxist orientation that Hemingway depicts the image of the great artist/hunter traveling the world and engaging in an imperial hunt as an alternative to war.

39 GULLASON, THOMAS A. "The 'Lesser' Renaissance: The American
Short Story in the 1920s." In *The American Short Story, 1900-1945: A
Critical History*. Edited by Philip Stevick. Boston: Twayne, pp. 71-101.
    Brief overview of Hemingway's contribution to the shaping of the
American short story. Covers early influences on the author and his
initial difficulties in getting his short fiction published. Also comments
on the seeming simplicity of his style, noting his technique of "layering"
meaning within texts.

40 HAINES, JAMES B. "More Re Hinkle's Polo Shirt Query." *Hemingway
Newsletter* 7 (January): 3.
    Responds to an earlier inquiry regarding the type of polo shirts
worn by Cohn in *The Sun Also Rises*. Describes the shirt as a standard
dress shirt for polo players because its button-down collar prevented it
from flapping up during play. Considers it a "sartorial symbol . . . of the
Princeton connection."

41 HANNUM, HOWARD L. "Dating Hemingway's 'Three-Day Blow' by
External Evidence: The Baseball Dialogue." *Studies in Short Fiction* 21,
no. 3 (Summer): 267-68.
    Points to references in Bill and Nick's discussion about baseball as
evidence that "The Three-Day Blow" and "The End of Something" are
prewar stories.

42 ____. "Soldier's Home: Immersion Therapy and Lyric Pattern in 'Big
Two-Hearted River.'" *Hemingway Review* 3, no. 2:2-13.
    Looks at Hemingway's use of a lyric sequence within the narrative
pattern of the text, contending that structurally the story resembles an
ode and that Nick's therapy follows a similar pattern.

43 HAUPTFUHRER, FRED. "*The Sun Also Rises* for TV." *People* 22, no.
10 (3 September): 28-31.
    Announces the upcoming four-hour miniseries version of the
novel starring Jane Seymour and Hart Bochner.

44 HAYS, PETER L. "Hemingway and London." *Hemingway Review* 4, no.
1 (Fall): 54-56.
    Looks at Jack London's literary influence on Hemingway in
subject matter, style, and focus on immediate action.

45 ____. "Self-Reflexive Laughter in 'A Day's Wait.'" *Hemingway Notes* 6,
no. 1 (Fall): 25.
    Sees Hemingway mocking his own heroic code in the story of a
little boy who bravely awaits his impending death from a moderate
fever.

46 HINKLE, JAMES. "Note on Hemingway and the Moral Majority."
    Hemingway Newsletter 8 (June): 4.
         Comments on a passage in Steve Shagan's 1983 *The Circle* in
    which a group of people representing the Moral Crusade discuss the
    banning of *The Sun Also Rises* from public schools.

47 ____. "Re Query on Passage from *SAR*." *Hemingway Newsletter* 7
    (January): 4.
         Responds to an earlier inquiry regarding Bill's speech on page 122
    of *The Sun Also Rises*. Interprets "Don't eat that, Lady–that's
    Mencken" as "the most directly obscene sentence in the book."

48 HOTCHNER, A.E. "When Hemingway Hurts Bad Enough, He Cries."
    In *Choice People: The Greats, Near Greats, and Ingrates I Have Known*.
    New York: William Morrow & Co., pp. 65-77.
         Recalls his first meeting with Hemingway in a Cuban bar, his later
    deep-sea fishing trip with him aboard the *Pilar*, the circumstances
    surrounding Hemingway's writing of *Across the River and into the Trees*,
    and their growing friendship.
         Pp. 397-406: "The Ghost of J. Edgar Hoover haunts the Corpse of
    Ernest Hemingway." Relates his embarrassment over the opening of the
    FBI file on Hemingway that revealed that Hemingway's claims of being
    persecuted by the FBI were not as psychotic as Hotchner had originally
    assumed.

49 HOUSTON, NEAL B. "Old Lady, Now Here Is Where the 'Wow' Is."
    American Notes and Queries 22, no. 5-6 (January-February): 78-80.
         Parallels Hemingway's handling of the homosexual motif in the
    unpublished "There's One in Every Town" with a similar version
    appearing in *Death in the Afternoon*.

50 "Individual Authors." *Journal of Modern Literature* 11, no. 3-4
    (November): 453-55.
         Descriptive listing of recent scholarly and critical studies on
    Hemingway.

51 JOHNSTON, KENNETH G. "Hemingway and Cézanne: Doing the
    Country." *American Literature* 56, no. 1 (March): 28-37.
         Describes Cézanne paintings on display during Hemingway's Paris
    days. A comparison of a pre-Cézanne piece ("Up in Michigan") with a
    post-Cézanne ("Big Two-Hearted River") clearly demonstrates the
    artist's influence on the young author regarding the selection,
    restructuring, and omission of detail. Reprinted with slight revision:
    1987.38.

52 ____. "Hemingway and Freud: The Tip of the Iceberg." *Journal of Narrative Technique* 14, no. 1 (Winter): 68-73.

Points to the similarities sin Freud's theories of the conscious, preconscious, and unconscious and Hemingway's iceberg principle in writing that seeks to make only one-eighth of a story explicit. According to Freud, "The poet's art consists essentially in covering up." Reprinted with slight revision: 1987.38.

53 ____. "'The Snows of Kilimanjaro': An African Purge." *Studies in Short Fiction* 21, no. 3 (Summer): 223-27.

Argues for a biographical interpretation of the story written by a craftsman who had long neglected his serious craft (fiction writing) in favor of nonfiction. Reads the story "as a report on the artistic and spiritual health of its author." Reprinted: 1987.38.

54 ____. "The Songs in Hemingway's 'The Snows. . . .'" *American Notes and Queries* 23, no. 3-4 (November-December): 46-48.

Looks at the way the Cole Porter lyric and Mother Goose melody underscore the motif of loss/betrayal in "The Snows of Kilimanjaro."

55 JONES, HORACE P. "Twain's *The Adventures of Huckleberry Finn*." *Explicator* 43, no. 1 (Fall): 43.

Takes exception to Hemingway's comment in *Green Hills of Africa* that Jim (of *Huckleberry Finn*) is stolen from the boys. "Jim belongs to no one on the raft; consequently, he could not have been stolen from anyone. His legal owner, Miss Watson, from whom he has run away, is way back up the river in Missouri."

56 KAISER, GERD. Stundenblätter. *Hemingway's Short Stories: Indian Camp, The Killers, The Battler, The Old Man at the Bridge*. Stuttgart, West Germany: Klett, 82 pp.

Annual Bibliography of English Language and Literature for 1985, p. 660.

57 KALIM, M. SIDDIQ. "The Motif of Peace in Hemingway." *Pakistan Journal of American Studies* 2, no. 2:22-28.

Overview article, commenting on Hemingway's fascination with "masculine" pursuits along with a summary treatment of the themes of war, peace, love, and sex in *The Sun Also Rises, A Farewell to Arms, For Whom the Bell Tolls*, and *The Fifth Column*.

58 KAZIN, ALFRED. "Hemingway and Fitzgerald: The Cost of Being American." *American Heritage: The Magazine of History* 35, no. 3:49-64.

Biographical essay emphasizing the influence of Cézanne, Matisse, and Stein on the young Hemingway, his fascination with violence, and his contribution to the American literary scene.

59 _____. "Hemingway the Painter." In *American Procession*. New York: Alfred A. Knopf, pp. 357-73.
Reprint of 1977.66. Reprinted: 1985.12.

60 KEINER, DAVID. "Two Alleged Errors of Dialogue Indentation in *Islands in the Stream*." *Analytical and Enumerative Bibliography* 8, no. 4:239-41.
Contends that no editor has the right to "correct" Hemingway's seeming confusing antimetronomic dialogue because it was both an intentional practice and a well-established technique in his writing.

61 KENNEDY, THOMAS E. "Nuts, Bolts, and Sheer Plod: An Interview with Gordon Weaver." *Western Humanities Review* 38, no. 4 (Winter): 363-37.
Novelist Gordon Weaver lists Hemingway as one of his literary influences. "Surely, Hemingway teaches you economy, that you don't need all that much space or that many words to create a whole cosmos in fiction."

62 KERNER, DAVID. "The Thomson Alternative." *Hemingway Review* 4, no. 1 (Fall): 37-39.
Responds to Thomson's reading of the textual confusions in "A Clean, Well-Lighted Place" (see 1983.115). Argues that Thomson's interpretation completely distorts Hemingway's characterizations of the two waiters.

63 KOBLER, J.F. *Ernest Hemingway: Journalist and Artist*. Studies in Modern Literature, no. 44. Ann Arbor, Mich.: UMI Research Press, 174 pp.
Examines the relationship between Hemingway's journalistic writing and his literary nonfiction and fiction. Compares the three in terms of content, ideas, and style and also looks at the process by which real events reported in Hemingway's journalism or nonfiction evolved into fiction. Particularly useful stylistic analysis of the differences in Hemingway's journalistic and artistic styles, looking at how the author adapted style to fit a specific medium.

64 KUBIE, LAWRENCE. "Ernest Hemingway: Cyrano and the Matador." *American Imago* 41, no. 1 (Spring): 9-18.
Written in 1934, this article was suppressed due to the personal nature of its approach, being viewed more as a psychological

examination of the author than the texts. In this psychoanalytic analysis of underlying Oedipal conflicts in Hemingway's works, Kubie looks at how the challenge of fear and the triumph over fear thematically tie the author's stories together. See 1984.75.

65 LACHMANN-KALITZKI, EVA. "Kindred Spirits: Ernst Toller Seen as Part of a New Spiritual 'Triumvirate.'" *Germanic Notes* 15, no. 3-4:47-51.
Brief analysis of Ernst Toller/Bertha von Suttner/Hemingway triumvirate, finding similar backgrounds and literary themes regarding war, peace, and politics.

66 LYNN, KENNETH. "Reader's Forum." *Georgia Review* 38, no. 3:668-69.
Lynn takes Cowley to task for believing everything that Hemingway ever told him, pointing out that "Hemingway was one of the great liars of his literary generation." Reasserts his claim that "Big Two-Hearted River" has nothing to do with Nick's previous war experiences. See 1984.12 and 1984.135.

67 McCOMAS, DIX. "The Geography of Ernest Hemingway's 'Out of Season.'" *Hemingway Review* 3, no. 2 (Spring): 46-49.
Using details from the text, McComas traces Peduzzi and the young couple's movements, showing how Hemingway's story about a man's divided loyalties is reflected in the setting itself for Cortina was claimed by both Italy and Austria. Includes map. See also 1985.18.

68 McNEELY, TREVOR. "War Zone Revisited: Hemingway's Aesthetics and *A Farewell to Arms*." *South Dakota Review* 22, no. 4 (Winter): 14-38.
In his detailed investigation, McNeely couples the twin poles of love and war in the novel with romanticism and realism, arguing that thinking (reflection) and falling in love are destructive since both falsify or romanticize reality. War always comes closer to "truth" in the Hemingway code. Also discusses Frederic's ambivalent feelings toward Catherine and his subconscious discontent with their affair.

69 McSWEENEY, KERRY. "Hemingway's Obsession." *Queen's Quarterly* 91, no. 4:877-90.
Survey of recent critical studies devoted to Hemingway's craft. Also quotes the author's own views on writing, excerpted from *Ernest Hemingway: Selected Letters, 1917-1961*.

70 MELLOW, JAMES R. *Invented Lives: F. Scott and Zelda Fitzgerald*. Boston: Houghton Mifflin Co., 569 pp.
Numerous references to Hemingway, his parents, wives Hadley Richardson and Pauline Pfeiffer, and sons. Reconstructs Hemingway's

relationship with Fitzgerald, their writings in relation to each other, and Fitzgerald's early championing of the young author and growing friendship with him based in part on hero worship.

71 MEYERS, JEFFREY. "Chink Dorman-Smith and *Across the River and into the Trees*." *Journal of Modern Literature* 11, no. 2 (July): 314-22.

Argues that Hemingway's World War I buddy and long time friend E.E. (Chink) Dorman-Smith served as the model for Cantwell, concluding that the novel "represents Hemingway's vicarious attempt to express and purge Chink's bitterness" over his military experiences.

72 ____. "Communications." *Bulletin of Bibliography* 41, no. 4 (December): 184.

Lists a number of errors in Hemingway's works, mainly in his spelling of foreign phrases, names, and places.

73 ____. "Hemingway's Second War: The Greco-Turkish Conflict, 1920-1922." *Modern Fiction Studies* 30, no. 1 (Spring): 25-36.

Provides historical background on the Greco-Turkish War along with an examination of how Hemingway's involvement in the war's aftermath resulted in the inspiration of three vignettes of *in our time*.

74 ____. "Kipling and Hemingway: The Lesson of the Master." *American Literature* 56, no. 1 (March): 87-99.

Influence study looking at Hemingway's literary debt to Kipling. Points out similarities in theme, subject, technique, and portrayal of an honor code.

75 ____. "Lawrence Kubie's Suppressed Essay on Hemingway." *American Imago* 41:1-18.

Analyzes Kubie's 1934 essay dealing with the underlying Oedipal conflicts in Hemingway's works (and in the author himself) that was suppressed by Hemingway and Scribner's editor Max Perkins. Meyers provides an extensive publishing history on the piece and also reprints it. See 1984.64.

76 ____. "Memoirs of Hemingway: The Growth of a Legend." *Virginia Quarterly* 60, no. 4:587-612.

Discusses Hemingway's deliberate imitation of his legendary image and the difficulties associated with differentiating fact from fiction. Reviews the numerous memoirs written by family, friends, and acquaintances over the years, warning readers that they are a minefield of slanted opinions, confused memories, half-truths, conflicting accounts, and rumor. Reprinted: 1989.33.

77 MILLER, LINDA PATTERSON. "Gerald Murphy and Ernest Hemingway: Part I." *Studies in American Fiction* 12, no. 2:129-44.

Biographical essay tracing Hemingway's split with friend Gerald Murphy. Drawing on correspondence between the two, Miller argues that Hemingway broke from Murphy primarily because Murphy supported his decision to separate from Hadley, a decision that Hemingway later deeply regretted. See also 1985.77 for additional discussion.

78 MILLER, PAUL. "Callaghan's *That Summer in Paris*: A Portrait of the Artist as a Young Man." *Canadian Literature*, no. 101 (Summer), pp. 176-79.

Chronicles Callaghan's reconstruction of his relationship with Hemingway in *That Summer in Paris*. Looks at Callaghan's eventual rejection of Hemingway's artistic vision in favor of a wider social consciousness.

79 MONTEIRO, GEORGE. "Hemingway's 'Symbolism of the Inconspicuous.'" *Hemingway Review* 3 (Spring): 22.

Draws attention to Erich Kahler's 1957 *The Tower and the Abyss: An Inquiry into the Transformation of the Individual* in which he comments on Hemingway's achievements in prose style.

80 _____. "Note on Alan Dugan Interview." *Hemingway Newsletter* 7 (January): 4.

Interview with poet Alan Dugan. Dugan considers Hemingway to be a "big hero" of the Liberation because unlike Camus, Sartre, and the other French intellectuals in Paris during World War II, Hemingway actively participated in the Liberation.

81 MOORE, ANN BRASHEAR. "Hemingway's *The Sun Also Rises* and Stein: A Stylistic Approach." *Káñina* 8, no. 1-2:111-17.

Argues that Stein's influence on the apprentice writer is overrated. Although Hemingway learned much about the craft of omission, repetition, and simplicity from Stein, his distinct treatment of dialogue and theme confirm that Hemingway experimented with and developed a style that was his own.

82 MORTON, BRIAN N. *Americans in Paris: An Anecdotal Street Guide*. Ann Arbor: Olivia & Hill Press, 313 pp.

Frequent references to places where Hemingway lived, wrote, and visited while in Paris, including favorite restaurants and bars.

83 MUROLO, FREDERICK L. "Another Look at the Nun and Her Prayers." *Hemingway Review* 4, no. 1 (Fall): 52-53.

Concludes that Hemingway's depiction of Sister Cecilia in "The Gambler, the Nun, and the Radio" as an overzealous sports fan who prays successfully not only for Cayetano's recovery but for sports teams is "a refreshing, ironic twist to an otherwise devastatingly pessimistic story."

84 NAGEL, JAMES, ed. *Ernest Hemingway: The Writer in Context.* Madison: University of Wisconsin Press, 246 pp.

A collection of essays given at a 1982 Hemingway conference at Northeastern University, in cooperation with the Hemingway Society and the John F. Kennedy Library. Contents:

Pp. ix-xvii: Introduction by James Nagel about the previous Hemingway conferences and the importance of these particular papers, stressing as they do the context for Hemingway's work.

Pp. 3-12: "Publishing Hemingway" by Charles Scribner, Jr. Discusses the author's relationship with this Scribner and his father. Much attention to Hemingway's rapport with Maxwell Perkins, beginning with *The Torrents of Spring,* and to the personal qualities of the author.

Pp. 13-18: "*Islands in the Stream*: A Son Remembers" by Patrick Hemingway. Focuses on the catching of the fish and the shark attack – both fictions, so far as Patrick knows. Insights into Hemingway's relationships with Martha Gellhorn, Marlene Dietrich, and others.

Pp. 19-27: "Reflections on Ernest Hemingway" by Tom Stoppard. From the perspective of the evanescence of literary reputation, Stoppard comments on Hemingway's craft of omission.

Pp. 31-52: "The Making of *Death in the Afternoon*" by Robert W. Lewis. Makes extensive use of manuscripts and writing history, beginning in 1925. Some comments on Hemingway's rivalry with William Faulkner.

Pp. 53-74: "The Tenth Indian and the Thing Left Out" by Paul Smith. Recasts Hemingway's Michigan years and his use of Indians in fiction. Close manuscript study of "Ten Indians," with attention to the theory of omission, and a closing comment on Prudence Boulton's death.

Pp. 77-106: "Grace under Pressure: Hemingway and the Summer of 1920" by Max Westbrook. Recounts evidence from family letters at University of Texas about the dissension between Hemingway and his mother, Grace Hall Hemingway, in 1920. Reprinted: 1987.95.

Pp. 107-128: "*A Farewell to Arms*: Pseudoautobiography and Personal Metaphor" by Millicent Bell. Studies the relationship between Frederic Henry and Catherine Barkley, concluding that "Frederic has only delusively attached himself to an otherness." Bell questions the passivity of both characters and terms their affair more maternal than passionate. Reprinted: 1987.6.

Pp. 129-44: "Women and the Loss of Eden in Hemingway's Mythology" by Carol H. Smith. Depicts Hemingway's use of women characters as a means of disillusioning the male character who is often idealistic about "love." Includes Catherine, Brett, Maria, and other women characters.

Pp. 147-64: "Exchange between Rivals: Faulkner's Influence on *The Old Man and the Sea*" by Peter L. Hays. Traces Hemingway's antagonism to Faulkner, as well as significant parallels in their lives as writers.

Pp. 165-78: "Ernest and Henry: Hemingway's Lover's Quarrel with James" by Adeline R. Tintner. Shows that Hemingway knew James's work well, particularly in *Across the River and into the Trees* and *The Sun Also Rises*.

Pp. 179-200: "Ernest Hemingway and Ezra Pound" by Jacqueline Tavernier-Courbin. Builds the aesthetic and personal relationship between the older poet and the young and impressionable Hemingway in Paris. Makes extensive use of Pound's letters from the Kennedy Library.

Pp. 201-236: "Invention from Knowledge: The Hemingway-Cowley Correspondence" by James D. Brasch. Pays clear tribute to Cowley for his role in charting of both modernism and Hemingway's strengths as writer. Much use of Cowley letters.

85 NAKJAVANI, ERIK. "The Aesthetics of Silence: Hemingway's 'The Art of the Short Story.'" *Hemingway Review* 3, no. 2 (Spring): 38-45.

Theoretical examination of Hemingway's preface, looking at the author's theory of omission within the context of the aesthetics of silence.

86 NELSON, GERALD B., and JONES, GLORY. *Hemingway: Life and Works*. New York: Facts on File, 183 pp.

Chronology of Hemingway's life and career, documented year by year (and sometimes day by day). Touches on important ideas, places, people, and events in the author's life. Includes selected bibliography of works by and about Hemingway.

87 NELSON, RAYMOND S. *Ernest Hemingway: Life, Work, and Criticism*. Fredericton, Nebr.: York Press, 43 pp.

Includes a brief biography, chronological list of his works, summaries of major works, and a critical overview of his contribution to twentieth-century literature.

88 NOLAN, CHARLES J., Jr., "Hemingway's Women's Movement." *Hemingway Review* 3, no. 2 (Spring): 14-22.

Argues that despite popular belief, Hemingway's fiction up to the late 1930s is sympathetic to the plight of women, especially those trapped in relationships with insensitive and boorish men who blame their own failures on the women in their lives. Pays particular attention to Hemingway's early short stories such as "Up in Michigan," "Out of Season," "Cat in the Rain," "The End of Something," and "Hills Like White Elephants." Reprinted: 1987.95.

89 ____. "Shooting the Sergeant: Frederic Henry's Puzzling Action." *College Literature* 11, no. 3 (Fall): 269-75.

In light of Henry's commitment to duty, which includes dealing with deserters, Nolan sees Henry's shooting as proper under military law.

90 OATES, JOYCE CAROL. "Ernest Hemingway: Man's Man? Woman-Hater? Our Greatest Writer?" *TV Guide* 32, no. 49 (8 December): 4-8.

Comments on Hemingway's impact on both American literature and culture, focusing on his writer-as-celebrity image and exaggerated sense of masculinity.

91 OGNIBENE, PETER J. "At the First Ski Spa, Stars Outshone the Sun and Snow." *Smithsonian* 15, no. 9 (December): 108-19.

Speaks briefly of Hemingway's attachment to Sun Valley, Idaho, beginning with the author's first visit in 1939.

92 PARKER, HERSHEL. "The Determinacy of the Creative Process and the Authority of the Author's Belated Textual Decisions." In *Flawed Texts and Verbal Icons*. Evanston, Ill.: Northwestern University Press, pp. 17-51.

Comments on Fitzgerald's well-known revisions of *The Sun Also Rises* and how information deleted in the initial opening disrupts the novel as a whole.

93 PAWLEY, Daniel. "Ernest Hemingway: Tragedy of an Evangelical Family." *Christianity Today* 28, no. 17 (23 November): 20-27.

Provides biographical data on Hemingway's Christian heritage and eventual rebellion against his family's rigorous faith.

94 PETRY, ALICE HALL. "Coming of Age in Hortons Bay: Hemingway's 'Up in Michigan.'" *Hemingway Review* 3, no. 2 (Spring): 23-28.

Argues that Hemingway's sympathy is with Liz Coates as he graphically depicts "the glaring disparity between male and female attitudes towards love and sex."

95 PHILLIPS, LARRY W., ed. *Ernest Hemingway on Writing*. New York: Scribner's; 140 pp.

Collection of Hemingway's comments and views on the craft of writing. Of little use to the scholar, but is probably of enough interest to the general reader and would-be writer to warrant publication.

96 PINSKER, SANFORD. "Revisionism with Rancor: The Threat of the Neoconservative Critics." *Georgia Review* 38, no. 2 (Summer): 243-61.

Takes exception to Kenneth Lynn's reading (see 1981.69) of "Big Two-Hearted River" as a "happy fishing trip" because of Lynn's failure to take into account Hemingway's own comments, which squarely place the story within the context of the war. See 1984.12, 1984.66, and 1984.135 for additional discussion.

97 RAEBURN, JOHN. *Fame Became of Him: Hemingway as Public Writer*. Bloomington: Indiana University Press, 231 pp.

Examines the development of Hemingway's celebrity mask which the author began shaping in the 1920s and perfected in the 1930s. Argues that *Death in the Afternoon* (1932) more than any other work "formulated his public personality" because it presents Hemingway in various appealing roles such as sportsman, manly man, world traveler, and heroic artist, thus laying the foundation for his public image which eventually eclipsed his private life. Speculates on why Hemingway actively cultivated the celebrity personality and its effects on his art.

98 RAMPERSAD, ARNOLD. "*Adventures of Huckleberry Finn* and Afro-American Literature." *Mark Twain Journal* 22, no. 2 (Fall): 47-52.

Speculates on the extent to which Hemingway's comment (on the importance of *Huckleberry Finn* being "the best book we've had. All American writing comes from that") applies to black American fiction.

99 REBOLI, NICOLA L. "Death as a Vehicle to Life in the Works of Ernest Hemingway." *Studi dell'Istituto Linguistico* 7:333-46.
    MLA Bibliography 1985, no. 8356, p. 217.

100 ROSENTHAL, HERMAN. "Report from Paris: Taking Liberties with an American Classic." *TV Guide* 32, no. 49 (8 December): 10-12.

Discusses the challenges for both the writer and performers in adapting *The Sun Also Rises* into a four-hour TV movie.

101 RUDAT, WOLFGANG E.H. "Jake's Odyssey: Catharsis in *The Sun Also Rises*." *Hemingway Review* 4, no. 1 (Fall): 33-36.

Looks at the way in the final car-ride scene that Jake exorcises himself of Brett by adopting a homosexual pose in order to avoid her attempt to castrate him psychologically. Thus Jake finally breaks the

Circean spell and "is able to put the past behind him and embrace the future."

102 RYAN, STEVEN T. "Prosaic Unity in *To Have and Have Not*." *Hemingway Review* 4, no. 1 (Fall): 27-32.
      Looks at the way Hemingway achieves unity in his experimental novel through a complex structure of opposites centered on the contrast between those female characters who know only a half-life and those who know what *Life* can be.

103 SAMUELSON, ARNOLD. *With Hemingway: A Year in Key West and Cuba*. New York: Random House, 183 pp.
      Journal-based account written more than half a century ago of the year Samuelson spent crewing for Hemingway aboard the *Pilar* in exchange for a writing tutorial. Gives a detailed account of day-to-day activities at the Whitehead Street home Hemingway shared with second wife Pauline, the author's time spent with Cuban cronies, and his frequent fishing trips with family and friends aboard the *Pilar*. Most of Hemingway's advice to the aspiring author has already been published over the years.

104 SCHUSTER, MARILYN R. "Reading and Writing as a Woman: The Retold Tales of Marguerite Duras." *French Review* 58, no. 1 (October): 48-57.
      Discusses the ways Duras's 1952 *Le Marin de Gibraltar* retells, through parody and inference, "The Snows of Kilimanjaro."

105 SCHWARTZ, NINA. "Lovers' Discourse in *The Sun Also Rises*: A Cock and Bull Story." *Criticism* 26, no. 1 (Winter): 46-69.
      Referring to Derrida, existentialism, and neo-Freudian theory, Schwartz explores "the dialectic of castration and desire" in the novel, arguing that Jake's impotence enables him to master Brett because he will never fulfill the desire that he has aroused in her. Discusses parallels between Romero's mastery of the bull and Jake's mastery of Brett, concluding that the ritual of the bullfight, in actuality, depicts "the symbolic destruction of man by woman."

106 SCHWENGER, PETER. "Reserve and Its Reverse." In *Phallic Critiques: Masculinity and Twentieth-Century Literature*. Boston: Routledge & Kegan Paul, pp. 36-50.
      Discusses Hemingway's preoccupation with the masculine role and its relation to his writing. Argues that despite the author's attention to "manly" themes and subject matter (especially the traditional masculine reserve), Hemingway's style preserves a feminine truth that the reader is made to feel can never be completely known.

107 SEELY, MIKE. "Re Hinkle's Polo Shirt Query." *Hemingway Newsletter*
7 (January): 3.
Responds to an earlier inquiry regarding the type of polo shirts
worn by Cohn in *The Sun Also Rises*. Describes the shirt as a standard
dress shirt for polo players because its button-down collar did not flap
up during play.

108 SHAMES, LAURENCE. "Hemingway's Briefcase." *Vanity Fair* 47, no. 8
(August): 17.
On the recent auctioning of Hemingway's briefcase, which sold for
$5,100.

109 SHAW, VALERIE. "The Splintering Frame." In *The Short Story, A
Critical Introduction*. New York: Longmans, pp. 227-69.
Looks briefly at Hemingway's lasting influence on the short-story
form, commenting on his ability to achieve a paradoxical sense of
detachment and intimacy in such stories as "Now I Lay Me" and others
from *Men without Women*.

110 SIPIORA, PHILLIP. "Hemingway's 'Hills Like White Elephants.'"
Explicator 42, no. 3 (Spring): 50.
Argues that Jig's apparent consent to the abortion at the end of
the story is actually the result of her inebriated condition and that
"nothing is resolved."

111 SLOAN, JAMES PARK. "A Toast to Hemingway: For Whom the
Nobel Tolled." *Bookworld* (*Chicago Tribune*), 11 November, pp. 31, 39.
Annual Bibliography of English Language and Literature for 1984,
p. 624.

112 SMITH, PAUL, and TAVERNIER-COURBIN, JACQUELINE.
"'Terza Riruce': Hemingway, Dunning, Italian Poetry." *Hemingway
Review* 3, no. 2 (Spring): 50-51.
Reprint of 1983.106.

113 SONNE, HARLY. "Problems of Knowledge in Fiction: Comments on
the Papers by Han Verhoeff and Gilbert Chaitin." *Style* 18, no. 3
(Summer): 302-11.
Discusses Hemingway's iceberg theory in light of what is omitted
from "Indian Camp." Contends that Uncle George is the real father of
the Indian woman's baby, thus solving the mystery of why her husband
commits suicide.

114 SPILKA, MARK. "A Source for the Macomber 'Accident': Marryat's
Percival Keene." *Hemingway Review* 3, no. 2 (Spring): 29-37.

Suggests Marryat's influence on Hemingway by pointing out parallels between Marryat's work and "The Short Happy Life of Francis Macomber," including deadly shooting accidents, hidden motives, and cowardice.

115 ____. "Victorian Keys to the Early Hemingway: Captain Marryat." *Novel* 17, no. 2 (Winter): 116-40.

Chronicles Hemingway's lifelong interest in the naval adventure novels of Frederick Marryat, British author and man of action. Looks at the recurring themes of masculine identity and warfare in Marryat's works and their influence on Hemingway's own writing.

116 STONEBACK, H.R. "Note on Hemingway in Thailand." *Hemingway Newsletter* 7 (January): 3.

Comments on Hemingway's popularity in Thailand. Many of his works have been translated, and he is included regularly in surveys and seminars.

117 STOUCK, DAVID. "*Many Marriages* as a Post-Modern Novel." *Midwestern Miscellany*, no. 12, pp. 15-22.

Begins his analysis of Anderson's *Many Marriages* with a brief look at Hemingway's parody of Anderson's style in *The Torrents of Spring*. "Hemingway's novel is exaggerated but it does point to an impulse in Anderson's writing toward experimental form, lyricism, and fantasy which constituted a sharp break from the dominant mode of realism in the American novel."

118 STRAUCH, EDWARD H. "*The Old Man and the Sea*: An Anthropological View." *Aligarh Journal of English Studies* 9, no. 1:56-63.

Sees Santiago's sea experience as a pilgrimage, pointing to the old fisherman's naturalistic and ritualistic way of life, the purity of his soul, the remoteness of his chosen sea destination, the suffering he undergoes to arrive there, and the sacrifice of the marlin as evidence of his interpretation.

119 STULL, WILLIAM L. "Richard Brautigan's *Trout Fishing in America*: Notes of a Native Son." *American Literature* 56, no. 1 (March): 68-80.

Numerous references to Hemingway and his influence on Brautigan's works, including *A Confederate General from Big Sur* and *Trout Fishing in America*. Pointing out similar themes, plot, characterization, and style, Stull concludes that in *Trout Fishing* "Hemingway's long shadow falls across nearly every page, symbolizing a lost literary promise that parallels the lost grandeur of virgin forests and clear streams."

120 SWAN, MARTIN. "*The Old Man and the Sea*: Women Taken for Granted." In *Visages de la Féminité*. St. Denis: Université de la Réunion, pp. 147-63.

Explores "classical misogyny" in the text through the negative portrayal of the four women characters: Santiago's wife, the female tourist, the sea, and the Portuguese man-of-war. Concludes that Hemingway's conception of woman as temptress, emasculator, and whore in his writing is taken too much for granted.

121 SWIFT, E.M. "In the Country He Loved." *Sports Illustrated* 61, no. 21 (5 November): 78-92.

Writes of his Idaho hunting and fishing trip with Jack Hemingway. Frequent references to the author and his attraction to the area.

122 TAVERNIER-COURBIN, JACQUELINE. "Fact and Fiction in *A Moveable Feast*." *Hemingway Review* 4, no. 1 (Fall): 44-51.

Relies on manuscript study in order to show that while Hemingway's memoirs are basically factual, they hardly represent an objective account because the author was still emotionally connected with his material.

123 TINTNER, ADELINE [R.]. "Wharton's Forgotten Preface to Vivienne de Watteville's *Speak to the Earth*: A Link with Hemingway's 'The Snows of Kilimanjaro.'" *Notes on Modern American Literature* 8, no. 2:item 10.

Gives evidence that Wharton may have sent Hemingway a copy of de Watteville's book about photographing wild animals in Africa which Hemingway "closely followed" in portions of "The Snows of Kilimanjaro."

124 TORREY, E. FULLER. *The Roots of Treason, Ezra Pound, and the Secret of St. Elizabeth's*. New York: Harcourt Brace Jovanovich, pp. 174-75, 181-82, 199, 210, etc.

Many references to Hemingway and his friendship and aid to Pound.

125 UNRUE, JOHN. "Hemingway: The Vital Principle." In *The Origins and Originality of American Culture*. Edited by Tibor Frank. Budapest: Akadémia Kiadó, pp. 261-67.

Looks at the way Hemingway translated his feelings about literary and rhetorical language into his own writings and the extent to which that process reveals character. Commenting briefly on stories appearing during the 1930s, Unrue shows that the author valued what was true and unaffected in both people and words.

126 WELLAND, DENNIS. "Idiom in Hemingway: A Footnote." *Journal of American Studies* 18, no. 3 (December): 449-51.

Discusses Nick's calculated reaction to Marjorie's innocent response of "I know it" in "The End of Something."

127 WELTER, JOHN. "More Letters from Papa." *Saturday Review* 10 (January-February): 12-13.

Parody of Hemingway's letters.

128 WHITE, WILLIAM. "For the Collector." *Hemingway Review* 3, no. 2 (Spring): 55-56.

Includes information on foreign editions and translations of interest to the collector.

129 _____. "For the Collector." *Hemingway Review* 4, no. 1 (Fall): 57-58.

Lists an array of books, tapes, and articles of interest to the Hemingway collector.

130 _____. "Hemingway: A Current Bibliography." *Hemingway Review* 3, no. 2 (Spring): 57-60.

Lists current items, including articles, reviews, books, and translations.

131 _____. "Hemingway: A Current Bibliography." *Hemingway Review* 4, no. 1 (Fall): 61-64.

Lists current items, including articles, books, new editions, and reviews.

132 _____. "Imitation Hemingway Contest: 7." *Hemingway Review* 4, no. 1 (Fall): 59-60.

Reprints "Paris in Spring" by Dave Eskes, winner of the Seventh International Imitation Hemingway Competition. Parody at its best (or worst).

133 _____. "A Misprint in Chapter vi of Hemingway's *In Our Time*." *Bulletin of Bibliography* 41, no. 1 (March): 50.

Locates a misprint near the end of the sketch.

134 WHITLOW, ROGER. *Cassandra's Daughters: The Women in Hemingway*. Westport, Conn.: Greenwood Press, 148 pp.

Argues that Hemingway's female characters have been consistently misread and oversimplified by critics. Whitlow examines the conventional categories associated with Hemingway's women (i.e., the ideal passive female figure, the bitch, and the marginalized woman), placing greater emphasis on the psychological. Defends Catherine

Barkley's and Maria's devotion as noble and therapeutic and argues that Brett Ashley's behavior is understandable in light of the disordered milieu in which she lives.

135 YOUNG, PHILIP. "Reader's Forum." *Georgia Review* 38, no. 3 (Fall): 669-70.

Attempts to set the record straight concerning Lynn's critical attack on Cowley's wound-theory reading of "Big Two-Hearted River" in his introduction to the 1944 *Portable Hemingway*. "Cowley's discussion of the widely known fishing story contains no war-victim material at all." The returned- soldier reading originated with Young in his 1952 *Ernest Hemingway*. See 1984.12 and 1984.66.

1985

1 ADAIR, WILLIAM. "Compass and Watch as Metaphors of Structure in *For Whom the Bell Tolls*." *Notes on Contemporary Literature* 15, no. 4 (September): 2.

Hemingway Review 9, no. 1 (Fall): 104.

2 _____. "*For Whom the Bell Tolls* as Family Romance." *Arizona Quarterly* 41, no. 4 (Winter): 329-37.

Looks at Hemingway's repetitive narrative structure in Jordan's prestory past – his childhood relationship with his family and his father's suicide are played out again in disguised form as Jordan too must undergo extreme psychological pressure. Sees the hero's "idealistic adventures . . . as compensation for his father's betrayal of the family."

3 _____. "Hemingway's Iceberg Method and Jake's Wound." *Notes on Contemporary Literature* 15, no. 5:11-12.

Looks at the reader's confusion over Jake's wound, the result of Hemingway's iceberg method of writing that seems to raise more questions than it answers.

4 ALDRIDGE, JOHN W. "*Dangerous Summer* a Bullish Performance by Hemingway." *Chicago Tribune Bookworld*, 16 June, p. 41.

Although written during the author's decline and edited extensively by Hotchner and Scribner's, Aldridge considers the book "far better than one had any right to expect."

5 ANDERSON, DAVID D. "American Regionalism, the Midwest, and the Study of Modern American Literature." *Society for the Study of Midwestern Literature Newsletter* 15, no. 3:10-20.

Suggests that we can better understand Hemingway and other writers whose works are grounded in the midwestern experience by examining the distinct regional dimensions of their writings. "The veneer of civilization for Hemingway's people is just that; love is an illusion as are the values of modern civilization, as Jake Barnes, Frederic Henry, and Robert Jordan recognize clearly and eloquently in the arms of Brett Ashley, in a Swiss rain, on a Spanish hillside."

6 ATHERTON, JOHN. "The Itinerary and the Postcard: Minimal Strategies in *The Sun Also Rises*." *Groupe de Recherches Anglo-Américaines de Tours*, no. 2, pp. 1-24.

Sees the entire novel as a prearranged trip in which "the reader is never taken anywhere that Jake has not been beforehand." Finds that Jake the narrator simply follows the itinerary of Jake the guide, shifting the responsibility for narration "elsewhere." Reprinted with minor revision: 1986.5.

7 BALEY, BARNEY. "Woolf and Hemingway." *Virginia Woolf Miscellany* 24:2-3.

Sums up Woolf's 1927 mixed review of *Men without Women*, which appeared in the *New York Herald Tribune* and infuriated Hemingway.

8 BARRON, JAMES. "Up in Michigan." *New York Times*, 24 November, sec. 10, p. 14.

Draws on details from Hemingway's short stories in his present-day tour of the author's early northern Michigan haunts.

9 BAWER, BRUCE. "Hemingway's Prelude to Paris." *New Criterion* 4, no. 2:34-40.

Begins with a negative review of Peter Griffin's *Along with Youth*, suggesting that Griffin is more interested in gossip than in how the author's early years shaped his later works. Also compares Hemingway's life and writings with T.S. Eliot's, commenting on the former's preoccupation with war not as "an ideological but an anthropological phenomenon – not a darkly revealing manifestation of twentieth-century Western society but an inescapable consequence of human character."

10 BEAVER, HAROLD. "The Big Splash: Hemingway and Scott Fitzgerald." In *The Great American Masquerade*. Totowa, N.J.: Vision and Barnes & Noble, pp. 156-74.

Concerned with the man behind the legendary mask. Comments on the gossipy nature of Hemingway's personal correspondence, his commitment to art, and his manipulation of his public image.

11 BENSON, JACKSON J. "Hemingway the Hunter and Steinbeck the Farmer." *Michigan Quarterly Review* 24, no. 3 (Summer): 441-60.

Biographical approach, pointing out similarities in background while also commenting on their different temperaments and worldviews. "Each represented a philosophy of modern existence so fundamental, yet so opposite, as to be like the two sides of the same coin."

12 BLOOM, HAROLD, ed. *Ernest Hemingway.* New York: Chelsea House, 233 pp.

Collection of mostly previously published essays by some of Hemingway's better known critics. Contents:

Pp. 1-5: Introduction by the editor speculates on Hemingway's place in the American literary tradition, commenting on Whitman's unacknowledged influence. Also comments on the enduring quality of Hemingway's works, considering the best (his short stories and *The Sun Also Rises*) to be "a permanent part of the American mythology."

Pp. 7-15: "Hemingway and His Critics" by Lionel Trilling. Reprint from *Partisan Review* 6 (Winter 1939).

Pp. 17-33: "Hemingway: Gauge of Morale" by Edmund Wilson. Reprint from *The Wound and the Bow* (Boston: Houghton Mifflin Co., 1941).

Pp. 35-62: "Ernest Hemingway" by Robert Penn Warren. Reprint from *Robert Penn Warren: Selected Essays* (Scribner's, 1966).

Pp. 63-84: "Observations on the Style of Ernest Hemingway" by Harry Levin. Reprint from *Contexts of Criticism* (Harvard University Press, 1957).

Pp. 85-106: "The Way It Was" by Carlos Baker. Reprint from *The Writer as Artist* (Princeton University Press, 1952).

Pp. 107-118: "The Death of Love in *The Sun Also Rises*" by Mark Spilka. Reprint from *Twelve Original Essays on Great American Novels.* Edited by Charles Shapiro (Wayne State University Press, 1958).

Pp. 119-36: "An Interview with Ernest Hemingway" by George Plimpton. Reprint from *Writers at Work: The Paris Review Interviews,* 2nd series (Paris Review, Inc., 1963).

Pp. 137-60: "For Ernest Hemingway" by Reynolds Price. Reprint from *Things Themselves* (Atheneum Publishers, 1972).

Pp. 161-71: "Mr. Papa and the Parricides" by Malcolm Cowley. Reprint from *And I Worked at the Writer's Trade* (Viking Penguin, 1963).

Pp. 173-92: "*Nada* and 'The Clean, Well-Lighted Place': The Unity of Hemingway's Short Fiction" by Steven K. Hoffman. Reprint of 1979.48.

Pp. 193-208: "Hemingway the Painter" by Alfred Kazin. Reprint of 1977.66. Reprinted: 1984.59.

Pp. 211-16: "Hemingway's Extraordinary Reality" by John Hollander. (New essay.) Comments on Hemingway's talent for short-story writing and gives a brief analysis of the symbolic title image and setting of "Hills Like White Elephants." Notes the story's resemblance "in the way in which dialogue and uninterpreted glimpse of scene interpret each other" to a 1960s Italian shooting script by Michaelangelo Antonioni.

13 BRENNER, GERRY. "Note on *Rinuce* and Research." *Hemingway Newsletter* 9 (January): 4.

Deduces from Kennedy Library materials that *rinuce* appearing four times in *A Moveable Feast* is actually a textual error. Hemingway intended *rima*.

14 BROSNAHAN, LEGER. "A Lost Passage from Hemingway's Macomber." *Studies in Bibliography: Papers of the Bibliographical Society of the University of Virginia* 38:328-30.

Locating a 100-word passage deleted from Scribner's 1938 and later printings of "The Short Happy Life of Francis Macomber," Brosnahan argues that this passage, appearing originally near the climax of the lion hunt along with a never-before-published sentence, should be restored to the text.

15 BRYER, JACKSON R. "Fitzgerald and Hemingway." In *American Literary Scholarship, an Annual: 1983*. Edited by Warren French. Durham, N.C.: Duke University Press, pp. 173-95.

Survey of criticism on both authors published during 1983. Bryer remarks on the "good news/bad news" situation in Fitzgerald and Hemingway studies for the year – texts or subjects thought to be completely exhausted continue to yield worthwhile scholarship while other studies seem blithely unaware of their redundancy.

16 BUCKLEY, REID. Review of *The Dangerous Summer*. *American Spectator* 18, no. 10 (October): 44-47.

Drawing on his own first-hand knowledge of the bullfights, Buckley criticizes Michener for inaccuracies in his "otherwise informative introduction." He likes some parts of the novel, but generally finds it to be an "overblown, overlong, overdramatic manuscript."

17 CAPELLÁN, ANGEL. *Hemingway and the Hispanic World*. Ann Arbor, Mich.: UMI Research Press, 327 pp.

Looks closely at the Hispanic world's influence on Hemingway, arguing that the author became a truly Spanish writer in source and attitude after his estrangement from his own country due to his experiences in the war. Speculates on Hemingway's indebtedness to such Hispanic authors as Cervantes and Pío Baroja and discusses at length his experiences in Spain and Cuba and personal observations through correspondence and conversations. Finds the Hemingway protagonist an essentially primeval man struggling in a modern world that seeks to destroy his natural environment.

18   CECCHIN, GIOVANNI. "Peduzzi Prototype." *Hemingway Review* 4, no. 2 (Spring): 54.

In response to McComas's article (see 1984.67). Cecchin identifies Peduzzi as "one of the Italian soldier-servants who attended the American ambulance drivers of Section Four billeted in the Lanificio Cazzola at Schio Vicenza." Shows once again Hemingway's reliance on actual experiences in his writings.

19   CHENEY, PATRICK. "Hemingway and Christian Epic: The Bible in *For Whom the Bell Tolls*." *Papers on Language and Literature* 21, no. 2 (Spring): 170-91.

Primarily concerned with biblical symbolism, contending that the novel should be read as an adaptation of the Christian epic in modern times. Although Jordan is not Christ, his death is a kind of crucifixion and represents modern man's adaption of Christianity to his own experience.

20   CHERRIN, BONNIE D. *The Ernest Hemingway Collection of Charles D. Field*. Stanford, Calif.: Stanford University Libraries, 108 pp.

Extensive bibliography of the Stanford University Libraries' recently acquired collection of items written by and about Hemingway, including first editions, translations, pamphlets, correspondence with Carlos Baker, and manuscripts of Hemingway's *Esquire* pieces.

21   COHEN, MILTON A. "Circe and Her Swine: Domination and Debasement in *The Sun Also Rises*." *Arizona Quarterly* 41, no. 4 (Winter): 293-305.

Provides background information on the Circe myth and then applies it to the story, finding that it strengthens and redefines Brett's character and role and illuminates the themes of sexual domination and debasement that permeate the story.

22   CORNELLIER, THOMAS. "The Myth of Escape and Fulfillment in *The Sun Also Rises* and *The Great Gatsby*." *Society for the Study of Midwestern Literature Newsletter* 15, no. 1 (Spring): 15-21.

Looks at the way both authors incorporate the myths of escape and fulfillment in their works, examining several of the characters' escapes (through alcohol or sexual encounters or accepting with dignity the cards one is dealt in life) and their quests to find meaning in the post-World War I wasteland.

23 COWLEY, MALCOLM. "Hemingway at Midnight." In *The Flower and the Leaf: A Contemporary Record of American Writing Since 1941*. New York: Viking, pp. 169-78.

Reprint with minor revision of introduction to the Viking *Portable Hemingway* (1944).

24 DEITCH, JOSEPH. "Portrait: Charles Scribner, Jr." *Wilson Library Bulletin* 59, no. 10:683-85.

Reminisces about Hemingway, remarking on the author's friendly manner and sensitivity about losing things.

25 DIEHL, DIGBY. "Hemingway: *A Moveable Feast*, the Third Annual Key West Literary Seminar." *Council for Florida Libraries Newsbrief: Hemingway Supplement*, pp. 1-4, 9-10.

*Hemingway Review 5, no. 2 (Spring): 58.

26 DONALDSON, SCOTT. "Dos and Hem: A Literary Friendship." *Centennial Review* 29, no. 2:163-85.

Drawing on their correspondence, biographies, and writings, Donaldson reconstructs Hemingway's relationship with Dos Passos from their early Paris friendship to their eventual break over the Spanish civil war. Donaldson goes on to explain the way each used his later work to attack the other and justify himself. Reprinted: 1987.95.

27 DOYLE, N. ANN, and HOUSTON, NEAL B. "Adriana Ivancich on Death." *Hemingway Review* 4, no. 2:53.

Pays attention to Ivancich's reporting in *La Torre Bianca* of a conversation she had with Hemingway concerning her near-death experience.

28 ____. "Ernest Hemingway, Adriana Ivancich, and the Nobel Prize." *Notes on Modern American Literature* 9, no. 1:item 5.

Comments on letters written to Ivancich revealing the author's anticipation of the Nobel prize as early as 1950 and the disruptions the 1954 prize brought to both his personal and professional life.

29 ____."Ernest Hemingway's Letters to Adriana Ivancich." *Library Chronicle of the University of Texas* 30:15-37.

Describes at length the sixty-five letters now housed in the Humanities Research Center at the University of Texas. Prohibited from quoting directly, the authors give a chronologically arranged synopsis of their contents, revealing an intimate portrait of the author as he discusses his love for Ivancich, financial concerns, the writing and filming of *The Old Man and the Sea*, and the winning of the Nobel prize.

30 ____. "Letters to Adriana Ivancich." *Hemingway Review* 5, no. 1 (Fall): 15-29.

Draws on Hemingway correspondence from 1950 to 1955 now available at the Harry Ransom Humanities Research Center in order to reconstruct Hemingway's relationship with the young Venetian woman whom he idealized.

31 EGRI, PETER. "The Fusion of the Epic and Dramatic: Hemingway, Strindberg, and O'Neill." *Eugene O'Neill Newsletter* 10, no. 1:16-22.

Briefly comments on the retrogressive motifs in *A Farewell to Arms* and *For Whom the Bell Tolls* that divert the dramatic action from the course of its intended goal. Sees Henry's experiences at Caporetto and the growing tension between Jordan and Pablo as prime examples. Reprinted with minor revisions in *Zeitschrift für Anglistik und Amerikanistik* 33, no. 4:324-30 and 1987.21.

32 FEASLEY, FLORENCE G. "Copywriting and the Prose of Hemingway." *Journalism Quarterly* 62, no. 1 (Spring): 121-26.

Points to the value of Hemingway's simplistic style, rhythm, and vivid imagery as a model for copywriters.

33 FISHKIN, SHELLEY FISHER. "Ernest Hemingway." In *From Fact to Fiction: Journalism & Imaginative Writing in America*. Baltimore: Johns Hopkins University Press, pp. 135-64.

Looks at the relationship between Hemingway's journalistic career and literary art. Points out the influence of the *Kansas City Star* style sheet that emphasized compression, brevity, and freshness on the apprentice author and his later success with *In Our Time*. Also looks at Hemingway's return to journalism during the Spanish civil war and his efforts to further the loyalist cause both through his writings and the documentary film *The Spanish Earth*.

34 FLEMING, BRUCE. "Writing in Pidgin: Language in *For Whom the Bell Tolls*." *Dutch Quarterly Review* 15, no. 4:265-77.

Objects to the Pidgin English spoken by the loyalist partisans because it distances both the reader and Jordan from the rest of the band and prevents him from fully interacting with his environment. Jordan remains a Montana college instructor on sabbatical, an outsider who never reconciles or comes to terms with his Spanish experience.

35 GAJDUSEK, ROBERT E. "Purgation/Debridement as Therapy/Aesthetics." *Hemingway Review* 4, no. 2:12-17.

Sees Hemingway's moral-aesthetic device of cutting away or purgation to be a continuous thematic thread running throughout his canon descended from a classical American literature rooted in Old Testament fundamentalist principles. Locates examples in Jake Barnes's missing phallus in *The Sun Also Rises*, Renata's purging love in *Across the River and into the Trees*, and Harry's gangrenous leg in "The Snows of Kilimanjaro."

36 GARDNER, RICHARD M. "Toward a Definition of Stereotypes." *Midwest Quarterly* 26, no. 4 (Summer): 476-98.
　　Identifies chapter 5 of *In Our Time* as completely devoid of stereotype.

37 GERLACH, JOHN. "The Twentieth Century: New Forms." In *Toward the End: Closure and Structure in the American Short Story*. University: University of Alabama Press, pp. 94-118.
　　Structural analysis focusing on the way endings influence the structure of short stories. Pays particular attention to compressed closure techniques in "Cat in the Rain" and "Hills Like White Elephants" and the badly constructed ending of "The Short Happy Life of Francis Macomber."

38 GRADOLI, MARINA. "Italy in Ernest Hemingway's Fiction." *Rivista di Studi Anglo-Americani*, pp. 145-52.
　　Sees Hemingway's use of Italy for the setting of *A Farewell to Arms* as incidental to the novel as a whole. However, in the later *Across the River and into the Trees*, Hemingway moves from that initial indifference to a desire to participate and become involved in the world around him. The author (and his heroes) "turn towards tradition and cultures other than his own with a different interest and even with nostalgia."

39 GRIFFIN, PETER. [M.] *Along with Youth: Hemingway, the Early Years*. New York: Oxford University Press, 258 pp.
　　Includes five unpublished early stories, "Crossroads," "The Mercenaries," "The Ash-Heel's Tendon," "The Current," and "Portrait of the Idealist in Love." Makes much use of Hadley Richardson's correspondence with Hemingway, not available previously, and other new letters. The resulting book, however, is not so different from other accounts of Hemingway's life as might be expected. Perhaps Griffin's second volume will move into areas in which he will evince more ability as biographer.

40 ＿＿＿. "The Young Hemingway: Three Unpublished Stories." *New York Times Magazine* (18 August):14-23, 59, 61.

Introduction by Griffin. Prints "The Mercenaries," "Crossroads," and "The Ash-Heel's Tendon."

41 GRIMES, LARRY E. *The Religious Design of Hemingway's Early Fiction*. Ann Arbor, Mich.: UMI, 156 pp.

Attributes the religious design in Hemingway's early works to the author's crisis of childhood faith. Defining the fifth dimension in aesthetic and religious terms, Grimes traces "the movement of Hemingway's characters toward life in the fifth dimension" through "three distinct stages: an innocent's fall into history; unsuccessful (ethical) or successful (playful) attempts at restoring meaning to life in history; and, for the successful, entrance into the world of play as religion." Includes bibliography.

42 GROSS, BARRY. "Yours Sincerely, Sinclair Levy." *Commentary* 80, no. 6 (December): 56-59.

Briefly comments on the anti-Semitism surrounding the character Robert Cohn. "Hemingway never lets the reader forget that Cohn is a Jew, not an unattractive character who happens to be a Jew but a character who is unattractive because he is a Jew."

43 HANSON, CLARE. *Short Stories and Short Fictions, 1880-1980*. London: Macmillan Press, pp. 74-77.

Comments briefly on Hemingway's stylistic and thematic achievements in the short-story form as exemplified by "A Clean, Well-Lighted Place" with its Conradian theme and finely etched setting.

44 HARPER, MICHAEL. "Men without Politics: Hemingway's Social Consciousness." *New Orleans Review* 12, no. 1 (Spring): 15-26.

Marxist reading of "The Light of the World," "Homage to Switzerland" and *The Sun Also Rises*, contending that Hemingway "is not interested in economics *per se*, but in how a socio-economic system corrupts human relationships and frustrates people's aspirations towards wholeness and integrity."

45 HAYS, PETER, and TUCKER, STEPHANIE. "No Sanctuary: Hemingway's 'The Killers' and Pinter's *The Birthday Party*." *Papers on Language and Literature* 21:417-24.

Influence study comparing Hemingway's short story with Pinter's later drama. Points out similarities in plot, character, conflict, and style, contending that in "The Killers" Nick "learns that man has lost Eden, that there is no sanctuary; Pinter believed the same and taught Stanley Webber that lesson in *The Birthday Party*."

46 HEAMAN, ROBERT J., and HEAMAN, PATRICIA B. "Hemingway's Fabulous Fisherman." *Pennsylvania English* 12, no. 1 (Fall): 29-33.

Compares the fishing episode in "Big Two-Hearted River" with fishing in *The Old Man and the Sea*, relating them both to the author's evolving attitudes regarding the process of writing. Claims that as Hemingway developed as a writer "he came more and more to identify the skill and discipline that go into fishing with the skill and discipline that go into writing and to discover that the value of both is not in what is achieved or what has been prepared for so much as it is in the process itself."

47 HEARST, BUNKY. "Fighting Chair: Hemingway Never Had It So Good." *Motor Boating & Sailing* 155:62.

Describes the *Pilar* in detail, commenting on its Spartan design compared to today's modern vessels decked out in the latest technology.

48 HEDEN, PAUL M. "Moving in the Picture: The Landscape Stylistics of *In Our Time*." *Language and Style* 18, no. 4 (Fall): 363-76.

Seeks to locate Cézanne's visual techniques in Hemingway's verbal art, focusing on passages from *In Our Time*. Identifies Cézanne's influence in four areas of the author's work: "depth composed with overlapping parallel planes; depth and tension composed with planes in juxtaposition; creation of 'flat depth'; and the purposeful use of detail."

49 HEIDELBERG, PAUL. "Yesterday: Boxer Hemingway Laced His Punches with Tips to His Sparring Partners." *Sports Illustrated* 63, no. 28 (23-30 December): 150-54.

James (Iron Baby) Roberts and Kermit (Geech) Forbes reminisce over their sparring matches with Hemingway in Key West.

50 HEMINGWAY, ERNEST. *The Dangerous Summer*. New York: Scribner's, 228 pp.

Heavily edited posthumous novel set in Spain during the bullfight season.

51 HEMINGWAY, JACK. "The Literary Life: The Short, Happy Files of a Young Reporter." *Esquire* 104, no. 4 (October): 193-200.

Hemingway's son introduces excerpts from *Dateline: Toronto*, pieces his father wrote while a reporter for the *Toronto Star Weekly* and *Daily Star* during the early 1920s.

52 HINKLE, JAMES. "What's Funny in *The Sun Also Rises*." *Hemingway Review* 4, no. 2 (Spring): 31-41.

Points to sixty humorous sections submerged in the text. Sees Jake's use of irony as a defense against living in a post-World War I world. Reprinted: 1987.7 and 1987.95.

53 HOUSTON, NEAL B. "Hemingway: The Obsession with Henry James, 1924-1954." *Rocky Mountain Review* 39:33-46.

Examines Hemingway's "sporadic obsession" with James's life and art, periodically vilifying and defending him over the years. Comments on his "bicycle" reference to James in *The Sun Also Rises*, his simultaneous praise and criticism of him in *Green Hills of Africa*, and his many references to him in correspondence.

54 JAIDEV. "A Note on the Narrational Perspective in *A Farewell to Arms*." *Indian Journal of American Studies* 15, no. 1 (Winter): 85-87.

Looks at the opposing narrative perspectives in the passage about Henry's distrust of abstractions such as sacred and glorious and the later chapter (34) in which he associates Catherine with goodness and courage. Contends that the first relates to Henry's narrow view of his war experiences while the latter refers to his broadened world vision.

55 JUNKINS, DONALD. "Hemingway's Contribution to American Poetry." *Hemingway Review* 4, no. 2 (Spring): 18-23.

Relates Hemingway's poetic prose back to Pound's principles of poetry found in *The ABC of Reading*. Suggests Hemingway's condensation and compactness, as demonstrated in "Cat in the Rain" and "The End of Something," to be his greatest contribution to poetry.

56 JUSTUS, JAMES H. "Hemingway and Faulkner: Vision and Repudiation." *Kenyon Review* 7, no. 4:1-14.

Concludes that although both authors shared similar dark visions of humanity, neither was paralyzed by them – instead they sought remedy through art. "The glory of such a world view is not its substance authorially prescribed but its substance authorially dramatized, enacted through art; the application of hard-won art is as consistent and pervasive as the vision it projects." Centers on *A Farewell to Arms* and *As I Lay Dying*.

57 KAMINSKY, STUART M. "Literary Adaptation: 'The Killers' – Hemingway, Film Noir, and the Terror of Daylight." *American Film Genres*. 2d ed. Chicago: Nelson-Hall, pp. 81-96.

A comparison of the original with the two film versions (each about twenty years apart) in light of the context of cultural and historical change. Reprinted with minor revision: 1989.38.

58 KAPLAN, E. ANN. "Hemingway, Hollywood, and Female Representation: *The Macomber Affair.*" *Literature/Film Quarterly* 13, no. 1:22-28.

Looks at the way Hollywood adapted "The Short Happy Life of Francis Macomber" to meet the genre requirements of the romance film.

59 KENNEDY, WILLIAM. "The Last Olé." *New York Book Review,* 9 June, pp. 1, 32-33, 35.

Review of *The Dangerous Summer.* Despite questionable editing, Kennedy concludes that the final version is true Hemingway.

60 KERNER, DAVID. "Counterfeit Hemingway: A Small Scandal in Quotation Marks." *Journal of Modern Literature* 12, no. 1 (March): 91-108.

After establishing the prevalence of antimetronomic dialogue in literature, Kerner argues that the waiters' lines in "A Clean, Well-Lighted Place" are correct as originally written and should never have been changed.

61 KLUG, M.A. "Horns of Manichaeus: The Conflict of Art and Experience in *The Great Gatsby* and *The Sun Also Rises.*" *Essays in Literature* 12, no. 1 (Spring): 111-24.

Compares the fear of failure and the tension between art and reality present in the two novels. Sees Gatsby and Romero as representative of the artist in conflict with reality while Nick and Jake portend the death of the artist.

62 KORT, WESLEY A. "Ernest Hemingway." In *Modern Fiction and Human Time.* Tampa: University Presses of Florida, pp. 25-41.

Discusses Hemingway throughout the book, but his chapter on Hemingway focuses on the critical attention to factors that obscure the depth of his writing, and on his consistent interest in the abstract issues – specifically here, human time. Kort reads *A Farewell to Arms,* for example, as a study in four kinds of time – "the time of Frederic Henry before the war and the love, the time of detachment and drifting. There are the contrasting times of war and love. . . . And finally, there is natural or cosmic time, large, complex, enfolding, which Henry does not adequately appreciate." Kort also discusses *In Our Time, For Whom the Bell Tolls,* and *The Old Man and the Sea.*

63 LAGENFELD, ROBERT. "Autobiography and Biography: Leicester Hemingway's *The Sound of the Trumpet.*" *Biography* 8 (Winter): 37-50.

Looks at Leicester Hemingway's autobiographical novel, finding that "aspects of Ernest's life and character are in some instances confirmed, embellished, or qualified." Sheds light on the suicide of Dr. Hemingway and the relationship between the two brothers.

64 LAMB,   ROBERT   PAUL.   "Eternity's   Artifice: Time   and Transcendence in the Works of Ernest Hemingway." *Hemingway Review* 4, no. 2 (Spring): 42-52.

Contends that Hemingway, like other modernist writers of a prophetic sensibility, "struggled in vain not to fall from mythic time into history; who, having fallen, sought to transcend historical process by both the themes and especially the structure of his prose; and who, after staring long and hard into the infiniteness of nonbeing was finally overwhelmed by the power of nothingness that lies beneath history and its conclusion." History prevails and there is no escape from man's fate (death) but there are ecstatic moments when time seems to stand still, when man is confronted with the possibility of his own death (such as during the bullfight). Lamb looks at Hemingway's preoccupation with those transcendent moments. The bullfighter strives to create the perfect moment while the writer struggles to transform the perfect moment into perfect prose.

65 LEEDS, B.H. Review of *The Dangerous Summer*. *Choice* 23, no. 3 (November): 447.

Considers the newly edited version a worthy addition to Hemingway's posthumous publications, of interest to general reader and scholar alike.

66 LEWIS, ROBERT W. "Note on Bourdon Gauge of Immorale." *Hemingway Newsletter* 9 (January): 3.

Suggests that in Rudy Wiebe's *Peace Shall Destroy Many*, the non-Mennonite school teacher who is reading *The Sun Also Rises* "thinks of herself as a displaced frustrated Lady Brett Ashley."

67 McDONNELL, THOMAS P. "Hemingway Reconsidered." *National Review* 37, no. 10 (31 May): 46-48.

In assessing the Hemingway legacy nearly twenty-five years after his death, McDonnell contends that the short fiction will last forever. Also remarks that the quintessential Hemingway novel, *The Sun Also Rises*, seems dated in places.

68 MacSHANE, FRANK. *Into Eternity, the Life of James Jones, American Writer*. Boston: Houghton Mifflin, 355 pp.

References to Hemingway throughout. See his comments on Jones, 192; see also 191-93 and 209-210.

69 MARKHAM, JAMES M. "Hemingway's Spain." *New York Times*, 24 November, sec. 10, pp. 15-16.

Draws on details from *For Whom the Bell Tolls* and *The Sun Also Rises* in his present-day tour of the author's old haunts.

70 MARTIN, W.R., and OBER, WARREN U. "Hemingway and James: 'A Canary for One' and 'Daisy Miller.'" *Studies in Short Fiction* 22, no. 4 (Fall): 469-71.

Points out parallels between the two stories, believing that in alluding to James's earlier story, Hemingway strengthens his "masterpiece of delicately structured pathos."

71 _____. "Lawrence and Hemingway: The Canceled Great Words." *Arizona Quarterly* 41, no. 4 (Winter): 357-61.

Suggests that Hemingway's passage in *A Farewell to Arms* about obscene abstract words such as "sacred, glorious, and sacrifice" is derived from a similar paragraph in Lawrence's *Lady Chatterley's Lover*.

72 MEYERS, JEFFREY. *Hemingway, A Biography*. New York: Harper & Row, 644 pp.

Massive biography attempting to cover the author's unfolding life history from Oak Park to Ketchum. Discusses Hemingway's works at some length, relating them thematically to the author and his life, relying frequently on Freudian psychology in his interpretation and commentary. Overall, too detailed and fragmentary a whole to provide a complete portrait of the author.

73 _____. "The Quest for Hemingway." *Virginia Quarterly Review* 61, no. 4 (Autumn): 584-602.

Account of the trials and tribulations he encountered while researching the above-cited *Hemingway, A Biography*. Reprinted: 1989.33.

74 _____. "Tolstoy and Hemingway: 'The Death of Ivan Ilych' and 'The Snows of Kilimanjaro.'" In *Disease and the Novel, 1880-1960*. New York: St. Martin's Press, pp. 19-29.

Argues that Hemingway consciously imitated Tolstoy's story in both subject and theme (disease, dying, revelation, and redemption), creating his own modernist and secularized version some fifty years later in "The Snows of Kilimanjaro."

75 MICHENER, JAMES A. "Introducing Hemingway." *Publishers Weekly* 227, no. 2 (11 January): 40-41.

Prints excerpts from Michener's introduction to *The Dangerous Summer*. See 1985.76.

76 ____. Introduction to *The Dangerous Summer*. New York: Scribner's, pp. 1-40.

Comments on his writing of a favorable review of *The Old Man and the Sea*, his one-time meeting with the author, and Hemingway's second commission by *Life* for a nostalgic essay on Spain that turned into the three-part series, *The Dangerous Summer*. Michener gives the publication history and the international bullfighting set's tempered response to the work along with definitions of selected bullfighting terminology helpful in understanding the novel. Interesting for what it tells about one older man's view of another older writer.

77 MILLER, LINDA PATTERSON. "Gerald Murphy and Ernest Hemingway: Part II." *Studies in American Fiction* 13, no. 1 (Spring): 1-13.

In her continuation of the Hemingway/Murphy relationship (see 1984.77), Miller begins with Hemingway's divorce from Hadley and gradual disassociation from the Murphys over the next six years. Believes Hemingway was put off by Gerald Murphy's "charm and the tendency to hyperbolize." Relies extensively on Murphy letters.

78 MONTEIRO, GEORGE. "Hemingway's Colonel." *Hemingway Review* 5, no. 1 (Fall): 40-45.

Looks at Cantwell's attitudes and actions in light of Walter Pater's influential nineteenth-century writings on the nature of aesthetic experience. Believes that the novel's "aestheticism implies not only a most practical, remarkable quotidian ethics but a system of self-defining morality."

79 MORGAN, GEORGE. "An American in Paris: Strategies of Otherness in *The Sun Also Rises*." *Cycnos* 2:27-39.

Sees Paris functioning symbolically for the individual characters as both a place of corruption and a source of restoration. "Alongside the Paris of drinking, dining and endless car rides, Hemingway evokes another Paris, a city which is more a state of soul, the mirror image of the spiritual condition of those citizens who temporarily inhabit and are conditioned by it."

80 MUNSON, GORHAM. *The Awakening Twenties: A Memoir-History of a Literary Period*. Baton Rouge: Louisiana State University Press, pp. 128-31, 157.

Discusses Hemingway's relationship with Scribner's and comments on his "first and best novel, *The Sun Also Rises*."

81 NAKAJIMA, KENJI. "To Discipline Eyes against Misery: On Hemingway's 'Chapter II,' *In Our Time*." *Kyushu American Literature* 26 (October): 11-19.

Looks at both Hemingway's revision of the piece in relation to the misery exposed in the Greek refugee evacuation and in the vignette's symbolic relation to the succeeding story. Sees the doctor in "The Doctor and the Doctor's Wife" as a "miserable refugee" and his wife as one of "the exotic and aloof minarets."

82 NORRIS, MARGOT. "The Animal and Violence in Hemingway's *Death in the Afternoon*." In *Beasts of Modern Imagination: Darwin, Nietzsche, Kafka, Ernest, & Lawrence*. Baltimore: Johns Hopkins University Press, pp. 195-219.

Sees Hemingway depicting the artist as sadist. Cruelty is transformed into culture as the matador creates art through torture. Norris challenges Hemingway's suppositions about the bullfight, calling into question the anthropocentrism and cultural chauvinism that sustain it.

83 OLDSEY, BERNARD. "El Pueblo Español: 'The Capital of the World.'" *Studies in American Fiction* 13, no. 1 (Spring): 103-110.

Considers the often-overlooked story to be a condensed novel, achieving its compression through the cinematic technique of crosscutting from character to character and scene to scene. Also looks at the way the theme of illusion and disillusion permeates the story.

84 OLIVER, CHARLES M. "Hemingway's Merger of Form and Meaning." *Language and Style* 18, no. 3 (Summer): 223-31.

Points to passages (usually of emotional intensity) in *For Whom the Bell Tolls*, *To Have and Have Not*, and *A Farewell to Arms* in which "the form–the repetition of words, the length of sentences, or the rhythm of the passage, 'tempo and sound, pause and flow'–merges with meaning and, therefore, enhances it." As in poetry, Hemingway balances meaning and form in order to strengthen the reader's emotional and imaginative response.

85 O'MEALLY, ROBERT G. "The Rules of Magic: Hemingway as Ellison's 'Ancestor.'" *Southern Review* 21, no. 3 (July): 751-69.

Traces Hemingway's long-lasting influence on Ellison in theme, style, and technique. Prints many of the comments Ellison made about Hemingway and his craft over the years. Considers the protagonist of *Invisible Man* to be a "brownskin cousin of Nick Adams, straining toward manhood in a world full of the blues." Reprinted: 1987.68.

86 PETRY, ALICE HALL. "Voice out of Africa: A Possible Oral Source for Hemingway's 'The Snows of Kilimanjaro.'" *Hemingway Review* 4, no. 2 (Spring): 7-11.

Suggests that anecdotes related to Hemingway during his 1933-34 African safari by Kenya-based pilot Beryl Markham may have served as the source for the short story.

87 PHILLIPS, LARRY W., ed. *F. Scott Fitzgerald on Writing*. New York: Scribner's, 136 pp.

Numerous references to Hemingway throughout, demonstrating Fitzgerald's respect and admiration for him as an artist.

88 PORTCH, STEPHEN R. "Silent Ernest." In *Literature's Silent Language: Nonverbal Communication*. New York: Peter Lang, pp. 89-116.

Looks at the function of silence in "Hills Like White Elephants" and "The Killers," two short stories in which dialogue punctuates silence. Analyzes Hemingway's sensitivity to nonverbal behavior and manipulation of nonverbal cues that result (for the alert reader) in the creation of meaning beyond the ambiguities of dialogue.

89 QUICK, JONATHAN R. "The Homeric Ulysses and A.E.W. Mason's *Miranda of the Balcony*." *James Joyce Quarterly*, 23, no. 1 (Fall): 31-43.

Suggests Hemingway included the reference to Mason's *The Four Corners of the World* in *The Sun Also Rises* because of the earlier author's break with the romantic tradition.

90 RAPHAEL, FREDERIC. "Art in Action." *Times Literary Supplement*, no. 4298, 16 August, p. 894.

Along with a review of recent critical studies, Raphael also looks at Hemingway's *The Dangerous Summer*. Finds that in editing the posthumous text, Scribner's "has removed bone and left flab."

91 Review of *The Dangerous Summer*. *Journal of Modern Literature* 12, no. 3-4 (November): 494.

Brings into question the extensive editing of the posthumous novel.

92 REYNOLDS, MICHAEL S. "Hemingway's Home: Depression and Suicide." *American Literature* 57, no. 4 (December): 600-610.

On the medical history of the family. Considers Hemingway's genetic inheritance (depression, diabetes, insomnia, etc.) to be a biological trap running through three generations. Reprinted: 1987.95.

93 ____. "Putting on the Riff." *Hemingway Review* 5, no. 1 (Fall): 30-31.

Draws from historical data on the Riffian War to explicate Jake Barnes's joke during the Burguete breakfast scene in *The Sun Also Rises*.

94 RUDAT, WOLFGANG E.H. "Brett's Problem: Ovidian and Other Allusions in *The Sun Also Rises*." *Style* 19, no. 3 (Fall): 317-25.

Discusses Brett's name (suggesting board, ski, and ship) in relation to the ending of the novel. Brett is not only a "plank nailed down by many men" but a ship that "will continue her voyage of meaningless motion and immediate gratification."

95 ____. "Cohn and Romero in the Ring: Sports and Religion in *The Sun Also Rises*." *Arizona Quarterly* 41, no. 4 (Winter): 311-18.

Compares Cohn and Romero, contending that Romero is a Jew and that Cohn possesses the necessary quality of the code hero–grace under pressure.

96 SAMUELSON, ARNOLD. "Fishing with Hemingway. Part I." *Motor Boat & Sailing* 155 (April): 91-94.

Excerpts from *With Hemingway: A Year in Key West and Cuba*. See 1984.103.

97 ____. "Fishing with Hemingway. Part II." *Motor Boat & Sailing* 155 (May): 65-68.

Excerpts from *With Hemingway: A Year in Key West and Cuba*. See 1984.103.

98 SCAFELLA, FRANK. "'I and the Abyss': Emerson, Hemingway, and the Modern Vision of Death." *Hemingway Review* 4, no. 2 (Spring): 2-6.

Argues for a reading of Nick Adams as a separate persona, contending that Nick the character is invented and should not be identified with Nick the author who likewise should not be identified with Hemingway.

99 SCALISE, MICHELLE. "Note on *F.T.A.* Puns." *Hemingway Newsletter* 9 (January): 3.

Points out three wry puns in the text of *A Farewell to Arms* involving Henry's ambulance ride, Catherine Barkley, and the incompetent captain-doctor who examines Henry's wounds.

100 SCHLUETER, PAUL, and SCHLUETER, JUNE, eds. "Hemingway, Ernest (1899-1961)." In *Modern American Literature*. Vol. 5 (2nd suppl. to 4th ed.). New York: Frederick Ungar, pp. 183-85.

Reprints excerpts from selected contemporary criticism on Hemingway in order to provide as broad an overview of his career as possible.

101 SCHOLES, ROBERT. *Textual Power: Literary Theory and the Teaching of English*. New Haven: Yale University Press, pp. 18-73.

Unites literary theory with teaching in order to encourage textuality (textual knowledge and textual skills) in the classroom. Scholes demonstrates through the short narratives of *In Our Time* how teachers can bring reading, interpretation, and criticism into their courses, moving students "from a submission to textual authority in reading, through a sharing of textual power in interpretation, toward an assertion of power through opposition in criticism."

102 SECOR, ROBERT, and MODDELMOG, DEBRA. "Conrad and Ernest Hemingway." In *Joseph Conrad and American Writers*. Westport, Conn.: Greenwood Press, pp. 150-58.

Bibliographic study devoted to Hemingway's connection with Conrad. Lists Hemingway's statements about Conrad in his writings, Conrad's works in Hemingway's library, and critical studies linking the two authors.

103 SLATOFF, WALTER J. *The Look of Distance: Reflections on Suffering & Sympathy in Modern Literature – Auden to Agee, Whitman to Woolf*. Columbus: Ohio State University Press, pp. 21-29.

Believes that the impact of the final line of "Indian Camp" derives not from Nick's naïveté but from the irony of such a statement in the context of the suffering and human savagery of *In Our Time*.

104 SOJKA, GREGORY S. *Ernest Hemingway: The Angler and Artist*. New York: Peter Lang, 180 pp.

Relying on Young's theory of the code hero for his critical base, Sojka explores Hemingway's angling aesthetic as a moral philosophy. Reads *The Old Man and the Sea, Islands in the Stream*, and such short fiction as "Big Two-Hearted River," along with Hemingway's articles about fishing, his letters, and his manuscripts, to make the theme of fishing well a crucial one in his oeuvre.

105 SPLAKE, T. KILGORE. "A Northern Monument to the Young Ernest Hemingway." *Midwestern Miscellany*, no. 13, pp. 7-9.

Briefly recounts his own visit to Seney, Michigan, relating it to Hemingway's earlier experiences in "Big Two-Hearted River."

106 STEINKE, JAMES. "Brett and Jake in Spain: Hemingway's Ending for *The Sun Also Rises*." *Spectrum* 27, no. 1-2:131-41.

Examination of Jake's quiet interval in San Sebastian near the end of the novel, abruptly interrupted by Brett's urgent telegram. Also looks at the way Jake's feelings prior to approaching Brett in Madrid help in interpreting their complex relationship.

107 ____. "Hemingway's 'In Another Country' and 'Now I Lay Me.'" *Hemingway Review* 5, no. 1 (Fall): 32-39.
Close comparison of the two war stories set in Italy, focusing on characters, events, and moment-by-moment effects. Questions the inclusion of "In Another Country" among the Nick Adams stories.

108 STOUCK, DAVID. "Sherwood Anderson and the Postmodern Novel." *Contemporary Literature* 26, no. 3 (Fall): 302-316.
Addresses Anderson's far-reaching influence on twentieth-century American literature, commenting briefly on Hemingway's parody of Anderson's thematic weaknesses and stylistic mannerisms in *The Torrents of Spring*. In doing so, "he highlighted aspects of Anderson's work that have become valued features of the contemporary postmodern novel: unreal, far-fetched scenes, ludicrous symbolism, comic book characters, loose plot, and myriad author's notes discussing the progress of the book with the reader."

109 TELOTTE, J.P. "A Consuming Passion: Food and Film Noir." *Georgia Review* 39, no. 2 (Summer): 397-410.
Suggests, in discussing one of the film versions of "The Killers," that a diner and a café make for ironic settings for the murder of Ole and the attempted murder of Reardon who are subject to destruction because of their appetites – desire for a beautiful woman and understanding.

110 THEROUX, PAUL. "Lord of the Ring." In *Sunrise with Seamonsters: Travels and Discoveries, 1964-1984*. London: Hamish Hamilton, pp. 76-82.
Reprint of *Encounter* 36 (February 1971): 62-66.

111 THORNBERRY, ROBERT S. "Hemingway's *Ce Soir* Interview (1937) and the Battle of Tervel." *Hemingway Review* 5, no. 1 (Fall): 2-8.
Reprints in English translation Hemingway's 1937 interview with the French communist newspaper *Ce Soir* in which he comments on his visit to Spain, the republican offensive on the Aragon front, and the controversial issue of foreign troops on Spanish soil.

112 TINTNER, ADELINE R. "The Significance of D'Annunzio in *Across the River and Into the Trees*." *Hemingway Review* 5, no. 1 (Fall): 9-13.

Contends that D'Annunzio's *Notturno* significantly influenced Hemingway's novel, pointing out as evidence Hemingway's modeling of Cantwell and Renata's relationship after D'Annunzio's relationship with his daughter Renata and Hemingway's identification with the author who too was a man of action as well as an artist.

113 TISA, JOHN. *Recalling the Good Fight: An Autobiography of the Spanish Civil War*. South Hadley, Mass.: Bergin & Garvey, pp. 93-95.
Memoir, mention of his relationship with Hemingway.

114 TOOLAN, MICHAEL. "Analyzing Fictional Dialogue." *Language & Communication* 5, no. 3:193-206.
Stylistic analysis of the dialogue found in "Cat in the Rain," determining that the gulf between the American couple is reflected in their stilted and uncooperative conversation. The typical mutual negotiation of dialogue is noticeably absent as the wife's indirect requests are met with resistance.

115 TRIPATHY, BIYOT KESH. "Into the Labyrinth: Crane, Hemingway, Mailer, Jones." In *Osiris N: The Victim and the American Novel*. Amsterdam: B.R. Gruner Publishing, pp. 171-226.
Finds similarities in theme, setting, plot, and characterization in Crane's *The Red Badge of Courage* and *A Farewell to Arms*. Sees Henry's movement through the plot as a mythic journey (or stages of a labyrinth) in which the victim/hero reaches the final threshold but fails to achieve true understanding. "His mind refuses to give him insights from experience to make the transition from personal love into a more inclusive and embracing love for God which would integrate the world with the person."

116 VERDUIN, KATHLEEN. "Hemingway's Dante: A Note on *Across the River and into the Trees*." *American Literature* 57, no. 4 (December): 633-40.
Argues that Hemingway's identification of Cantwell with Dante is based on the popular Byronic view of the great poet rather than intimate knowledge of his writings.

117 WARD, J.A. "Anderson and Hemingway." In *American Silences*. Baton Rouge: Louisiana State University Press, pp. 35-77.
Looks at both authors' fascination with silence in their first books, *Winesburg, Ohio* and *In Our Time*. Focuses on their depiction of silent characters, the necessary and desirable withdrawal from society, and the problems associated with verbal communication. Concludes that the silences found in these two early texts "are the silences that are the

necessary preliminary conditions for the important works of James Agee, Walker Evans, and Edward Hopper."

118 WEISS, DANIEL. "Ernest Hemingway: The Stylist of Stoicism." In *The Critic Agonistes: Psychology, Myth, and the Art of Fiction*. Edited by Eric Solomon and Stephen Arkin. Seattle: University of Washington Press, pp. 133-60.

Loosely organized posthumous essay written in 1962 on psychological issues in Hemingway's life and work such as his fascination with death and violence, the formative experience of the war on his art, and the Hemingway code and stoic consciousness. Provides an overview of the author's major works with an extended treatment of *The Sun Also Rises* in comparison to Eliot's *The Waste Land*.

119 WHITE, WILLIAM, "For the Collector." *Hemingway Review* 4, no. 2 (Spring): 58.

Includes information on books and new editions. A brief note by Susan Beegel lists other items also of interest to collectors.

120 _____. "For the Collector." *Hemingway Review* 5, no. 1 (Fall): 60-64.

Includes information on Hemingway films, videotapes, and other items of interest to the collector.

121 _____. "Hemingway: A Current Bibliography." *Hemingway Review* 4, no. 2 (Spring): 61-63.

List of current items, including articles, dissertations, books, new editions, and translations.

122 _____. "Hemingway: A Current Bibliography." *Hemingway Review* 5, no. 1 (Fall): 60-64.

List of current items, including articles, reviews, books, and new editions.

123 _____. "Imitation Hemingway Contest: 8." *Hemingway Review* 5, no. 1 (Fall): 55-57.

Reprints both the winning and runner-up entries in the Eighth International Imitation Hemingway Competition: Peter Applebome's "The Tollway Belle's for Thee" and Richard S. Simmons's "Rest in the Afternoon." Parody at its best (or worst).

124 _____. ed. *Dateline: Toronto, The Complete Toronto Star Dispatches, 1920-1924*. New York: Scribner's, 478 pp.

White includes 172 "identifiable articles" Hemingway published in either the *Toronto Star Weekly* or the *Toronto Daily Star* between February of 1920 and September of 1924. Unsigned pieces and those with bylines other than "by Ernest M. Hemingway" or "By E.M. Hemingway" are noted in the table of contents. Only twenty-nine of these pieces appeared in White's 1967 *By-Line: Ernest Hemingway*.

125 WILLY, TODD G. "The Covenants of Venery: Political Mythopoeism in Ernest Hemingway's *The* [sic] *Green Hills of Africa*." *South Atlantic Quarterly* 84 (Spring): 141-60.
   Attacks both the safari genre itself and Hemingway's contribution to it. Willy defines the "monotonous formula" of the safari book as racist, sexist, imperialist, and graceless. He then goes on to show how *Green Hills of Africa* is more successful than most in employing the familiar conventions.

126 YARDLEY, JONATHAN. "Ten Books That Shaped the American Character." *American Heritage* 36, no. 3 (April-May): 24-31.
   Includes *In Our Time* because a book by Hemingway "is absolutely mandatory" on such a list. Comments on the far-reaching impact of Hemingway's style "that we now hear at every turn, in novels and stories, in newspapers and magazines, in advertisements and speeches, in movies and television."

127 YOUNG, ROBERT D. "Hemingway's Suicide in His Works." *Hemingway Review* 4, no. 2 (Spring): 24-30.
   Discounting Philip Young's well-known death-wish theory, Robert D. Young (drawing liberally from the Hemingway canon) argues that the author adopted a fiesta approach to life – drinking, loving, writing, and fishing – as a shield against inevitable death. "Rather than pursue death, Hemingway was aware of death and pursued life."

1986

1 ADAIR, WILLIAM. "Lying Down in Hemingway's Fiction." *Notes on Contemporary Literature* 16, no. 4:7-8.
   Points out numerous instances of lying down in Hemingway's works, arguing that such a minor action serves not only as a structuring device but as a means to convey escape, retreat, or defeat.

2 A.G. Review of *The Garden of Eden*. *West Coast Review of Books* (September): 32.
   Feels that the few good parts are far outweighed by the novel's major flaws of redundancy and skeletal characterization.

3 ALDRIDGE, JOHN W. "*The Sun Also Rises*: Sixty Years Later." *Sewanee Review* 94, no. 2 (Spring): 337-45.

Speaks of Hemingway's continued popularity. In commenting on the author's minimalist style, Aldridge relates *The Sun Also Rises* to "Big Two-Hearted River" in suggesting that the real story behind the novel is too disturbing to tell. Therefore, language is used as a barrier to guard against nihilism.

4 ALLEN, WILLIAM RODNEY. *Walker Percy: A Southern Wayfarer.* Jackson: University Press of Mississippi, 160 pp.

Comments on Hemingway's influence on both Percy and his writing, believing that Percy eventually rejected Hemingway's stoical response as inadequate and reminiscent of his own father's approach to life.

5 ATHERTON, JOHN. "The Itinerary and the Postcard: Minimal Strategies in *The Sun Also Rises.*" *Journal of English Literary History* 53, no. 1 (Spring): 199-218.

Reprint with only minor revision of 1985.6.

6 BAKKER, J. *Ernest Hemingway in Holland, 1925-1981: A Comparative Analysis of the Contemporary Dutch and American Critical Reception of His Work.* Amsterdam: Rodopi, 191 pp.

Provides a chronologically organized summary and commentary of nearly all reviews appearing in Dutch newspapers, journals, and periodicals from 1925 to 1981. In comparing them with the American reception found in Robert O. Stephen's *Ernest Hemingway: The Critical Reception* (see 1977.104), Bakker reveals similarities and differences in the Dutch and American responses to the author but finds surprisingly more consensus than divergence. Bakker also includes summaries of twenty-four general articles on the author appearing in Dutch newspapers and journals.

7 BALASSI, WILLIAM. "The Writing of the Manuscript of *The Sun Also Rises*, with a Chart of Its Session-by-Session Development." *Hemingway Review* 6, no. 1 (Fall): 65-78.

Records the sixty-seven writing sessions that resulted in the composition of the novel along with descriptions of the contents of each of the seven notebooks and the thirty-two-page text that began the original narration. Collates the manuscript with the Scribner's edition to show additions, deletions, contradictions, and errors.

8 BEASLEY, CONGER, Jr. "Hemingway and the *Kansas City Star.*" *Society for the Study of Midwestern Literature Newsletter* 16, no. 1 (Spring): 1-7.

Overview of Hemingway's six-month apprenticeship as a cub reporter for the *Kansas City Star.*

9 BEEGEL, SUSAN. "The Death of El Espartero: An Historic Matador Links 'The Undefeated' and *Death in the Afternoon.*" *Hemingway Review* 5, no. 2 (Spring): 12-23.

Locates a source for Manuel of "The Undefeated" in a discarded manuscript fragment of *Death in the Afternoon* that details the 1894 fatal goring of Manuel Garcia, known as El Espartero. Suggests that Hemingway may have been researching *Death in the Afternoon* as early as 1924 while writing "The Undefeated."

10 BELL, MILLICENT. "Narrative Gaps/Narrative Meaning." *Raritan* 6, no. 1 (Summer): 84-102.

Contends that by filling in gaps in Hemingway's narratives, especially with biographical detail, we are losing the larger context of the stories. For example, defining "Big Two-Hearted River" within the frame of war precludes a reading of the story as a ritual abstraction of humanity's recovery from all loss and suffering.

11 BENDIXEN, ALFRED. "Restoring the Hemingway Image." *New Leader* 69, no. 7 (7 April): 26-27.

Favorable review of *The Garden of Eden* but questions the extent and methodology behind Jenks's editing of Hemingway's posthumous novel.

12 BENSTOCK, SHARI. *Women of the Left Bank: Paris, 1900-1940.* Austin: University of Texas Press, pp. 171-73.

A revisionary account of American and British modernism, focused on women writers and salons and bookstores they operated. Benstock does not ignore the standard figures (she includes a discussion of the attraction of Gertrude Stein for Hemingway, and suggests that the former's *A Novel of Thank You* might have some bearing on their relationship) but her attention is on Djuna Barnes, Kay Boyle, Natalie Barney, Sylvia Beach, H.D., Jean Rhys, Stein, Wharton, and others of their respective circles.

13 BLOOM, HAROLD, ed. *American Fiction 1914-1945.* New York: Chelsea House, 464 pp.

Pp. 285-99: "Hemingway: Valor against the Void" by Ihab Hassan. Reprint from *The Dismemberment of Orpheus* (New York: Oxford University Press, 1971), pp. 80-109.

Pp. 301-313: "Ernest Hemingway: The Meaning of Style" by John Graham. Reprint from *Ernest Hemingway.* Edited by Arthur Waldhorn. New York: McGraw-Hill, 1973.

Pp. 315-29: "Human Time in Hemingway's Fiction" by Wesley A. Kort. Reprint of 1980.49.

14 BRASCH, JAMES D. "Hemingway's Doctor: José Luis Herrera Sotolongo Remembers Ernest Hemingway." *Journal of Modern Literature* 13, no. 2 (July): 185-210.

From various interviews given from 1970 through 1984, Brasch reconstructs Herrera's nearly twenty-year relationship with Hemingway as the author's personal physician and friend. Herrera recounts Hemingway's activities during the Spanish civil war and his support of Castro during the Cuban Revolution. See also 1987.26 and 1987.9.

15 BRAUDY, LEO. "Above It All: Lindbergh and Hemingway." In *The Frenzy of Renown: Fame & Its History*. New York: Oxford University Press, pp. 19-28.

Looks at the increasing difficulties both Lindbergh and Hemingway had in balancing their public and private lives. Concludes that for Hemingway, "the more famous he became, the less sure he was that his public image supplied an identity with which he could be comfortable."

Pp. 535-47: "Suicide and Survival." Examines Hemingway's suicide in light of his legendary status along with a further assessment of the problems associated with Hemingway's keeping his private life separate from his public celebrity.

16 BROWN, NANCY HEMOND. "Aspects of the Short Story: A Comparison of Jean Rhys's 'The Sound of the River' with Ernest Hemingway's 'Hills Like White Elephants.'" *Jean Rhys Review* 1, no. 1:2-13.

Hemingway Review 9, no. 1 (Fall): 105.

17 BRUCCOLI, MATTHEW. J. "Hemingway 'Theft' Identified." *Hemingway Newsletter* 12 (June): 4.

Identifies the source of the line, "They were coming up on Mestre fast, and already it was like going to New York the first time you were ever there in the old days when it was shining, white and beautiful," from chapter 5 of *Across the River and into the Trees*, as probably the last sentence of Fitzgerald's 1932 "My Lost City."

18 ____, ed. *Conversations with Ernest Hemingway*. Jackson: University Press of Mississippi, 204 pp.

Collection of forty newspaper and magazine interviews and public statements beginning with the New York *Sun's* article on the first wounded American at the Italian front and ending with several Cuban "conversations" including George Plimpton's well-known Havana interview. As a whole, they cover a range of topics from Hemingway's involvement in the Spanish civil war to his writing habits and his winning of the Nobel prize.

19 BUDICK, E. MILLER. "*The Sun Also Rises*: Hemingway and the Art of Repetition." *University of Toronto Quarterly* 56, no. 2 (Winter): 319-37.

Examines the novel's narrative structure, arguing that "Hemingway superimposes Jake's story on a set of biblical and historical narratives which suggest how Jake's problems represent a more general crisis in American literature and culture. In particular, he produces from behind Jake's autobiography, which itself hides behind the story of Robert Cohn, another story of which Jake's story and also Cohn's are unconscious replications. This is the story of America's quest for the promised land, which, in Hemingway's views . . . represented a serious misreading of the scriptural texts on which America had constructed its self-identity and which had led to a subsequent miswriting of American history and literature."

20 BURGESS, ANTHONY. "The Joys of a New Marriage: After Four Wives, Hemingway Knew a Lot about His Subject." *Life* 9 (June): 91-93.

Attempts to put the events and characters of *The Garden of Eden* within a biographical context.

21 BUSCH, FREDERICK. "Islands, Icebergs, Ships beneath the Sea." In *When People Publish*. Iowa City: University of Iowa Press, pp. 97-112.

Discusses the stylistic strength of "After the Storm" in the context of Hemingway's later reworking of it in the much-flawed *To Have and Have Not*. Traces Hemingway's influence on novelist John Hawkes, showing how the image of the sunken ship and drowned woman from "After the Storm" appear over and over in Hawkes's works.

22 CAMPBELL, JAMES. "Arms and the Young Man." *Times Literary Supplement*, no. 4348, 1 August, pp. 837-38.

Along with a review of recent critical studies, Campbell also looks at Hemingway's dispatches collected in White's *Dateline: Toronto*. Comments on Hemingway's emerging talent that was evident even in these early journalistic endeavors.

23 CASILLO, ROBERT. "The Festival Gone Wrong: Vanity and Victimization in *The Sun Also Rises*." *Essays in Literature* 13, no. 1 (Spring): 115-33.

Examines Cohn's role as scapegoat and outsider in the novel, his ostracism a result of the jealousy and rivalry of the in-group. However, "far from being 'other' or different, Cohn represents the code in its basest aspects of egotism, envy, and vanity; he is the projected and unacknowledged image of the confusion within the in-group."

24 COLLINS, WILLIAM J. "Taking on the Champion: Alice as Liar in 'The Light of the World.'" *Studies in American Fiction* 14, no. 2 (Autumn): 225-32.

Provides background information on the boxer in order to prove that both whores are not telling the truth about their relationship with him. Their differing responses represent their opposing worldviews. While Peroxide retreats into fantasy, Alice's response is more realistic, forcing "her to accept what she is now in a world she never made."

25 "A Conversation with Patrick Hemingway." *Clockwatch Review* 3, no. 2:5-9.

Interview with Hemingway's second son in which he comments on his father's enduring popularity and place in modern art, the numerous memoirs and biographies that have appeared over the years and his own projected efforts in that direction, and the controversy over the publication of *The Garden of Eden*.

26 CUMMINGS, DON. "A Master in the Making." *Maclean's* 99, no. 2 (13 January): 47.

Review of *Dateline: Toronto*. Sees Toronto's influence on the young writer in these early dispatches, which are still amazingly fresh and clear despite the passage of sixty years.

27 CURRAN, RONALD. Review of *The Dangerous Summer*. *World Literature Today* 60, no. 1 (Winter): 115.

Questions the editing of the posthumous novel by Hotchner and Scribner's, suggesting that what results may be *their* Hemingway.

28 DILLARD, ANNIE. "Natural History: Annotated Booklist." *Antaeus*, no. 57 (Autumn): 283-301.

Dillard includes *Green Hills of Africa* in her list of twentieth-century works "out of the mainstream."

29 DOCTOROW, E.L. "Braver Than We Thought." *New York Times Book Review*, 18 May, pp. 1, 44-45.

Review of *The Garden of Eden*. Contends that in spite of questionable editing, there are enough clues in the posthumous novel to suggest that Hemingway was experimenting toward a greater truth in his development of character and theme, leaving behind the romance and literary bigotry of earlier works. Reprinted: 1987.95.

30 DRABECK, BERNARD A., and ELLIS, HELEN E., eds. *Archibald MacLeish: Reflections*. Amherst: University of Massachusetts Press, pp. 27-28, 29-30, 42, 57-67.

Reminiscences about his friendship with Hemingway and their Paris days together, Hemingway's dislike of Joyce, and his supposedly close friendship with Pound.

31 DYER, JOYCE. "Hemingway's Use of the Pejorative Term 'Nigger' in 'The Battler.'" *Notes on Contemporary Literature* 16, no. 5:5-10.
    Argues that Hemingway uses the term "nigger" to mislead readers and destroy stereotypes for "it is the servile 'nigger' who challenges our ability to spot deception."

32 EBY, CECIL D. "Bothering to Explain Hemingway's 'How Do You Like It Now, Gentlemen?'" *Hemingway Review* 5, no. 2 (Spring): 47-48.
    Attributes the title of Lillian Ross's 1950 *New Yorker* profile of Hemingway entitled "How Do You Like It Now, Gentlemen?" to an anecdote recounted in Claud Cockburns's 1956 autobiography, *In Time of Trouble*. Hemingway repeated the phrase four times during the interview.

33 "Ernest Hemingway." *Journal of Modern Literature* 13, no. 3-4 (November): 482-86.
    Annotated bibliography of recent books, articles, and dissertations on Hemingway.

34 FELLNER, HARRIET. *Hemingway as Playwright: The Fifth Column*. Ann Arbor, Mich.: UMI Research Press, 123 pp.
    Good discussion of Hemingway's only play, as published and as produced. Important background provided as well for Hemingway's personal life during the Spanish civil war, his journalism during that conflict, and his political and propagandistic activities.

35 FLEMING, ROBERT E. "Perversion and the Writer in 'The Sea Change.'" *Studies in American Fiction* 14, no. 2 (Autumn): 215-20.
    Argues that allusions to Pope's *An Essay on Man* and Shakespeare's "Ariel's Song" in *The Tempest* point to the real meaning–Hemingway's exploration of the writer and his art. In transforming other character's experiences into art, Phil performs his own "sea change."

36 FLORICK, JANET L., and RAABE, DAVID M. "Longfellow and Hemingway: The Start of Something." *Studies in Short Fiction* 23, no. 3 (Summer): 324-26.
    Contends that Hemingway's "The End of Something," about a young couple's breakup, is indebted in both setting and subject matter to Longfellow's poem "The Fire of Drift-Wood."

37 FLYNN, ELIZABETH A. "Gender and Reading." In *Gender and Reading: Essays on Readers, Texts, and Contexts*. Edited by Elizabeth A. Flynn and Patrocinio P. Schweickart. Baltimore: Johns Hopkins University Press, pp. 267-88.

Flynn examines the interpretive strategies of college freshmen through their responses to Joyce's "Araby," Woolf's "Kew Gardens," and "Hills Like White Elephants." Finds that "male students sometimes react to disturbing stories by rejecting them or by dominating them, a strategy, it seems, that women do not often employ. ... women more often arrive at meaningful interpretations of stories because they more frequently break free of the submissive entanglement in a text and evaluate characters and events with critical detachment."

38 GAJDUSEK, ROBERT E. *Hemingway's Paris*. New York: Scribner's, 182 pp.

Reprint of 1978.31 with only minor revisions. Covers not just the 1920s, but rather extends through the liberation of Paris. Many excerpts from Hemingway's letters, *A Moveable Feast*, etc. Walks and maps. Many photos.

39 GLADSTEIN, MIMI REISEL. "Hemingway." In *The Indestructible Woman in Faulkner, Hemingway, and Steinbeck*. Ann Arbor, Mich.: UMI Research Press, pp. 47-73.

Gladstein's approach to the problem of Hemingway's characterization of women is mythic, keyed to our understanding of Demeter and Persephone. She aligns what she sees as his four indestructible women – Brett, Pilar, Marie, and Renata – with women she thinks influenced him as a developing writer (his mother, Agnes von Kurowsky, Hadley), noting the similarities in the roles Hemingway gives them fictionally.

40 HANNUM, HOWARD L. "Nick Adams and the Search for Light." *Studies in Short Fiction* 23, no. 1 (Winter): 9-18.

Study of character, theme, light and dark imagery, and Christian and literary allusions in the story. Suggests the two whores, in arguing over their supposed relationship with the boxer Stan Ketchel, are actually reenacting the Ketchel-Johnson fight, with Peroxide (Ketchel) up against the heavier opponent, Alice (Johnson).

41 HARRELL, DAVID. "A Final Note on Duff Twysden." *Hemingway Review* 5, no. 2 (Spring): 45-46.

Verifies that Duff Twysden, the model for Brett Ashley of *The Sun Also Rises*, died at the age of forty-six in Santa Fe, New Mexico, from tuberculosis. Twysden was cremated and no service was held.

Points out the numerous variations of her name but fails to deduce which is correct.

42 HART, JEFFREY. "For Whom the Bell Tolled." *Commentary* 82 (December): 59-62.
    Brief plot summary and discussion of *For Whom the Bell Tolls* in the context of the Spanish civil war viewed in retrospect.

43 HAYS, PETER L. "Note on Santiago and Lear." *Hemingway Newsletter* 11 (January): 3.
    Hears echoes of *King Lear* in Santiago's line, "But I killed the shark that hit my fish," in *The Old Man and the Sea*.

44 HELLMAN, LILLIAN. *Conversations with Lillian Hellman*. Edited by Jackson R. Bryer. Jackson: University Press of Mississippi, 298 pp.
    Many references to Hemingway; see 142-43, on the power of his personality.

45 HEMINGWAY, ERNEST. "An African Betrayal." *Sports Illustrated* 64, no. 18 (5 May): 58-72.
    Excerpts of passages from *The Garden of Eden* restructured to form the short story of a boy and his father on an elephant hunt.

46 _____. *The Garden of Eden*. New York: Scribner's, 247 pp.
    Heavily edited posthumous novel dealing with, among other themes, androgyny and bisexuality. The young novelist David Bourne finds both relief from his destructive marriage and a soulmate in the adoring Marita.

47 _____. "Hemingway on Writing: 'Remembering Accurately.'" *New York Times Book Review*, 27 April, pp. 1, 32-33.
    Prints excerpts from *The Garden of Eden*, Hemingway's most recent posthumous work.

48 HEMINGWAY, JACK. *Misadventures of a Fly Fisherman: My Life with and without Papa*. New York: McGraw-Hill, 326 pp.
    Suffused with memories and accounts of his father, John N. Hemingway has managed to write his own story. This is required reading for anyone interested in either Hemingway or his work. The memories of Hemingway during the 1920s and 1930s are especially informative, as well as Jack's impressions of his mother, Hadley Richardson, of Pauline Pfeiffer, of Martha Gellhorn, and of Mary Hemingway.

49 HEMINGWAY, LORIAN. "Ernest Hemingway's Farewell to Art." *Rolling Stone*, no. 475 (5 June): 41-42, 72.

Questions the publication of Hemingway's posthumous works (against the author's "unwritten" wishes) and considers the latest addition to the Hemingway canon, *The Garden of Eden*, "not just bad, but god-awful."

50 ____. "Leicester: The Other Hemingway." *Clockwatch Review* 3, no. 2:12-16.

Fond recollections of her time spent in Bimini with her Uncle Leicester Hemingway, Ernest's younger brother. "When I think of *Hemingway* I think of Les. He was the embodiment of all that was truly good in the family."

51 HERNDON, JERRY A. "'The Snows of Kilimanjaro': Another Look at Theme and Point of View." *South Atlantic Quarterly* 85, no. 4 (Autumn): 351-59.

Sees Harry's dream-flight at the end of the story as a vision of redemption.

52 HILY-MANE, GENEVIÈVE. "Point of View in Hemingway's Novels and Short Stories: A Study of Manuscripts." *Hemingway Review* 5, no. 2 (Spring): 37-44.

Manuscript study centered on Hemingway's experimentation with point of view. Discusses shifts in first- and third- person narration in several works, including *A Farewell to Arms*, *For Whom the Bell Tolls*, and "Hills Like White Elephants."

53 HINKLE, JAMES. "'Dear Mr. Scribner' – About the Published Text of *The Sun Also Rises*." *Hemingway Review* 6, no. 1 (Fall): 43-64.

Focuses on textual problems, finding over 4,000 differences between Hemingway's finished typescript and Scribner's published edition. Includes an appendix of the differences, citing major deletions, sentence and word changes, and copyediting revisions.

54 ____. "Scribner, Scribners, Scribner's." *Hemingway Review* 6, no. 1:42.

Attempts to sort out the confusion regarding the proper form of the publisher's name. "In short: the man is *Scribner*, the adjective is *Scribner*, the noun and short firm name is *Scribners*, the official firm name is *Charles Scribner's Sons*, and *Scribner's* is almost never right."

55 HITCHENS, CHRISTOPHER. "American Notes." *Times Literary Supplement*, no. 4335, 2 May, p. 472.

Announces the upcoming publication of the posthumous *The Garden of Eden*, discussing briefly the controversy over Scribner's heavy-handed editing.

56 HOLCOMBE, WAYNE C. "Philip Young or Youngerdunger?" *Hemingway Review* 5, no. 2 (Spring): 24-33.

Summarizes Young's well-known psychoanalytic criticism of Hemingway's works, taking exception to Young's approach because of its excessive reliance on the subconscious and its distance from literary criticism.

57 HOLMESLAND, ODDVAR. "Structuralism and Interpretation: Ernest Hemingway's 'Cat in the Rain.'" *English Studies* 67, no. 3 (June): 221-33.

In his structural analysis of the story, Holmesland argues against the orthodox interpretation of the cat as symbol of the wife's unfulfilled desire for a child. ". . . [T]he meaning of the cat cannot be defined more explicitly than as a metaphor for the wife's instinctual desire for a vital openness to life. . . . All that can be said is that it reflects her need to experience emotional fertility and is not attached to a definable object."

58 HOWELL, JOHN M. "McCaslin and Macomber: From Green Hills to Big Woods." *Faulkner Journal* 2, no. 1:29-36.

Traces Faulkner's use of the dog/lion and dog/woman analogies and their role in developing the theme of courage in "The Bear" back to Hemingway's earlier "The Short Happy Life of Francis Macomber" and *Green Hills of Africa*.

59 "How Would You Put a Glass of Ballantine Ale into Words?" *Clockwatch Review* 3, no. 2:31.

Reprint of Hemingway's 1959 *Life* Ballantine Ale advertisement.

60 "Individual Authors." *Journal of Modern Literature* 13, no. 3-4 (November): 482-86.

Descriptive listing of recent scholarly and critical studies on Hemingway.

61 JOHNSTON, GEORGE SIM. Review of *The Garden of Eden*. *American Spectacular* (September): 44-45.

A mixed review; still, Johnston is pleasantly surprised that despite all the negative publicity surrounding its publication, "the book is not only an absorbing narrative but contains some of Hemingway's best writing."

62 JOHNSTON, KENNETH G. "'A Way You'll Never Be': A Mission of Morale." *Studies in Short Fiction* 23, no. 4 (Fall): 429-35.

Argues that Nick's ostensible mission, to boost the morale of the Italian troops, is a front invented by his doctors who are really interested in boosting Nick's own morale and restoring his confidence by sending him back into the battle zone. Reprinted with slight revision: 1987.38.

63 JOSEPHS, ALLEN. "In Papa's Garden." *Boston Review* 11, no. 3 (June): 20-21.

Favorable review of *The Garden of Eden*, positive that the novel "reveals a more imaginative talent, a more profound psychological vision, and a more ambitious attempt at understanding some parts of the human condition than we had generally given Hemingway credit for." Reprinted in part: 1986.64.

64 ____. Review of *The Garden of Eden*. *Hemingway Review* 6, no. 1 (Fall): 112-14.

Reprint from 1986.63.

65 ____. "*Toreo*: The Moral Axis of *The Sun Also Rises*." *Hemingway Review* 6, no. 1 (Fall): 88-99.

Considers the spiritual dimensions of the *toreo* which make it not only the center of the novel but also the center of the author's artistic vision. Sees characters revolving around the center in concentric circles at varying distances—from Romero who is nearest the center to the uncomprehending Cohn, the farthest figure. Traces Hemingway's transformation of the historical Cayetano Ordóñez into the mythic Romero. Reprinted: 1987.7.

66 KAZIN, ALFRED. "The Wound That Will Not Heal: Writers and the Spanish Civil War." *New Republic*, no. 3736 (25 August), pp. 39-41.

Touches on Hemingway's involvement in the Spanish civil war and his writing of *The Fifth Column* and *For Whom the Bell Tolls*. Comments on the failure of those *many* who supposedly supported the republic to actually defend it.

67 KOBLER, J.F. "British Reviews." *Hemingway Review* 5, no. 2:61-62.

Annotated bibliography of selected British reviews of Hemingway's works.

68 LANCASHIRE, DAVID. Review of *Dateline: Toronto. Smithsonian* 17, no. 2 (May): 160.

Considers it an extraordinary collection revealing Hemingway's early talent as a writer, but chides the editor for failing to give background information on the articles.

69   LAZAREV, LAZAR. "'Nothing Stands between the Friendship of Our Countries': Correspondence between Ernest Hemingway and Konstantin Simonov." *Soviet Literature*, no. 1 (454): 130-37.

Includes an introduction reconstructing the occasion of the brief correspondence between Hemingway and Russian journalist and author Konstantin Simonov. Reprints their letters in which Hemingway invites Simonov to visit him in Cuba.

70   LEEDS, B.H. Review of *Dateline: Toronto*. *Choice* 23, no. 8 (April): 1213.

Finds the collection of use to scholars and of interest to the general reading public. The emerging art of Hemingway shows through even in these early journalistic endeavors.

71   ____. Review of *The Garden of Eden*. *Choice* 24, no. 1 (September): 122.

Grants that the novel is tiresome in places, but believes it frequently sparkles with some of the author's best writing.

72   LYNN, KENNETH S. "Hemingway's Wars." *New Republic*, no. 3705 (20 January), pp. 6, 40.

Responds to Lewis's "Who's Papa?" (see 2 December), defending his reading of "Big Two-Hearted River" as a story about the protagonist's personal war and not about the trauma of being wounded at Fossalta.

73   McCONNELL, FRANK. "Stalking Papa's Ghost." *Wilson Quarterly* 10, no. 1:160-72.

Looks at Hemingway's monumental impact on contemporary writers such as Bellow, Mailer, Vonnegut, and Pynchon, concluding that Hemingway's notion of the code, a separate peace, and the antiheroic hero strongly influenced the course of American literature in the 1950s, 1960s, and 1970s.

74   MacLEISH, ARCHIBALD. *Reflections*. Edited by Bernard A. Drabeck and Helen E. Ellis. Amherst: University of Massachusetts Press, 291 pp.

Many references to Hemingway in this volume of transcribed and edited reminiscences, taped by the editors (MacLeish did not want to write his own autobiography). On Hemingway in Paris, 44-45, 57-67; and on writing, 32, 35, 185. Other references.

75   MARTIN, ROBERT A. "Hemingway's Sun as Title and Metaphor." *Hemingway Review* 6, no. 1 (Fall): 100.

Shows how the meaningless activity of the characters in *The Sun Also Rises* and the pointless circularity of their lives is reflected in the thematic pattern of the sun's rising and setting.

76 MERRIMAN, MARION, and LERUDE, WARREN. *American Commander in Spain, Robert Hale Merriman and the Abraham Lincoln Brigade*. Reno: University of Nevada Press, 255 pp.

Many references to Hemingway because Merriman was at least partially the model for Jordan in *For Whom the Bell Tolls*. His writing quoted on several military actions (133-34, 137, 140-41); radio broadcasts (131-36); described (132-33). Other references.

77 MEYERS, JEFFREY. "Tonsorial." *National Review* 38, no. 9 (23 May): 44-45.

Review of *The Garden of Eden*. Considers the novel worth reading "for the light it casts on Hemingway's second marriage (to Pauline Pfeiffer), his hair fetishism, and his sexual fantasies – though anyone who picks up the novel for descriptions of kinky sex will be seriously disappointed." Reprinted with slight revision: 1987.57.

78 MICHAELS, LEONARD. "What's a Story?" *Ploughshares* 12, no. 1-2:199-204.

Sees the bullfight scene in *Death in the Afternoon* in which Hernandorena is gored as the perfect crafting of the transformation through transition, resulting in the transformation of the bullfighter without changing his character.

79 MIKHAILOV, PYTOR. "Bloodshedding Corrida." *Soviet Life*, no. 8 (August): 56-57.

Comments briefly on Hemingway's support of the republican cause during the Spanish civil war.

80 MILLER, PAUL. "Paris of the 1920s through Midwestern Novelists' Eyes." *Midamerica* 13:84-93.

Comments briefly on Hemingway's literary apprenticeship in Paris and the tremendous influence of that period on his art.

81 MONTEIRO, GEORGE. "'This Is My Pal Bugs': Ernest Hemingway's 'The Battler.'" *Studies in Short Fiction* 23, no. 2 (Spring): 179-83.

Locates a possible source for the unorthodox relationship between the three characters in Melville's *Benito Cereno*.

82 MOORHEAD, MICHAEL. "Hemingway's 'The Short Happy Life of Francis Macomber' and Shaw's 'The Deputy Sheriff.'" *Explicator* 44, no. 2 (Winter): 42-43.

Contends that Irwin Shaw modeled, in part, his character Macomber (in "The Deputy Sheriff") after Hemingway's protagonist.

83 MORELAND, KIM. "Hemingway's Medievalist Impulse: Its Effect on the Presentation of Women and War in *The Sun Also Rises*." *Hemingway Review* 6, no. 1 (Fall): 30-41.

Contending that the novel resembles a distorted medieval romance, Moreland analyzes how the actions and requests of Lady Brett, the new modern woman, skew the conventions of courtly love and make true knighthood an impossibility for her suitors, the new modern men.

84 MORROW, LANCE. "A Quarter-Century Later, the Myth Endures." *Time* 128, no. 8 (25 August): 70.

Expounds on Hemingway's mythic legend and continued popularity.

85 MORTON, BRIAN. "The Highest Thing on the Mountain." *Times Educational Supplement*, no. 3652 (27 June), p. 22.

Reviews several of the recent biographies along with the author's own *The Garden of Eden*. "Hemingway was never bolder in technique or in subject and for all its ineptitudes *The Garden of Eden* is a remarkable hymn to the imagination."

86 MOSELEY, MERRITT. "Faulkner's Benjy, Hemingway's Jake." *College Literature* 13, no. 3 (Fall): 300-304.

Compares the scene of Jake Barnes (*The Sun Also Rises*) standing naked before a mirror and crying over his disfigurement with a similar scene involving Benjy Compson in *The Sound and the Fury*.

87 NAGEL, JAMES. "Hemingway Guidelines for Permission and Publication: Background and Comment." *Hemingway Review* 5, no. 2 (Spring): 34-36.

Prints established guidelines concerning permission to quote from both published and unpublished Hemingway materials.

88 NAKAJIMA, KENJI. "Literary Bravery in Hemingway's 'Chapter III' and 'Chapter IV' of *In Our Time*." *Kyushu American Literature* 27:47-56.

Sees the author's sincere consciousness of the gap between everyday language and reality as an ineffable act of bravery equal to that "of a soldier who objectively looks at the destructive reality of war and at his own emotions as well."

89 NAKJAVANI, ERIK. "The Aesthetics of the Visible and the Invisible: Hemingway and Cézanne." *Hemingway Review* 5, no. 2 (Spring): 2-11.

Attempts to explain, through phenomenological theory and Cézanne's aesthetic vision, the nature and consequence of Hemingway's "affinity" with the painter, paying close attention to each artist's preoccupation with the visible.

90 NELSON, RAYMOND [S.]. "Five Formerly Unpublished Hemingway Stories." *International Fiction Review* 13, no. 2 (Summer): 87-89.

Summarizes and discusses short stories written after Hemingway's return to America from Italy that were rejected by *Redbook* and *The Saturday Evening Post*. Even in these early sketches, Hemingway's talent for detail and fascination with violence shine through.

91 "Note on New *OMS* Source (?)." *Hemingway Newsletter*, no. 11 (January): 3.

Summarizes Gregorio Fuentes's account of how Hemingway selected the title for *The Old Man and the Sea*. "On the way to Pinar del Rio, they came on an old man and a child struggling to capture a blue marlin. The fishermen were losing strength rapidly but, when Hemingway and Fuentes offered assistance, the old man refused and swore at them until they backed off."

92 OLSON, RAY. Review of *The Garden of Eden*. *Booklist* 82, no. 14 (15 March): 1042.

Favorable review. Feels that while scholars will immerse themselves in the novel's autobiographical implications, others will simply enjoy it for the quality of Hemingway's prose style and steamy subject matter.

93 PAUL, ANGUS. "Hemingway Scholar Offers New View on the Story 'Up in Michigan.'" *Chronicle of Higher Education* 32, no. 1 (5 March): 5, 10.

Summarizes Paul Smith's contentions that Hemingway may have written the story in Chicago in early 1919, earlier than previously thought. Cites *Saturday Evening Post* contributor H.W. Howe as a possible influence on the young Hemingway.

94 PIZER, DONALD. "The Hemingway-Dos Passos Relationship." *Journal of Modern Literature* 13, no. 1 (March) 111-28.

Traces Hemingway's long and complex relationship with Dos Passos, beginning with their initial friendship in the early 1920s and ending with their differing opinions over the Spanish civil war. Concentrates on their later autobiographical portraits and fictional caricatures of each other, contending they represent "a largely unconscious attempt by each writer to project into the other some of the tormenting anxieties of his own psychic life and thus of his work as a whole."

95 PLIMPTON, GEORGE. "The Art of Fiction: E.L. Doctorow." *Paris Review* 28, no. 101:22-47.
    Interview with E.L. Doctorow. Doctorow feels the successful writing strategies that served Hemingway so well early in his career eventually restricted and limited his later literary endeavors.

96 POOLEY, ERIC. "Papa's New Baby: How Scribner's Crafted a Hemingway Novel." *New York* 19, no. 17 (28 April): 50-60.
    Discussion of Tom Jenks's editing of the original manuscript of *The Garden of Eden* from 1,500 pages to just 247.

97 PRESCOTT, PETER S. "Reconstructing Hemingway." *Newsweek*, 19 May, p. 71.
    Review of *The Garden of Eden*. Recommends the novel for what it has to say about writing.

98 Review of *Dateline: Toronto*. *New Yorker* 61 (3 February): 105-6.
    "Although these writings are sixty years old, they are as fresh as morning, and a pleasure to read."

99 REYNOLDS, MICHAEL S.. "Fitzgerald and Hemingway." In *American Literary Scholarship: An Annual, 1984*. Edited by J. Albert Robbins. Durham, N.C.: Duke University Press, pp. 175-89.
    Survey of criticism on both authors published during 1984. Reynolds comments on the uneven quality of Hemingway scholarship for the year.

100 ____. "A Supplement to *Hemingway's Reading: 1910-1940*." *Studies in American Fiction* 14, no. 1 (Spring): 99-108.
    Lists ninety-three more entries to the Hemingway library, brought to light through Baker's *Ernest Hemingway: Selected Letters, 1917-1961* and the Hadley Richardson-Hemingway correspondence recently opened to the public at the Kennedy Library. Finds no new surprises.

101 ____. *The Young Hemingway*. New York: Blackwell, 291 pp.
    The best of the new biographies, Reynolds's first installment of a projected multivolume study focuses on Hemingway's boyhood and youth, ending with his first marriage to Hadley Richardson and their departure for France and the expatriate literary scene in 1921. Offers a valuable account, both more accurate and directed than other recent biographical attempts, of Hemingway's formative years, showing that

the author was a product of his culture – influenced by the values and lifestyle of Oak Park and Theodore Roosevelt.

102 ROTHER, JAMES. "Close-Reading Hemingway: Risking Mispronounced Stresses in *The Sun Also Rises*." *Hemingway Review* 6, no. 1 (Fall): 79-87.

Looks at the role of Georgette in the novel, contending that "like the other figures in *The Sun Also Rises* both major and minor, her inner core is not explication-soluble."

103 ROVIT, EARL, and BRENNER, GERRY. *Ernest Hemingway*. Rev. ed. Boston: G.K. Hall, Twayne Publishers, 214 pp.

Revision of original 1963 edition with an additional chapter on Hemingway's posthumous works. Includes a discussion of problems in editing and publishing of *A Moveable Feast*, *The Dangerous Summer*, *Islands in the Stream*, and *African Journal* as well as a summary analysis of the texts themselves. Also includes a new annotated bibliography of primary and secondary sources and an expanded notes and reference section.

104 ROWE, ANNE E. "The Last Wild Country." In *The Idea of Florida in American Literary Imagination*. Baton Rouge: Louisiana State University Press, pp. 92-106.

Discusses the appeal that Key West's colorful setting, primitive frontier qualities, and history had for Hemingway and how this area, with its striking contrasts between the poor natives and the idle rich tourists, influenced his writing of *To Have and Have Not*. Rowe also summarizes much of the critical controversy surrounding the novel.

105 RUDAT, WOLFGANG, E.H. "Hemingway's Brett: Linguistic Manipulation and the Male Ego in *The Sun Also Rises*." *Journal of Evolutionary Psychology* 7, no. 1-2:76-82.

Analyzes the thematic significance of Brett's name and the name of her real-life counterpart, Lady Duff Twysden. With *duff* as an English version of "dough" and *Brett* signifying the colloquial German for "skis" or "boards," Rudat argues that "Duff/dough is a loaf of bread shared by many men, just as Brett is a board nailed down, a ski tread on, by many men."

106 SALTER, JAMES. "Ernest Hemingway's Last Farewell." *Book World – Washington Post*, 1 June, pp. 1, 2.

Review of *The Garden of Eden*. Praises Jenks's extensive editing of the novel, which still retains both Hemingway's strengths and weaknesses.

107 SCAFELLA, FRANK. "*The Sun Also Rises*: Owen Wister's 'Garbage Pail,' Hemingway's Passage to the 'Human Soul.'" *Hemingway Review* 6, no. 1 (Fall): 101-111.

Drawing on correspondence initiated by Wister in 1928, Scafella traces Wister's attempts at moral/paternalistic instruction. In advising Hemingway on his craft, Wister points out the author's "vices" in language, style, and preoccupation with "factual" recreation rather than with "truths."

108 SCHULTZ, PHILIP. "On Writing 'The Hemingway House at Key West.'" *Clockwatch Review* 3, no. 2:21.

Schultz sums up the difficulties he had in writing his poem "The Hemingway House at Key West," eventually realizing that in actuality he was writing an elegy for his own father who had died when the poet was eighteen. Discovered that writing, as Hemingway suggested, was a good way of exorcising ghosts and grief.

109 SHAW, JAMES. "The Spanish Civil War Fifty Years Later: High Points of the Literature." *Choice* 23, no. 7 (March): 1005-1018.

Bibliographical essay devoted to a number of works treating the Spanish civil war. Includes references to *By-Line: Ernest Hemingway*, *For Whom the Bell Tolls*, *The Fifth Column*, and *The Spanish Earth*.

110 SHEED, WILFRID. "A Farewell to Hemingstein." *New York Review of Books* 33, no. 10 (12 June): 5-6, 8, 10, 12.

Reviews *The Garden of Eden* and *Dateline: Toronto* along with several recent critical studies on Hemingway. Sheed calls *The Garden of Eden* "weird" and speculates on Gertrude Stein's influence on it.

111 SIZEMORE, MARY. "The Old Man and His Columns." *Tennessee Alumnus* 66 (Summer): 27.

*Hemingway Review 6, no. 1 (Fall): 120.

112 SMIRNOFF, MARC. "Wilson and Hemingway." *New York Times Book Review*, 28 September, p. 45.

An unknown critic with the initials M.R., in an April 1924 issue of *the transatlantic review*, was actually the first (rather than Edmund Wilson as previously thought) to take note of Hemingway's talent.

113 SMITH, PAUL. "Hemingway's Apprentice Fiction: 1919-1921." *American Literature* 58, no. 4 (December): 574-88.

Traces Hemingway's early development as a writer in this study of the thirteen pieces written during the author's "Chicago period." Identifies three distinct styles (Chicago, Italian, and Michigan) and gives examples of each in his analysis of their characteristic features.

114 STARK, BRUCE. "Ernest Hemingway: Writer, Man, & Myth." *Clockwatch Review* 3, no. 2:25-30.

Beginning with the Paris years, Stark gives a broad survey of Hemingway's life and writings along with commentary on his impact on American literature and culture.

115 STEINBERG, SYBIL. "Hemingway. *The Garden of Eden.*" *Publishers Weekly* 229, no. 14 (4 April): 51.

Laments the posthumous publication of the novel with its skeletal plot, limited characterization, and awkward prose.

116 STETLER, CHARLES. "Hemingway's Women: A Warning to the Well Intentioned." *Cat's Eye II* 3:26.

*Hemingway Review 5, no. 2 (Spring 1986): 60.

117 _____. "Notes Towards Future Hemingway Criticism." *Gypsy* 4:54-64.

*Hemingway Review 5, no. 2 (Spring 1986): 60.

118 STONEBACK, H.R. "From the Rue Saint-Jacques to the Pass of Roland to the 'Unfinished Church on the Edge of the Cliff.'" *Hemingway Review* 6, no. 1 (Fall): 2-29.

Treatment of the pilgrimage motif and Jake Barnes's spirituality, tracing his pilgrim route from Paris to such places as Bayonne, Roncevaux, and Pamplona.

119 SVOBODA, FREDERIC JOSEPH. Review of *The Dangerous Summer*. *Hemingway Review* 5 (Spring): 49-50.

Contends that "while *The Dangerous Summer* was seriously flawed journalism in 1960, its edited version is a compelling reading experience in 1985, whatever its remaining flaws."

120 SYLVESTER, BICKFORD. "Winner Take Nothing: Development as Dilemma for the Hemingway Heroine." *Pacific Coast Philology* 21, no. 1-2:73-80.

Drawing from a range of Hemingway's female characters, Sylvester creates a composite portrait of the Hemingway heroine as she develops toward self-realization. "For Hemingway's protagonists, the only way to maturity is through a romantic individual union with natural order, an order larger than society, larger than mankind. And it is an order to which the heroine must contribute only at great cost to the part of her self which does not directly need that union."

121 TALESE, GAY. "Ernest Hemingway." *Esquire* 105, no. 6 (June): 259.

Briefly considers Hemingway's impact on both American culture and literature.

122 TRENT, BILL. "Hemingway: Could His Suicide Have Been Prevented?" *Canadian Medical Association Journal* 135 (15 October): 933-34.

Refers to the author's long-standing fascination with death and penchant for living life on the edge, contending that Hemingway did not want his suicide prevented.

123 TSURUTA, KINYA. "The Twilight Years, East and West: Hemingway's *The Old Man and the Sea* and Kawabata's *The Sound of the Mountain.*" In *Explorations: Essays in Comparative Literature.* Edited by Matoto Ueda. Lanham, Md.: University Press of America, pp. 87-99.

In his comparison of the two works, Tsuruta looks at the way each author presents "a hero at the penultimate stage of his life struggling to live out his final days in the fullest way he knows." Analyzes the interconnection of spatial locale and time as he examines the way the protagonists confront death or the crisis of old age.

124 UPDIKE, JOHN. "Books: The Sinister Sex." *New Yorker,* 30 June, pp. 85-88.

Review of *The Garden of Eden,* finding that some places, as when "the elephant lumbers toward death and Catherine dips in and out of madness and David speaks his goodbyes in his heart, are among Hemingway's best, and the whole rounded fragment leaves us with a better feeling about the author's humanity and essential sanity – complicated, as sanity must be – than anything else published since his death."

125 VEACH, MARLENE S. Review of *The Garden of Eden. Best Sellers* 46:168.

"Sustaining incredible events, retelling, reshaping the same kinds of details without creating boredom attest to Hemingway's artistry. Much of his writing is simple and beautiful or simply beautiful."

126 WAINWRIGHT, J. ANDREW. "The Far Shore: Gender Complexities in Hemingway's 'Indian Camp.'" *Dalhousie Review* 66, no. 1-2 (Spring-Summer): 181-87.

Close reading of narrative voice, characterization, and symbolism in the short story. Finds Hemingway affirming the "essential female life-qualities" while criticizing male limitations.

127 WALDHORN, ARTHUR. Review of *The Garden of Eden. Library Journal* 111, no. 10 (1 June): 140.

"As fiction, the book utterly fails – clumsily plotted, thematically vague and indecisive, the characters unfleshed caricatures."

128 WALLACE, EMILY MITCHELL. "Some Friends of Ezra Pound: A Photographic Essay." *Yale Review* 75, no. 3 (June): 331-56.
Comments on Hemingway's longtime friendship with Pound and their mutual respect for each other.

129 WHITE, WILLIAM. "For the Collector." *Hemingway Review* 5 (Spring): 54-56.
Lists an array of books, tapes, and articles of interest to the Hemingway collector.

130 ____. "Hemingway: A Current Bibliography." *Hemingway Review* 5, no. 2 (Spring): 57-61.
Lists current items, including books, articles, new editions, and reviews.

131 ____. "Hemingway: A Current Bibliography." *Hemingway Review* 6, no. 1 (Fall): 118-20.
Lists current items, including articles, reviews, books, and new editions.

132 ____. "Imitation Hemingway Contest: 9." *Hemingway Review* 6 (Fall): 116-17.
Reprints the winning entry in the Ninth International Imitation Hemingway Competition, Mark Silber's "The Snooze of Kilimanjaro." Parody at its best (or worst).

133 "Why Hemingway Burned Letters." *Wolf Magazine of Letters* (Cleveland, Ohio) 52 (December-January): 11-12.
*Hemingway Review 6, no. 2 (Spring 1987): 60.

134 WILHEM, ALBERT E. "Dick Boulton's Name in 'The Doctor and the Doctor's Wife.'" *Names* 34, no. 4 (December): 423-25.
Examines the semantic overtones of Boulton's name, including identifying him as a maker of crossbows–thus interpreting Boulton as "an invader from the Indian camp who attacks the Doctor on his own ground and destroys all peace and security."

135 WILKINSON, MYLER. *Hemingway and Turgenev: The Nature of Literary Influence*. Ann Arbor, Mich.: UMI International Research Press, 126 pp.
Relying on Harold Bloom's theory of *clinamen* (poetic misreading) in his *The Anxiety of Influence*, Wilkinson compares Hemingway's writings with Turgenev's. Focusing primarily on *Fathers and Sons* and *The Sun Also Rises*, Wilkinson contends that both Turgenev and Hemingway "worked out of personal visions which had to

confront the problem of nihilism in the modern world. They dealt with the question of man's place in a natural world without intrinsic meaning – the existential question of how man will make choices and define himself within a context that lacks a priori meaning." Also explores similarities in style and theme found in *A Sportsman's Sketches* and some of Hemingway's early short stories. Includes appendices on Hemingway and Isaac Babel, Hemingway's borrowing records from Sylvia Beach's library, and an inventory of Hemingway's readings of Turgenev's works.

136 WILSON, EDMUND. *The Fifties*. Edited by Leon Edel. New York: Farrar, Straus, Giroux, pp. 98, 123, 253, 302, 339-42.
    Wilson recollects Hemingway's boxing match with Morley Callaghan (339-42) and makes other comments.

137 WINCHELL, MARK ROYDEN. "Fishing the Swamp: 'Big Two-Hearted River' and the Unity of *In Our Time*." *South Carolina Review* 18, no. 2 (Spring): 18-29.
    Focuses on the negative attitude toward domestic life that serves to unify the sketches and stories into an integrated whole. "Whether viewed from a male or female perspective, however, the clear message of *In Our Time* is that domestic bliss is a fraud and an illusion."

138 WRIGHT, WILLIAM. *Lillian Hellman, The Image, The Woman*. New York: Simon & Schuster, 507 pp.
    References to Hemingway, particularly during the Spanish civil war.

139 WYLDER, DELBERT E. Review of *The Dangerous Summer*. *North Dakota Quarterly* 54 (Spring): 268-70.
    Laments Hemingway's repetitious descriptions of bullfights and lack of objectivity.

140 YAMAMOTO, SHOH. "Hemingway's Macomber Story: Its Structure and Meaning." *Poetica* (Tokyo) 23:98-115.
    Structural analysis of "The Short Happy Life of Francis Macomber" along with an examination of the omniscient point of view. Opens with a brief account of Hemingway's growing popularity in Japan.

141 YOUNG, THOMAS DANIEL. *Conversations with Malcolm Cowley*. Literary Conversations Series. Jackson: University Press of Mississippi, 224 pp.
    Collection of previously published interviews. Many references to Hemingway and his writing, including Cowley's editing of *The Portable Hemingway* in 1944 and Hemingway's antifascist address to the Second

American Writers Congress. Reprints the Cowley portions of "The Importance of Knowing Ernest" interview with Denis Brian. See *Esquire* 77 (February 1972).

1987

1 ADAIR, WILLIAM. "Hemingway's Debt to *Seven Pillars of Wisdom* in *For Whom the Bell Tolls.*" *Notes on Contemporary Literature* 17, no. 3 (May): 11-12.

   Citing parallels in plot, characterization, descriptive detail, and action imagery, Adair argues that *For Whom the Bell Tolls* was significantly influenced by T.E. Lawrence's earlier account of guerrilla warfare in *Seven Pillars of Wisdom*.

2 _____. "Hemingway's *The Sun Also Rises.*" *Explicator* 45, no. 3:48-49.

   Points to Jake's dislike of nearly all of the characters in the novel as evidence that he suffers from xenophobia.

3 BARTLETT, BERTRICE. "Negatives, Narrative, and the Reader." *Language and Style* 20, no. 1 (Winter): 41-61.

   Looks briefly at the way Hemingway's use of negatives in "Big Two-Hearted River" reveals Nick's internal struggle.

4 BELL, PEARL K. "Fiction Chronicle." *Partisan Review* 54:99-114.

   In surveying postwar American novels, Bell reviews *The Garden of Eden*, finding it genuinely moving in those places that describe in detail the writer at work. "How passionately Hemingway wanted us to know that nothing else – wars, wine, or women – could ever matter so much!"

5 BELLAVANCE-JOHNSON, MARSHA, and BELLAVANCE, LEE. *Hemingway in Key West*. Ketchum, Idaho: Computer Lab.
   *Hemingway Review 9, no. 1 (Fall): 105.

6 BLOOM, HAROLD, ed. *Ernest Hemingway's "A Farewell to Arms."* New York: Chelsea, 164 pp.

   Collection of mostly previously published material. Includes a chronology and bibliography. Contents:

   Pp. 1-8: Introduction by Harold Bloom. Brief overview of literary influences on Hemingway, including Twain and Whitman, and an evaluation of Hemingway's position in American literature. Also links *A Farewell to Arms* to Walter Pater's aesthetic impressionism via Joseph Conrad's influence.

   Pp. 9-24: "The Novel as Pure Poetry" by Daniel J. Schneider. Reprint from *Modern Fiction Studies* 14, no. 3 (Autumn 1968).

Pp. 25-32: "Tragic Form in *A Farewell to Arms*" by Robert Merrill. Reprint from *American Literature* 45, no. 4 (January 1974).

Pp. 33-48: "*A Farewell to Arms*: A Dream Book" by William Adair. Reprint of 1975.1.

Pp. 49-59: "Going Back" by Michael S. Reynolds. Reprint from 1976.72.

Pp. 61-75: "Hemingway's 'Resentful Cryptogram'" by Judith Fetterley. Reprint of 1976.24. Reprinted also: 1977.33 and 1978.28.

Pp. 77-96: "The Sense of an Ending in *A Farewell to Arms*" by Bernard Oldsey. Reprint of 1977.86.

Pp. 97-112: "Frederic Henry's Escape and the Pose of Passivity" by Scott Donaldson. Reprint from 1983.86.

Pp. 113-29: "Pseudoautobiography and Personal Metaphor" by Millicent Bell. Reprint from 1984.84.

Pp. 131-48: "Catherine Barkley and the Hemingway Code: Ritual and Survival in *A Farewell to Arms*" by Sandra Whipple Spanier. (New Essay.) Relying on *The Garden of Eden* and the unpublished manuscripts of *A Farewell to Arms* to further support her argument, Spanier suggests that Catherine's honor and courage exemplify the Hemingway code. As Frederic's mentor, Catherine must teach him "by example how to survive in a hostile and chaotic world in which an individual can gain at most a limited autonomy through scrupulous adherence to roles and rituals of one's own devising."

7 ____. *Ernest Hemingway's "The Sun Also Rises."* New York: Chelsea, 184 pp.

Reprints eleven essays, prefaced with Bloom's introduction and indexed. Contents:

Pp. vii-viii: Editor's note on selections.

Pp. 1-8: Introduction by Harold Bloom.

Pp. 9-24: "The Wastelanders" by Carlos Baker. Reprint from *The Writer as Artist* (Princeton: Princeton University Press, 1952).

Pp. 25-37: "The Death of Love in *The Sun Also Rises*" by Mark Spilka. Reprint from *Twelve Original Essays on Great American Novels*, edited by Charles Shapiro (Detroit: Wayne State University Press, 1958).

Pp. 39-49: "Implications of Form in *The Sun Also Rises*" by William L. Vance. Reprint from *The Twenties*, edited by Richard E. Langford and William E. Taylor (Deland, Fla.: Everett Edwards Press, 1966).

Pp. 51-60: "Ernest Hemingway and the Rhetoric of Escape" by Robert O. Stephens. Reprint from *The Twenties*, edited by Richard E. Langford and William E. Taylor (Deland, Fla.: Everett Edwards Press, 1966).

Pp. 61-70: "Meyer Wolfsheim and Robert Cohn: A Study of Jewish Type and Stereotype" by Josephine Z. Knoff. Reprint from *Tradition: A Journal of Orthodox Jewish Thought* 10, no. 3 (1969).

Pp. 71-90: "Hemingway's Morality of Compensation" by Scott Donaldson. Reprint from *American Literature* 43, no. 3 (November 1971).

Pp. 91-101: "The End of *The Sun Also Rises*: A New Beginning" by Carole Gottlieb Vopat. Reprint from *Fitzgerald/Hemingway Annual* 1972.

Pp. 103-115: "*The Sun Also Rises*: One Debt to Imagism" by Linda W. Wagner. Reprint from *Journal of Narrative Technique* 2, no. 2 (May 1972).

Pp. 117-32: "False Dawn: *The Sun Also Rises* Manuscript" by Michael S. Reynolds. Reprint from 1980.79. Reprinted: 1983.86.

Pp. 133-49: "What's Funny in *The Sun Also Rises*" by James Hinkle. Reprint of 1985.52. Reprinted: 1987.95.

Pp. 151-67: "*Toreo*: The Moral Axis of *The Sun Also Rises*" by Allen Josephs. Reprint of 1986.65.

8 BLUE, ADRIANNE. "Papa and Son." *New Statesman* 113, no. 2916 (13 February): 30-31.

Questions the heavy-handed editing of *The Garden of Eden*, which leaves the novel thin and unconvincing.

9 BRASCH, JAMES D. "Professor Brasch's Reply." *Journal of Modern Literature* 14, no. 1:149-51.

Response to Aden Hayes's criticism (see 1987.26) of Brasch's earlier "José Luis Herrera Sotolongo Remembers Ernest Hemingway" (see 1986.14). Defends his position concerning Hemingway's alleged sympathies for Castro.

10 BREDAHL, A. CARL. "The Body as Matrix: Narrative Pattern in *Green Hills of Africa*." *Midwest Quarterly* 28, no. 4 (Summer): 455-72.

Sees consumption and transformation as dominant images in the text and in the motivation of the narrator. In relating the creative act to the hunt, Bredahl considers it to be another kind of consumption – consuming experience and transforming it into art. Sees the narrator moving "from sickness to health as a result of his ability to perceive shape and pattern and to consume the meat of his experience."

11 BROWN, JOHN L. Review of *The Garden of Eden*. *World Literature Today* 61, no. 1 (Winter): 102.

Considers much of the novel dated and familiar Hemingway territory.

12 BURKHART, ROBERT E. "The Composition of *The Torrents of Spring.*" *Hemingway Review* 7, no. 1 (Fall): 64.

Confirms that Hemingway spent only one week during November of 1925 writing *The Torrents of Spring.*

13 BURNS, GRANT. *The Sports Pages: A Critical Bibliography of Twentieth-Century American Novels and Stories Featuring Baseball, Basketball, Football, and Other Athletic Pursuits.* Metuchen, N.J.: Scarecrow Press, items 228-230, 271, 304-6, 450, 491, 554.

Several of Hemingway's short stories are listed in this sports fiction bibliography, including "The Battler," "Fifty Grand," "The Undefeated," and "Big Two-Hearted River." Provides a brief plot summary for each entry.

14 CARPENTER, HUMPHREY. *Geniuses Together: American Writers in Paris in the 1920s.* London: Unwin Hyman, pp. 62, 70, 146-48, 150-53, 178-79, 181, 193, 215-16, etc.

More than a hundred references to Hemingway, personal and aesthetic, seeing him as a key figure in Paris life in the 1920s. Comments on writing prowess, *The Sun Also Rises*, *In Our Time*, other.

15 CLEMENS, JOHN K., and MAYER, DOUGLAS F. "Ernest Hemingway: Authority versus Influence." In *The Classic Touch: Lessons in Leadership from Homer to Hemingway.* Homewood, Ill.: Dow Jones-Irwin, pp. 187-94.

In analyzing effective corporate management styles, Clemens and Mayer point to Robert Jordan in *For Whom the Bell Tolls* as the perfect example of the "people approach" to overhauling an ailing organization, balancing authority, and influencing situations.

16 CONLON, RAYMOND. "*The Fifth Column*: A Political Morality Play." *Hemingway Review* 6, no. 2 (Spring): 11-16.

Considers the play to be Hemingway's "only truly ideological work," with the protagonist Phillip Rawlings torn between his desire for personal happiness (represented in Dorothy Bradley) and commitment to the republic. As a classic example of the divided self, Phillip's growth and development politically resemble Everyman's.

17 COOPER, STEPHEN. *The Politics of Ernest Hemingway.* Ann Arbor, Mich.: UMI Research Press, 164 pp.

Cooper chooses the term "libertarian" to describe Hemingway's politics, which he sees as focused on championing personal liberty–free from infringements from either the Left or the Right. He appeared to be conservative in that he hated big business and served during the war to protect the United States, yet he was allied with communism at times and preferred to live outside the United States. His opposition to fascism and censorship was liberal; his dislike of the New Deal and centralized government was conservative.

18 CUNLIFFE, MARCUS. "A Source for Hemingway's Macomber?" *Journal of American Studies* 21, no. 1 (April): 103.

   Suggests Teeling's dedication to H.K. Macomber in his travel narrative *American Stew: Impressions of the United States* as the source for the name "Macomber" in "The Short Happy Life of Francis Macomber."

19 DAVISON, RICHARD ALLAN. "The Cohn/Hemingway Collection." *Collections* 2:65-82.

   MLA Bibliography 1988, p. 249.

20 DONALD, DAVID HERBERT. *Look Homeward, A Life of Thomas Wolfe*. Boston: Little, Brown, 578 pp.

   Many references to Hemingway: as mentor, 277-78; compared to, 223, 240-41, 352; Wolfe's view of, 210, 278, 353; others.

21 EGRI, PETER. "Epic Retardation and Diversion: Hemingway, Strindberg, and O'Neill." *Neohelicon* 14, no. 1:9-20.

   Reprint with minor revision of 1985.31.

22 ELLSWORTH, RON. Review of *Dateline: Toronto*. *Queen's Quarterly* 94, no. 1 (Spring): 218-19.

   Values the collection for the glimpse it offers of the future novelist and short-story writer.

23 FLEMING, ROBERT E. "Portrait of the Artist as a Bad Man: Hemingway's Career at the Crossroads." *North Dakota Quarterly* 55, no. 1 (Winter): 66-71.

   Believes that Hemingway's inclusion of several writers in his works during the 1930s suggests that he may have been reevaluating the role of the writer and his responsibility to his fellow human beings at this low point in his career. Concentrating on Richard Gordon of *To Have and Have Not*, Fleming argues that writers must contend both with the "risk of violating the dignity of the human soul" and the public and critical demands for formula writing.

24 FORD, HUGH. *Four Lives in Paris*. San Francisco, Calif.: North Point Press, 286 pp.

   Scattered references to Hemingway in Ford's short biographies of George Antheil, Harold Stearns, Kay Boyle, and Margaret Anderson. Includes the story of Hemingway's review of Antheil's music (28-29),

Stearns's involvement with Hemingway's early fiction (109-11) and Hemingway's kindness to him and other references.

25 GAJDUSEK, ROBERT [E.]. "Elephant Hunt in Eden: A Study of New and Old Myths and Other Strange Beasts in Hemingway's *Garden*." *Hemingway Review* 7, no. 1 (Fall): 15-19.

Explores Hemingway's treatment of sexual inversion and its relation to identity. Gajdusek is particularly interested in the male relinquishment of power (which is depicted not only in *The Garden of Eden* but in almost all of Hemingway's major novels) and the need for men to balance the masculine and feminine sides of their nature.

26 HAYES, ADEN. "Comments on James Brasch's 'José Luis Herrera Sotolongo Remembers Ernest Hemingway.'" *Journal of Modern Literature* 14, no. 1 (Summer): 147-49.

Put off by the error-riddled and unsubstantiated text. See 1986.14 and 1987.9.

27 ____. "Have You Heard This Hemingway Story?" *Hemingway Review* 7, no. 1:37.

Draws attention to H.L. Woods's 1976 account in his memoir *Wings over Asia* of a 1941 incident in Lashio, Burma, in which Gellhorn publicly humiliated Hemingway.

28 HAYES, ADEN and WYLDER, DELBERT E. "Jake Barnes and the Cork-Oak Trees." *Hemingway Review* 6, no. 2:33.

Believe that Jake Barnes probably saw "plain old *quercus robber*" (deciduous oaks) rather than the cork oaks he claims to have seen during his bus ride to Burguete.

29 HAYS, PETER L. "Hemingway as *Auteur*." *South Atlantic Quarterly* 86, no. 2 (Spring): 151-58.

Comments on Hemingway's cinematic techniques (pictorial presentation coupled with seeming objectivity) which invite the reader to respond – to make connections and judgments.

30 HEMINGWAY, ERNEST. "I Guess Everything Reminds You of Something." *Family Circle* 100, no. 15:116-17.

Prints the previously unpublished short story collected in *The Complete Short Stories of Ernest Hemingway: The Finca Vigía Edition* (1987).

31 ____. "A Train Trip." *Esquire* 108, no. 6 (December): 162-71.

Prints the previously unpublished short story about a young boy's initiation into the harsher realities of life.

32 HEMINGWAY, JOHN; HEMINGWAY, PATRICK; and HEMINGWAY, GREGORY [H.] Foreword to *The Complete Short Stories of Ernest Hemingway*. New York: Charles Scribner's Sons, Macmillan, pp. xi-xiii.
Describes life in the Finca Vigía, in Cuba, beginning in 1940. Brief.

33 HENDRICKSON, PAUL. "Papa's Boys [Part I]." *Washington Post*, 29 July, pp. D1-D2.
Drawing on biographical data and an interview with Gregory, Patrick, and Jack Hemingway, Hendrickson attempts to reconstruct the author's relationships with his three sons.

34 ____. "Papa's Boys [Part II]." *Washington Post*, 30 July, pp. C1, C6.
See 1987.33.

35 HOPCRAFT, ARTHUR. "Who's Doing What, and to Whom?" *Listener* 117, no. 2998 (February): 27.
Review of *The Garden of Eden*. Questions the editing of the posthumous novel and considers the book, although at times reminiscent of the famous Hemingway style, overall unsatisfactory.

36 JENKS, TOM. "Editing Hemingway: *The Garden of Eden*." *Hemingway Review* 7, no. 1 (Fall): 30-33.
Reveals very little about the actual editing process but does state that "when there was any chance that a change might injure the author or the work, then no change was made." Also claims that he cut away only the excesses that had interfered with the telling of the true story.

37 JOHNSTON, KENNETH G. "Hemingway's Search for Story Titles." *Hemingway Review* 6, no. 2 (Spring): 34-37.
Scours manuscripts, typescripts, letters, and Baker's biography for discarded titles to a number of Hemingway's short stories. For example, "The Matadors" became "The Killers" and Hemingway rejected "The Great Man" in favor of "The Battler."

38 ____. *The Tip of the Iceberg: Hemingway and the Short Story*. Greenwood, Fla.: Penkevill Publishing, 296 pp.
Collection of mostly previously published material. Contents:
Pp. 1-5: Introduction. "The Story-Teller." Reprint with slight revision of 1984.52.
Pp. 11-25: "Hemingway and Cézanne: Patches of White." Reprint with slight revision of 1984.51.
Pp. 29-38: "'Out of Season': The Tip of the Iceberg." Reprint from *Literature and Psychology* 21 (1971): 41-46.

Pp. 41-46: "'The Revolutionist': The Bitter Nail Holes of Mantegna." Reprint with slight revision from *Journal of Narrative Technique* 1 (May 1971): 86-94.

Pp. 49-60: "'Indian Camp': In the Beginning." Revised reprint of 1978.40. Expanded.

Pp. 63-71: "'Cross-Country Snow': Freedom and Responsibility." Revised reprint of 1981.55. Discusses the function of snow in the short story as a symbol of freedom, purity, illusion, and innocence.

Pp. 75-82: "'Soldier's Home': Conflict on the Home Front." (New Essay.) Begins by relating the events in the story to Hemingway's own postwar experiences. Discusses the symbolic significance of the title image and photographs at the beginning of the story in relation to Krebs's coming of age.

Pp. 85-92: "'The Undefeated': The Moment of Truth." (New Essay.) Locates a source for the story in the aging matador Manuel García Lopez, "Maera." Hemingway shows Manuel abiding by the code of honor and killing by the rules despite his wound and humiliation by the jeering crowd. Suggests that the defiant and uncompromising matador may represent the struggling Hemingway at the beginning of his career.

Pp. 95-102: "'The Three-Day Blow': Tragicomic Aftermath of a Summer Romance." Reprint of 1982.45.

Pp. 105-111: "'The Killers': The Shaping of a Classic." Reprint of 1982.44.

Pp. 115-22: "'In Another Country': The Strategy of Survival." (New Essay.) Shows how the introductory paragraph anticipates both stylistically and thematically the rest of the story. Through simple diction and sentence structure, repetition and setting, Hemingway aligns the story's form with the themes of alienation, isolation, and death.

Pp. 125-34: "'Hills Like White Elephants': A Matter of Life and Death." Reprint with slight revision of 1982.43.

Pp. 137-43: "'Now I Lay Me': The Great Awakening." Reprint from *Hemingway Notes* 1 (Fall 1971): 7-10.

Pp. 147-58: "'Wine of Wyoming': Disappointment in America." Reprint from *American Literature* 9 (November 1974): 159-67.

Pp. 161-67: "'A Clean, Well-Lighted Place': Black on Black." (New Essay.) Sees the story as "Hemingway's version of the spiritual wasteland." Looks at how setting, character, and dialogue blend in order to depict man's fate in the twentieth century, of being lost in a "moral wilderness."

Pp. 171-79: "'A Way You'll Never Be': A Mission of Morale." Reprint with slight revision of 1986.62.

Pp. 183-92: "'Fathers and Sons': The Past Revisited." (New Essay.) Begins by providing a biographical base for the story, then analyzes the cyclical nature of the destructive communication patterns that result in the fathers' failing to provide guidance for their sons.

Pp. 195-204: "'The Snows of Kilimanjaro': An African Purge." Reprint of 1984.53.

Pp. 207-213: "'The Short Happy Life of Francis Macomber': Charge and Countercharge." Reprint with slight revision of 1983.57.

Pp. 217-229: "'The Denunciation': The Aloof American." Reprint of 1979.52.

Pp. 233-43: "'The Faithful Bull' and 'The Good Lion': Fables for Critics." Reprint with slight revision of 1977.68.

Pp. 249-55: Afterword. "Career in Eclipse." (New Essay.) Looks at Hemingway's decline in later years, commenting on his winning of the Nobel prize and the final short stories, "Black Ass at the Cross Roads" and "Get a Seeing-Eyed Dog." The last view of the Hemingway hero in the short fiction is of "a blind man groping in the darkness, descending the stairs leading to the fire below."

39 JONES, ROBERT B. "Mimesis and Metafiction in Hemingway's *The Garden of Eden*." *Hemingway Review* 7, no. 1 (Fall): 2-13.

Examines the novel on both mimetic and metafictional levels, exploring "the nature and evolution of authentic selfhood in its examination of Catherine's and David Bourne's individual crises of gender (identity)," as well as the novel's status as art and text. Argues that David's decision to put the elephant story before the honeymoon narrative signals the recovery of his identity as both a man and a writer.

40 JUNKINS, DONALD. "Hemingway's Bullfighter Poems." *Hemingway Review* 6, no. 2 (Spring): 38-45.

Selects nine passages from *Death in the Afternoon* and relines them into the shape of poems in order to demonstrate the poetic qualities of Hemingway's prose.

41 KAIN, GEOFFREY. "Hemingway: The Syntax of Resistance and the Symbolism of Style." *Waiguou* 50, no. 4: 70-74.

Hemingway Review 9, no. 1 (Fall): 107.

42 KEMP, PETER. "Chopping and Changing." *Times Literary Supplement*, no. 4375 (6 February), p. 135.

Considers the story about the elephant hunt to be the best part of *The Garden of Eden*.

43 KERNER, DAVID. "Hemingway's Trail to British Anti-Metronomic Dialogue." *Literary Research* 12, no. 4:187-214.

More on Hemingway's use of antimetronomic dialogue in "A Clean, Well-Lighted Place," establishing the typographical convention within the context of British literature.

44 KUMAR, SUKRITA PAUL. "Woman as Hero in Hemingway's *The Sun Also Rises*." *Literary Endeavor* 6, no. 1-4:102-8.
    Explores Brett's relationships with Cohn, Mike Campbell, Romero, and Jake, concluding that the "novel paves the way for complete androgynous relationships through an acceptance and absorption of the new values as well as the new female ideal."

45 LESCAZE, LEE. "Genius for Decisive Moments." *Wall Street Journal*, 22 December, p. 17.
    Review of *The Complete Short Stories of Ernest Hemingway: The Finca Vigía Edition*. Contends that the twenty-one stories (including fragments and later works) that Scribner's added to Hemingway's original 1938 collection fail to meet the quality of the author's earlier short stories.

46 LEVINE, SUZANNE JILL. "Vistas of Dawn in the (Tristes) Tropics: History, Fiction, Translation." *World Literature Today* 61 (Autumn): 548-53.
    Comments on the "heavily Hemingwayesque vignettes" of Guillermo Cabrera Infante's *View of Dawn in the Tropics*. Discusses how the author transforms Hemingway's description of Cuba in *Green Hills of Africa* into the subtext of his last vignette.

47 LEWIS, ROBERT W. "Have You Read This Article?" *Hemingway Review* 7, no. 1 (Fall): 13.
    Brings attention to an article appearing in *Granta* (Winter 1986) by Martha Gellhorn detailing her recent two-week visit to Cuba.

48 _____. "Hemingway's Lives: A Review." *Hemingway Review* 7, no. 1 (Fall): 45-62.
    Review essay contrasting and comparing Griffins's *Along with Youth*, Reynolds's *The Young Hemingway*, and Meyers's *Hemingway: A Biography*–three biographies all appearing in the mid-1980s.

49 _____. "Scribner, Scribners, Scribner's Revisited." *Hemingway Review* 6, no. 2:54-55.
    Attempts to set the record straight concerning the proper form of the publisher's name. After consulting the *Chicago Manual*, *Words into Type*, and the *MLA Handbook*, Lewis concludes that the most acceptable shortened form is *Scribner*.

50 LOVE, GLEN A. "Hemingway's Indian Virtues: An Ecological Reconsideration." *Western American Literature* 22, no. 3 (Fall): 201-13.

Contends that in much of Hemingway's fiction primitivism is presented in opposition to the earth (human will in ascendancy over the natural order). Concludes that even the greatest primitive Hemingway hero, Santiago of *The Old Man and the Sea*, "represents the indisputable tragic hero, strongly affirming the spirit of man in conflict with natural laws."

51 LYNN, KENNETH SCHUYLER. *Hemingway*. New York: Simon & Schuster, 702 pp.

Lynn's chief distinction is applying decades-old psychological theory to Hemingway's life – and not being ridiculed for that application. He retells a familiar story, bringing a reasonable amount of authentication to his tale; but his work is not distinguished nor is his writing exemplary. What has made Lynn's biography of Hemingway newsworthy is partly his telling of a story that readers have been conditioned to expect: something was awry in the Hemingway household, and making Grace Hall Hemingway the villain, whether for dressing Hemingway in girls' clothing or for restricting his essential freedom and then rejecting him on his birthday, is a common ploy. Lynn's prose is heavy with highly charged adjectives: "desperate," "compulsive," "intense." That these adjectives are often inappropriately used needs to be said.

52 McLAUGHLIN, ROBERT L. "'Only Kind Thing Is Silence': Ernest Hemingway vs. Sinclair Lewis." *Hemingway Review* 6, no. 2 (Spring): 46-53.

Reconstructs their relationship through meetings and references to each other in correspondence and in their writings, concluding that once again Hemingway allowed his professional jealousy to take over.

53 MAGAW, MALCOLM O. "The Fusion of History and Immediacy: Hemingway's Artist-Hero in *The Garden of Eden*." *Clio* 17, no. 1 (Fall): 21-36.

In his comparison of Robert Bourne with Jake Barnes of *The Sun Also Rises*, Magaw argues that Bourne is Hemingway's "final portrait of the artist as a young man and hero – a portrait that coalesces the early Jake Barnes/Pedro Romero hero in his *aficion*-imbued Eden before and outside time, on the one hand; with the post World War II man in tune with history, with time, and with memory, on the other hand. When these two twentieth-century Adams merge, they form a mid-century Hemingway artist-hero, a new Adam in a new Garden of Eden."

54 MAKOWSKY, VERONICA A. "Caroline Gordon: Amateur to Professional Writer." *Southern Review* 23, no. 4:778-93.
    Comments briefly on Allen Tate's friendship with Hemingway during their Paris days.

55 MARTIN, JOHN STEPHEN. "Vision and Visibility: The Phenomenology of Power and the American Literary Consciousness of Self." *Canadian Review of American Studies* 18, no. 2:181-96.
    Considers "Big Two-Hearted River" to be "a paradigm of modernist parody."

56 MARTIN, ROBERT A. "Hemingway's *For Whom the Bell Tolls*: Fact into Fiction." *Studies in American Fiction* 15, no. 2:219-25.
    Contends that Hemingway relied extensively on his own observations and experiences as a war correspondent during the Spanish civil war in writing *For Whom the Bell Tolls*. Locates sources for the people, places, and events in Hemingway's novel, including Robert Merriman, a graduate student in economics at Berkeley who serves as the model for Robert Jordan.

57 MEYERS, JEFFREY. "Fetishism and Sodomy." *Spectator*, 21 February, pp. 30-31.
    Reprint with minor revisions of 1986.77.

58 ____. "Imaginative Portraits of Hemingway." *Bulletin of Bibliography* 44, no. 4 (December): 253-54.
    Lists novels, poems, stories, and plays about Hemingway, including works by Dos Passos, Fitzgerald, Pound, and Cummings.

59 MILLER, DONALD L. "Fighting in Spain: A Conversation with Steve Nelson." *Salmagundi*, no. 76-77 (Fall-Winter): 113-32.
    1986 interview with Steve Nelson, commander of the Lincoln Battalion. Nelson reminisces about the Spanish civil war, his initial endorsement of *For Whom the Bell Tolls*, and his later withdrawal, under Communist party pressure, of that endorsement.

60 MILLER, L.C. "The Evolution of a Production Concept: *Three Americans in Paris*." *Communication Education* 36, no. 2 (April): 172-77.
    Discusses his recent stage production of *Three Americans in Paris*, featuring the lives and writings of Stein, Anderson, and Hemingway.

61 MITGANG, HERBERT. "Annals of Government: Policing America's Writers." *New Yorker*, 5 October, pp. 47-90.

Surveys the files of several authors, including Hemingway's FBI files that trace his Cuban activities during World War II and later associations with the Castro government. Reprinted with minor revision: 1988.63.

62 MOLESWORTH, CHARLES. "Hemingway's Code: The Spanish Civil War and World Power." *Salmagundi*, no. 76-77 (Fall-Winter): 84-100.

Summarizes the Hemingway code ("the hero must not be afraid to die or to kill, but he must never delight in killing nor mistake it for anything but what it is") and then relates it to his writings of the Spanish civil war, including *For Whom the Bell Tolls*, *The Fifth Column*, and "The Denunciation." Provides a firm historical grounding and argues against well-known readings of Hemingway's political vision by Trilling, Bessie, and others. "Hemingway was devoted to the Republican cause not out of any explicit or complicated political stance or argument, but rather out of a cultural and emphatically nationalistic identification with the Spanish people. Never blind to the extent and consequences of Russia's involvement and ulterior motives, he nevertheless knew that the guns in the hands of his friends were supplied by the Soviet Union."

63 MONTEIRO, GEORGE. "Ernest Hemingway, Psalmist." *Journal of Modern Literature* 14, no. 1 (Summer): 83-95.

Manuscript study of Kennedy Library materials, revealing that Hemingway's reading of King David's "Twenty-Third Psalm" affected his writing of "Neothomist Poem," *A Farewell to Arms*, and "A Clean, Well-Lighted Place." Finds the religious subtext of *A Farewell to Arms* made explicit in "A Clean, Well-Lighted Place."

64 NAGEL, JAMES. "Literary Impressionism and *In Our Time*." *Hemingway Review* 6, no. 2:17-26.

Discusses the impressionistic movement already established by the 1880s and its influence upon the style, structure, and themes of *In Our Time*. In attempting to capture in literature the "empirical sensations of actually being present at a scene," Hemingway is consciously working out of the impressionistic tradition adopted by such late-nineteenth-century American authors as Crane and Bierce.

65 NAKAJIMA, KENJI. "The Bullfight, A Test of Manhood: On Hemingway's 'Chapter IX,' *In Our Time*." *Kyushu American Literature* 28 (October): 19-27.

Looks at the role of masculinity in the bullring and Hemingway's revision of the piece after actually witnessing a bullfight. Concludes that the author retains much of the inexperienced vision of the earlier version because it captures the theme of grace under pressure.

66 NOLAN, CHARLES J., Jr. "Catherine Barkley: Hemingway's Scottish Heroine." *Hemingway Review* 7, no. 1 (Fall): 43-44.

Identifies both Catherine Barkley and Helen Ferguson as Scottish, suggesting that their friendship may predate the war. Such a firm relationship accounts for Catherine's commitment to Fergy and Fergy's strong reaction to Henry's seduction and impregnation of Catherine.

67 OLSON, RAY. Review of *The Complete Short Stories of Ernest Hemingway: The Finca Vigía Edition*. *Booklist* 84, no. 3 (1 October): 169-70.

Questions the "completeness" of the edition but has some praise for the contents.

68 O'MEALLY, ROBERT G. "The Rules of Magic: Hemingway as Ellison's 'Ancestor.'" In *Speaking for You: The Vision of Ralph Ellison*. Edited by Kimberly W. Benston. Washington, D.C.: Howard University Press, pp. 245-71.

Reprint of 1985.85.

69 PEELER, DAVID P. *Hope among Us Yet: Social Criticism and Social Solace in Depression America*. Athens: University of Georgia Press, pp. 155-56, 167, 268.

Views Hemingway as usually remote from the social novelists or the proletarian writers, except in the anomalous *To Have and Have Not*.

70 PINSKER, SANFORD. Review of *The Garden of Eden*. *Southern Humanities Review* 21, no. 4 (Fall): 381-83.

Finds the work, like his other posthumous publications, to be disappointing.

71 PRITCHARD, WILLIAM H. "Fictional Places." *Hudson Review* 39, no. 4 (Winter): 644-56.

In a brief mention of the posthumous *The Garden of Eden*, Pritchard feels the "novel has enough of the authentic Hemingway style to make it hard to decide whether mainly that style goes pure and deep, or is mannered to the edge of silliness. But I have trouble deciding that even with vintage Hemingway."

72 PUTNAM, ANN. "Dissemblings and Disclosure in Hemingway's 'An Alpine Idyll.'" *Hemingway Review* 6, no. 2 (Spring): 27-33.

Attempts to show how the peasant's grotesque tale functions as a lens through which to interpret the implied story of the skier/narrator. Points to the bundle of letters and the protagonist's interest in the affairs of others as she raises the question: "Has there been some lapse, some estrangement or omission in the narrator's own life for which the peasant's story acts as a reminder of perhaps other, more subtle kinds of blindness?"

73 ____. "'Wine of Wyoming' and Hemingway's Hidden West." *Western American Literature* 22, no. 1 (Spring): 17-32.

Contends that Hemingway's ambivalent attitude toward place in general and the West in particular is brought out in the short story centered on the motif of betrayal. Like much of Hemingway's other fiction, "Wine of Wyoming" reflects the author's unsuccessful search for a place to call home.

74 REYNOLDS, MICHAEL S. "Fitzgerald and Hemingway." In *American Literary Scholarship: An Annual 1985*. Edited by J. Albert Robbins. Durham, N.C.: Duke University Press, pp. 169-86.

Survey of criticism on both authors published during 1985. Reynolds comments on the steadily increasing interest in Hemingway scholarship.

75 REYNOLDS, STANLEY. "Adam and Evil." *Punch* 292 (11 February): 43.

Despite flaws in the ending and elsewhere, Reynolds finds the posthumous *The Garden of Eden* sparkling from time to time with the old Hemingway touch.

76 RUDAT, WOLFGANG E.H. "Jake Barnes, Chaucer's Pardoner, and the Restaurant Scene in Ernest Hemingway's *The Sun Also Rises*." *Cithara* 26, no. 2 (May): 48-55.

Correlates sex with food in the restaurant scene near the end of the novel, arguing that Nick successfully staves off Brett's attempt at psychological castration by adopting a homosexual pose. Rudat further concludes that the restaurant and taxi-ride scenes are allusions to the ending of Chaucer's *Pardoner's Tale*, which also deals with a sexually incapacitated man.

77 SANGWAN, SURENDER SINGH. "Humour in Hemingway's Short Stories." *Panjab University Research Bulletin* 18, no. 1 (April): 55-57.
Hemingway Review 9, no. 1 (Fall): 110.

78 SCAFELLA, FRANK. "Clippings from *The Garden of Eden*." *Hemingway Review* 7, no. 1 (Fall): 20-29.

Liberally quoting from the manuscripts, Scafella explores David's identity as a writer and the central quality or *mystère* of his work (his soul), Catherine's decline, and Marita's role as David's soulmate.

79 SMITH, PAUL. "Hemingway's Luck." *Hemingway Review* 7, no. 1
    (Fall): 38-42.
        Contrary to the image of Hemingway as deliberate craftsman,
    Smith points out instances in which sheer luck accounted for fortunate
    eleventh-hour revisions and editorial lapses, including the deletion of
    the original conclusion to "Big Two-Hearted River" and the introductory
    chapter of *The Sun Also Rises*. Also gives instances in which
    Hemingway's luck worked against him.

80 _____. "Impressions of Ernest Hemingway." *Hemingway Review* 6, no. 2
    (Spring): 2-10.
        Comments on a variety of topics, including: Hemingway's
    ambivalent relationship with his parents; the difficulties of separating
    the man from his art; the importance of Gertrude Stein, Hadley
    Richardson, and the mysterious girl (muse) in the café to *A Moveable
    Feast*; and Hemingway's affinity with Cézanne.

81 SMITH, PETER A. "Hemingway's 'On the Quai at Smyrna' and the
    Universe of *In Our Time*." *Studies in Short Fiction* 24, no. 2 (Spring):
    159-62.
        Looks at the seven anecdotes making up "On the Quai at Smyrna"
    that function as miniparables on "the often senselessly brutal universe
    that Nick Adams and the other characters of *In Our Time* must learn to
    live in."

82 SOLOMON, BARBARA PROBST. "Where's Papa? Scribner's *The
    Garden of Eden* Is Not the Novel Hemingway Wrote." *New Republic*
    196, no. 9 (9 March): 30-34.
        Laments the "editorial violations" and wonders if Hemingway
    would have written such a disjointed and trivial novel.

83 SPILKA, MARK. "Hemingway's Barbershop Quintet: *The Garden of
    Eden* Manuscript." *Novel* 21, no. 1 (Fall): 29-55.
        Drawing heavily on manuscript materials, Spilka laments Jenks's
    extensive editing of important scenes and subplots that tie the narrative
    together. Relates the themes of androgyny and lesbianism in the novel
    to Hemingway's own life and credits Kipling's *Jungle Books* as the
    source of the elephant-hunt tale. Finally, the novel is "about a writer's
    bravery – about Hemingway's bravery as he saw it in the daily struggle to
    transcend his own terrible dependencies and passivities."

84 _____. "Original Sin in 'The Last Good Country.'" In *The Modernists:
    Studies in a Literary Phenomenon, Essays in Honor of Harry T. Moore*.
    Edited by Lawrence B. Gamache and Ian S. MacNiven. Rutherford,
    N.J.: Fairleigh Dickinson University Press, pp. 210-33.

Discusses the blue heron episode that was the factual base for "The Last Good Country" and the circumstances surrounding the writing of the story. Relies heavily on biographical background and manuscript revisions in his examination of the story and the notion of "original sin" (meaning "doing things you will regret not having done, and getting into trouble for doing them") brought out in it. Spilka suggests that Nick's violation of the game laws falls into this category. Also explores Nick's relationship with Littless, refuting critics' claims of sublimated incest in favor of a natural bond based on childhood affection and nurturing regard.

85 SPUFFORD, FRANCIS. "Strange Fruit." *London Review of Books* 9, no. 3 (5 February): 14-15.

Sees *The Garden of Eden* as a kind of domestic novel exploring some unexpected, though consistently interesting, avenues.

86 STEINBERG, SYBIL. Review of *The Complete Short Stories of Ernest Hemingway: The Finca Vigía Edition*. *Publishers Weekly* 232, no. 18 (30 October): 51.

Values the collection for drawing together, in some instances, material that was previously unavailable or difficult to find.

87 STOLTZFUS, BEN. "A Post-Lacanian Reading of Hemingway's *The Garden of Eden*." *American Journal of Semiotics* 5, no. 3-4:381-95.
   *American Literary Scholarship 1988.

88 SUMMERLIN, TIM. "Baseball and Hemingway's 'The Three-Day Blow.'" *Arete* 4, no. 2:99-102.

Explicates the story's references to baseball (specifically the "bonehead" play by Heini Zimmerman) in relation to the larger *nada* theme of *In Our Time*.

89 SYMONS, JULIAN. *Makers of the New: The Revolution in Literature, 1912-1939*. London: Deutsch, 295 pp.

Many references to Hemingway, including: his initiation into the expatriate scene in Paris; his relationship with his first publisher, Robert McAlmon, and with mentor Gertrude Stein; the publication of *Three Stories & Ten Poems* and *In Our Time*; and his later success with *The Sun Also Rises*.

90 TAVERNIER-COURBIN, JACQUELINE. "Hemingway and Company." *Canadian Review of American Studies* 18, no. 3 (Fall): 387-91.

In her survey of recent Hemingway criticism, Tavernier-Courbin also includes a review of *Dateline: Toronto* and *The Garden of Eden*. Considers the first an invaluable tool for those interested in

Hemingway's stylistic development but questions Scribner's editing of the posthumous *The Garden of Eden*. Praises those passages about the elephant hunt in Africa but finds the rest of the novel "singularly dull."

91 TICHI, CECILIA. "Opportunity: Imagination Ex Machina II." In *Shifting Gears: Technology, Literature, Culture in Modernist America.* Chapel Hill: University of North Carolina Press, pp. 215-22.

Contends that "the famous Hemingway style was essentially the achievement, in novels and stories, of the engineers' aesthetic of functionalism and formal efficiency." Comments on the influence of the *Kansas City Star* style sheet on the young author and compares his severe verbal economy with the efficient architecture of Frank Lloyd Wright who too disliked the nonfunctional and ornamental.

92 TRUEHEART, CHARLES. "Documents Show FBI Kept Files on Leading U.S. Writers." *Washington Post*, 30 September, pp. A1, A7.

Mentions Hemingway as one of the authors monitored by the FBI.

93 VEIKHMAN, G.A. "Derivatives of English Question-Answer Units." *Zeitschrift für Anglistik und Amerikanistik* 35:326-37.

Quotes single lines from *A Farewell to Arms*, *The Old Man and the Sea*, and "The Killers" in a linguistic study of question-answer structures.

94 VERDUIN, KATHLEEN. "The Lord of Heroes: Hemingway and the Crucified Christ." *Religion and Language* 19, no. 1 (Spring): 21-41.

Looks at Hemingway's treatment of masculinity in relation to Christ and how the author translates the themes of pain, heroic suffering, valor, and death associated with the Crucifixion into his own writings [see "Today is Friday"]. "Hemingway's dramatization of the Crucifixion ... may be taken as a paradigm for Hemingway's subsequent heroes, nearly all of whom bear in some way the imprint of Calvary."

95 WAGNER, LINDA W., ed. *Ernest Hemingway: Six Decades of Criticism*. East Lansing: Michigan State University Press, 341 pp.

Collection (entirely different from Wagner's *Five Decades*) of previously published essays and reviews of Hemingway's writing, dating from 1925 to 1986, with the inclusion of three unpublished essays.

Pp. 1-8: Introduction by Linda W. Wagner. Surveys biography, writing aesthetic, career as writer, and accessibility of manuscripts and letters. Wagner points out that criticism of Hemingway's writings since the opening of the Hemingway Room in the John F. Kennedy Library has changed immeasurably.

Pp. 9-17: "Hemingway's Home: Depression and Suicide" by Michael S. Reynolds. Reprint of 1985.92.

Pp. 19-40: "Grace under Pressure: Hemingway and the Summer of 1920" by Max Westbrook. Reprint of 1984.84.

Pp. 41-59: "Dos and Hem: A Literary Friendship" by Scott Donaldson. Reprint of 1985.26.

Pp. 61-63: "Tough Earth" by Paul Rosenfeld. Reprint from *New Republic* 45 (25 November 1925).

Pp. 65-76: "The Structure of *In Our Time*" by Robert M. Slabey. Reprint from *South Dakota Review* 3 (Autumn 1965).

Pp. 77-92: "What's Funny in *The Sun Also Rises*" by James Hinkle. Reprint of 1985.52.

Pp. 93-112: "'An Image to Dance around': Brett and Her Lovers in *The Sun Also Rises*" by Sam S. Baskett. Reprint of 1978.4.

Pp. 113-38: "Hemingway's Beginnings and Endings" by Bernard Oldsey. Reprint of 1980.69 and 1981.86.

Pp. 139-45: "Hemingway and *Vanity Fair*" by C. Hugh Holman. Reprint from *Carolina Quarterly* 8 (Summer 1956).

Pp. 147-54: "The Social Basis of Hemingway's Style" by Larzer Ziff. Reprint of 1978.98.

Pp. 155-62: "Semantics and Style–With the Example of Quintessential Hemingway" by Richard L. McLain. Reprint of 1979.63.

Pp. 163-64: "Review of *Men without Women*" by Dorothy Parker. Reprint from *New Yorker* (1927). Thought Hemingway's career peaked with *The Sun Also Rises* (critics prefer novels to short-story collections) and so she feared for his next book. Happily, *Men without Women* lives up to his earlier promise: it is "a truly magnificent work." She admires Hemingway's "unerring sense of selection."

Pp. 167-69: "On Hemingway" by Claude McKay. Reprint from *A Long Way from Home* (New York: Furman, 1937).

Pp. 171-85: "Catherine Barkley and Retrospective Narration in *A Farewell to Arms*" by James Nagel. (New Essay.) Another argument for the validity of Catherine's role in this controversial novel comes from Nagel's insistence that Hemingway's choice of retrospective narration changes the dynamics of Catherine and Frederic. Henry's retelling the story is to allow him to come to terms emotionally with the events. Nagel disagrees with Brenner's interpretation that Frederic plans suicide, concluding that "he is now prepared to resume living once again . . . and to end his fixation on loss and pain."

Pp. 187-93: "A Téssera for Frederic Henry: Imagery and Recurrence in *A Farewell to Arms*" by Gwen L. Nagel. (New Essay.) Focuses on manuscript changes that allow Hemingway to present a consistent Frederic Henry. She also assesses the imagery of clothing and Hemingway's use of pronouns.

Pp. 195-204: "Hemingway and the Ambulance Drivers in *A Farewell to Arms*" by Robert A. Martin. (New Essay.) Studies Hemingway's naming of the ambulance drivers for larger thematic import. Because Hemingway was careful and conscious of every detail in his writing, his attention to the root meanings of both sets of ambulance drivers' names – which differ radically from each other – is plausible.

Pp. 205-7: "Hemingway: Work in Progress" by Malcolm Cowley. Reprint from *New Republic* 92 (20 October, 1937).

Pp. 209-219: "Hemingway's Women's Movement" by Charles J. Nolan, Jr. Reprint of 1984.88.

Pp. 221-37: "*For Whom the Bell Tolls* as Mythic Narrative" by John J. Teunissen. Reprint of 1976.88.

Pp. 239-55: "The Mask of Death, the Face of Life: Hemingway's Feminique" by Robert D. Crozier, S.J. Reprint of 1984.14.

Pp. 257-72: "Hemingway's Poetry: Angry Notes of an Ambivalent Overman" by Nicholas Gerogiannis. Reprint of 1980.30 and 1981.86.

P. 273: "Review of *The Old Man and the Sea*" by William Faulkner. Reprint from *Shenandoah* (Autumn 1952).

Pp. 275-87: "The Poem of Santiago and Manolin" by Linda W. Wagner. Reprint from *Modern Fiction Studies* 19 (Winter 1973).

Pp. 289-92: "The Hemingway Obituary" by John Wain. Reprint from *Observer* (9 July 1961). Admires Hemingway for his proficiency in writing the classic fable. No matter how simple his work seems, its meaning is profound. A very physical writer, he is a poet, deeply compassionate, caring about humanity and its fate.

Pp. 293-95: "Hemingway: The Dye That Did Not Run" by Nelson Algren. Reprint from *Nation* (1 June 1964). *A Moveable Feast* shows that Hemingway was "a tolerant opponent and a mean competitor." Above all, he was a great writer.

Pp. 297-311: "Are We Going to Hemingway's *Feast*?" by Gerry Brenner. Reprint of 1982.9.

Pp. 313-24: "'Bimini' and the Subject of Hemingway's *Islands in the Stream*" by Joseph M. DeFalco. Reprint of 1977.27.

Pp. 325-31: "Braver Than We Thought" by E.L. Doctorow. Reprint of 1986.29.

96 WAGNER-MARTIN, LINDA, ed. *New Essays on "The Sun Also Rises."* Cambridge: Cambridge University Press, 134 pp.

A collection of five previously unpublished essays and an introduction, which bring Hemingway's 1926 novel, *The Sun Also Rises*, into a 1980 critical paradigm. Contents:

Pp. 1-18: Introduction by Linda Wagner-Martin. Provides cultural context and aesthetic ideas for the novel; surveys critical reception of the book as well.

Pp. 19-41: "Humor in *The Sun Also Rises*" by Scott Donaldson. Provides a different reading for a novel usually considered highly serious. Donaldson shows the various kinds of humor – irreverence, ethnic humor, inside jokes, witty dialogue, humorous self-disparagement, and the clear humor of Bill Gorton, modeled on humorist Donald Ogden Stewart.

Pp. 43-64: "The *Sun* in Its Time: Recovering the Historical Context" by Michael S. Reynolds. Places Hemingway's novel in the mid-1920s, culturally, economically, politically, and socially. Reynolds provides new insights about the author's sense of aggrieved morality, as well as the times.

Pp. 65-82: "Brett Ashley as New Woman in *The Sun Also Rises*" by Wendy Martin. Reads this protagonist in light of social and economic reform of the early twentieth century. Reynolds said that Brett was not a new woman, so Martin's essay works both against the previous essay and toward the following one.

Pp. 83-107: "Decoding the Hemingway Hero in *The Sun Also Rises*" by Arnold E. Davidson and Cathy N. Davidson. Using forms of deconstruction, the Davidsons read the novel as a conundrum of sexual and emotional allegiances. They point to various signs that provide alternate codes for Hemingway's characters and make the novel remain interesting because of its self-contradictions.

Pp. 109-29: "Afterthoughts on the Twenties and *The Sun Also Rises*" by John W. Aldridge. Provides retrospective views of both.

97 WALDHORN, ARTHUR. Review of *The Complete Short Stories of Ernest Hemingway: The Finca Vigía Edition*. *Library Journal* 112, no. 19 (15 November): 90.

Chides the editors for failing to publish the *complete* short stories and for failing to come up with a fresh approach to reordering them – either thematically, chronologically, or stylistically.

98 WALDMEIR, JOSEPH J. "And the Wench Is Faith and Value." *Studies in Short Fiction* 24, no. 4 (Fall): 393-98.

Demonstrates the ways in which the religious symbolism of "In Another Country" foreshadows that of *The Old Man and the Sea*. Taking examples from Hemingway's early war stories (including "Soldier's Home" and "Now I Lay Me") of abortive attempts to hang on to outworn values in times of chaos, Waldmeir contends that "Hemingway was no less concerned with religion in his very early work than he was in his late work, though the concern shifts from negation toward the affirmation of secular religion by the time we reach *The Old Man and the Sea*."

99 WALKER, WARREN S. "Annual Bibliography of Short Fiction Interpretation." *Studies in Short Fiction* 24:329-74.

Lengthy bibliography that includes some critical items on Hemingway (p. 348).

100 WANG, SHOUYI. "Hemingway's Linguistic Style and Art." *Waiguoyu* 2, no. 48 (April): 41-45.
   *Hemingway Review 9, no. 1 (Fall): 111.

101 WELLAND, DENNIS. "The Language of American Fiction between the Wars." In *American Literature Since 1900*. Edited by Marcus Cunliffe. New York: Peter Bedrick Books, pp. 29-51.
   Numerous references to Hemingway and his contribution to American literature. Comments on the author's language, style, and celebrity image along with a brief overview of his fiction.

102 WESCOTT, GLENWAY. Foreword to *Four Lives in Paris*, by Hugh Ford. San Francisco: North Point Press, xv-xviii.
   Section on Hemingway as a young writer ("immensely good-looking, animated, and hardworking. The French used to say he had *esprit* – a rather light, pointed, and quotable way of talking"). Hemingway had little understanding of character, especially the character of women, thus making his short stories better than his novels.

103 WHITE, WILLIAM. "For the Collector." *Hemingway Review* 6, no. 2 (Spring): 56-57.
   Looks at the effect of "simplified spelling" on the opening paragraph of "A Clean, Well-Lighted Place" and briefly discusses a new find, a 1949 edition of *Game Fishing of the World* in which Hemingway's brief "Cuban Fishing" appears.

104 ____. "Hemingway: A Current Bibliography." *Hemingway Review* 6, no. 2 (Spring): 58-60.
   Lists articles, reviews, books, and new editions.

105 YIDONG, ZHANG. "Hemingway's and Sholokhov's Viewpoints on War." *International Fiction Review* 14, no. 2 (Summer): 75-78.
   Compares *A Farewell to Arms* and *For Whom the Bell Tolls* with *The Quiet Don* and *The Destiny of Man*, pointing out similarities in setting, theme, and plot. "In all of the four works, a similar pathetic sentiment appears, as well as the idea of fatalism."

106 ZAPF, HUBERT. "Reflection vs. Daydream: Two Types of the Implied Reader in Hemingway's Fiction." *College Literature* 14, no. 2 (Spring): 101-119.
   Demonstrates the shifting role of the implied reader depending on appellative structure in Hemingway's fiction. Shows how the daydream pattern of response in "The Short Happy Life of Francis Macomber," *The Old Man and the Sea*, and *A Farewell to Arms* draws the reader into the imaginative world of the text. "He is not primarily led to question the premises of this world but to follow the immanent logic of the

developing narrative." Nevertheless, texts such as *The Sun Also Rises* and "Big Two-Hearted River" require the reader to reflect upon, detect, and interpret ambiguous or incomplete textual information. Reprinted: 1988.103.

1988

1 ABBOTT, H. PORTER. "Autobiography, Autography, Fiction: Groundwork for a Taxonomy of Textual Categories." *New Literary History* 19, no. 3 (Spring): 597-615.

Looks at the problems associated with defining autobiography in relation to other categories of literature. Comments briefly on *A Moveable Feast*, a kind of autobiography broken into a collection of distinct units with little "desire for sincere, or even authentic, textual self-recovery."

2 BARBOUR, JAMES. "Fugue State as a Literary Device in 'Cat in the Rain' and 'Hills Like White Elephants.'" *Arizona Quarterly* 44, no. 2 (Summer): 98-106.

Deciphers Hemingway's sympathetic portrayal of the female characters in the two short stories through the author's use of the fugue technique, a barrage of seemingly confusing, conflicting, and disparate imagery and symbolism designed to convey the jumbled inner state of the protagonist and also link characters to parallel systems of meaning within the story.

3 BÉCEL, PASCALE. "Hemingway and Brancusi: A Relationship between Writer and Sculptor?" *West Virginia University Philological Papers* 34:83-94.

MLA Bibliography 1988, p. 250.

4 BEEGEL, SUSAN F. *Hemingway's Craft of Omission, Four Manuscript Examples*. UMI Research Press, 124 pp.

Focusing on three of Hemingway's short stories – "Fifty Grand," "A Natural History of the Dead," "After the Storm" – and a fourth selection, a disordered passage from *Death in the Afternoon*, Beegel contends that the changes Hemingway made as he revised and polished his fiction were judicious, insightful, and often accomplished through omission. "Fifty Grand" begins with a personal anecdote that is later deleted; "A Natural History of the Dead" retains the initial memory of corpses during World War I but changes reminiscence into fiction; the early autobiographical context of "After the Storm" is omitted entirely; and the *Death in the Afternoon* passage also follows the same procedures.

Beegel's point is that Hemingway's revision becomes a true "re-vision," and that omission is his usual route to the change.

5 BENDER, BERT. "Hemingway: Coming to the Stream." In *Sea-Brothers: The Tradition of American Sea Fiction from Moby-Dick to the Present*. Philadelphia: University of Pennsylvania Press, pp. 167-75.

Compares Hemingway's vision of life with Thoreau's, finding that although both saw at the center a certain savagery, Hemingway rejected Thoreau's naturalistic view shaped by religion. Hemingway's simplistic style and fascination with violence and pain "derived from his seemingly innate grasp of the basic, violent biological realities."

Pp. 175-98: "Hemingway's Sea Men." Discusses the progressive struggles of Hemingway's three sea protagonists (Thomas Hudson of *Islands in the Stream*, Harry Morgan of *To Have and Have Not*, and Santiago of *The Old Man and the Sea*) to meet and overcome the central meanness of life and complications of modern time.

6 BENNETT, WARREN. "The Poor Kitty and the Padrone and the Tortoise-Shell Cat in 'Cat in the Rain.'" *Hemingway Review* 8, no. 1:26-36.

Maintains that the wife's situation is like that of the poor kitty; she is a homeless figure in search of a loving place to share with a sensitive and kindly padrone of her own generation.

7 BIER, JESSE. "Tornado in a Thimble." *Analytical & Enumerative Bibliography*, n.s. 2, no. 2:58-60.

Reasons that controversy over the mislineation of the waiters' speeches in "A Clean, Well-Lighted Place" really reflects the deeper issue of the author's "infallibility."

8 BIGSBY, CHRISTOPHER. "E Pluribus Unisex? Gender and Identity in the U.S. Novel." *Encounter* 80, no. 3 (March): 54-57.

Comments briefly on Lynn's biography (see 1987.51), which connects Hemingway's sexual ambivalence in his works to his life. Points out, however, that Hemingway is simply following an American tradition "in his tendency to seek a sexual correlative for his social, moral, and even political convictions."

9 BRENNER, GERRY. "Fitzgerald and Hemingway." In *American Literary Scholarship: An Annual, 1986*. Edited by David J. Nordloh. Durham, N.C.: Duke University Press, pp. 156-79.

Survey of criticism on both authors published during 1986. Brenner comments on Hemingway's steadily increasing popularity among critics and scholars.

10 BRIAN, DENIS. *The True Gen*. New York: Grove Press, 356 pp.

Popularized account of the writer, presented in Brian's own usually highly colored prose or in the words of interviewees or writers. Brian's juxtaposition of random comments, grouped under general headings, creates an effect that is almost incoherent at times. Not all of the interviewees are as credible as one might hope.

11 "Brief Mention." *American Literature* 60:323.

Mentions the publication of *The Complete Short Stories of Ernest Hemingway: The Finca Vigía Edition*, which contains *The First Forty-Nine* (1938), fourteen later published stories, four unpublished stories, three unpublished scenes from uncompleted works, a foreword by Hemingway's sons, and a preface by Charles Scribner, Jr.

12 BROMWICH, DAVID. "Hemingway's Valor." *Grand Street* 7, no. 2 (Winter): 185-217.

Broad overview of Hemingway's contribution to American literature as well as commentary on the author's current critical and popular reputation.

13 CHAFE, WALLACE. "Punctuation and the Prosody of Written Language." *Written Communication* 5, no. 4 (October): 395-426.

Looks at the way writers use punctuation to make overt the "covert prosody" of written language. Comments on the difficulties associated with relating punctuation units to intonation units in Hemingway's writing because of the author's reliance on open punctuation.

14 CHAPPLE, RICHARD. "Ivan Turgenev, Sherwood Anderson, and Ernest Hemingway: *The Torrents of Spring* All." *New Comparison* 5 (Summer): 136-49.

*MLA Bibliography 1988, p. 251.

15 COOPER, STEPHEN. "Politics over Art: Hemingway's 'Nobody Ever Dies.'" *Studies in Short Fiction* 25, no. 2 (Spring): 117-20.

Compares "Nobody Ever Dies" with the earlier "The Revolutionist" in order to show the effect of the Spanish civil war on Hemingway's writing. Finds the irony in the earlier story replaced with a serious devotion to a cause. Contends that although propagandistic, "Nobody Ever Dies" also reflects Hemingway's "old skepticism toward ideologues" and "bitterness about the military inefficiency that contributed to the loyalist defeat."

16 COX, JAMES M. "*In Our Time*: The Essential Hemingway." *Southern Humanities Review* 22, no. 4 (Fall): 305-20.

Laments the overemphasis on biographical interpretation of Hemingway's works. Looks at the way the discontinuous form of *In Our Time* contributes to the collection's overall impact and theme centered on the trap of life.

17 CURTIS, MARY ANN C. "*The Sun Also Rises*: Its Relation to *The Song of Roland*." *American Literature* 60, no. 2 (May): 274-80.

After establishing Hemingway's familiarity with the French epic, Curtis compares the Spanish section of the novel with the poem, finding numerous similarities in character, structure, and plot.

18 DAVIS, ROBERT MURRAY. Review of *The Complete Short Stories of Ernest Hemingway: The Finca Vigía Edition*. *World Literature Today* 62, no. 2 (Spring): 281-82.

Feels that "even the worst of the stories in the latest collection deserves more honorable treatment than Scribner and the estate have given them in this deplorably shoddy piece of work."

19 DAVISON, RICHARD ALLAN. "Hemingway, Steinbeck, and the Art of the Short Story." *Steinbeck Quarterly* 21, no. 3-4 (Summer-Fall): 73-84.

In a comparative study of the two authors, Davison shows how both, despite their distinct styles, shared similar views on the craft and artistic goals of short-story writing. Points out their similarities in economic style, objective point of view, and attention to sensuous detail.

20 _____. "The Publication of Hemingway's *The Spanish Earth*: An Untold Story." *Hemingway Review* 7 (Spring): 122-30.

Focuses on the unusual circumstances surrounding the publication of the script of Hemingway's documentary film *The Spanish Earth* by an unknown high-school student. Quotes liberally from telegrams, letters, and other materials related to the publication.

21 DeFAZIO, ALBERT J., III. "Hemingway Bibliography." *Hemingway Review* 8, no. 1:68-77.

List of current items, including articles, books, reviews, and new editions.

22 DESNOYERS, MEGAN FLOYD. "News from the Hemingway Collection." *Hemingway Review* 7, no. 2:166-68.

Outlines photocopying policies for the Hemingway collection at the Kennedy Library in Boston, in addition to giving an itemized list of Hadley Richardson's correspondence now available for research and announcing the future availability of the manuscript of *African Journal*.

23 DONALDSON, SCOTT. *John Cheever, A Biography*. New York: Random House, pp. 37, 61, 351, etc.

Scattered and comparatively frequent references to Hemingway, whom Cheever admired and considered an influence on his writing.

24 DOYLE, N. ANN, and HOUSTON, NEAL B. "Hemingway: A Final Meeting with Adriana Ivancich at Nervi." *Hemingway Review* 8, no. 1 (Fall): 58-61.

Verifies that Hemingway and Ivancich continued to correspond even during the "scandal" of *Across the River and into the Trees* and that Mary Hemingway was present during their last meeting at Nervi in 1954, attesting to a rather more mundane relationship than previously thought.

25 DUNN, DOUGLAS. "Thinking about Women." *Times Literary Supplement*, 3-9 June, p. 612.

In his brief assessment of feminism's impact on male writers, Dunn says of *The Garden of Eden*, "Of all Hemingway's novels, it is the least tainted by male-centred sensationalism, even if its erotic occasions are guided by fiction and obsession into the overstatement of human truth."

26 FLEMING, ROBERT E. "The Importance of Count Mippipopolous: Creating the Code Hero." *Arizona Quarterly* 44, no. 2 (Summer): 69-75.

Suggests that Count Mippipopolous of *The Sun Also Rises* is an early code hero despite his wavering in character between a brash American gangster and a soft-spoken man of the world. Mippipopolous's scars are his stigmata, proving that he is a wise man whose philosophy of life (i.e., to be satisfied with the limited pleasures of life) is to be heeded.

27 FLORA, JOSEPH M. "Hemingway's 'The Strange Country' in the Context of *The Complete Short Stories*." *Studies in Short Fiction* 25, no. 4 (Fall): 409-20.

In his examination of "The Strange Country," Flora finds the fragment to be a particularly satisfying conclusion for the latest collection because it makes use of many familiar Hemingway themes, motifs, and characters.

28 GAGGIN, JOHN. *Hemingway and Nineteenth Century Aestheticism*. Ann Arbor, Mich.: UMI Research Press, 132 pp.

Examines nineteenth-century aestheticism's literary impact on Hemingway and includes much of the author's canon in the analysis. Gaggin finds the aesthetic tradition's focus on the primacy of art and its advocacy of detached observation, devotion to craft and style, and "art

for art's sake" philosophy clearly influential to both the modern period
and Hemingway's own development as an author. Provides an overview
of the movement along with Hemingway's acquaintance with it.

29 GAJDUSEK, LINDA. "Toward Wider Use of Literature in ESL: Why
and How." *TESOL Quarterly* 22, no. 2 (June): 227-57.
    Combines current ESL (English as a Second Language) theory
with practical classroom techniques in order to encourage mature ESL
students to arrive at increasingly complex understandings of literary
texts. Uses "Soldier's Home" to illustrate both the theoretical approach
and classroom activities.

30 GANZEL, DEWEY. "A Geometry of His Own: Hemingway's 'Out of
Season.'" *Modern Fiction Studies* 34, no. 2 (Summer): 171-83.
    Considers "Out of Season" significant for its initial treatment of
the "theme of anomie" (loss of self) and its use of the disjunctive point
of view. Compares the first version of the story appearing in the 1923
Three Stories & Ten Poems with the version in the 1925 *In Our Time*,
discussing in detail significant changes made by Boni and Liveright in
their later edition.

31 GIRGUS, SAM B. "Portnoy's Prayer: Philip Roth and the American
Unconscious." In *Reading Philip Roth*. Edited by Asher Z. Milbauer and
Donald G. Watson. London: Macmillan Press, pp. 126-43.
    Comments briefly on the "hard-boiled-dom" found in *A Farewell to
Arms* and *The Sun Also Rises*, contrasting the Hemingway code hero
with Roth's Portnoy in light of Freudian psychology. "In spite of his
neurosis and weakness, Portnoy works toward an ideology of love and
growth as opposed to mere resistance and distance."

32 GOODWIN, DONALD W. "Hemingway: Scenes from New York and
Havana." In *Alcohol and the Writer*. Kansas City, Mo.: Andrews &
McMeel, pp. 50-72.
    Discusses Hemingway's drinking habits. Believes that although he
had a certain amount of control over his drinking, Hemingway was still
an alcoholic.

33 HAMALIAN, LEO, and BALIOZIAN, ARA. "Hemingway in Istanbul."
Ararat 29, no. 2 (Spring): 40-45.
    Prints extracts from *Dateline: Toronto* – Hemingway's dispatches
written from Constantinople at the time of the Greco-Turkish conflict.

34 HAMID, SYED ALI. "A Separate Peace: Nature of Alienation in
Hemingway's Short Fiction." *Panjab University Research Bulletin* 19, no.
1 (April): 51-57.

MLA Bibliography 1988, p. 251.

35 HANNUM, HOWARD L. "The Case of Doctor Henry Adams."
Arizona Quarterly 44, no. 2 (Summer): 39-57.
Takes issue with the overwhelming negative criticism leveled at
Dr. Adams (Nick's father) in stories such as "Indian Camp," "The
Doctor and the Doctor's Wife," and "Ten Indians," maintaining that
many of his actions can be explained away. Contends that for Nick and
readers alike, Dr. Adams remains an unsympathetic character that we
all turn away from.

36 ____. "Hemingway's Revenge and the Vulcan Myth." *Studies in Short
Fiction* 25, no. 1 (Winter): 73-76.
Sees "Up in Michigan" in relation to the feud Hemingway had with
his mother, which resulted in his banishment from Windemere Cottage
in the summer of 1920. Argues that Hemingway restructures the Vulcan
myth in his story in order to punish his mother for her unjust
accusations.

37 HANSEN, ERIK ARNE. "Ernest Hemingway's 'The Fall of Troy in
Spain.'" *Dolphin* 16:54-87.
MLA Bibliography 1988, p. 250.

38 HARDY, RICHARD E., and CULL, JOHN G. *Hemingway: A
Psychological Portrait*. New York: Irvington, 92 pp.
Reprint with only minor revision of 1977.45. Still contains
biographical inaccuracies and little documentation.

39 HAYS, PETER L. "Hemingway, Nick Adams, and David Bourne: Sons
and Writers." *Arizona Quarterly* 44, no. 2 (Summer): 28-38.
Looks at the ambivalent father/son relationships found in the
Nick Adams stories and *The Garden of Eden* in which love is present
but respect is not, comparing them with Hemingway's relationship with
his own father.

40 ____. "Robert Frost 'Happiness' Line is *FWBT*?" *Hemingway
Newsletter*, no. 16 (June), p. 2.
Notes "a striking coincidence between a line in Hemingway's *For
Whom the Bell Tolls*, published in 1940, and a poem of Frost's published
in the *Atlantic* in September, 1938: 'Happiness Makes Up in Height for
What It Lacks in Length.' As Jordan muses about his relationship with
Maria, he concludes, 'Love her very hard and make up in intensity what
the relation will lack in duration and continuity.'"

41 HEMINGWAY, JACK. "Historic Houses: Hemingway in Idaho."
    Architectural Digest 45, no. 4 (April): 142-47.
        Tour of the Hemingway house in Ketchum, Idaho. Includes
    interior and exterior photographs.

42 HEMINGWAY, PATRICIA SHEDD. *The Hemingways Past and
    Present and Allied Families*. Baltimore: Gateway Press, 858 pp.
        *Hemingway Review 9, no. 1 (Fall): 103.

43 "Hemingway's House on Whitehead." *Southern Living* 23, no. 6:24.
        Brief description of Hemingway's Key West home on Whitehead
    Street. Includes photos.

44 HINZ, EVELYN J., and TEUNISSEN, JOHN J. "*Islands in the Stream*
    as Hemingway's *Laocoön*." *Contemporary Literature* 29, no. 1 (Spring):
    26-48.
        Sees the novel as Hemingway's exploration of the limitations of
    narrative and pictorial art forms. Contends that the author is evaluating
    his own literary contribution through the use of pictorial analogues.

45 JAY, PAUL, ed. *The Selected Correspondence of Kenneth Burke and
    Malcolm Cowley, 1915-1981*. New York: Viking, pp. 185, 188, 189, 190,
    223, 240, 246, 280-83, 297, 346-47.
        Scattered references to Hemingway, his works, and Cowley's *Life*
    article on him.

46 JOHNSTON, KENNETH G. "The Silly Wasters: Tzara and the Poet in
    'The Snows of Kilimanjaro.'" *Hemingway Review* 8, no. 1:50-57.
        Manuscript study identifying Malcolm Cowley as the American
    poet conversing with dadaist writer Tristan Tzara in the satiric flashback
    section of the short story.

47 KASTELY, JAMES L. "Toward a Politically Responsible Ethical
    Criticism: Narrative in *The Political Unconscious* and *For Whom the
    Bell Tolls*." *Style* 22, no. 4 (Winter): 535-58.
        Examines the contradictory ethical-political situation presented in
    Hemingway's novel. Although Jordan is clearly antifascist, Hemingway
    provides an unbalanced view of the atrocities in the war, focusing on
    those mainly committed by the republican side. Feels the central
    concern of the novel is not Jordan's blowing of the bridge but his
    "education as a potential writer. And Pilar's narrative of the republican
    atrocities is essential to that education"—to complete his understanding
    of the war.

48 KENNEDY, J. GERALD. "Life as Fiction: The Lure of Hemingway's Garden." *Southern Review* 24, no. 2 (Spring): 451-61.

Comments on the autobiographical dimensions of Hemingway's fictionalized account of his professional and private life in *The Garden of Eden*. Relies extensively on unpublished manuscripts of the posthumously published novel.

49 KERNER, DAVID. "The Origins of Hemingway's Anti-Metronomic Dialogue." *Analytical & Enumerative Bibliography*, n.s. 2, no. 1:12-28.

Locates numerous examples of the practice in O'Henry, London, and others to show that it was both common and intentional and should never have been "corrected" by Scribner's in Hemingway's "A Clean, Well-Lighted Place."

50 LARSEN, KEVIN S. "Rounds with Mr. Cervantes: *Don Quijote* and *For Whom the Bell Tolls*." *Orbis Litterarum* 43:108-128.

Notes a number of parallels, including motif (arms vs. letters), conflict (chivalric ideals vs. "modern" reason, traditional combat vs. technologically updated warfare), and character (Jordan and Quixote, Pablo and Sancho Panza, Maria and Dulcinea) in the two novels in order to illustrate "not only how closely he [Hemingway] had read *Don Quixote*, but also his attempt at systematic oneupmanship, his almost consuming desire in his 'novel of Spain' to out-Cervantes Mr. C. and beat him at his own game."

51 LIGGERA, JOSEPH J. "Rereading *Across the River and into the Trees*." *West Virginia University Philological Papers* 34:94-101.

MLA Bibliography 1988, p. 250.

52 LOCKRIDGE, ERNEST. "Faithful in Her Fashion: Catherine Barkley, the Invisible Hemingway Heroine." *Journal of Narrative Technique* 18, no. 2 (Spring): 170-78.

Argues against the traditional interpretation of Catherine Barkley as the self-effacing dream girl. Lockridge points to her ability to see through Henry's posturing and put him in his place as evidence to the contrary. Concludes that Catherine's vision, rather than Frederic's, motivates their relationship. "It is Catherine's effort to resurrect her lost love, not the narrator's pursuit of a sexual liaison which grows into love, that is the whole novel's primary mover."

53 LUDINGTON, TOWNSEND. "Spain and the Hemingway–Dos Passos Relationship." *American Literature* 60, no. 2 (May): 270-73.

Attributes one cause of their collapsed friendship to an initial friction over differing visions of Spain and its rituals (bullfighting).

54 LYNN, KENNETH S. "Adulthood in American Literature." *Daedalus* 117, no. 3 (Summer): 283-98.

Concludes his essay with a brief assessment of the emphasis on youth and the level of immaturity found in modern American literature. "Dreiser, on the one hand, versus Hemingway and Fitzgerald, on the other: American literature in the early twentieth century was torn between a willingness to confront 'what it means to be a man' and a desire to postpone that confrontation as long as possible."

55 McIVER, BRUCE. "Hemingway in Soca Valley." *Acta Neophilogica* 21:17-18.

MLA Bibliography 1988, p. 250.

56 MADISON, ROBERT D. "Hemingway and Selous: A Source for 'Snows'?" *Hemingway Review* 8, no. 1:62-63.

Points to a possible source for the plot, setting, and title of "The Snows of Kilimanjaro" in J.G. Millais's 1919 biography *Life of Frederick Courtenay Selous, D.S.O.*

57 MARTIN, LAWRENCE H., Jr. "Crazy in Sheridan: Hemingway's 'Wine of Wyoming' Reconsidered." *Hemingway Review* 8, no. 1:13-25.

Chronicles the story's critical reception and virtual eclipse as well as discussing biographical implications and Hemingway's aesthetic principle of truthfulness. Concludes that "even in the trivialities of life in Sheridan, Wyoming, the story reiterates the inevitability of suffering and destruction."

58 MARTIN, ROBERT A. "The Way It Wasn't: Hemingway and Gellhorn in Burma." *Hemingway Review* 8, no. 1:40-41.

Prints Gellhorn's response to H.L. Wood's account of her alleged disrespectful treatment of Hemingway at the C.N.A.C. hotel at Lashio, Burma, in his 1987 memoir, *Wings over Asia*. "I was never disrespectful to E.H. . . . No doubt my silence (contemptuous) infuriated him even more but during the China period, our honeymoon comically, there was as peaceful a relation as at any time."

59 MERRILL, ROBERT. "EXTRA, Demoting Hemingway: Feminist Criticism and the Canon." *American Literature* 60, no. 2:255-68.

Argues against Lawrence Buell's March 1987 essay (see *American Literature* 59) supporting feminist revisionism and the demotion of Hemingway. Merrill warns of the dangers of questioning the criteria of aesthetic value that determine the canon.

60 MEYERS, JEFFREY. "Hemingway's Primitivism and 'Indian Camp.'" *Twentieth Century Literature* 34, no. 2 (Summer): 211-22.

After summing up previous critical readings of why the Indian husband kills himself, Meyers offers his own interpretation based on Hemingway's attitude toward primitivism and knowledge of anthropology. The husband cannot stand the defilement of his wife's purity by the white men, "which is far worse than her screams. In an act of elemental nobility, he focuses the evil spirits on himself, associates his wife's blood with his own death-wound, and punishes himself for the violation of taboo."

61 MIALL, DAVID S. "Affect and Narrative: A Model of Response to Stories." *Poetics* 17, no. 3 (June): 259-72.

Uses Virginia Woolf's "A Summing Up" and Hemingway's "Cat in the Rain" in an experimental study of how the affective modes (self-reference, anticipation, and domain crossing) help in shaping our response to ambiguities and conflicts in literature.

62 MILLER, LINDA PATTERSON. "'Nourished at the Same Source': Ernest Hemingway and Gerald Murphy." *Mosaic* 21, no. 1 (Winter): 79-91.

Discusses in what ways both were influenced by the artistic movements of Paris during the early 1920s. Compares "Hills Like White Elephants" with Murphy's precisionist-cubist painting *Watch*. Although Hemingway did not subscribe to the precisionist painters' portrayal of machinery as an ordering principle in one's personal life, he was preoccupied with the notion of learning to live rightly or orderly in a chaotic world. Goes over briefly the reasons for their breakup, including Hemingway's resentment toward Murphy for the role he played in the author's break with first wife Hadley Richardson.

63 MITGANG, HERBERT. "Ernest Hemingway." In *Dangerous Dossiers: Exposing the Secret War against America's Greatest Writers*. New York: Donald I. Fine, pp. 61-71.

Reprint with minor revision from 1987.61.

64 MODDELMOG, DEBRA A. "The Unifying Consciousness of a Divided Conscience: Nick Adams as Author of *In Our Time*." *American Literature* 60, no. 4 (December): 591-610.

Shows that despite Hemingway's facade of being a brave man, his most constant enemy was himself and his own fear – at least as he represents the self in the character of Nick Adams. A good summary of attitudes and critical responses through the last half-century, without much new information or insight.

65 NAGEL, JAMES. "Kitten to Waxin: Hadley's Letters to Ernest Hemingway, May 1926." *Journal of Modern Literature* 15, no. 1 (Summer): 146-58.
   *Hemingway Review 9, no. 2 (Spring): 195.

66 NAKAJIMA, KENJI. "The Role of the Bullfight Spectators in 'Chapter XI' of Hemingway's *In Our Time.*" *Kyushu American Literature* 29:13-22.
   *Hemingway Review 9, no. 2 (Spring): 195.

67 NAKJAVANI, ERIK. "Ernest Hemingway's Robert Jordan and Carlos Fuentes' Lorenzo Cruz: A Comparative Study." *Selected Proceedings of the Pennsylvania Foreign Language Conference.* Edited by Gregorio C. Martin. Pittsburgh: Duquesne University, Department of Foreign Languages.
   *Hemingway Review 9, no. 2 (Spring): 196.

68 ———. "Knowledge as Power: Robert Jordan as an Intellectual Hero." *Hemingway Review* 7, no. 2 (Spring): 131-46.
   In looking at the origin and nature of power and its relationship to knowledge and application to Robert Jordan in *For Whom the Bell Tolls*, Nakjavani draws on the theories of Marx and Foucault. Examines Jordan's power as a militant intellectual, his knowledge of Spain and the Spanish language, and the nature of his political beliefs.

69 OATES, JOYCE CAROL. "The Hemingway Mystique." In *(Woman) Writers: Occasions and Opportunities.* New York: E.P. Dutton, pp. 301-9.
   Oates assesses Hemingway's impact on both American literature and culture, with much attention paid to the "exaggerated sense of maleness" found in *The Sun Also Rises*.

70 OLIVER, CHARLES M., and WATSON, WILLIAM BRAASCH. "Introduction to the Spanish Civil War Issue." *Hemingway Review* 7, no. 2:2-3.
   Provides a brief overview of Hemingway's involvement in the Spanish civil war.

71 OPPENHEIM, ROSA. "The Mathematical Analysis of Style: A Correlation-Based Approach." *Computers and the Humanities* 22:241-52.
   *Hemingway Review 9, no. 2 (Spring): 196.

72 O'SULLIVAN, SIBBIE. "Love and Friendship/Man and Woman in *The Sun Also Rises.*" *Arizona Quarterly* 44, no. 2 (Summer): 76-97.
   Examines the changing gender-role patterns, seeing Brett as an example of the New Woman who breaks from nineteenth-century traditional sex roles by uniting love with friendship.

73 PARRISH, ROBERT. "Hemingway and How to Write for the Movies [Parts I and II]." In *Hollywood Doesn't Live Here Anymore*. Boston: Little, Brown, pp. 83-102, 109-118.
    Hemingway Review 9, no. 2 (Spring): 196.

74 PASSEY, LAURIE. "Hemingway's 'Hills Like White Elephants.'" *Explicator* 46, no. 4 (Summer): 32-33.
    Briefly discusses the way the various denotative and connotative definitions of the anise image magnify the couple's conflict and lack of communication.

75 PEROSA, SERGIO, ed. *Hemingway E Venezia*. Florence: Leo S. Olschki.
    MLA Bibliography 1988, p. 249. English Contents:
    Pp. 31-56: "'Ernie, Dear Boy': The End of the Affair" by Scott Donaldson.
    Pp. 73-78: "Hemingway's Discoveries in Rapallo and Cortina" by Paul Smith.
    Pp. 79-100: "'See You Around': Hemingway's Cartographic Modernism" by William Boelhower.
    Pp. 111-18: "Hemingway's Modernism: Troping and Narrating" by Sonja Bašić.
    Pp. 173-90: "An Interim Report on Hemingway's Posthumous Fiction" by Roger Asselineau.

76 RAEITHEL, GERT. "Aggressive and Evasive Humor in Hemingway's Letters." *Humor* 1-2:127-34.
    MLA Bibliography 1988, p. 250.

77 REYNOLDS, MICHAEL. *"The Sun Also Rises": A Novel of the Twenties*. Boston: Twayne, 106 pp.
    Extended monograph on this important novel, locating it historically and thematically. Reynolds's discussions of structure, character, and narrative method are excellent.

78 ROBINSON, FORREST. "Hemingway's Invisible Hero of 'In Another Country.'" *Essays in Literature* 15, no. 2 (Fall): 237-44.
    Considers the narrator to be heroic for his active approach to healing–transcendent healing through the creative act of writing.

79 ROESSEL, DAVID. "The 'Repeat in History': Canto XXVI and Greece's Asia Minor Disaster." *Twentieth Century Literature* 34, no. 2 (Summer): 180-90.

Summarizes briefly Hemingway's views of the Greco-Turkish War as evidenced in his *Toronto Star* dispatches, in "On the Quai at Smyrna," and in Pound's incorporation of those views in *The Cantos*.

80 ROHRKEMPER, JOHN. "The Great War, the Midwest, and Modernism: Cather, Dos Passos, and Hemingway." *Midwestern Miscellany* 16:19-29.

Examines the ways Cather's *One of Ours*, Dos Passos's *Three Soldiers*, and Hemingway's *In Our Time* "explored the striking contrast between the American Midwest and war-ravaged Europe while at the same time finding harmony in theme and style through experimentation with the modernist technique of juxtaposition."

81 RUDAT, WOLFGANG E.H. "He 'Just Lay There': Bill Gorton as Wounded Preacher in *The Sun Also Rises*." *Wascana Review* 23, no. 1 (Spring): 22-30.
    MLA Bibliography 1988, p. 250.

82 _____. "Hemingway's Jake and Milton's Adam: Sexual Envy and Vicariousness in *The Sun Also Rises*." *Journal of Evolutionary Psychology* 9, no. 1-2:109-119.

Discusses Brett's attempted psychological castration of Jake, finding allusions to *Paradise Lost* in Jake's tantrum directed at Brett earlier on. Contends that Jake eventually exorcises Brett and the need for vicarious sexual pleasure (successfully fending off her attempt to un-Adam him) and becomes his own man.

83 _____. "Mike Campbell and 'These Literary Chaps': Palimpsistic Narrative in *The Sun Also Rises*." *Studies in the Novel* 20, no. 3 (Fall): 302-315.

Argues that with Romero, Brett has finally found the sexual fulfillment she has been lacking with her other lovers. Rudat, detecting allusions to Shakespeare's Falstaff, interprets Mike Campbell as a parody of Falstaff who resents both himself and Brett for his sexual inadequacies.

84 SCHNITZER, DEBORAH. "Conceptual Realism." In *The Pictorial in Modernist Fiction from Stephen Crane to Ernest Hemingway*. Ann Arbor, Mich.: UMI Research Press, pp. 63-158.

Contrasts "conceptual realism" with "ocular realism" and "total representation." Bases her discussion of writers Crane, Woolf, Lawrence, Matthiessen, Joyce, Stein, and Hemingway on their relationship to the three major art movements of the nineteenth and twentieth centuries: impressionism, postimpressionism, and cubism. Comments on Hemingway's fiction, pp. 118-38.

85 SHULMAN, JEFFREY. "Hemingway's Observations on the Spanish Civil War: Unpublished State Department Reports." *Hemingway Review* 7, no. 2 (Spring): 147-51.

Summaries of two conversations Hemingway had with American Ambassador Claude G. Bowers regarding the evacuation of American medical personnel and American wounded and the status of the loyalist resistance.

86 SMILEY, PAMELA. "Gender-Linked Miscommunication in 'Hills Like White Elephants.'" *Hemingway Review* 8, no. 1:2-12.

Looks at the way gender-linked patterns of communication function in the story to produce two characterizations of Jig (nurturing/creative/affectionate or manipulative/shallow/hysterical) and the American (cold/hypocritical/oppressive or stoic/sensitive/intelligent).

87 SMITH, PAUL. "The Doctor and the Doctor's Friend: Logan Clendening and Ernest Hemingway." *Hemingway Review* 8, no. 1:37-39.

Locates a source for the *nada* ending, one of the discarded variant conclusions of *A Farewell to Arms*, in Clendening's 1928 *The Human Body*.

88 THORN, LEE. "*The Sun Also Rises*: Good Manners Make Good Art." *Hemingway Review* 8, no. 1:42-49.

Argues that Cohn and Romero represent opposite extremes of Hemingway's code/etiquette/aesthetic. Further argues that Hemingway's development of an aesthetic based on etiquette opposes the traditional ethic- or moral-based aesthetic.

89 TING, NAI-TUNG. "Hemingway in China." *Sino-American Relations: An International Quarterly* 14, no. 2:20-45.

MLA Bibliography 1988, p. 250.

90 URGO, JOSEPH R. "Hemingway's 'Hills Like White Elephants.'" *Explicator* 46, no. 3 (Spring): 35-37.

Looks at gender-linked resources in the story, contending that the man's cultural authority, as demonstrated through his reliance on language, money, science, and reason is undermined by Jig's natural sensibility and creativity.

91 V.W.M. Review of *The Garden of Eden*. *Kliatt: Young Adult Paperback Book Guide*, January, p. 10.

Despite Hemingway's simplistic style, V.W.M. feels that the posthumous novel, containing themes that deal with sexual ambivalence, will appeal to only the most sophisticated of adolescents.

92 WAGNER, LINDA W. "Ernest Hemingway, F. Scott Fitzgerald, and Gertrude Stein." In *Columbia Literary History of the United States*. Edited by Emory Elliot. New York: Columbia University Press, pp. 873-86.

Surveys the three important modernist writers in light of their 1980s reputations, and finds that the work of Stein is becoming more important than that of Fitzgerald and nearly equal to that of Hemingway. Describes careers and products of each writer, in the context of their times, and shows the surprising similarities among the three.

93 ____. "Hemingway's Search for Heroes, Once Again." *Arizona Quarterly* 44, no. 2 (Summer): 58-68.

Reveals Hemingway's rich literary heritage by tracing Jake Barnes's name and other elements of *The Sun Also Rises* to the Bible and the *Chanson de Roland*. Notes that although a definite resolution is reached by the end of the novel, nothing is answered and happiness and heroes are conspicuously absent.

94 WATSON, WILLIAM BRAASCH. "Hemingway's Spanish Civil War Dispatches." *Hemingway Review* 7 (Spring): 4-92.

Publishes thirty dispatches Hemingway wrote on the Spanish civil war between March 1937 and May 1938 for the North American Newspaper Alliance (NANA). Watson includes a detailed introduction on the subject, style, and editing of the collection along with maps and further notes for each individual dispatch.

95 ____. "'Humanity Will Not Forgive This!': The *Pravda* article." *Hemingway Review* 7, no. 2 (Spring): 114-18.

Reprints Hemingway's 1938 *Pravda* article condemning murderous fascists. Watson speculates on Hemingway's reasons for writing the propaganda piece, citing his admiration for the communist leadership and his desire to write openly.

96 ____. "In Defense of His Reporting from Spain: A Hemingway Letter to NANA." *Hemingway Review* 7, no. 2 (Spring): 119-21.

Reprints Hemingway's letter to John N. Wheeler, general manager of the North American Newspaper Alliance, summing up and defending his work as a correspondent in Spain.

97 ____. "'Old Man at the Bridge': The Making of a Short Story." *Hemingway Review* 7, no. 2 (Spring): 152-65.

Looks at the way Hemingway transformed the field notes (intended for a news dispatch) of a real-life encounter with an old refugee at the Amposta bridge into the short story.

98 _____. "A Variorum Edition of Dispatch 19." *Hemingway Review* 7 (Spring): 93-113.
Follows the transformation of "Flight of Refugees" (dispatch 19) from field notes to the final printed version in order to show the complex process of composing and communicating the dispatches.

99 WEIMANN, ROBERT. "Text, Author-Function, and Appropriation in Modern Narrative: Toward a Sociology of Representation." *Critical Inquiry* 14, no. 3 (Spring): 431-47.
Quotes Hemingway's well-known passage on the obscenity of abstractions such as "sacred, glorious, and sacrifice" from *A Farewell to Arms* in his discussion of the gaps and links in fictional discourse and the author's iceberg principle.

100 WICKES, GEORGE. "Where Did Cantwell Steal the Passage?" *Hemingway Newsletter*, no. 16 (June): 3.
Identifies the source of the line, "They were coming up on Mestre fast, and already it was like going to New York the first time you were ever there in the old days when it was shining, white and beautiful," from chapter 5 of *Across the River and into the Trees*, as probably Fitzgerald's description of New York in *The Great Gatsby*.

101 YANNELLA, PHILIP R. "Work and Character: American Literature and the Middle Class." In *Cross-Cultural Studies: American, Canadian, and European Literatures: 1945-1985*. Ljubljana, Yugoslavia: Filozofska Fakulteta, pp. 19-23.
Finds in Hemingway's writings a validation of the middle-class value system – supporting the work ethic (including the work of professional writers) and the importance of character.

102 YARDLEY, JONATHAN. "Dispatches of Rare Distinction." *Book World* (*Washington Post*), 6 November, p. 3.
Contains a single picture of Hemingway with Janet Flanner in Paris, 1945. Flanner contributed to *The New Yorker Book of War Pieces: London 1939-Hiroshima 1945*.

103 ZAPF, HUBERT. "Reflection vs. Daydream: Two Types of the Implied Reader in Hemingway's Fiction." *College Literature* 15:289-307.
Reprint of 1987.106.

1989

1 BEEGEL, SUSAN F., ed. *Hemingway's Neglected Short Fiction: New Perspectives*. Ann Arbor, Mich.: UMI Research Press, 373 pp.

A collection of previously unpublished essays on the less-often-studied stories by Hemingway. Prefaced by a chronology; followed by a list of contributors, a very complete bibliography, and a good index. Accurate headnotes for each essay.

Pp. 1-18: Introduction by Susan F. Beegel. Explains why these stories deserve attention. In Beegel's words, "unpublished, uncollected, unauthoritative," some of Hemingway's short stories have simply fallen between categories and reasons for study. This collection of essays tries to use these fictions as the avenue "for exploring the many complexities of Hemingway's art."

Pp. 19-30: "'The Mercenaries': A Harbinger of Vintage Hemingway" by Mimi Reisel Gladstein. Studies this very early story for its themes, style, and techniques that foreshadow his later, more polished work. A story of men without women, "The Mercenaries" are soldiers of fortune (one named Rinaldi), whose concepts of bravery are called into question. Gladstein criticizes the story for its "inconsistencies of characterization, problems with tone, and slippage in point of view."

Pp. 31-41: "Uncle Charles in Michigan" by Susan Swartzlander. Discusses Hemingway's use of James Joyce's "Uncle Charles principle," a way of using diction and syntax to reflect multiple characters in a single, third-person, omniscient voice. The story studied is "Up in Michigan."

Pp. 43-60: "Ethical Narration in 'My Old Man'" by Phillip Sipiora. Using theories of rhetoric from Aristotle and Quintilian, Sipiora creates a narrative understanding for this intricate story that previous readings have oversimplified.

Pp. 61-73: "'Out of Season' and Hemingway's Neglected Discovery: Ordinary Actuality" by James Steinke. Reads this often-discussed story as "a comedy of everyday errors," unrelated to the guide's eventual suicide or the couple's marital problems.

Pp. 75-98: "Hemingway's Italian *Waste Land*: The Complex Unity of 'Out of Season'" by Bickford Sylvestor. Discusses Hemingway's attempt to rewrite Eliot's *The Waste Land*, complete with a corrupted Fisher King whose encounter with the young knight leaves him confused.

Pp. 99-105: "'A Very Short Story' as Therapy" by Scott Donaldson. Treats the story in relation to Hemingway biography, and traces changes through three versions as the author distances himself from the failed relationship with Agnes von Kurowsky. *A Farewell to Arms* benefits from what Hemingway learned here.

Pp. 107-121: "The Bullfight Story and Critical Theory" by Bruce Henricksen. The six bullfight vignettes from *In Our Time* are here read as a single short story, with Henricksen showing the linear development of both plot and voice, even while the "story" resists the expected unity and harmony of a single fiction.

Pp. 123-29: "From the Waste Land to the Garden with the Elliots" by Paul Smith. Places "Mr. and Mrs. Elliot" as a powerful, intentionally satiric assault on the wealthy intellectuals (as well as the Tom Eliots and Chard Powers Smiths). More importantly, Smith sees the story as the first of Hemingway's treatments of the writer divided between his sexual and creative impulses.

Pp. 131-40: "Hemingway's 'On Writing': A Portrait of the Artist as Nick Adams" by Lawrence Broer. Studies the fragment "On Writing" from "Big Two-Hearted River," published separately in 1972. Broer compares Hemingway's use of Nick in this excerpt to Joyce's use of Daedalus in *Portrait of the Artist as a Young Man*, and draws from his aesthetic here to explain other Nick Adams stories.

Pp. 141-47: "The Writer on Vocation: Hemingway's 'Banal Story'" by George Monteiro. Comments on the satiric short story and its allusions to the *Forum*. Concludes that it "gathers considerable biographical significance when it is seen for the ironic gesture towards its author's own self-conscious need for exorcism that it was at least partly intended to be."

Pp. 149-61: "Hemingway and Turgenev: *The Torrents of Spring*" by Robert Coltrane. Hemingway's novella, a satire of Sherwood Anderson's *Dark Laughter*, can also be read in relation to the novella by Turgenev with the same title and as a text in which Hemingway expressed his disguised sexual and artistic frustrations.

Pp. 163-83: "'An Alpine Idyll': The Sun-Struck Mountain Vision and the Necessary Valley Journey" by Robert E. Gajdusek. Provides a reading that stresses the cyclic nature of death and birth, as well as seasonal change.

Pp. 185-94: "Waiting for the End in Hemingway's 'A Pursuit Race'" by Ann Putnam. Provides an existential reading of this 1927 story, one that blends humor and terror in the Poe tradition – and central to the Hemingway canon.

Pp. 195-207: "A Semiotic Inquiry into Hemingway's 'A Simple Enquiry'" by Gerry Brenner. Stresses the story's similarity to such other narratives as "Hills Like White Elephants" and "The Sea Change," puzzles whose interpretation "pivots on an unarticulated word and on the sensitivity of readers' responses to sign-laden dialogue."

Pp. 209-224: "'Mais Je Rests Catholique': Communion, Betrayal, and Aridity in 'Wine of Wyoming'" by H.R. Stoneback. Stresses Hemingway's concern with Catholicism, read here as a parable of communion and aridity in the *Waste Land* mode.

Pp. 225-45: "'That's Not Very Polite': Sexual Identity in Hemingway's 'The Sea Change'" by Warren Bennett. Connects this narrative with *The Garden of Eden*. Instead of finding that the girl's lesbianism is the crux of the narrative, Bennett believes the male protagonist has found that his relationship with her has been "unmanly" and that his identity has been shattered in that understanding.

Pp. 247-53: "'A Natural History of the Dead' as Metafiction" by Charles Stetler and Gerald Locklin. In this story, ahead of its time in philosophy and technique, Hemingway combines the genres of satiric essay and graphic fiction to achieve "metafiction." The story calls attention to its status as artifact and raises questions about the relationship of fiction to reality.

Pp. 255-62: "'Homage to Switzerland': Einstein's Train Stops at Hemingway's Station" by Michael S. Reynolds. Discusses Hemingway's cryptic compression within its triptych (three different protagonists). The story seems to predict Samuel Beckett's *Waiting for Godot*.

Pp. 263-82: "Repetition as Design and Intention: Hemingway's 'Homage to Switzerland'" by Erik Nakjavani. Views the riddles of the story as its key, finding an intricately constructed tale of "universal homelessness and the isolation of the individual."

Pp. 283-90: "Myth or Reality: 'The Light of the World' as Initiation Story" by Robert E. Fleming. Reads that the notion of the grotesque has dominated our impressions, and asserts that the real focus of the story should be on the two young protagonists and their possible initiation.

Pp. 291-302: "Up and Down: Making Connections in 'A Day's Wait'" by Linda Gajdusek. It is not simply comic, but it is rather a "deeply involved and involving" story about "the need to reconcile opposites."

Pp. 303-311: "Illusion and Reality: 'The Capital of the World'" by Stephen Cooper. Shows that the story treats many of Hemingway's characteristic subjects ("the bullfight, life in Spain, initiation into manhood, the disillusionment that comes with experience, the nature of fear, the necessity of facing death alone") in different ways.

Pp. 313-27: "Hemingway's Spanish Civil War Stories, or the Spanish Civil War as Reality" by Allen Josephs. Studies yet again the five Spanish civil war stories, "The Denunciation," "The Butterfly and the Tank," "Night Before Battle," "Under the Ridge," and "Landscape with Figures."

Pp. 329-38: "The Hunting Story in *The Garden of Eden*" by James Nagel. Identifies the story as the "heart" of the novel, *The Garden of Eden*, Hemingway's elegy for Hemingway.

Pp. 339-50: "Hemingway's Tales of 'The Real Dark'" by Howard L. Hannum. Discusses the last of Hemingway's stories published during his lifetime, "Get a Seeing-Eyed Dog" and "A Man of the World," both about blind protagonists for whom the formula–and the magic–of enduring life has failed.

2 BELLAVANCE-JOHNSON, MARSHA, and BELLAVANCE, LEE. *Ernest Hemingway in Idaho*. 2d ed. Ketchum, Idaho: Computer Lab. *Hemingway Review* 9, no. 1 (Fall): 104.

3 BENSON, JACKSON J. "Criticism of the Short Stories: The Neglected and the Oversaturated–an Editorial." *Hemingway Review* 8, no. 2 (Spring): 30-35.

Surveys the status of Hemingway short-story criticism. Is pleased that the availability of manuscript materials at the Kennedy Library along with new critical strategies have had a revitalizing effect on scholarship plagued by repetition and irrelevancy. Calls for periodic evaluations of criticism in order to ensure that the best and most useful won't sink into the sheer volume.

4 BEVERSLUIS, JOHN. "Dispelling the Romantic Myth: A Study of *A Farewell to Arms*." *Hemingway Review* 9, no. 1 (Fall): 18-25.

Finds that for Henry, self-knowledge can be achieved only through reassessing his total life in light of the way he behaves. Contends that the real subject of the novel "is not love as such, but one man's attempt, in the name of love, to escape from the oppressive world in which he finds himself and discover a more tolerable world." His retreat, however, brings only emptiness and boredom, a fact realized long before Catherine's death.

5 BRENNER, GERRY. "Fitzgerald and Hemingway." In *American Literary Scholarship: An Annual, 1987*. Edited by James Woodress. Durham, N.C.: Duke University Press, pp. 147-71.

Survey of criticism on both authors published during 1987. Brenner comments on the sheer volume of Hemingway scholarship for the year, but adds that scholars are still reluctant to apply recent critical theory to the texts.

6 BROWN, FRIEDA S.; COMPITELLO, MALCOLM ALAN; HOWARD, VICTOR M.; and MARTIN, ROBERT A., eds. *Rewriting the Good Fight: Critical Essays on the Literature of the Spanish Civil War*. East Lansing, Mich.: MSU Press, 266 pp.

Essays given as part of the Conference in Modern Literature in November of 1987, "International Literature of the Spanish Civil War." Several concern Hemingway's involvement in that conflict and his fiction.

Pp. 175-84: "Hemingway and the Spanish Civil War or the Volatile Mixture of Politics and Art" by Allen Josephs. Compares Hemingway's involvement with that of Lorca and Picasso, saying that Hemingway was–of the three–the most political. Josephs discusses his work in *The Spanish Earth*, his fiction, his great love for Spain, and his embarrassment at having to choose the political side he did. His narrative strategy, to write *For Whom the Bell Tolls* as a novel of nostalgic memory rather than as a political novel, was a way of disguising what his real politics were. Hemingway was never naive about such issues, but he was trying desperately to write good fiction.

Pp. 199-214: "Intellectuals as Militants: Hemingway's *For Whom the Bell Tolls* and Malraux's *L'Espoir*: A Comparative Study" by Erik Nakjavani. Discusses Hemingway's work as a manifestation of the "mode of existence of the intellectual militant" and the character of Robert Jordan as the personification of that character. Author concludes that Jordan is a composite figure, and therefore blurs many individual traits; and he is also given the romantic task of blowing the bridge, which further blurs his beliefs.

7 BRYER, JACKSON [R.]. *Sixteen Modern American Authors*. Vol. 2, *A Survey of Research and Criticism since 1972*. Duke University Press, 832 pp.
   *Books in Print: Supplement 1989-90. Vol 1., p. 271.

8 BUSH, GLEN P. "Hemingway's Quest for Living." *Lost Generation Journal* 9, no. 1 (Spring-Summer): 4-5.
   Overview of Hemingway's fascination with the code and desire to live rightly in a disordered world.

9 CONRAD, BARNABY. *Hemingway's Spain*. San Francisco: Chronicle Books, 144 pp.
   Over one hundred photographs (by Loomis Dean) of people, places, and events, giving the reader an inside look at Spain as Hemingway saw it. Photos are accompanied by quotes taken from several sources, including Hemingway's correspondence and works. Conrad's introduction discusses the author's long association with Spain.

10 CONSIGNY, SCOTT. "Hemingway's 'Hills Like White Elephants.'" *Explicator* 48, no. 1 (Fall): 54-55.
   Interprets the curtain as a demarcation between the artificial world of the bar and the real world outside.

11 DeFAZIO, AL [BERT J., III]. "Hemingway Bibliography." *Hemingway Review* 8, no. 2 (Spring): 55-65.
   List of recent items, including articles, reviews, dissertations, and translations.

12 _____. "Hemingway Bibliography." *Hemingway Review* 9, no. 1 (Fall): 104-112.

Lists articles, books, and reviews as recent as 1989.

13 DESNOYERS, MEGAN FLOYD. "News from the Hemingway Collection." *Hemingway Review* 9, no. 1 (Fall): 96-97.

Lists and describes manuscripts, typescripts, galleys, and other *A Farewell to Arms* materials in the collection. Also announces recent acquisitions from the estate of Mary Hemingway and the opening of *The Garden of Eden* materials.

14 _____. "News from the Kennedy Library." *Hemingway Review* 8, no. 2 (Spring): 53-54.

Includes information on recent acquisitions, research grants, archival internships, and donations.

15 DONALDSON, SCOTT. "The Jilting of Ernest Hemingway." *Virginia Quarterly Review* 65, no. 4 (Autumn): 661-73.

Pieces together Hemingway's affair with Agnes von Kurowsky. Donaldson considers her eventual rejection a severe blow that drove him to excel and shaped his subsequent relationships with others.

16 "Ernest Hemingway Honored on New Stamp." *Lost Generation Journal* 9, no. 1 (Spring-Summer): 2-3.

Remarks on the commemorative ceremonies in addition to technical information on the stamp's design and release. Also includes a broad overview of his life and works.

17 FITCH, NOEL RILEY. "A Draw for Artists." *Arete* 2, no. 1 (July-August): 83-85.

Comments on the attraction of Paris for such painters and writers as Picasso, Joyce, and Hemingway. "Here were the teachers, the little magazines and presses, the salons and schools. In short, here was an audience."

18 FLEMING, ROBERT E. "American Nightmare: Hemingway and the West." *Midwest Quarterly* 30, no. 3 (Spring): 361-71.

Looks at Hemingway's ambivalent attitude toward the West in "Wine of Wyoming," "The Gambler, the Nun, and the Radio," "The Snows of Kilimanjaro," "A Man of the World," *For Whom the Bell Tolls*, and *Across the River and into the Trees*. "In his fiction, Hemingway associated the West with a painful confrontation between romance and reality, in which reality usually won. The resulting depiction of the West saw a soothing pastoral scene giving way to one that was infinitely more troubling."

19 ____. "The Endings of Hemingway's *Garden of Eden*." *American Literature* 61, no. 2 (May): 261-70.

Close attention to manuscript materials makes Fleming's study of Hemingway's controversial novel useful. He describes the extant manuscript, not only the segment Tom Jenks, the Scribner editor, shaped into the published novel. Hemingway's seven-page "provisional ending" chapter brings Catherine and David back together, unhappy after Catherine's illness, David's ministrations more those of a nurse than a lover. The chapter closes with talk of a mutual suicide pact, a denouement more in keeping with the tone of the book than the passage Jenks has chosen as closing.

20 FYATT, CHARLES M. "Errol Flynn Steals the Show in *The Sun Also Rises*." *Lost Generation Journal* 9, no. 1 (Spring-Summer): 22.

Comments on Zanuck's 1957 film adaptation of the novel in which Flynn's successful portrayal of the comic/tragic Mike Campbell echoed the actor's own personal and professional decline.

21 GAJDUSEK, ROBERT E. "*A Farewell to Arms*: The Psychodynamics of Integrity." *Hemingway Review* 9, no. 1 (Fall): 26-32.

Discusses Hemingway's exploration of the self in the novel, of what it means to be whole (to establish an authentic identity) in a stressful world.

22 ____. "Here's an Answer to Query about Cantwell Passage." *Hemingway Newsletter* 17 (January): 7.

Identifies sources of the line, "They were coming up on Mestre fast, and already, it was like going to New York the first time you were ever there in the old days when it was shining, white and beautiful," from chapter 5 of *Across the River and into the Trees*, in Thomas Wolfe's "Four Lost Men" and Alfred Tennyson's *Idylls of the King*.

23 GILBERT, SANDRA M., and GUBAR, SUSAN. *No Man's Land, the Place of the Woman Writer in the Twentieth Century*. Vol. 2, *Sexchanges*. New Haven, Conn.: Yale University Press, 472 pp.

Discusses *A Farewell to Arms*, *The Sun Also Rises*, and *The Garden of Eden* as examples of male writing that questions accepted gender patterns, albeit implicitly. During war, men are to be wounded or killed, as Jake Barnes illustrates. *Garden* shows most convincingly the necessity for women to avoid the usurpation of male roles, as David Bourne's horror at Catherine's sexual practices shows. They see much of Hemingway's writing as being prompted by the "male 'disease of modern life.'"

24 HAYS, PETER L. "Hunting Ritual in *The Sun Also Rises*." *Hemingway Review* 8, no. 2 (Spring): 46-48.

Looks at the elaborate ceremony surrounding Romero's killing of the bull, concluding that it is a form of religious worship that also partakes of ancient hunting rituals, thereby joining the secular and religious aspects of *The Sun Also Rises*.

25 HINKLE, JAMES. "Twenties Paris in 1989." *Arete* 2, no. 1 (July-August): 90-91.

Discusses the changes that have occurred in Paris over the past seventy years. References to Hemingway.

26 HOTCHNER, A.E. *Hemingway and His World*. New York: Vendome Press, pp. 208.

*Hemingway Review 9, no. 2 (Spring): 183.

27 HOUK, WALTER. "Will the Real Herrera Brothers Please Stand Up?" *Hemingway Review* 9, no. 1 (Fall): 98-99.

Clears up the confusion over Hemingway's friends the Herrera brothers in Fuentes's *Hemingway in Cuba*.

28 JOHNSON, PAUL. "Hemingway: Portrait of the Artist as an Intellectual." *Commentary* 87, no. 2 (February): 49-59.

Broad overview of Hemingway's life and career, drawing on biographies by Kenneth S. Lynn, Jeffrey Meyers, and Carlos Baker.

29 KERNER, HUGH. "Small Ritual Truths." In *A Homemade World: The American Modernist Writers*. New York: Alfred A. Knopf.

Reprint of 1975 edition.

30 LELAND, JOHN. *A Guide to Hemingway's Paris*. Chapel Hill, N.C.: Algonquin Books, 124 pp.

Useful descriptive annotations of addresses, people's names, and miscellanies, complete with walking tours and photographs. Louis Rubin's foreword stresses Hemingway's ability to describe the sensuous.

31 LEWIS, ROBERT W. "The Inception and Reception of *A Farewell to Arms*." *Hemingway Review* 9, no. 1 (Fall): 91-95.

Discusses Hemingway's writing of the novel, begun in Paris and continued in Key West, Arkansas, and Wyoming. Also provides an overview of the broad critical response to the novel since its publication.

32 MANGUM, BRYANT. "The Hemingway Code and Ten-Word Telegrams." *Lost Generation Journal* 9, no. 1 (Spring-Summer): 9-10.

Connects the telegrams and postcards sent by the various characters to the larger themes of moral value brought out in the novel.

33 MEYERS, JEFFREY. *The Spirit of Biography*. Ann Arbor, Mich.: UMI Research Press, 315 pp.
    Reprint of 1983.81, 1984.76, and 1985.73.

34 MONTEIRO, GEORGE. "The Hit in Summit: Ernest Hemingway's 'The Killers.'" *Hemingway Review* 8, no. 2 (Spring): 40-42.
    Compares Henry's lunchroom to a bullring and Max and Al to matadors, believing that it is the indirection of "The Killers" that parodies the actual bullfight. Contends that in order to maintain their domination and entertain themselves, the killers deliberately upset the routine of the lunchroom.

35 NAGEL, JAMES, and VILLARD, HENRY S. *Hemingway in Love and War: The Lost Diary of Agnes von Kurowsky, Her Letters & Correspondence of Ernest Hemingway*. Boston: Northeastern University Press, 303 pp.
    Covers just what the title says. Villard recounts his time spent at the American Red Cross Hospital in Milan where he convalesced with the wounded Hemingway. Attempts to set the record straight concerning Hemingway's relationship with the beautiful Red Cross nurse who served in part as the model for Catherine Barkley. Comments on the influence Hemingway's Italian experiences (both his wounding in the field and his eventual jilting by von Kurowsky) had on his writings.

36 NAKJAVANI, ERIK. "Hemingway on Nonthinking." *North Dakota Quarterly* 57, no. 3 (Summer): 173-98.
    Explores in detail (function, extent, achievement, psychotropic technique and soteriological method, effect on the act of writing) the notion of *nonthinking* in Hemingway's works. Describes nonthinking as the way "fictional characters *in extremis* respond to the inevitable human discovery that certain problems of life cannot be merely thought, thought out, or thought away." It serves as a way out of extreme (mind-destroying) situations. Looks at *The Sun Also Rises*, *For Whom the Bell Tolls*, *Islands in the Stream*, and others.

37 NOLAN, CHARLES J., Jr. "Heller's Small Debt to Hemingway." *Hemingway Review* 9, no. 1 (Fall): 77-81.
    Finds echoes of characters and situations from *A Farewell to Arms* in *Catch-22*, contending that both authors "use war as a metaphor to document the modern existential condition."

38 OLIVER, CHARLES M., ed. *A Moving Picture Feast: A Filmgoer's Hemingway*. New York: Praeger, 186 pp.

   Collection of mostly new material. Contents:

   Pp. xi-xvi: Introduction by Robert W. Lewis. Comments on Hemingway's often reluctant involvement in the movie industry. Provides an overview of the collection.

   Pp. 3-11: "Hemingway's Cinematic Style" by Eugene Kanjo. Pays attention to the cinematic qualities (montage, slow-motion imagery, close-up, etc) in *Paris 1922*. Discusses Hemingway's quest for the fourth and fifth dimension in prose through an analysis of "Soldier's Home."

   Pp. 12-18: "Novelist versus Screenwriter: The Case for Casey Robinson's Adaptations of Hemingway's Fiction" by Gene D. Phillips. Compares Robinson's film scripts for "The Short Happy Life of Francis Macomber," "My Old Man," and "The Snows of Kilimanjaro" with Hemingway's original stories, noting that despite some major changes (especially in the endings), each is "a respectable rendition of the author's fiction."

   Pp. 19-25: "Hollywood Publicity and Hemingway's Popular Reputation" by Frank M. Laurence. Reprint with slight revision of *Journal of Popular Culture* 6 (1972).

   Pp. 26-31: "Death in the Matinée: The Film Endings of Hemingway's Fiction" by Frank M. Laurence. Reprint with slight revision of 1974.25.

   Pp. 32-37: "Filming Novels: The Hemingway Case" by George Bluestone. Discusses the aesthetic relationship between fiction and cinema, Hemingway's dislike of nearly all the film adaptations of his work, and the limitations of the Hemingway code.

   Pp. 41-53: "Inventing from Knowledge: Some Notes toward a Remake of *For Whom the Bell Tolls*" by John Garrick. Comments on Hemingway's "highly personalized" view of the Spanish civil war and finds those elements that lend validity to the novel (narrative pace, characterization) missing from Paramount's 1943 film version. Offers suggestions for improvement.

   Pp. 54-63: "Larding the Text: Problems in Filming *The Old Man and the Sea*" by Linda Dittmar. Finds that even with Hemingway's involvement in the project, the tension between written language and the audiovisual nature of cinema was never resolved. Contends that all involved, from Hemingway to the Hollywood producers, were naive in assuming that a literal fidelity to the text was possible.

   Pp. 64-75: "Marriage as Moral Community: Cinematic Critiques of Hemingway's *To Have and Have Not*" by Thomas Hemmeter and Kevin W. Sweeney. Relying on a dialogical approach, Hemmeter and Sweeney examine the original with its three subsequent adaptations, paying particular attention to the idea of moral community and Harry's changing moral predicament.

Pp. 76-90: "Hemingway and *The Spanish Earth*" by John Garrick. Discusses Hemingway's involvement both in the Spanish civil war and the making of the documentary, a propaganda piece juxtaposing peaceful village life with the brutality of war.

Pp. 91-113: "*The Sun Also Rises*: The NBC Version" by Frank M. Laurence. Detailed comparison of the 1984 television adaptation with the novel, including an appendix describing the eighty-three scenes which make up the NBC version and their relationship to the novel. Discusses ratings, publicity, and the largely female audience for this miniseries, which sacrificed art for entertainment.

Pp. 114-21: "Hemingway's Hollywood Paris" by Hugh Ford. Laments King's telescoping of important scenes, deletion of minor characters, and substitution of the original cynical ending of *The Sun Also Rises* with an upbeat one because of the major themes lost in the process.

Pp. 125-34: "Literary Adaptation: 'The Killers' – Hemingway, Film Noir, and the Terror of Daylight" by Stuart Kaminsky. Reprint with slight revision of 1985.57.

Pp. 135-40: "'That Hemingway Kind of Love': Macomber in the Movies" by Robert E. Morsberger. Reprint with slight revision of 1976.65.

Pp. 141-47: "'Soldier's Home': A Space Between" by Marianne H. Knowlton. Pays attention to the fundamental thematic differences between the story and film versions. In the original, Krebs comes to recognize his individuality while the film emphasizes his common identity with the rest of the returning soldiers. And in a reversal of motivation, in the film version "we are left with the sense that Krebs must move on, not because society has failed 'the good soldier,' but because Harold Krebs has devastatingly failed himself."

Pp. 148-61: "Hemingway, Film, and U.S. Culture: *In Our Time* and *The Birth of A Nation*" by Stanley Corkin. Finds many similarities in the works (desire to reveal the "real" experience, behaviorism, alienated characters) due to the common influence of being created in the mechanistic world of the early twentieth century rather than any influence one might have had on the other.

Pp. 163-78: "Film Bibliography" compiled by Bruce Crawford and Lisa Middents. Extensive list of articles, reviews, books, theses, and screenplay typescripts.

39 PATE, CAROLYN KALLSEN. "Destroyed but Not Defeated: A Hemingway Theme." *Lost Generation Journal* 9, no. 1 (Spring-Summer): 6-8.

Distinguishing between "destroyed" and "defeated," Pate examines the ways in which Santiago's comment that "a man can be destroyed but not defeated" functions as a controlling idea in three other stories: "The

Capital of the World," "The Short Happy Life of Francis Macomber," and "The Undefeated."

40 PHELAN, JAMES. *Reading People, Reading Plots: Character, Progression, and the Interpretation of Narrative.* Chicago: University of Chicago Press, pp. 165-88.

Phelan uses "the case of Catherine Barkley" to illustrate his thesis that character is the multichromatic linchpin of all fiction, incorporating mimetic, thematic, and synthetic elements as the reader "progresses" through the text. In Hemingway's *A Farewell to Arms*, Catherine reflects the author's sexism and makes the reader attend to various interpretive strategies. Phelan uses Judith Fetterley's reading as one focal point.

41 PLIMPTON, GEORGE, ed. Introduction to *The Best of Bad Hemingway: Choice Entries from the Harry's Bar & American Grill Imitation Hemingway Competition.* San Diego: Harcourt Brace Jovanovich, 163 pp.

Plimpton provides an overview of the contest along with a brief discussion of the Hemingway style (so easily parodied) and Hemingway's own early parody of Sherwood Anderson in *The Torrents of Spring.* Collection includes the best entries in the competition from the past eleven years as well as selected parodies of Hemingway from such well-known authors as F. Scott Fitzgerald and E.B. White.

42 PRICE, ALAN. "'I'm Not an Old Fogey and You're Not a Young Ass': Owen Wister and Ernest Hemingway." *Hemingway Review* 9, no. 1 (Fall): 82-90.

Quoting liberally from correspondence between the two recently made available, Price attempts to set the record straight concerning Wister's "filching" of galleys of *A Farewell to Arms* and alleged unsolicited suggestions for revision. Wister comes off as generous and supportive rather than interfering.

43 RALEIGH, RICHARD. "Papa's Place." *Lost Generation Journal* 9, no. 1 (Spring-Summer): 13.

Recounts his visits to Hemingway's old haunts, including Sloppy Joe's in Key West.

44 RENZA, LOUIS A. "The Importance of Being Ernest." *South Atlantic Quarterly* 88, no. 3 (Summer): 661-89.

Looks at the stories of *In Our Time* (and their relation to the act of writing) in light of *A Moveable Feast.* Comments on Hemingway's desire in the later collection to return to the earlier experience of writing "truly."

45 REYNOLDS, MICHAEL S. *Hemingway: The Paris Years*. New York: Basil Blackwell, 391 pp.

Vivid and excruciatingly detailed account of Hemingway's life in Paris, from late 1921 to late 1925. Most of those years include Hadley Richardson, Hemingway's first wife, and his first child, John Nicanor; more importantly for literary history, they include *in our time*, *In Our Time*, poems, the composition of *The Sun Also Rises*, *The Torrents of Spring*, and the crucial world of modernist writing–Ford Maddox Ford, Gertrude Stein, Sylvia Beach, F. Scott Fitzgerald, Ernest Walsh, Ezra Pound, Sherwood Anderson–and modernist living. The years have never been brought to life in such modest, and humbling, detail. This second volume of Reynolds's projected full biography follows *The Young Hemingway*, and it builds on its own remarkable accomplishment. Impressive and helpful notes and index.

46 ROSCO, JERRY. "An Expatriate Feud: Wescott and Hemingway." *Lost Generation Journal* 9, no. 1 (Spring-Summer): 28-29.

Records Hemingway's dislike of Glenway Wescott as evidenced in his reference to him in *The Sun Also Rises* and later correspondence. After achieving international recognition, however, Hemingway's animosity toward Wescott seems to have faded.

47 RUDAT, WOLFGANG E.H. "Jacob Barnes and Onan: Sexual Response in *The Sun Also Rises* and *For Whom the Bell Tolls*." *Journal of Evolutionary Psychology* 10, no. 1-2:50-58.
Hemingway Review 9, no. 1 (Fall): 110.

48 ____. "Sexual Dilemmas in *The Sun Also Rises*: Hemingway's Count and the Education of Jacob Barnes." *Hemingway Review* 8, no. 2 (Spring): 2-13.

Argues that in the closing cab-ride scene, Brett is attempting to psychologically castrate Jake by making demands on him that he cannot fulfill, just as she'd tried to do earlier with the impotent count. That Brett is unsuccessful is evidenced by Jake's deliberate homosexual pose.

49 SCHWENGER, PETER. "The Masculine Mode." In *Speaking of Gender*. Edited by Elaine Showalter. New York: Routledge, pp. 101-112.

Uses Yukio Mishima and Ernest Hemingway to illustrate writers whose style and subject matter create a "masculine mode," "an attempt to render a certain *maleness of experience*." Cites Jake Barnes and Nick Adams as examples of characters choosing the reserved language that is, paradoxically, very intimate.

50 SIMMONDS, ROY S. "The British Critical Reception of Hemingway's *The Garden of Eden*." *Hemingway Review* 8, no. 2 (Spring): 14-21.

Surveys the British response to Hemingway's posthumous novel. Quotes liberally from a variety of reviewers who overall consider the book less than satisfying.

51 SMITH, PAUL. "A Note on a New Manuscript of 'A Clean, Well-Lighted Place.'" *Hemingway Review* 8, no. 2 (Spring): 36-39.

Raises more questions about the controversial dialogue of the story. Describes the 1932 typescript, now available at the University of Delaware Library, which assigns the line, "You said she cut him down," to the Older Waiter.

52 _____. "Open Letter to Mike Reynolds." *Hemingway Review* 9, no. 1 (Fall): 100-101.

In attempting to explicate Hemingway's enigmatic "A Divine Gesture," Smith dismisses historical relevance. Instead, Smith considers it to be "partly a joyous celebration of his new love in Chicago, and partly a stiff index finger to his Father in Oak Park."

53 _____. *A Reader's Guide to the Short Stories of Ernest Hemingway.* Boston: G.K. Hall, 407 pp.

Gives composition and publication history, sources and influences (significant events, places, people, other authors), and critical studies for fifty-five short stories, arranged chronologically from "Up in Michigan" (1921) through "A Man of the World" (1957).

54 SOLOTAROFF, ROBERT. "Sexual Identity in *A Farewell to Arms*." *Hemingway Review* 9, no. 1 (Fall): 2-17.

Explores the sexual conflict within Henry–the feminine component of the male identity–and Catherine Barkley's role in bringing out Henry's "femininity" (i.e., pulling him away from his place in the male world).

55 STANTON, EDWARD F. *Hemingway and Spain: A Pursuit.* Seattle: University of Washington, 258 pp.

Stanton retraces Hemingway's footsteps in Spain, combining biography, literary criticism, and personal observation in his chronicle of Hemingway's forty-year love affair with that country. Places Hemingway's evolving prose style, code of honor, and life within the context of his Spanish experience, drawing on unpublished letters and manuscripts only recently made available. Treats *The Sun Also Rises, For Whom the Bell Tolls, Death in the Afternoon,* and other works set in Spain. Includes some photographs and a selected bibliography.

56 STONEBACK, H.R. "Hemingway's Paris." *Arete* 2, no. 1 (July-August): 86-89.

Discusses Hemingway's love of "the real Paris" (not the superficial Paris of the Lost Generation) and permanent presence there.

57 ____. "Jeopardy in the Evening: For Whom the Telly Tolls." *Hemingway Review* 8, no. 2 (Spring): 66-67.
   Details the inclusion of a Hemingway category on the popular television show *Jeopardy!*

58 ____. "'Lovers' Sonnets Turn'd to Holy Psalms': The Soul's Son of Providence, the Scandal of Suffering, and Love in *A Farewell to Arms*." *Hemingway Review* 9, no. 1 (Fall): 33-76.
   Attempts to set the critical record straight by "correcting" previous explications of the novel. Touches on such topics as the time lapse between the events of the novel and its narration, name-and-identity wordplay, misreadings of key passages, religious imagery, symbolic landscape, and rejected titles.

59 ____. "Memorable Eggs 'in Danger of Getting Cold' and Mackerel 'Perilous with Edge-Level Juice': Eating in Hemingway's Garden." *Hemingway Review* 8, no. 2 (Spring): 22-29.
   Begins by linking the egg passage of the title to Henry James's *A Little Tour in France* and then traces Hemingway's use of the egg motif throughout *The Garden of Eden*. Concludes that the broken eggs and tinned mackerel with its unpleasant aftertaste "tell us of a movement from the happiness of the Garden to a mixed-up omelet, to a canned happiness."

60 STRONG, PAUL. "Gathering the Pieces and Filling in the Gaps: Hemingway's 'Fathers and Sons.'" *Studies in Short Fiction* 26, no. 1 (Winter): 49-58.
   Discusses in what ways Hemingway's earlier Nick Adams stories often look forward to the later stories in interconnected and clarifying patterns. Suggests that the final pages of "Fathers and Sons" hint at a reconciliation between Nick and his father.

61 STRYCHACZ, THOMAS. "Dramatizations of Manhood in Hemingway's *In Our Time* and *The Sun Also Rises*." *American Literature* 61, no. 2 (May): 245-60.
   Pays attention to the author's use of space (camps, clearings, houses, hotels, etc.) as an arena (proving ground) and the audience's role in evaluating and legitimizing the ritual performances of manhood. "Mastery of the arena bestows power on him, failure invites humiliation: in either case the process implies a loss of authority to the audience." Thus the whole notion of the autonomous male and fashioning of male identity is undermined.

62 SYLVESTER, BICKFORD. "Cantwell's 'Suicide' and 'Mental Illness.'" *Hemingway Review* 8, no. 2 (Spring): 49-50.

Bothered by the contents of an editorial introduction to a Hemingway story in an American literature anthology because it perpetuates outdated assumptions about Hemingway's vision and falls into the biographical trap of confusing his life with his art.

63 ____. "Hemingway-Malraux Exchange Reported." *Hemingway Newsletter* 18 (June): 2.

Contains excerpts from Eric Downton's 1987 *Wars without End* regarding a debate Hemingway had in Madrid in 1937 with André Malraux over the importance of the Spanish civil war in comparison to projected wars against Mussolini and Hitler.

64 SYLVESTER, BICKFORD, and STEPHENS, D.G. "Have You Read This One?" *Hemingway Review* 8, no. 2 (Spring): 68.

Points out Bruce Jay Friedman's 1970 burlesque of *The Old Man and the Sea* in his own novel *The Dick*.

65 WAGNER-MARTIN, LINDA. *The Modern American Novel, 1914-1945: A Critical History.* Boston: Twayne, pp. 27-34, 39-40, 43-45, 68, 72-75, 129, etc.

Numerous references to Hemingway as a central figure in American modernism. Special attention to his aesthetic, his shorter fiction, *A Moveable Feast*, *The Sun Also Rises*, *For Whom the Bell Tolls*, and other works.

66 WALDMEIR, JOSEPH. "Chapter Numbering and Meaning in *For Whom the Bell Tolls*." *Hemingway Review* 8, no. 2 (Spring): 43-45.

Points to similarities in physical resemblance as well as shared masculine traits and sexual ambivalence as evidence that Hemingway had Gertrude Stein primarily in mind when he developed the character of Pilar.

67 WARD, L.E. "Hemingway on Film." *Lost Generation Journal* 9, no. 1 (Spring-Summer): 14-22.

Reviews several of the film adaptations of Hemingway's works, including Paramount's 1932 *A Farewell to Arms* and Warner Brothers' 1944 *To Have and Have Not*. "It would seem that Hollywood should have done better by him – and by us; yet, at times, it seems equally, that it could have done worse. The quantity is there; although that is more rueful, than helpful."

68 WILLIAMS, DAVID. "The Poetics of Impersonality in *A Farewell to Arms*." *University of Toronto Quarterly* 50, no. 2 (Winter): 310-33.

Sees Henry as "Hemingway's version of Eliot's impersonal poetics with the metaphysical mask taken off." Henry's self-serving impersonality allows him to present himself as victim, devoid of responsibility for his own fate. Contends that in adopting such a philosophy, Hemingway was not paying homage but instead delivering "a devastating critique on the ruling poetics of that time."

69 WOOD, DELORIS. "Hemingway Stamp Dedication Set at Hemingway's Home in Key West, July 17, 1989." *Lost Generation Journal* 9, no. 1 (Spring-Summer): 30.

Comments on both the stamp dedication ceremonies and the Whitehead Street home Hemingway shared with second wife Pauline in the 1930s, now a museum.

70 WOOD, TOM. "Cablese – Used in Paris." *Lost Generation Journal* 9, no. 1 (Spring-Summer): 11-12.

Outlines the use of the ten-word telegram in early newspaper reporting and speculates on its influence on young authors. References to Hemingway's own talent in writing "cablese."

71 ____. "On the Road to Pamplona." *Lost Generation Journal* 9, no. 1 (Spring-Summer): 23-25.

Recounts his journey to Pamplona. Some references to Hemingway.

Index